The Criminal Conversation
of Mrs Norton

Also by Diane Atkinson

Elsie and Mairi Go to War

*Love and Dirt: The Marriage of Arthur Munby
and Hannah Cullwick*

DIANE ATKINSON

THE CRIMINAL CONVERSATION OF MRS NORTON

preface
publishing

Published by Preface 2012

10 9 8 7 6 5 4 3 2 1

First published in Great Britain in 2012 by Preface Publishing

20 Vauxhall Bridge Road
London, SW1V 2SA

An imprint of The Random House Group Limited

www.randomhouse.co.uk
www.prefacepublishing.co.uk

Addresses for companies within The Random House Group Limited
can be found at www.randomhouse.co.uk

The Random House Group Limited Reg. No. 954009

A CIP catalogue record for this book is available from the British Library

ISBN 978 1 84809 301 0

The Random House Group Limited supports The Forest Stewardship Council (FSC®), the leading
international forest certification organisation. Our books carrying the FSC label are printed on
FSC® certified paper. FSC is the only forest certification scheme endorsed by the leading
environmental organisations, including Greenpeace. Our paper procurement
policy can be found at www.randomhouse.co.uk/environment

Typeset in Sabon by Palimpsest Book Production Limited
Falkirk, Stirlingshire

Printed and bound in Great Britain by Clays Ltd, St Ives PLC

For Pauline and Peter Tanner

Contents

Caroline Sheridan's Family Tree

Richard Brinsley Sheridan 1751–1816 — m 1773 — Elizabeth Ann 'Eliza' Linley 1754–1792

Thomas Sheridan 1775–1817 — m 1805 — Caroline Henrietta Callander 1799–1851

Hester Jane 'Hecca' Ogle 1776–1817 — m 1795 — Charles Brinsley Sheridan 1796–1843 unm

Mary 1792 illegitimate daughter of Lord Edward Fitzgerald

Caroline Elizabeth Sarah 1808–1877 — m 1827 — George Chapple Norton 1800–1875

Jane Georgiana 1809–1884 — m 1830 — Edward Adolphus Seymour 12th Duke of Somerset 1804–1885
— 3 daughters + 2 sons

Thomas Berkeley 1811–1826 unm

Francis Cynric c.1815–1843 unm

Charles Kinnaird 1817–1847 unm

Helen Selina 1807–1867 — m 1825 — Price Blackwood 4th Baron Dufferin and Clandeboye 1794–1841

Richard Brinsley 1806–1888 — m 1835 — Marcia Maria Grant 1815–1884
— 6 sons and 3 daughters

Frederick 1826–1902 — m 1862 — George Hay Earl of Gifford 1818–1862

Fletcher Cavendish Charles Conyers Norton 1829–1859

Thomas Brinsley Norton 1831–1877 — m 1854 — Maria Chiara Elisa Federigo 1837–1892

William Charles Chapple Norton 1833–1842

Carlotta 1854–1931

Richard 1855–1943
— 2 marriages 4 daughters + 2 sons

Sir William Stirling Maxwell 1818–1878 — m 1865 — Lady Anna Maria Leslie Melville ?–1874
— m 1877

George Norton's Family Tree

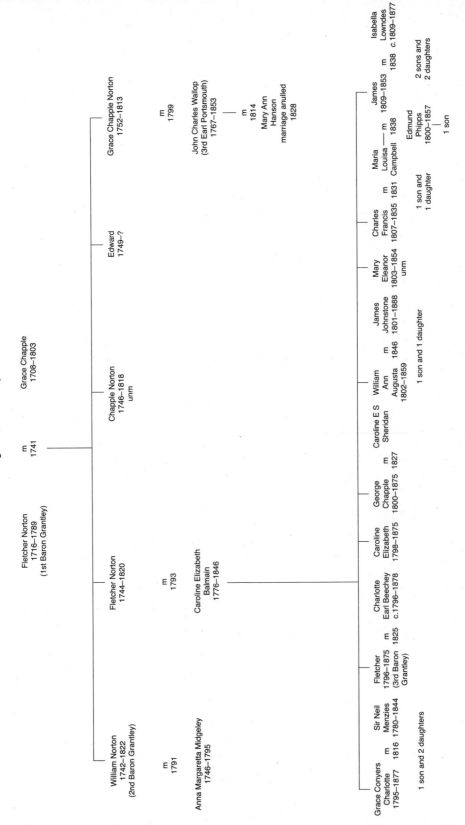

Fletcher Norton 1716–1789 (1st Baron Grantley) — m 1741 — Grace Chapple 1708–1803

William Norton 1742–1822 (2nd Baron Grantley) — m 1791

Chapple Norton 1746–1818 unm

Edward 1749–?

Grace Chapple Norton 1752–1813 — m 1799

John Charles Wallop (3rd Earl Portsmouth) 1767–1853 — m 1814 — Mary Ann Hanson — marriage anulled 1828

Fletcher Norton 1744–1820 — m 1793 — Caroline Elizabeth Balmain 1776–1846

Anna Margaretta Midgeley 1746–1795

Grace Conyers Charlotte 1795–1877 — m 1816 — Sir Neil Menzies 1780–1844

1 son and 2 daughters

Fletcher 1796–1875 (3rd Baron Grantley) — m 1825 — Charlotte Earl Beechey c.1796–1878

Caroline Elizabeth 1798–1875

George Chapple 1800–1875 — m 1827 — Caroline E S Sheridan

William Ann Augusta 1802–1859 — m 1846 — James Johnstone 1801–1888

1 son and 1 daughter

Mary Eleanor 1803–1854 unm

Charles Francis 1807–1835 — m 1831 — Maria Louisa Campbell

1 son and 1 daughter

James 1809–1853 — m 1838 — Isabella Lowndes c.1809–1877

2 sons and 2 daughters

Edmund Phipps 1800–1857

1 son

View from the Jury Box in the Court of Common Pleas.

Aug[t] 25th 1826.

Prologue

The Trial of the Nineteenth Century

At an early hour yesterday morning, both the public and private entrances to the Court were thronged with people eager to procure any place from which they could hear the smallest portion of a trial which has excited so much interest. Their patience and perseverance, however, were but ill-rewarded, for the galleries of the body of the Court were filled before the public doors were thrown open, so high a sum as five and in some cases we believe even ten guineas having been given for a seat. The Court is peculiarly small . . . the heat and the overcrowding can be very imperfectly imagined.

Morning Chronicle, 23 June 1836

The twenty-second of June 1836, a warm drizzly day in London. A light wind cooled the men waiting impatiently at the big doors of the medieval Westminster Hall.[1] At half past nine the crowd, murmuring with anticipation, pushed into the adjacent Court of Common Pleas: 'a simultaneous rush was made and it appeared as if the doors had given way to the pressure from without, confusion and uproar prevailed'.[2] A clearly annoyed Lord Chief Justice Sir Nicholas Conyngham Tindal took his seat. He ordered the doors to be shut and that only those with subpoenas be allowed in, and warned that unless silence prevailed he would adjourn the trial.

The case of Norton vs Melbourne was said to be motivated more by politics – the desire of the Tories to bring down the Whig government – than the hurt feelings of a husband allegedly cuckolded by the man who happened to be the prime minister of Great Britain. Lord Melbourne, in his fifties, was being sued by the Honourable George Norton, in his mid-thirties, for having had 'criminal conversation' (sexual relations) with Norton's wife, the beautiful and well known writer Caroline Norton. Melbourne was raffish, urbane and witty; there was something of the Regency masher about him. He was old enough to be Caroline's father and had indeed known her father, Tom Sheridan, and even her famously rackety grandfather, the playwright-turned-Whig-politician Richard Brinsley Sheridan, author of *The Rivals* and *The School for Scandal,* those two great comedies of the English stage.

The legal complaint was that Melbourne had denied Norton the benefits of 'domestic harmony and affections', which led to a dereliction of Caroline's conjugal duties and Norton's conjugal rights. Damages of ten thousand pounds (almost a million today) were demanded from the prime minister for the loss of Mr Norton's enjoyment of his wife's body. This was the second time Lord Melbourne had been sued for criminal conversation with another man's wife, but on the previous occasion it had been settled away from the gaze of the press and the public when Melbourne paid off his lover's husband. Now the timing could not have been worse for the prime minister, or better for the Tories who were itching to bring down the reforming Whigs. Lord Melbourne through his legal team denied the charge and was pleading not guilty.

Rumours had circulated about Lord Melbourne and Mrs Norton for three or four years, and their affair had been the subject of satirical lampoons, although the cartoons were tamer than those of a previous generation, when Rowlandson and Gillray had been in their heyday. Some drawings punned and played with Lord Melbourne's family name, Lamb, which became Lambkin, while Mrs Norton was the 'Norty One'. The cuckolded husband was depicted as a wide-eyed gormless goat. As the trial drew near *The Times* speculated that Melbourne's political career would soon be over. A rhyming couplet entitled 'For Better For Worse' in *The Satirist* whetted readers' appetites, but held back on lewd imagery: '"Nay pr'ythee, dear Norton, ne'er rave and curse / Remember you took me for better or worse."/"I know it," said Norton, but then, "Madam, look you. / You proved on trial much worse than I took you!"'[3]

The court was impatient for the preliminaries to be over and wanted to hear the details. The case had all the ingredients of a scandal – sex and politics at the highest level, royal connections, great celebrity, a gorgeous and clever wife, a grumpy and doltish husband and an older richer lounge-lizard of an adulterer – and would not disappoint. The mood was boisterous, high spirits threatening to tip out of control.

Designed by John Soane in the 1820s, the forty-foot-square room was 'filled to suffocation' with members of the public and inquisitive junior barristers who had taken the day off and whose attitude Charles Dickens, reporting for the *Morning Chronicle,* found unbearable. He wrote in his account the following day of their 'very indecent behaviour', and thought them guilty of having only 'a very imperfect understanding of the behaviour of gentlemen' in court. Dickens wrote to a friend that he was so exhausted by his shorthand recording of the fourteen-hour proceedings that he struggled to get out of bed the next day. The jury of ten merchants, a banker and a retired admiral, and the witnesses had to barge their way in to take their places, buffeted by the clamouring spectators.

During the proceedings every man in court would leave the building from time to time to answer calls of nature and take refreshment. There were no public lavatories or dining places, nor had there been even before the great fire of 1834, which had destroyed the Houses of Parliament. In the summer of 1836 Westminster Hall stood almost alone in a blitzed landscape of charred ruins, like a giant tooth in an otherwise empty mouth blasted by decay. The officials, barristers and the jury availed themselves of the facilities of Bellamy's Tavern and Chophouse nearby or Howard's coffee house, the haunt of Members of Parliament, or sought the cover of bushes or the ruined buildings. With the exception of female witnesses called to give evidence – in this case the Nortons' servants – such occasions were all-male affairs. Food was available from coffee stalls, pie shops or street vendors.

On George Norton's formidable legal team was Sir William Follett, a king's counsel of precocious talent in his early forties. Mr John Bayley, in his sixties, a very experienced master of the common law, who had a 'clue to its labyrinth,' would open the pleading, while Mr Richard Crowder assisted.[4] For Lord Melbourne was the attorney general, Sir John Campbell, a man in his fifties whose physical presence made an impression on everyone: 'he was as thick set as a navvy and as hard as nails and full of vigour'. Mr Serjeant Thomas Noon Talfourd and Mr Frederic Thesiger, a KC and one of the most popular leading counsels of his day, assisted Campbell. Both were in their early forties and well liked. (The congeniality of Talfourd's home life was much admired by Charles Dickens, who was a frequent guest at his house. The place swarmed with children and cats and crackled with fun, and Dickens made him the model for the idealistic Tommy Traddles in *David Copperfield*.)[5]

A mix of distinguished experience and eager ambition, these six lawyers were at the height of their powers in 1836, pacing the floor of the Court of Common Pleas in Westminster Hall, where civil cases had been heard for hundreds of years. Both sides anticipated a lengthy and lucrative trial.

The action was the cause célèbre of that year. Not since the trial of Queen Caroline, the estranged wife of George IV, accused of adultery in 1820, had there been such a controversial case. Then the public had rallied round their increasingly eccentric and put-upon queen, believing she was being persecuted by a hypocritical husband who was no better than she was. The bill to divorce her was passed by the House of Lords, but fearing riots if it was ratified by the Commons, it was dropped.[6] Outside in New Palace Yard couriers were waiting to convey news of the Norton vs Melbourne case to British embassies all over Europe and America, where diplomats were anxious to know the prime minister's fate.[7] The prize was the vindication of a husband's jealousy and a fortune in damages. The personal cost was potentially immense for both parties: for Caroline, the loss of her children and her reputation; for the prime minister the collapse of the government and the end of his political career.

George Norton, thirty-six, a barrister who did not practise, was the younger brother and heir-in-waiting to the childless third Lord Grantley of Wonersh, Baron of Markenfield in Yorkshire. Norton and his wife Caroline had three sons: Fletcher, aged seven, five-year-old Brinsley and eighteen-month-old William. Norton doubted the paternity of Brinsley, who had been born in 1831, the first year of his wife's alleged affair, and was also unhappy that his youngest child had the same Christian name as Melbourne. A criminal conversation trial was the first stage in the dismantling of a marriage. Until 1857 divorce could only be granted by an act of Parliament. A trial was an alternative to duelling, which had been outlawed in 1815 but persisted in semi-secrecy for at least another thirty years.[8] The damages awarded could be crippling, and if they were not paid the defendant was liable to arrest and incarceration in a debtors' prison, only to be freed when the debt was paid.

Norton was a dull and unprepossessing husband whose political career had stalled and then ended in 1830 three years into his stormy marriage. He had insisted his vivacious wife use her considerable charms to procure a cushy job for him from Melbourne, who had visited their house three or four times a week for nearly five years. Caroline got Norton not one but two good jobs without much difficulty. In the afternoon, when Melbourne would usually visit, the servants were instructed that Caroline and her visitor were not to be disturbed. Melbourne had everything that Norton had not: he was a lord, wealthy, witty, good-looking and very charming. Hovering in the background was George Norton's brother, Fletcher, Lord Grantley, in his late thirties, married for eleven years but childless, who had been wounded at Waterloo while serving as a young officer in the Grenadier Guards and was thereafter sarcastically known as Waterloo Grantley.[9] Grantley had a reputation as a malevolent puppeteer determined to bring down Lord Melbourne and the government, and at the same time rid his family of his too-clever-by-half sister-in-law. An important friend of the Nortons was Lord Wynford, a judge whose gout required him to be carried into the House of Lords in an armchair. Wynford was George Norton's godfather, his father's executor and trustee of the Grantley estate, and deeply involved in the bringing of the case. He was in court.[10]

None of the named parties was in court. George Norton was with his clan at their London home in Mayfair; Lord Melbourne was going about his prime ministerial business in Downing Street, seeming insouciant but nervous of the outcome; Mrs Norton was in hiding at her mother's home, a grace-and-favour apartment at Hampton Court Palace where the Sheridans had lived since the death of their father in 1817. Unable to appear in public because of the scandal generated by the case, she had arranged for her elder brother to send a messenger on horseback with news of the proceedings.

Opening the case, George Norton's leading counsel Sir William Follett went straight on the attack. He reminded the court of the 'painful task' that had been imposed upon him and was sure 'gentlemen that in justice to all parties – the plaintiff, the defendant and the lady herself, you will dismiss as far as you possibly can from your minds the idle rumour and talk to which this case has given rise – that you will approach it as you would a trial between two persons whose names were wholly unknown to you – that you act upon the evidence alone which I shall adduce on the part of the plaintiff; and if that satisfies you of the guilt of the defendant, you will fearlessly so pronounce your verdict'. The Nortons' marriage had been happy 'at least on the part of Mr Norton, of the most unbounded affection'. Follett described how quickly the friendship between Lord Melbourne, 'a man of high rank', and the 'unfortunate' Mrs Norton, a woman of 'beauty, talents and accomplishments', had blossomed. He was a 'constant visitor' to the Nortons' home in Storey's Gate, which looked on to Birdcage Walk, a five-minute walk from Dorset House in Whitehall, where Melbourne had worked as home secretary, and also from 10 Downing Street, to which he moved when he became prime minister in 1834. It was a convenient stopping-off point on his way home across St James's Park to his house in South Street near Park Lane. Norton's barrister suggested that Lord Melbourne had insinuated his way into the young couple's lives by 'taking advantage of his high position to lull suspicion asleep, to introduce himself into the family of Mr Norton as his benefactor, his patron and his friend, to inflict the deepest injury one man can inflict upon another'.

It had been obvious to everyone who saw them together that Caroline was infatuated with Melbourne and he was flattered by the adoration of the dark-haired beauty. By way of explaining the large amount of time they spent together she would say that Melbourne and her father had been friends, which was true. Both Thomas Sheridan and Melbourne had been born in the 1770s, and he had stories to share with her. Now in her late twenties, Caroline's memories of her father were fading: he had died in South Africa in 1817, when she was nine, where her parents had gone in search of a cure for his tuberculosis four years before. Melbourne and Caroline conversed about her poetry and prose, and he enjoyed her brilliant mimicry and racy Sheridan wit. Unlike her Tory husband, Caroline, who inherited her Whig politics from her father and grandfather, had been active in the campaign supporting the passing of the Catholic Emancipation Act (1829) and the Great Reform Act (1832). George Norton and his family had opposed these reforms and had been disgruntled at Caroline's insistence on taking her own line and expressing her political views in society.

Sir William Follett promised to produce evidence that shortly after Melbourne and Caroline's first meeting 'criminal inter-course commenced between them and was continued for a very considerable time afterwards'. George Norton's magistrate's duties in Whitechapel meant he was away from home most of the day, often returning at seven o'clock in the evening to learn that the prime minister had visited that afternoon or was still with his wife in the drawing room. Often Melbourne would stay and join the Nortons for dinner.[11]

Follett reminded the jury that circumstantial evidence could lead to a guilty verdict in cases of adultery, citing the judgment of an earlier case: 'it is not necessary to prove the direct act of adultery because . . . it is very rarely indeed that the parties are surprised in the act . . . because if it were otherwise, there was not one case in a hundred in which the act had been committed where such proof were attainable'. The rules for circumstantial evidence were not hard and fast, and he reminded the jurors of factors such as 'the station and character of the parties, the state of general manners, and by many other incidental circumstances apparently slight and delicate in themselves but which may have important bearings in the decision of particular cases'. Follett ended by quoting that the only general rule that could be laid down 'is that the circumstances must be such as would lead the guarded discretion of a reasonable and just man to come to the conclusion'. Everything would hinge on the jury having the qualities of a reasonable and just man.

Follett made much of the fact that Lord Melbourne would enter 2 Storey's Gate via the back door and not the front: 'in what way, I ask, did he come as a visitor when Mr Norton was not at home? It does appear rather extraordinary – the house opens into Birdcage Walk. Was that the visit of a friend, or like any other person coming to the house?' When Lord Melbourne visited the blinds were drawn and no other visitors – not even the most 'intimate friends and relations' were admitted. Mrs Norton told her servants never to enter the room unless she rang or sent for them, and the drawing room in which she saw Melbourne was always locked from the inside. Caroline Norton made elaborate preparations to receive Lord Melbourne, dressing carefully, arranging her hair, pencilling her eyebrows and rouging her face. And 'while he was in the house she has frequently gone up to her bedroom with her hair and her dress disordered, and having put herself to rights, washed her hands and arranged her dress and hair, she would come downstairs again to Lord Melbourne'. Great importance was given to a handful of brief but essentially uninteresting notes Lord Melbourne had sent to Mrs Norton. 'How are you?' one asked. Another announced, 'I will call about half past four. Yours.' Another, 'I shall not be able to call today, but I probably shall tomorrow. Yours.' They were hardly passionate, but Follett injected into their discovery as much moral outrage as he could summon.

Follett went on to allege that criminal conversation had also taken place elsewhere and promised to produce evidence of Mrs Norton visiting Lord Melbourne's house in South Street, travelling there in the carriage of a young female friend whom Caroline would then send off for half an hour's drive round Hyde Park. The lawyer thundered, 'Where was she in Lord Melbourne's house? In what room? Who was with her? What was she doing – a 'young and beautiful woman in such extraordinary and suspicious circumstances?' There had also been occasions on which Caroline was ill and confined to her bedroom when the prime minister had been admitted and spent hours alone with her with the door bolted. Follett asked the jury to remember the 'manners of the present day' when they heard more of this later.

In households like the Nortons' and Lord Melbourne's, and indeed wherever servants were employed, maids and footmen knew a lot about their masters and mistresses. Privacy as we understand it now did not exist for people like Caroline Norton. The women who laid her fire in the morning also took away her chamber pot, and made and changed her bedding and personal linen, bathed and dressed her, while men waited on her at table and drove her carriage. They knew when she and George had sex, and when she had her period. At 'crim con' trials servants were the star witnesses, and real or imagined grievances could decide a case. Servants who had been dismissed were especially dangerous. Sir William Follett called a string of servants employed by or still working for George Norton, who offered detailed and colourful accounts of the Norton marriage and the damage it had suffered at the hands of the nation's prime minister.

The servants, who had been interviewed by clerks and agents

paid for by Norton's brother Lord Grantley, supplied plenty of circumstantial evidence which George's team expected to win the case for them. Follett titillated the jury with a few tales of servants going to Mrs Norton's bedroom, finding the door bolted and hearing Lord Melbourne's voice. They had seen 'kisses passing between the parties', noticed his arm draped round her neck, her hand on his knee, found her kneeling on the floor at his feet, and many more 'familiarities and such things as would make you wonder'. Mrs Norton had even been seen lying on the floor, 'and her clothes in a position to expose her person' alone with Lord Melbourne.

Bodily fluids were regularly brought up at such proceedings as evidence of adultery. It was his 'painful duty', said Follett, to produce witnesses who had seen 'those marks which are the consequence of intercourse between the sexes. We shall show those marks existed on the day linen which will be shown to have existed on her gown; from which, and the other facts I have stated, there can, I apprehend, be no doubt of the guilty connection of these parties.'

Follett now called a string of witnesses – a Norton cousin and a motley crew of male and female servants who had worked for the couple during the period of the alleged affair – who were questioned and cross-examined by both legal teams. Trinette Elliot, a lady's maid who had served her mistress for two years from 1831, supplied details of Caroline's rouging and heavy use of pocket handkerchiefs whenever Melbourne visited. Ellen Monk, who had been a nurse to the three boys for six months in 1834, described seeing Lord Melbourne with Mrs Norton in her bedroom when she was unwell. Looking faint when she was called, Eliza Gibson, a housemaid, was allowed to sit down to be questioned. During the six months she worked at Storey's Gate in 1833 she had also sometimes acted as Mrs Norton's lady's maid and noted how often she rouged and re-rouged and needed to tidy her 'dishevelled appearance and tumbled hair'.

Thomas Bulliman, a footman who had worked for George Norton for only a month in the summer of 1833, told the court about Caroline's carriage rides with her friend Sophia Armstrong. Bulliman had worked for Colonel Armstrong, Sophia's father, for nearly two years before going to the Nortons. His duties included accompanying Miss Armstrong, who was driven round the park for thirty minutes after taking Caroline to Melbourne. Mrs Norton was then picked up and taken back to Storey's Gate. Thomas Tucker succeeded Bulliman as the Nortons' footman at Christmas 1833 and stayed for eight months. He told of turning visitors away when Lord Melbourne was with Caroline, delivering notes to him at Downing Street and letting him into the house shortly after being summoned by notes from his mistress.

John Fluke, coachman and groom to the Nortons from 1830 to 1834, was the most entertaining and certainly the slipperiest witness to be called. He had also worked in the house, answering the door and running errands. Initially his evidence was the most damning for Mrs Norton, but under careful cross-examination by Melbourne's team Fluke came apart at the seams. He preferred to play to the public in the gallery rather than answer questions clearly. One story has the tone of a bodice-ripper novel. Returning from an errand to buy theatre tickets, Fluke knocked twice on the door of the drawing room to deliver them to his mistress. Receiving no answer and thinking no one was there, he walked into the room and found the prime minister 'sitting in a chair on the left [hand side of the room] at the fire with his elbows on his knees, his head reclining on his hands, and his face turned towards Mrs Norton. She was lying down on the right side with her feet towards the door, and her head upon the hearth rug. Mrs Norton, the moment I got into the middle of the room, when I was going to deliver the message, shifted herself with her hands, and rose up a little. Lord Melbourne looked at her and she looked again at his lordship, she then turned round, and never said anything, but gave me a bow as much as to say, "That is enough," after I had delivered my message. Mrs Norton's clothes were up and I saw the thick part of her thigh.' No words were spoken and Fluke turned round and left the room, scuttling downstairs to tell the rest of the servants what he had seen.

Anticipating this potentially disastrous tale, Melbourne's team had done their homework and proceeded to lead the witness into destroying his own credibility. It became apparent Fluke was a man who was fond of a drink – cheerfully admitting he had a few before he came into court set off shrieks of laughter in the public gallery. He was manoeuvred into divulging that he had been beset with financial problems and his family life was in chaos. While he was working for the Nortons part time, he also owned a small livery stable hiring out horses and gigs by the day, but the business collapsed and he was saddled with debts. In 1834 Fluke was dismissed by the Nortons for drunkenness after the last in a string of incidents. On what turned out to be his last day in their employment he drove George Norton to his work in court, and unusually Caroline accompanied her husband. It was usual for the coachmen to have a drink together while they waited, but Fluke cheerfully admitted, 'to tell the truth I got a drop too much. Mr and Mrs Norton fell out [on the way home] and of course they put the spite on me and I was discharged.' Caroline was angry because he almost lost control of the carriage: 'you could not please her very easily . . . the black horse threatened to gallop, and I could not get him into a trot; horses will break sometimes, you can't help it'. Fluke was exposed as a disgruntled servant who had been nursing a grudge for the past two years. Melbourne's team had spoken to people who had heard him blame Mrs Norton for his dismissal and call her 'a d----d b---h' [damned bitch].

A depressing picture emerged of Fluke's circumstances after leaving the Nortons. He revealed that his fortunes had taken a slide and he had been living in a cellar in Covent Garden with his pregnant wife and three surviving children of ten, selling old clothes and cobbling shoes. Born in Worcestershire in 1795, he joined the 73rd Regiment of Foot when he was eighteen and served in the East Indies and fought at Waterloo. He told the court he was a veteran injured in action, slashed in the hip, but Fluke had actually been wounded in India in 1817 – almost 'unmanned' – leaving him incontinent, and was discharged from the army in 1819 with a pension of sixpence a day. He had enlisted for an indefinite period, hoping to make the army his life, but at twenty-four, the young man was left on his own suffering from an untreatable and embarrassing condition.[12]

At the time of the trial Fluke was looking after the horses of Captain Charles Francis Norton of the 52nd Regiment of Foot while he was posted to the East Indies. Charles had put in a good word for Fluke with his brother George, and that is how Fluke came to be a witness in court that day. His cockiness, his behaviour while he was employed by George Norton and the fact that he had worked for the family for several years suggest a man ripe to be groomed to give evidence against the woman who had dismissed him.

But he was no match for Melbourne's lawyers. Under cross-examination Fluke cheerfully revealed that he and other servants had been put up by Lord Grantley at the Grantley Arms and other lodgings in Wonersh, the village owned by him near his country seat. Frequently tipsy, Fluke had been heard to boast that he was 'the principal witness against the Premier of England' and was expecting to receive five or six hundred pounds when the trial was over (now between forty and fifty thousand pounds). John Fluke denied having made such remarks, but the damage was done and all present could see that he had been coached by Lord Grantley's lawyers and also encouraged to 'fish up evidence' to support Norton's case by looking for other disgruntled servants.

One of the servants he fished up and spent time with at Wonersh was Ann Cummins. She was recently widowed with three children when she went to work for the Nortons as a nurse and sometimes lady's maid in the autumn of 1831. She left Storey's Gate at the end of 1834. During her time there the Nortons' second son Brinsley was born in 1831 and William two years later. Questioned by Mr Crowder, she told the court of a conversation she had overheard between her mistress and Lord Melbourne, who paid a call on Mrs Norton some days after Brinsley's birth. This was intended to plant the idea in the minds of the jury that Melbourne might have been the father of the child. 'Mrs Norton took the baby and kissed him and asked Lord Melbourne if it were not a handsome baby; and he patted it on the head and kissed it, and said it was not like Norton.'

Cummins' personal life was also in something of a muddle. Out of work since leaving the Nortons, Fluke had found her living in a lodging house in Tottenham Court Road with her children. A man by the name of Owen, a tailor, was the father of the child she was carrying when she left the Norton household. He had promised to marry her, but they were broke and would not do so 'until trade gets good'. As a widowed Roman Catholic with an illegitimate baby who had asked to swear on the Cross before she gave her evidence, she may not have made a good impression on the jury. She came across as an evasive witness whose memory seemed vague when she was asked to recall conversations with her landlady at Wonersh. Probed by Frederic Thesiger, she said that she had been driven out of

London, 'teased' by visits from an agent working for Lord Melbourne and a messenger from Mrs Norton, and was forced to admit that she had been staying at Wonersh at Lord Grantley's expense. Awkwardly for Norton's legal team, Thesiger got her to admit she had also been 'tormented' by their own clerks and threatened by Norton (a magistrate) that he would send a policeman to take her to the country. Terrified, she fled to Lord Grantley at Wonersh, where she was paid five pounds for her trouble, received a pound a week for the month she was there, and got three pounds to pay for the carriage that took her back to London. Ann Cummins took her three children and young baby with her but left Mr Owen behind. Under Thesiger's cross-examination she admitted that at Wonersh she had discussed details of the case with John Fluke and his wife, and had been 'examined' five times for her appearance in court.

Even Norton's legal team did not have it all their own way with their well-rehearsed witness. Despite Follett coaxing her several times to believe the 'marks' on Mrs Norton's linen evidence of her 'connexion' with Lord Melbourne, Ann Cummins stubbornly refused to admit that she had been suspicious of an affair. And though she had seen Mrs Norton's hand on his knee, when her mistress made a point of explaining to her that 'the freedom between them was owing to Lord Melbourne's having been so well-acquainted with her father', she had believed Caroline.

Several hours into the trial the jury was told of a row between George Norton and his brother-in-law Richard Brinsley Sheridan, who lived in magnificent style at Frampton House in Dorset. The two did not get on, and George Norton was not invited to join his wife and children and all the Sheridan family for Easter 1836 at Frampton a couple of months before the trial. To her husband's outrage, Caroline was determined to go with the children and leave him behind. Martha Morris, a nurse to the three Norton children, painted a picture of the tension in her employers' marriage. As far as she knew, up to the time of the row her master and mistress had been living 'in the usual terms of matrimonial affection and perfect harmony', a decorous way of saying they still shared a bed and were having sex. On the evening of 28 March 1836, the night before Caroline and the boys were due to leave for Frampton, she and George went out to dinner; the row about the visit continued in the carriage home and until the early hours of the morning. At 3 a.m. Norton went up to the nursery and woke Morris to say that the children would not be going to Dorset the next day and that his 'orders were not to be disobeyed'. A short time later, still in her evening finery, Caroline visited the nursery and asked Morris what her husband had said.

At 7 a.m., when George left the house to go to his office in Whitechapel, Caroline walked the short distance to her sister Lady Seymour's house in nearby Spring Gardens to tell her what had happened and that the children were not allowed to visit Frampton. What Caroline did not know was that George Norton had arranged for Martha Morris to take the boys to a lodging house in Upper Berkeley Street that morning. When Caroline returned home she was shocked to find her children and their nurse gone. Interrogating the servants for the address, she found the place, arriving in 'a state of the greatest affliction' and went into a 'state of the deepest agony' when she was told that her husband had left orders that no one be allowed to see the children. She begged to see them for an hour, but his wishes were obeyed and she reluctantly left in 'great distress'. She spent the night with her sister Georgiana not knowing that the boys had gone back to their home in Storey's Gate that evening before being taken to Wonersh the next morning. From that day on Caroline Norton had never seen her children.

Eight and a half hours in a stuffy and crowded court were

taking their toll on Sir John Campbell, who asked the judge to adjourn the proceedings until the next morning. He was 'quite exhausted, so much so, that it was impracticable that he should be in such a state of exhaustion to do justice to his client which the importance of the case demanded, or that the jury could listen with that degree of attention to the arguments he should feel himself bound to address to them'.

Follett may have felt he had his opponent on the ropes and objected. The jurors said they wanted to continue, and the judge adjourned the court for fifteen minutes so that the attorney general 'might refresh himself'. There was no closing statement from the prosecution. Getting to his feet, Campbell, whose words would be the last that the jury would hear, apart from the judge's summing-up, said he was 'sure . . . his client would be delivered from the unfounded charge that had been brought against him'. He had called no witnesses, he explained, because no case had been made against his client – there was 'no proof whatever in the evidence which had been submitted'. He agreed that the offence Lord Melbourne was accused of was 'a high crime . . . the violation of the marriage vow was one of the greatest crimes', but warned the jury that because of the gravity of the accusation 'the proof ought to be clear and convincing'.

Campbell went to the heart of his defence by urging the jury to look at the character of each of the witnesses and assess the credibility of their accounts: 'they must believe that the adulterous act was really committed and completed between the parties, for nothing short of that proof could entitle the plaintiff to a verdict'. The attorney general agreed that his client and Mrs Norton had an 'intimacy', but insisted that it was 'of innocent friendship', had been sanctioned by Mr Norton, and that there were many examples of him encouraging his wife's friendship with the powerful man who had exercised his right of patronage more than once in Norton's favour. He attacked the prosecution's case as entirely politically motivated: 'Mr Norton was evidently under some delusion, and had been made a tool of by others for political motives . . . It has been put into the plaintiff's mind by some insinuating rogue by whom he had been played upon. Someone had laid hold of him, and for indirect purposes advised him to bring forward this charge, of which he had never dreamed before.'

Campbell referred to the presence of Lord Grantley in court just a few yards from him. He wondered aloud why Grantley had not been called as a witness and why he had chosen to 'remain mute on the bench' and asked if he was there from curiosity or was there 'to grace the cause'. The head of the family and paymaster to all, he said, was the man directing and coordinating the attack on Lord Melbourne. A man of ultra-Tory views but with little ability as a politician, he was surely there to remind the witnesses that he would be paying them, but only if his brother's case was won. Campbell pointed out that the leader of the Tory party, Sir Robert Peel, was also in court, proving that politics was at the heart of the drama.

The evidence against the prime minister was a string of stories told by 'discarded servants – a race most dangerous in all cases, but particularly in cases of this sort'. What they said they had seen and heard related to the period from 1831 to the end of 1834 during which time some of them had been dismissed by the Nortons for being drunk or 'in the family way'. No evidence was offered of any moments of criminal conversation in 1835 and 1836 by anyone who still worked for them or had left for a better position. Campbell reminded the jury of the questionable value of testimony given by servants years after the alleged events: 'In a discovery made by a servant, it was important to show that it was promptly communicated to the party injured. If it is not made until after a quarrel or dismissal from the service, or after a long interval, the evidence labours under great suspicion.'

If George Norton had known of the intimate moments when they had happened in the early 1830s, Campbell asked, why had he done nothing about the heinous crime which had been committed against him before now? He also asked why the servants had not reported the matter to their master at the time, and why they had waited in some cases five years to report it to him and the agents acting for his brother. Campbell pointed out that of the string of witnesses Sir William Follett had called only two were 'respectable gentlemen' – a Norton uncle and a family friend and barrister, who both described the happy early years of the marriage. The rest were a ragtag bunch, some of whom had been fished up by Lord Grantley's agents and paid to give evidence. Their stories were garbled, had been coached and 'were wholly unworthy of belief, or . . . spoke to facts utterly immaterial'.

Campbell reiterated John Fluke's evidence and blasted it with his attorney general's scorn: 'this man said that he . . . saw Mrs Norton lying on the rug, like a Spartan virgin, exposing her thigh without making any effort to adjust her dress and they looked at each other, and he delivered his message and she nodded to him and he went away. Was this credible? Was it to be supposed that the act of adultery had taken place, and that when Fluke came in she should continue in that posture and make him a bow, or that she should lie like a statue, without any effort to recompose her dress, for the mere purpose of allowing Mr Fluke to gratify his curiosity? The most profligate woman could not have behaved in such a manner.'

The attorney general thanked the jury for asking whether the Nortons were sleeping together at the time of the alleged adultery, to which the answer was yes. This proved that a 'depravity' between her and Melbourne could not have taken place: 'everyone knew that after a woman surrendered her person to a paramour, she looked down upon her husband with loathing and abhorrence'. He said that Mrs Norton 'continued to the last fond of her husband', and he declared to God that for him this was the most convincing proof of her innocence.

Campbell argued that the frequency of Lord Melbourne's visits and the fact that he used the back rather than the front door – quite reasonable considering how well known he was – did not add up to adultery. Mrs Norton's beauty, literary accomplishments and conversation were widely known, and when Lord Melbourne had no domestic engagements why should he not 'cultivate friendship without being suspected to abuse confidence'? He reiterated that the matter was not a personal one; that Mr Norton had willingly been duped for party-political purposes. The attorney general concluded by saying that Lord Melbourne had instructed him to make clear in the 'most emphatic and solemn manner, that he had never had any criminal intercourse' with Mrs Norton, nor had he done anything 'in the slightest degree to abuse the confidence of Mr Norton'.

By the time Judge Tindal began his summing-up, urging the jury not to give a guilty verdict if they only suspected guilt, but consider the case as 'men of sense and discrimination', the midsummer light which had flooded into the top-lit room was starting to fade and the candles and oil and gas lamps had been lit. Tindal asked the jurors to 'apply to the evidence the same degree of guarded and temperate discrimination as they would to the ordinary transactions of life'. With regard to the amount of damages demanded he declined to guide them, believing they were 'men of the world and of good sense'. It had been a long day: by half-past eleven everyone in the room was exhausted by the battle that had been waged before them, and just wanted it to end. The place blazed with a muggy light and reeked of the fug of stale bodies.

The foreman of the jury, Robert Stafford, a merchant who lived nearby in Smith Square, gave the verdict immediately.

'My Lord, we are agreed. It is my duty to say that we have agreed to a verdict for the defendant.' It was twenty minutes before midnight. There were shouts of 'Bravo' from one end of the court and 'loud cheers and hisses from a different part of the room'. Tindal got to his feet angered by this 'disgraceful conduct' and asked the police to seize anyone in contempt of court. Silence prevailed for a short time, but when the verdict reached the crowd gathered outside in New Palace Yard there was uproar.

For Lord Grantley and the expensive legal team he had taken to Westminster Hall this was a disaster, while Lord Melbourne's lawyers must have been stunned and relieved. It was clear to everyone in court that the most damning evidence had been supplied by servants hired by George, some dismissed on Caroline's orders, then bought and paid for by Grantley. John Fluke, a cheeky swindler, had enjoyed his day in court but had undermined his paymaster's efforts. His tipsy casualness had enlivened the proceedings and pricked the pomposity of Follett's line of questioning. The jury had listened to his saucy evidence and not been shocked by it; sometimes they laughed.

The verdict could have gone in Norton's favour, but the jury was clearly convinced that Norton's feelings had been manipulated by his family in an attempt to bring down Lord Melbourne and his government. The jury saw the bringing of the case and the demand for damages as politics and extortion. The fact that George Norton had not resigned his well-paid job as a magistrate, obtained for him by Melbourne, seemed significant. The Honourable George Norton had been shown to be a man lacking in honour. The day after the trial and for many days that followed the newspapers featured transcripts of the proceedings, and the 'Unfortunate George Norton' became a laughing-stock, a 'noodle' with only a questionable right to call himself a gentleman. However, although Lord Melbourne and Caroline

Norton had been found not guilty of adultery, Caroline's reputation was ruined. Polite society and the wider public made their own decisions: the trial itself, regardless of the outcome, had branded the Honourable Mrs Norton a dishonourable and scandalous woman. It was a label she would never quite shake off for the rest of her life.

Following the trial Caroline consulted lawyers to see if she could divorce George Norton. She learned to her dismay that he could not sue her for adultery as she had been proved innocent, and that the only way she could divorce George was to sue him for adultery, which would be difficult to prove. There was also the added complication of the time in 1835 when Caroline had left George after a row. By returning to him she had apparently condoned his behaviour, which meant that she was unable to seek a divorce from him ever after. They were stuck with each other until one of them died. Estranged and living apart from her husband, Caroline had no automatic right to see her children, and he was immovable on the point. Caroline would not be able to change his mind, so she set about changing the law.

I

Caroline Sheridan and George Norton

That is not a child I would care to meet in a dark wood!

Richard Brinsley Sheridan

Well made, though not tall . . . with a fine ruddy complexion.

Joan Gray Perkins

Caroline Elizabeth Sarah Sheridan was born in London on 22 March 1808 to the sound of coughing. Her father Thomas Sheridan was riddled with consumption, the 'white death'. The antique name for pulmonary tuberculosis was phthisis, in Greek 'to waste away', which describes the effect of the disease, which is a bacterial infection of the lungs and other organs and was the single biggest killer in nineteenth-century Britain. It killed Tom's beautiful mother, the singer Miss Eliza Linley, 'whose bewitching melody went straight to the heart', when Tom was seventeen. It was said at the time that the road from Hot Wells in Bristol, where she died aged thirty-seven, to Wells Cathedral, where she was buried sixteen miles away, was lined with mourners. Tom Sheridan died in his forties, leaving his thirty-seven-year-old widow with seven children aged from eleven to a babe in arms. Tuberculosis also blighted the lives of Caroline's two youngest brothers, Frank and Charlie, killing them in their thirties.

Caroline was the third child of a famously beautiful mother, also named Caroline. Her father was the eldest son of Richard Brinsley 'Sherry' Sheridan, who had eloped with Tom's mother and fought two duels over her. Tom inherited his mother's dark hair and good looks, playing the part of Regency buck with enthusiasm and success. Known as Dazzle, he was a talented comic actor and singer who wrote poetry and melodrama. Never a keen student, at Harrow school he had 'wit and humour but no knowledge' and was popular, 'the idol of the young men who pronounced him the cleverest man in the place'.[1] Tom was allowed to run wild as a child, his father preoccupied and his mother's health delicate for years, bouts of tuberculosis followed by periods of remission were the rhythm of their family life.[2] Eliza Sheridan was slowly dying and in no position to guide her irrepressible son when he needed the firmest of hands.

Tom's parents were estranged for much of his childhood. Although their relationship had begun as a romantic and passionate love affair followed by an elopement, his father's affections strayed the year Tom was born, when Sheridan started an affair with another great beauty of the day, Frances Anne Crewe. He then conceived a passion for Harriet Ponsonby, Lady Duncannon, which ended his marriage in all but name. Eliza was wounded by her husband's infidelities and what she called the 'duplicity of his conduct . . . my heart is entirely alienated from him'. She had a fling with the Duke of Clarence, later William IV, who was infatuated with her brittle beauty, and in 1790 fell in love with Lord Edward Fitzgerald, an Irish nationalist and army officer nearly ten years younger than her. (In 1798 he would die in the struggle for Irish independence.) Their child Mary was born on 30 March 1792; three months later Eliza died of tuberculosis. Fitzgerald agreed that Tom's father should adopt the baby and bring her up as his own child, but Mary was delicate and died at seven months.[3]

Three years later Richard Brinsley Sheridan, forty-three, married eighteen-year-old Hester Jane Ogle, known as Hecca, daughter of the dean of Winchester. She was as much of a handful as his own son, who was a year older than his new stepmother. George Canning, a close friend of Sheridan and under-secretary for foreign affairs, found Hecca 'wilder and more strange in her air, dress and manners than anything human, or at least anything female I ever saw'.[4] In 1796 Charles Brinsley Sheridan was born, stepbrother to twenty-one-year-old Tom.

Running through Tom Sheridan's life were his eagerness to please and his need to entertain. Finding it almost impossible to be serious, he was happier inhabiting a comic character from one of his father's plays than being himself. When his father suggested to him that it was time he took a wife, he answered, 'Yes, sir, but whose?' Harriette Wilson, London's most famous courtesan, would not travel alone in a hackney carriage with Tom Sheridan in case he molested her.[5]

Tom Sheridan's working life was spent in his father's shadow. Sometimes he performed on the stage, but mostly he managed his father's theatre in Drury Lane, nursing it from one financial crisis to another. In the first two years of the nineteenth century, showing how highly he regarded both father and son, King George III wrote several times to Richard Sheridan about how the precociously talented Tom's life seemed to be close to coming off the rails, and despairing that the father had instructed his son to refuse any help the King offered him: 'I am more anxious than I can express about Tom's welfare. It is indeed unfortunate that you have been obliged to refuse these things for him.'[6] Eventually a position came up in the autumn of 1803 that did meet with the father's approval, and Tom was allowed to accept a commission in the Prince of Wales' own regiment, the 10th Light Dragoons, and became aide-de-camp to Lord Moira, army commander-in-chief in Scotland, for three years. Despite having friends in the highest of places – the Prince of Wales financed three of his attempts – Tom Sheridan was never elected a Member of Parliament, failing twice at Liskeard in 1802 and 1804 and twice at Stafford in 1806 and 1807.[7]

Caroline Henrietta Callander was born in Dublin in 1779 and so was four years younger than Tom. She and her sisters were brought up by their aunts at Ardkinglas in Scotland. Fanny Kemble remarked that she was more beautiful than anybody but her own three daughters.[8] Caroline, who was 'sensible, amicable and gentle', met Tom Sheridan in Edinburgh in 1805 while he was working for Lord Moira. Just as his father had eloped with his mother, Tom eloped with Caroline to Gretna Green, where they were married on Midsummer's Day 1805, and then more formally in London on 29 November at St George's Church, Hanover Square.[9] When Caroline walked down that aisle she was four months pregnant with their son Richard Brinsley, who was born on 29 April 1806. Tom's father Sherry was enchanted by his new daughter-in-law, finding her 'lovely and engaging and interesting beyond measure'.[10] However, the rumbustious Tom soon found his new bride's apparent perfection trying, insisting that 'her extreme quietness and tranquillity is a defect in her character' and accusing her 'of such an extreme apprehension of giving trouble . . . as to be an absolute affectation'. Mocking her sweet nature in a letter to one of his fellow guests on their honeymoon at Inverary Castle he wrote, 'if she were to set her clothes on fire, she would step to the bell very quietly, and say to the servant, with great gentleness and composure "Pray William is there any water in the house?" "No Madam; but I can soon get some." "Oh dear, I dare say the fire will go out of itself."'[11]

Caroline Sheridan was a poet and budding novelist, and the young Sheridans were often broke, frequently on the cadge, borrowing money, paying it back, taking out another loan straightaway. Despite settling the financial future of his younger son, Charles Brinsley, Sherry never secured Tom's financial future and even expected him to borrow money to bail his father out of a string of financial difficulties. Sherry's fondness for drink and gambling made money disappear. Caroline had to wait for her long-living rogue of a father (Sir Walter Scott called him 'a swindler of the first order') to die in 1831 before she received the inheritance her mother, Lady Elizabeth Macdonnell, had left her. In May 1806 the young Sheridans gave a gala for the christening of Richard Brinsley, whose godparents were the Prince of Wales and the Countess of Westmoreland. There was a 'sumptuous dinner for thirty-six persons' and in the evening a masque acted by the artistes of the Opera House and Drury Lane Theatre. The day ended with 'a ball and supper in a distinguished style of taste, elegance and variety'.[12]

A year before Tom Sheridan married Caroline Callander he had had a dalliance with Mrs Elizabeth Campbell, the wife of a Jamaican plantation owner. The Campbells had moved to England in the mid-1790s because of Elizabeth's delicate health. Tom met the couple in Edinburgh in the autumn of 1803; they had been married for thirteen years when he arrived in their lives. Elizabeth Dunston had married Peter Campbell, ten years older than her, when she was sixteen and had three daughters, one of whom had died. A beauty and 'a woman of the greatest accomplishments', she was the same age as Tom and feeling restless in her marriage when she met Lord Moira's dashing new aide-de-camp. The rules about paying social calls were looser in Edinburgh than London, and Tom found he could visit the Campbells 'at all hours and at all times'.

The affair was discovered by the Campbells' housekeeper Mary Brotherton during the evening of 29 February 1804, two days after Peter Campbell had gone to London, when Tom Sheridan was found in her master's bedroom. Hearing all the commotion Mrs Campbell came out of her room and asked what was going on, and Mary, talking from a position of strength, told her mistress she was surprised that Mrs Campbell was asking her 'when she knew what she had done'. Mrs Campbell 'put out her hand and begged Mary Brotherton to be her friend'. The housekeeper acquiesced, but only 'in everything that was right, but never in anything that was wrong'. Elizabeth Campbell and Tom Sheridan were off the hook, but only for as long as Mary Brotherton kept quiet.

Not long after that illicit night of passion Tom met his future wife and they moved to London. In 1806 he had a brief spell as muster-master general for Ireland before his father gave him a quarter-share in Drury Lane Theatre and appointed him manager. While running Drury Lane and also managing the Lyceum, he and his father were also trying, and failing, to get Tom elected as an MP. Artistically, Tom's career was more successful: his poetry was praised and he was working on a 'grand ballet', which was performed the following year. How much Caroline knew about her husband's life before their elopement is unknown, but by the time his private life became public property in July 1807 – when Peter Campbell learned what had happened three years before, and sued Tom for criminal conversation with his wife with damages of fifteen hundred pounds – Caroline Sheridan had two children under two, Richard Brinsley and Helen Selina. Some time during the ensuing and embarrassing hearing she became pregnant with Caroline. Three babies in three years.

Tom Sheridan appeared in a contemporary cartoon as a young blade in uniform being threatened by a candlestick-wielding crone. He did not defend the case, although his lawyer John Curwood tried to get the damages reduced by reminding the jury 'he is a person having no fortune at all' whose father was well known 'in every corner of the country' and from whom he had inherited 'wit, genius and taste' but 'I fear, nothing more'. If the jury awarded the maximum damages his client would be ruined, 'immured in the walls of a prison and the country would lose the benefit of his talent'. Curwood accepted that Tom would have to pay something, but pleaded with the jury 'not to give way to those prejudices which naturally arise out of a case of this sort'. The lawyer did his best, but the jury awarded Peter Campbell the full amount for 'Trespass, Assault and Criminal Conversation.' [13]

Tom and his father scrabbled around to pay the damages, borrowing money from actor chums and Sherry's agent Richard Peake. The loyal and long-suffering Peake received frantic scrawled notes from Tom begging him to advance money, presumably to keep his young family afloat: 'I am in town [London] again tomorrow night. Do not for God's sake forget me.' Tom tried gambling his way out of trouble. One night he was playing cards at Watier's Club in Piccadilly when his fellow masher Beau Brummell breezed in and came to his rescue. The dandy and diarist Thomas Raikes described how Brummell took Tom's place at the table, offering to share the winnings and adding two hundred pounds in counters to the ten pounds Tom was playing with. Brummell did brilliantly and in ten minutes won fifteen hundred pounds. He gave half the winnings to Tom and told him to 'go home and give your wife and brats supper and never play again'. Caroline Sheridan was to become another one of those 'brats'. [14]

When she was born Caroline was 'a queer, dark-looking little baby' with lots of black hair. Her mother wrote to one of her brothers she was 'stout and strong and the prettiest infant I ever saw'. [15] There was no lavish christening gala as there had been for her brother; money was still being borrowed to pay off the damages to keep her father out of prison. Every pound would have to be repaid within a specified time and with interest.

But despite all the efforts made on his behalf and his own ingenuity in dodging those charged with seizing him and his goods in lieu of the debt, Tom was arrested on 3 June 1808 and sent to the Fleet Prison near Ludgate Hill. The conditions there were awful, 'crowded with women and children, being riotous and dirty', an alcohol-fuelled and disease-ridden environment.[16]

Eventually bonds were drawn up, money was advanced, the lawyers' bills grew and Tom was released and could return to work, no longer in fear of Campbell's bailiffs. But the debt would hang over the Sheridans' heads for some time. And life got much harder for Tom and his family the day after a bill to dissolve the Campbells' marriage was debated by the House of Lords. On 24 February 1809 the Sheridan family's most important asset, Drury Lane Theatre, went up in smoke. The scenery caught fire and the whole place was reducing to a charred ruin, the flames lighting up the windows of the House of Commons 'as strongly as if it had been in the Speaker's garden'. When Sherry was told about the fire he was listening to a speech in the House and reacted to the news calmly, declining the offer that the sitting be adjourned. He left the Commons and sat in Drury Lane to watch his theatre burn down. When asked why he was taking it so well, he apparently replied, 'A man may surely be allowed to take a glass of wine by his own fireside.' The loss was three hundred thousand pounds (now nineteen million pounds) and only forty thousand was insured. Sheridan and his dependants faced an uncertain financial future. Drury Lane Theatre was rebuilt in three years, but rows and financial muddles meant that Tom and his father were excluded from the management of the new building. Taking umbrage, which he often took, at what he felt was shabby treatment, Sherry refused to go and see his own son's work when it was performed in the new building in 1813.[17]

Shortly after the fire Tom's wife became pregnant with their fourth child, Jane Georgiana, known as Georgy, who was born on 5 November 1809.[18] Tom's health had been failing long before the theatre caught fire; he was consumptive and being 'blistered'. Generations of doctors insisted that blistering was a good treatment despite the agony it caused the debilitated patient. 'The successive application of blisters seems the best. In many cases it will provoke and maintain suppuration at the surface. The practice is undoubtedly painful; but when the local lesions are recent, large in size and threaten to remain in the acute condition, such treatment is more beneficial than any other.'

Blistering was one of a number of painfully pointless treatments that consumptive patients had to endure. Another was bleeding, a panacea for all kinds of illnesses, which dangerously weakened those already very ill with tuberculosis. Cupping, which was supposed to draw out the infection, was worse. A cut was made in the flesh over the suspected site – in Tom's case it would have been his chest or back – and a hot glass with a roughened edge was placed over the wound. As the glass cooled and contracted, blood and sometimes pus and other 'necrotic material' oozed out through the open wound. The theory was that the noxious cause of the illness would be drawn out and the patient cured.[19]

During 1809 Tom and his pregnant wife sailed from Portsmouth to Spain on the battleship HMS *Audacious* to try to recover his health. Dry sunny climates were recommended for consumptives, and when they returned to England in September newspapers reported that Tom's health had considerably improved. He returned to running the Lyceum.[20] The following year he went on his own to Sicily in search of the sun, but his condition worsened and there were fears he might die. When he returned in July 1810 *The Times* reported that he had 'not much benefited by his foreign excursions.'[21] In his absence Tom's father and his wife Caroline, whom he had appointed to speak and act on his behalf, had successfully seen off an attempt by the Lord Mayor of London to build a theatre which could have threatened Drury Lane and Lyceum Theatres. This is Caroline Sheridan's mother taking on some of Tom's professional responsibilities in addition to her own domestic duties. Even with a couple of maids to help her run their home in South Audley Street, four children under the age of four represented a treadmill of daily chores.

In 1811, aged three, and with her father's poor health looming over family life like a black cloud, Caroline makes an appearance in family history. She was plonked on a table and proudly shown off to her famous grandfather. Like any three-year-old she became shy when confronted with an unfamiliar old face at close quarters. She looked 'frightened out of her wits' and stared at him 'with her enormous black eyes'. Unsettled by the intensity of her innocent scrutiny, the great dramatist and politician announced, 'That is not a child I would care to meet in a dark wood.'[22]

A fifth child, Thomas Berkeley, was born in London on 30 April 1811.[23] Since the autumn of 1805, Mrs Sheridan had been almost continuously pregnant and now had five children. By February 1812 Tom Sheridan had lost a great deal of weight, and was no longer the imposing fellow of the past. He was 'ill in spirits' and looked 'as thin as a Highland crop of oats'.[24] His appearance was disturbing to all who saw him, and yet he still persisted with the idea of a career in public life: 'I am mad about politics.'[25]

In September Tom and Caroline sailed to Madeira in another attempt to get him better. He was anxious to put his affairs in order with Richard Peake: 'Dick, I am very ill and wish to leave nothing unsettled that I can avoid.'[26] Being agent to Sherry, and personal banker to his son required endless patience, a thick skin, nerves of steel and a huge admiration for both that was sorely tested on a regular basis. Peake was often the mediator in their volatile and fractious relationship; coped with them

when they were racketing about town being drunk and dis-
orderly, sorting out the scrapes they got themselves into; fielded
bad news; and bailed them out financially. Tom begged Peake
for money and turned nasty when he was refused; ugly scenes
were described in notes written in the weeks before Mr and
Mrs Sheridan left for Madeira: 'I really can bear it no longer
and this moment I am so beset by the servants [who wanted
their wages] that I know not how I shall get out of the house
without giving them money.' Peake had been tested to the limit
and harsh words had been exchanged. Tom tried to make
amends: 'I think when you used the word swindler to me you
ought not to be surprised at a drunken man's anger.' [27]

Madeira did not restore his health, and by the spring of 1813
Tom and his wife were back in London and reunited with their
five children, who had been cared for by relatives. Tom now
successfully lobbied the Duke of York for a position at the Cape
of Good Hope, and in November 1813 Tom and Caroline set
off for the last time in search of the sun. They took their eldest
daughter Helen, who was six years old. Brinsley, seven years
old, five-year-old Caroline, Georgy aged four and two-year-old
Tommy were sent with servants by steam packet from St
Katherine's Dock to be looked after by their mother's sisters
Fanny and Georgy on the Callander estate at Craigforth in
Stirlingshire. This was the last time they would see their father.

Tom and his wife knew he was a dying man and this was his
last chance. One of the features of consumption is s*pes phthisica*,
also known as 'the hope of the tuberculous', an irrational
optimism of the patient that he is recovering. [28] Tom's post as
colonial paymaster was an attractive one for him: the duties
were light and the salary of a thousand pounds a year was
generous. The climate was warmly recommended for consumptives, although the voyage was anything but easy.

It could take three months for letters to reach London from

the Cape.[29] In May 1815 Tom sent his father an 'exceeding good account' reporting that he and his wife were well and she was 'quite recovered'. This refers to the birth of their sixth child, Francis Cynric, known as Frank, born there in February 1815.[30]

On 7 July 1816 'the eminent individual' Richard Brinsley Sheridan, aged sixty-five, died 'after a severe and protracted illness' at his London house in Savile Row. As befitted a man of his extraordinary literary talent, who at the height of his political prowess seemed destined to become prime minister, he was buried near the monument to Shakespeare in Poet's Corner, Westminster Abbey.[31] His wife Hecca was too ill to attend. There was no inheritance for Tom and his young family, although Sheridan's younger son Charles would be well provided for when his mother died the following year.

In 1817 another child was born at the Cape, Charles Kinnaird known as Charlie, in the final months of his father's life. On 8 September Tom made his will in 'the full possession of his intellect and senses of a sound mind'. It was a short document, less than a page: there was little to bequeath and nothing he had the energy to itemise. All his 'property, effects and chattels in this colony and elsewhere' were left to his wife, 'to be enjoyed by her during her natural life and after her demise to devolve upon and to go to the children he has begotten by her to be divided in equal portions'. The seven children's names were written in the margin.[32] Tom Sheridan died four days after his will was written. On 17 November 1817, two months later, *The Times* reported Tom's demise. The brief obituary noted 'he possessed talents, that if his health had permitted might have raised him at least to hereditary distinction; as a companion he was animated, good humoured, and full of anecdote'. *The Times* also mentioned that his wife Caroline had been taken ill and 'broke a blood vessel'.

Bereft, frail, alone with three small children, Caroline had to find a ship to take them home. She wrote to her sisters Fanny and Georgy and her brother-in-law Charles Brinsley Sheridan, tactfully reporting that her husband had 'suffered little' and informing them that she would be travelling on the *Albion*. Charles told a cousin in Dublin that 'her life has been a course of unparalleled devotion and attachment to my poor brother'. Caroline sounded lost and in need of their help: 'I am sure you would teach me better than anyone I know how all these things coming in such a sad succession ought to be borne.'[33]

In December Caroline Sheridan, Helen, Frank and Charlie arrived home after a journey lasting ten weeks. Their ship stopped at St Helena and Caroline took the children to get a look at Napoleon: ten-year-old Helen remembered him walking in his garden: 'he was enormously fat with a large straw hat'.[34] Her late husband's father and stepmother were dead; her own mother had long since died, and there was little she could hope for from her father, whom she had not seen for years. All she could expect was a share of her mother's will when he died, which he showed no sign of doing. Her only hope was that royal favour would grant her a pension for her husband's brief career at the Cape.

At the end of January 1818, four months after he had died, Tom Sheridan's body arrived in England on the *Abeona*. It is intriguing that Tom's body was repatriated. Sailors did not like to carry corpses on board ship – their own comrades were always buried at sea – thinking it brought bad luck. Usually only the bodies of persons of note like Nelson were repatriated; the return of a civilian was a rarity. Caroline had Tom's body embalmed and coffined with myrrh and camphor to mask the smell.[35] He was buried with his mother in the nave of Wells Cathedral.[36]

The Irish writer Tom Moore wrote sensitively about his old friend Sheridan's troubled but lovable son, whom he felt at times had paid a high price for his father's reputation, pride and ferociously held principles. Moore was sure that Tom, and thereby his young family, had been 'the victim of the distinction of his situation', at times prevented by his father from taking well paid positions offered by royal patrons. Tom paid 'dearly for the glory of being the son of Sheridan. His popularity in society was unexampled . . . he had many manly and intelligent qualities that deserved a better destiny. There are indeed, few individuals whose lives have been so gay and thoughtless whom so many remember with cordiality and interest.'[37]

Fanny and Georgy Callander brought Caroline, Tommy and Georgy to London to be reunited with their mother and sister Helen, whom they had not seen for four years, and to meet their two brothers Frank and Charlie for the first time. Brinsley was twelve and showing the Sheridan talent for public speaking as a prize-winning pupil at Reverend Lanphier's school 'for the sons of persons of distinction and respectability' at Sunbury-on-Thames. Caroline, known to her siblings as Car or Cary, was ten years old, and for some years had been taught together with the youngest son of an old family friend, Lord Kinnaird, at Glenrossie. Caroline was thus better educated than most girls of her age, as the lessons given to young Kinnaird by his male tutor were based on a more academically rigorous curriculum.

The patronage of Tom's old friend the Duke of York saved Caroline and the children from serious embarrassment; he arranged a small pension for her (which she was entitled to bequeath to her children) and somewhere to live. In 1820 she and her seven children moved into a grace-and-favour apartment at Hampton Court Palace. This would be their first settled home, and Mrs Sheridan lived there until she died in 1851. The Sheridans lived on the north side of the palace opposite what is now called Cardinal Wolsey's kitchen, their own kitchen looking onto Tennis Court Lane. Their neighbours were often titled, sometimes the widows of generals and admirals, now reduced to employing only a couple of servants. Strings had been pulled for the Sheridans as the waiting list was long. King William IV, Victoria's predecessor, called the place the 'Quality Poorhouse'. The residents were always complaining about the cold and damp and how ruinously expensive it was to keep warm. Charles Dickens described the arrangements: 'There was a temporary air about their establishments, as if they were going away the moment they could get anything better; there was also a dissatisfied air about themselves, as if they took it very ill that they had not already got something better. Callers, looking steadily into the eyes of their receivers, pretended not to smell cooking three feet off; people, confronting closets accidentally left open . . . visitors, with their heads against a partition of thin canvas and a page and a young female at high words on the other side. There was no end to the social accommodation bills which the gypsies of gentility were constantly drawing upon, and accepting for, one another.'[38]

Caroline and her siblings were talented at singing, drawing and writing, making their own collections of poetry and prose. The apartment at Hampton Court was the first time they had all lived together and they were a striking bunch, a theatrical troupe. Good-looking, dark-haired, all with 'splendid real Irish blue eyes like Brinsley and Georgie . . . or dark as the night, like Caroline's'.[39] From an early age they had shown off their Sheridan performing genes: 'even in the nursery they were fond of private theatricals', and the children spent many hours preparing plays.[40]

As a child Caroline was not as conventionally pretty as her elder and younger sisters, but as she grew older she developed striking looks, often deployed to great effect. She had the charm that had got her grandfather and father into such muddles with ladies over the years. There was the 'dark burning gaze . . . and long eyebrows', the eyes 'enormous with long sweeping eyelashes and darkly shadowed eyelids which she had a trick of keeping constantly lowered'.[41]

Caroline and Helen showed a special talent for poetry and drawing and had their first book published when Helen was twelve and Caroline eleven. Her brother Brinsley's godmother, Lady Westmorland, had given Caroline an illustrated *Dandy Book,* which contained caricatures of foppish men. The girls wrote rhymes and illustrated their own version, calling it *The Dandies' Rout.* Marshall, the publisher of the *Dandy* books, saw theirs, offered to publish it and gave them fifty copies. To be an author at such a tender age was remarkable and was the beginning of Caroline's long career in poetry, song and prose.

Caroline remembered her mother at this time; her lonely sadness and the struggle to bring up seven children on her own. The family had a roof over their heads and her mother's small pension, but the children needed to be educated; careers had to be found for the four sons, and husbands for the three girls, for whom there would be no dowries.

> In thy black weeds, and coif of widow's woe;
> Thy dark expressive eyes all dim and clouded
> By that deep wretchedness the lonely know;
> Stifling thy grief, to hear some weary task
> Conned by unwilling lips, with listless air
> Hoarding thy means, lest future need might ask
> More than the widow's pittance then could spare.
> Hidden, forgotten by the great and gay,
> Enduring sorrow, not by fits and starts
> But the long self-denial day by day,
> Alone amidst thy brood of careless hearts!
> Striving to guide, to teach, or to restrain
> The young rebellious spirits crowding round,
> Who saw not, knew not, felt not for thy pain,
> And could not comfort – yet had the power to wound.

Caroline was passionate and self-willed, in other words a handful, and these words, part of a much longer poem, *The Dream,* were written when she was thirty-two and regretted how she had sometimes behaved towards her widowed and beleaguered mother. Encouraged by her uncle Charles, whose *Thoughts on the Greek Revolution* had recently been published, and buoyed up by the attention she and Helen received from *The Dandies' Rout,* Caroline was determined to become a writer. In 1823, when she was fifteen and Georgy fourteen, they were sent to Miss Taylor's, a boarding school at Shalford, a neat village surrounded by watery meadows a mile from Guildford.[42]

In 1822, supported by a recommendation from George Canning, recently appointed governor general of Bengal, Mrs Sheridan had got her eldest son Brinsley, who was sixteen, a place at the East India College in Hertfordshire, established in 1806 to prepare young men for service in India.[43] He needed to attend the college for 'further improvement in liberal and suitable learning' to become a 'writer', the most senior kind of clerk in the East India Company. If his 'behaviour and attainments' were satisfactory the plan was for Brinsley to work in Madras. Such a position could be very lucrative. Brinsley attended the college for two years and set off for Madras in 1824. When he left his mother did not expect to see him ever again: 'I must not look forward to seeing his return from Asia.' Most young men who went to make their fortunes in India stayed for good. But Brinsley came back eight years later. Meanwhile, Tommy, Frank and Charlie were sent to Mr Walton's school in nearby Hampton village.[44]

During this time the Sheridans went to Brighton to take the bracing air and this is where Caroline attracted her first admirer, a Captain Fairfield. He was a 'clever, handsome and good-natured man'. They met on Marine Parade, the place to promenade in the town, made fashionable by the Prince of Wales. However, her mother stopped Fairfield in his tracks, burning the valentine he sent to Caroline. Mrs Sheridan would have asked around, made enquiries about who his people were, and if he had any prospects. Even though there were no dowries for her girls, she expected them to do better than a young officer like Fairfield. Marriage was a business where love need not play a part. Caroline spent the rest of the time in Brighton in a state of 'suppressed wrath'.[45]

In 1824 Caroline and some of the other young ladies at Miss Taylor's were taken to nearby Wonersh Park by their governess, whose brother was agent to Lord Grantley, to have tea with Lady Grantley and her husband's sisters. The family owned the village of Wonersh and the land around. During one of Caroline's visits to the house she was spotted by Lord Grantley's younger brother George Norton, but the person who usually demanded most of her attention was Norton's eccentric sister William Augusta, who took her name rather seriously. She had 'masculine habits', wore pantaloons, and instead of having fashionable tumbling ringlets frame her face, preferred a fierce Eton crop. Augusta was five years older than Caroline and became obsessed with her. She played to Caroline on the violin and 'amused herself with my early verses and my love of music and took more notice of me than of my companions'. Flattered by the attentive twenty-one-year-old, Caroline was shocked when her governess told her that they would not be able to visit Wonersh again until George Norton had written to her mother asking for her hand in marriage. She was underwhelmed by George and had barely noticed him. Despite her daughter's reluctance, Mrs Sheridan accepted the offer but insisted he wait for three years. Caroline was horrified at the prospect of marrying a man she barely remembered seeing, but it was her mother's right and duty to secure a husband for her and there had been no other interest. Perhaps Mrs Sheridan was playing for time, hoping someone else would come along. After years of money troubles with Tom, and no money with which to make a better match, Caroline's mother had made her decision.[46]

On 4 July 1825, to the dismay of the Blackwood family, Captain Price Blackwood, an officer in the Royal Navy and heir to the fifth Baron Dufferin and Clandeboye, married Helen, the eldest Sheridan girl, by licence, at St George's, Hanover Square. They had expected him to marry money, but he chose love, captivated by her beauty, poetry and songs. Helen grew to love him and found him a 'good kind little husband'. Blackwood was thirty-one, and she was not yet eighteen so still a minor. While his navy pay was small, his prospects were good, and Mrs Sheridan was happy with the match. The Duke of York stood in for her late father on Helen's wedding day. The number of witnesses' signatures is a clue to the size of the wedding: Caroline, Mrs Sheridan, an aunt and a close friend were there; from his side only the groom's friend Charles William Vane, third Marquess of Londonderry, signed the register, perhaps a sign of his family's displeasure. The situation was so awkward that the young couple left England immediately for Florence, where their son Frederick was born a year later.[47]

Before the wedding, Caroline and Helen had been starting to make a name for themselves with their songs and ballads. The Sheridans were always hard up, and writing poetry and composing songs was one of the few genteel ways for young ladies to earn money. Since leaving Miss Taylor's Caroline had penned dozens of popular songs and ditties designed to make the bosom heave. The titles suggest the market she was aiming for: 'Dry up that sparkling tear', 'Rosalie my love awake!', 'The home where my childhood played', 'Never forget me love', 'Love me still', 'When I first loved thee', and 'When I think of you love'. Perhaps her brief encounter with Captain Fairfield inspired her lyrics.[48]

Tommy, the second eldest boy, left Mr Walton's school at Hampton in 1823, and joined the Royal Navy as a midshipman.

He was twelve years old, and royal patronage had secured his place. But his life and career in the navy was a brief one: in 1826 he fell to his death from the rigging of HMS *Diamond* off Rio de Janeiro.[49]

With one daughter married, Mrs Sheridan turned her attention to Caroline, who had gone through her first season in London in 1825 without any further requests for her hand. George Norton renewed his offer in 1826, which was again accepted. Although he was not the heir to the Grantley estate, Norton's elder brother and his wife were childless and thought likely to remain so, and when he died George would inherit the title. The role of the girl's father in such matters was usually pre-eminent, but Mrs Sheridan was having to make these important decisions on her own.

The absent presence of Tom Sheridan in the story of Caroline's adult life is compelling. The family's circumstances were straitened by his early death, and they became beholden to relations and friends, dependent on their kindness and patronage. The widowed Caroline Sheridan, dealing with George Norton, a barrister, and his elder brother Lord Grantley, whose circle included the best legal brains of the day, cannot have found it easy. Her elder daughter Helen's marriage had helped, but up against the Norton clan, with no money for Caroline's dowry, and no husband to help broker the marriage, Mrs Sheridan and Caroline were always at a serious disadvantage.

Caroline was the opposite of her prospective husband. She was an extraordinarily attractive young woman, equal in beauty to her sisters. A gifted writer who had been earning money for some years by her pen, she was confident, with a cheeky talent for mimicry. Her self-esteem was higher than considered seemly for young ladies and she could be 'stormy-tempered with a reckless and specious tongue'. A combination of her mother's gentle beauty and quiet literary prowess, and her father's dramatic impulses and love of showing-off, had given her a reputation as bossy, high-handed and an outrageous flirt. In a man these qualities were admired but in a woman were considered dangerous. Caroline could also be 'magnanimous and generous in defeat, and was 'uninterested in paying back old scores' when the 'ungovernable outburst of resentment against them had subsided'.[50]

On 31 August 1800 George Chapple Norton had been born at Abbey Hill House in Edinburgh's New Town. Conceived in the eighteenth century and born in the nineteenth, Chapple was the maiden name of his father's mother Grace. George's father was the Honourable Fletcher Norton, second son of Fletcher Norton, attorney general of England in 1762 and speaker of the House of Commons in 1770, who became the first Lord Grantley in 1782.

The Honourable Fletcher Norton, a lawyer, was appointed one of the barons of the Scottish Exchequer in 1776, a position he held until his death in 1820. A handsome salary of three thousand pounds a year allowed him a comfortable life in Edinburgh's most fashionable suburb. He had moved north to settle in Scotland at a time 'when prejudices then against England and Englishmen were strong and deep'. Feelings were still raw after the Scottish defeat and the English brutality at Culloden in 1745. Baron Norton was respected as a judge and liked as a man. His 'perspicacity easily discovered the true merits of any cause before him'. Fletcher Norton's own father, George's grandfather, who died long before George was born, was a bluff cantankerous Yorkshireman, careless of whom he offended. His contemporaries both inside and outside Parliament disliked him for his greed and called him Sir Bull-Face Double Fee.[51]

George's father was forty-nine when in July 1793 he married seventeen-year-old Caroline Elizabeth Balmain, the daughter of a wealthy Scottish merchant and commissioner of excise in Edinburgh. They had eight children, four sons and four daughters, of whom George was the fourth child and second son. Fletcher Norton's 'gentlemanly pleasantness of manner, made his society to be universally coveted'. He supported musical and literary projects, including sending Alexander Campbell on a twelve-hundred-mile trip around Scotland collecting two hundred Gaelic poems and songs. Baron Norton was also a devout follower of the Scottish Episcopalian Church.

The first child was Grace Conyers Charlotte, born 27 March 1795, then just one year later on 4 July 1796 came Fletcher, heir to his uncle's title; Caroline Elizabeth arrived in 1798, and George at the cusp of the new century. Two sisters followed: William Augusta Ann in 1802 and Mary Eleanor in 1803; then two brothers, Charles Francis in 1807, and James in 1809. The boys were taught at home by tutors until they were dispatched on their various ways: Fletcher served in the Grenadier Guards, knowing that he would inherit estates in Yorkshire and Surrey and become the third Lord Grantley. Fletcher's proud boast was that he was wounded at Waterloo, but his military career came to an awkward end. In 1821 he insulted the wife of a fellow officer, calling her 'what she ought not to be'. Her husband challenged him to a duel and both parties and their seconds travelled to France since duelling was illegal in England. A few shots were fired in the Bois de Boulogne and no one was hurt, but on their return his commanding officer insisted Fletcher Norton resign from the regiment or face a court martial. He left the Guards, and when his uncle died in 1822 took up the life expected of a member of the aristocracy.[52]

Fletcher's younger brother Charles became an officer in the 52nd Regiment of Foot, while George and James were sent to Oxford, after which George trained as a lawyer and James became a clergyman. In the opinion of their widowed mother almost all her sons married well: Fletcher married Charlotte Earle, a daughter of Sir William Beechey, a successful portraitist, in 1825; Charles became the husband of Maria Louisa Campbell, daughter of Sir Colin Campbell, lieutenant governor of Nova Scotia and Ceylon, in 1831; and the Reverend James married Isabella Lowndes, only child of Thomas Lowndes of Barrington Hall, Essex in 1838.

Grace Norton, by all accounts a very disagreeable person, married a first cousin, Sir Neil Menzies in 1816. William Augusta, who preferred to look more like a man than a young lady of the Regency, eventually married her cousin James Johnstone of Alva in 1846 when she was forty-three. Caroline and Mary Eleanor died unmarried, living much of their lives in Madeira for the sake of their health.[53]

When twenty-four-year-old George Norton first spotted the schoolgirl Caroline Sheridan at Wonersh House he was a lawyer who had been admitted to the Middle Temple in 1820. In 1825 he was called to the Bar and took chambers at Garden Court in the Temple, the hub of London's legal community, where he was looked after by an elderly housekeeper. George got little work. It is likely that he had been shunted into the law; his father would have expected one of his four sons to follow him, and his father before him, into the profession, and it was expected George would carry on the family tradition of winning high office. But instead he preferred an undemanding and modestly paid role as a commissioner of bankrupts, dealing with arrangements to repay creditors. This was a job his future mother-in-law had got for him. Mrs Sheridan was skilful at manoeuvring her children, and now her son-in-law-to-be, into suitable situations. Given that from the outset it was accepted that his brother would not have children, George did not make much effort in his career, simply waiting for his turn as Lord Grantley to come.

In 1826 George Norton was shoehorned into the parliamentary seat of Guildford, a mile or so from his brother's estate, the third Norton in succession to represent the town. Being a Member of Parliament gave him access to influence and was an indicator of high social status. Government ministers were paid, but salaries for MPs were not introduced until 1911. George, Lord Grantley and their closest family friends were not just Tories, they were Ultra Tories, whose heyday began in 1827 and lasted until 1834. The Ultras were part of a group of politicians, journalists and intellectuals who rejected the changes in British life associated with the Enlightenment, industrialisation and urbanisation. They disliked many Tories, whom they thought were far too liberal, and loathed the Whigs with a passion. They opposed plans to widen the electoral franchise, or dismantle the many restraints under which Catholics were obliged to live. For several years the Ultras enjoyed a sympathetic hearing from the conservative Tory press.[54] This was the family Caroline Sheridan was marrying into: as different to her own as it was possible to be.

Wedding Bells

You are come at last, and look handsomer, I declare, than I expected.

Caroline Sheridan to George Norton on their wedding day

On Monday 30 July 1827 Caroline Sheridan married George Chapple Norton at St George's, Hanover Square in Mayfair. The bride and her family travelled by carriage from the house her mother had rented in Great George Street where Helen had been launched into marriage. The bridegroom was due in a cabriolet from Wilton Place in Belgravia, where the Nortons had a new house at number 10.[1] Twenty-two years earlier Mrs Sheridan had stood at the same altar with Tom. Hanover Square was a century old, laid out in 1713; by 1725 St George's had been completed to the designs of John James and was a grand and glittering place. Caroline and George walked in separately through the towering six-column Corinthian portico, an impressive entrance to their new life together.

Wedding dresses in the 1820s were whiter and grander confections of the kind of garments women ordinarily wore, still influenced by the love of all things classical. Taffeta was popular during the 1820s and especially suitable for wedding gowns as it helped the skirt to stand away from the body and create a strong silhouette, and also caused the fashionably exuberant sleeves to billow out. The neckline would have hovered modestly above the cleavage; the waist was cut high under the breasts and a shapely transition from bodice to skirt was assisted by a corset. Flounces danced their way across the hem of the dress. Caroline's hair was dark and glossy, parted in the centre and piled high, recalling the elaborate coils of Roman ladies.[2] Gentlemen's clothing and wedding garb also created a shapely silhouette. Shoulders were tailored to look large, emphasised with puffs at the top of the sleeves; waists were narrow. Military officers had long worn girdles or 'vests' to cinch their waists to a narrowness approaching that of the ladies. A shirt with cravat, tailored trousers full on the hips and tapering tightly to the ankle, a curvy crowned hat over curled hair and sideburns finished the look.

Caroline and George were married by licence, a sign of their status. Most couples wed after banns were read for three consecutive Sundays, which was cheaper. Those who could afford it preferred to be married by licence.[3] Ten years after his death Tom Sheridan made a brief appearance at the wedding. It was declared that because Caroline was a minor she was marrying 'by and with the consent of Caroline Henrietta Sheridan, widow and natural mother and guardian appointed to the said minor in the last will and testament of Thomas Sheridan.'[4] George arrived very late: his horse had bolted and run away with him in his cabriolet.[5] When he eventually arrived, Caroline greeted him sarcastically, upset by the wait and anxiety that he might not turn up: 'Well, Mr Norton, you are come at last, and look handsomer, I declare, than I expected.' One of the bridesmaids, the Honourable Mary Elizabeth Fox, remembered George: 'the poor man was much the shyest and most confused of the two'.[6] Of the dozen witnesses only one was a Norton. The rest were

Caroline's family and friends including her mother and sisters Helen and Georgy, aunt Georgy, who had looked after the family in Scotland when her parents were at the Cape, uncle Charles the Graecophile, and her brothers Frank, who was twelve, and ten-year-old Charlie. Brinsley was in Madras.

Giving Caroline away was Douglas Kinnaird, with whom the Sheridans had close ties stretching back to the previous century. His father, the seventh Lord Kinnaird, had invited Caroline to share lessons with his youngest son when she was being looked after by her Callander aunts, and her youngest brother Charlie was named after him. Douglas Kinnaird was a writer and politician, a raffish fellow with radical politics who had known Byron at Cambridge and handled his finances. After 1816 he was in charge of publishing Byron's work. Kinnaird was not married but had a mistress, an actor and singer, with whom he had had a son in 1814. He joined the management committee of the Sheridan family's greatest asset, the newly rebuilt Drury Lane Theatre, in 1815. The following year Kinnaird and his mistress gave Byron two bottles of champagne and a cake as parting gifts before the poet left England for ever. In response to Caroline's grandfather's death in 1816, Kinnaird commissioned Byron to write 'Monody on the Death of the Right Hon R.B. Sheridan'. Penned while Byron was staying at the Villa Diodati with the Shelleys, this was read at Drury Lane Theatre later that year. Kinnaird was the first person in England to hear of Byron's death from septicaemia at Missolonghi. Not many people could claim to have been a bad influence on Byron, but Kinnaird could.[7]

The famous and battle-scarred Charles Vane, third Marquess of Londonderry was a guest. A friend of Caroline's brother-in-law Captain Price Blackwood, he had been present at the marriage of Blackwood to her sister Helen. Not many men survived a bullet in the cheek, but this happened to Londonderry in 1796, when he was eighteen and a young captain. He was fighting with the Austrian army against the French when he was wounded at Donauörth in Bavaria. The bullet entered the right side of his face and passed under his nose, coming to rest under his left eye, where it remained. His sight and hearing were affected for the rest of his life but he still sought out danger, pursuing a thrilling and lengthy military career. From 1801 to 1814 he was Member of Parliament for Londonderry, where his family had great estates. His bravery was matched only by his vanity, which earned him the nickname of the 'golden peacock'. This old soldier was the grandest guest at the ceremony, a grizzled old warhorse who had packed more into his life than anyone else present.[8]

The groom had waited three years for this day, and his family were displeased that he was marrying the pretty young girl standing by his side. But George had stood his ground and kept his promise. There are no extant portraits of George Norton, but he was apparently 'rather dull and slow and lazy' and had a reputation for being late for everything, which he lived up to.[9]

After the wedding breakfast the couple went on honeymoon. On their return they went to live in George's chambers in Garden Court in the Temple, with only his doddery old housekeeper to look after them. For a lively nineteen-year-old woman, life in the cloistered world of lawyers, inky clerks and wrinkled old retainers was a shock. The Sheridans didn't have much money but they had always lived in airy and elegant homes. Caroline found herself in a ghetto-like ramshackle world of offices and chambers built in a medley of styles. In his first novel, *The Pickwick Papers*, Charles Dickens painted a picture of the neighbourhood where the pretty young bride had to make her home: 'low-roofed, mouldy rooms, where innumerable rolls of parchment, which have been perspiring in secret for the past century, send forth an agreeable odour, which is mingled every day with the scent of dry rot, and by night with the various exhalations which arise from the damp cloaks, festering umbrellas and the coarsest tallow candles'.[10]

Sketch of attitude of a young person of resolved mind

The Honourable Mr and Mrs Norton

Too splendidly, magnificently, furiously beautiful. Cleopatra
sailing on the Nile . . . Mr Norton rather fidgeting around her.
Mrs Sullivan to Mr Sullivan

T
he newly-weds set off for Edinburgh and a tour of
Scotland, a place Caroline loved and had not visited for
ten years. George was there for the shooting, and his
wife to be introduced to her new in-laws. They travelled on the
Northern Mail Coach to Edinburgh. This set off at half past
seven every morning from the galleried Bull and Mouth coaching
inn off St Martin's le-Grand in the City of London. It took
forty-five exhausting hours to get there over bumpy roads and
in cramped seats as the carriage rattled and lurched and buffeted
them and their fellow passengers on the four-hundred-mile drive
north. As well as the lack of comfort and privacy there was the
fear of being held up by highwaymen. Though the turnpike
highways they followed were safer than other roads, newspaper
reports of places 'swarming' with men intent on 'plunder and
violence' on the route through Lincolnshire were concerning.[1]

In Edinburgh Caroline had her first meeting with George's
mother and they got on well. But few of his six siblings liked
her, apart from his brother Charles, taking their lead from Lord

Grantley. George's eldest sister, Lady Menzies, 'a hard-tempered Scotswoman', took against her from the beginning, disliking the amount of attention her husband Sir Neil showed Caroline. Augusta was as strange as ever in her pantaloons, while Caroline, Mary Eleanor and James were suspicious of their bubbly new sister.[2] One night George drank too much and they had a row in their bedroom when Caroline admonished him for a 'silly and ridiculous' opinion he had expressed that evening. He kicked his new bride in the side, which was painful for several days. Caroline was too afraid to sleep with him and sat up all night in an adjoining room.

Gossip about Caroline and her sisters had preceded her. This was when armies of servants delivered up-to-the-minute news from one Mayfair drawing room to another, and when letters could reach Edinburgh and answers be back in London via mail coach in four days. The Sheridan girls had ruffled feathers, not just with their looks but also by their cockiness. Lady Cowper, sister of the man who would become Lord Melbourne, noted, 'the Sheridans are much admired but are strange girls. They swear and say all sorts of things to make the men laugh. I am surprised so sensible a woman as Mrs Sheridan should let them go on so. I suppose she cannot stop the old blood coming out. They are remarkably good looking . . . and certainly clever.'[3]

Norton family talk turned to John Wallop. The Nortons were involved in a fourteen-year legal battle which was in its final stage. They wanted to get Wallop's second marriage declared illegal and annulled, so that the dowry of his first wife, Grace Norton, could be returned. This may have been the first Caroline had heard of this queer tale. In 1799 George's aunt Grace Norton became the Countess of Portsmouth when she married John Charles Wallop, the third earl, a man some believed was insane. The bride was forty-seven, her groom thirty-two. His great wealth and the grandeur of his title calmed any quibbles about the state of his mind.

When John Wallop was six he had been tutored by Jane Austen's father George at Chawton, but he was academically weak and extremely vulnerable. Physically awkward and a bad stammerer, he experienced wild mood swings. In 1790, when he was twenty-three, his father the second Earl of Portsmouth, mindful of his son's right to succeed to the title but concerned at the 'weakness of his mind', had a deed drawn up leaving some of his wealth to his younger children, and appointed trustees to take care of John's interests. One of the trustees was a London lawyer called John Hanson of Chancery Lane. After his wedding to Grace Norton, John Wallop took no part in running his own affairs: Grace provided money as he needed it and paid a minder to look after him. Male servants on the family estate Hurstbourne Park watched him, but it could be a dangerous business. There was no possibility of any children – Grace's age was the main factor, but also he was sexually like a child. The succession of the title and the estate was not in doubt; his younger brother, Newton Fellowes, Baron Wallop, was waiting in the wings.

When people encountered Lord Portsmouth for the first time he seemed 'polite and complaisant', but his mood could quickly change and he often assumed 'a very peculiar look', ranting and raving and attacking the servants. On one occasion he stormed the room of a coachman with a broken leg and insisted he get out of bed and go to work. The poor man said he could not, at which point Portsmouth threw himself onto the bed, 'snatched up George's leg, and broke it a second time'. Another servant, John Baverstock, rushed in. He heard the leg snap and George scream, 'You have broke my leg,' to which Lord Portsmouth replied, 'I don't care for that.' Bravely, Baverstock 'pull'd my lord off George's leg'.

Portsmouth fancied himself a coachman and would drive madly, whipping the horses fiercely until they careered off the road, narrowly avoiding killing himself, the horses and anyone who got in their way. He would also go out with a team of carthorses and a dung cart to spread manure. Drinking with the men at the end of the day, he would behave childishly by throwing beer at them and pinching them and pulling their ears. He had an obsession with brown horses and would buy every one he came across, one of many trials Grace had to manage. Her husband's mood swings often had a sado-masochistic bent. He repeatedly approached two of the maids, insisting that they bleed him with lancets, which they declined because 'there was an appearance of some amorous idea attached to this action'. Coachman Charles Webb worked out how to avoid being beaten, how to stop his employer bleeding him with the scalpels Portsmouth habitually carried around, and having to take pails of blood from the horses: 'I used to threaten him that I would not tell him when there was a black job [the earl's term for a funeral] and he would let me alone.' Another of the dark compulsions which gave Portsmouth a reputation for 'having the disposition of a Vampyre which was to be fed nothing but the prey of death' was a love of corpses and funerals. He would haunt undertakers' premises, attend funerals uninvited, insist on ringing the church bells and muscle his way into the pulpit and conduct the service. In a murder-ously playful mood he once threw the bell rope around the neck of the bell ringer's son. The boy narrowly escaped being dragged up by the rope and hanged. On jaunts to Southend, Bognor and Portsmouth he had to be removed from slaughter-houses.

When Grace died in 1813 Wallop's behaviour was callous: he was obsessed with getting his hands on another wife as soon as possible. In the early days of March 1814 he went to London to see John Hanson (who had been Lord Byron's trustee since childhood and was also his banker) to 'express a desire to be married again'. Hanson refused to give his permission unless Portsmouth married one of his own daughters. The untrustworthy trustee moved quickly to bag his wealthy but wild prize: he brokered the deal with the earl and put the offer to his twenty-four-year-old daughter Mary Ann, who said she would give Portsmouth her answer in two days' time. When the eager suitor returned on 7 March, scruffy, dishevelled and in mourning black, he was told that she would wed him only on condition they married that morning. Hanson had arranged the dodgiest of weddings, drawing up a deed of marriage settling a great deal of money on the bride. This was witnessed by Lord Byron, William Rowland Alder and others in on the conspiracy. Portsmouth signed the deed he did not bother to read and was 'hurried away to the church, unshorn, without clean linen, without any clothes on him suitable to so cheerful a ceremony'. The clerk at St George's Church in Bloomsbury was surprised to see them, but the marriage was solemnised there and then. Wallop was so disengaged from what was going on that he did not know which of the two Hanson girls he was marrying. After the ceremony the happy couple went to Hampshire, where Mary Ann took to the role of Countess of Portsmouth with relish.

The marriage was a cruel and ugly farce. Mary Ann's lover, Rowland Alder, a gambler and ladies' man, immediately moved into the family home. He was introduced to the earl and his servants as a physician, which only Portsmouth believed; actually he was a barrister, an imposing man with a reputation as a duellist. He joined the countess in the marital bed. The earl would creep into bed with them when they were asleep and cuddle up to her, a simple man-child who had never had sex. Portsmouth was afraid of Alder, who bullied him into thinking he was 'a powerful man and must submit to him'. The servants often saw their master being beaten and whipped by the countess, Alder, her brothers, and sister Laura, who would give him black eyes and strike him across the face with a whip. In the most dreadful betrayal of trust, John Hanson, whose successful firm in Chancery Lane allowed him to afford a fine house in Bloomsbury Square, moved his entire family into Hurstbourne Park and began spending the earl's fortune as fast as he could.

Meanwhile, the earl's younger brother and the Nortons had joined together to commence the labyrinthine legal process of having John Wallop declared insane and the marriage fraudulent. A three-way wrangle, which would last for fourteen years, ensued between the heir-in-waiting, Newton Fellowes, whose position was threatened by Portsmouth's new wife and any children she had; the Hansons, who insisted the marriage was legal and were determined to hang on to the Wallop title and fortune; and the Nortons, who wanted Grace's dowry returned.

George Norton's elder brother Fletcher duly took over the case when he inherited the Grantley title in 1822. Before that happened, with great gusto he personally abducted the Earl of Portsmouth off the street in Edinburgh, where the Hansons had taken him six months earlier, apparently not realising his late wife's family lived there. Matters had come to a head because Lady Portsmouth was about to give birth. Fletcher learned that his uncle was allowed to take a walk along Princes Street without any of his minders so he hid in the Royal Hotel. When Portsmouth appeared, Grantley darted out and got his uncle into a carriage waiting nearby, which took them to Haddington in the east of Edinburgh. There they transferred to Fletcher's chariot, which brought them 'with the utmost speed, travelling day and night towards London', clattering through the gates into Wonersh Hall fifty-one hours later. The Hansons sent their people to Wonersh to get the earl back but were unsuccessful. Protected by his own family, he returned to Hurstbourne; when his wife and her baby daughter arrived from Edinburgh they were prevented from entering the grounds by a large gang of labourers 'for the purpose of opposing, by force if necessary that entrance on which her Ladyship was expected to insist'. The stand-off lasted for several days until she withdrew to London.[4]

The work of Lord Portsmouth's younger brother for a second *inquirendo lunatico* now paid off (the first, held in 1815, had bizarrely declared he was sane and capable of managing his own affairs), and the Commission of Lunacy looked again at the earl's mental state. The cost of all this to the earl's family was a staggering twenty-five thousand pounds (now two and a quarter million pounds), but worth paying to prevent their entire estate being ransacked by the Hansons. A jury listened to evidence for three weeks in February and March 1823, at the Freemasons' Hall in Bishopsgate, London and came to the unanimous verdict that he was of 'unsound mind and condition and incapable of managing himself and his affairs'. It would take another five years to have the marriage annulled, and the daughter born to the countess, fathered by Alder, declared illegitimate.[5]

On their return to London, George and Caroline Norton moved out of Garden Court and rented a house at 2 Storey's Gate in Westminster, close to Parliament and Downing Street, and next to an entrance to St James's Park. George, who was still a new Member of Parliament, believed he was where the political action was. Caroline knew Storey's Gate well: it was close to where her mother had rented a house in 1825 from which to launch her daughters into the world. Mrs Sheridan needed to find a husband for young Georgy and scout around for suitable situations for her sons Frank and Charlie. When they left Dr

Walton's it was hoped to send them to Eton to finish them off, a good school from which to embark on a career perhaps in the diplomatic service. Caroline's sister Helen Blackwood and her young son had returned from Italy and were living at Hampton Court Palace, while Captain Price Blackwood was away with the Royal Navy. Already disappointed with the man her husband had turned out to be, Caroline had family close enough to be considered neighbours.

The house, long-since demolished, with its balcony over-looking Birdcage Walk, was certainly an improvement on George's musty, dusty chambers, but the couple was short of money and he was short of temper. Caroline had only brought the interest on fifty-seven pounds a year to the marriage, her share of her father's pension from his time at the Cape. George had no briefs and relied on an allowance from his elder brother. She was happy to lose herself in her literary work and earned money from the songs she wrote: 'The Soldier'; 'Why Should I Sing of Days Gone By?'; 'Oh Sad, Sad is the Heart' and 'Love Not!' She was writing for the market of the day, but her own feelings of despair and disappointment can be seen in the lyrics.[6]

Soon Caroline's family saw the consequences of George's bad temper stoked by drink. The Blackwoods were staying with the Nortons when they heard a furious row break out between them. They had all been to a ball together and retired to their rooms when George picked a fight by making coarse remarks about one of Caroline's female relations, who was married but still danced, a practice he said no husband ought to allow. Caroline defended the lady and George ordered her to bed. When she ignored him, 'he suddenly sprang from the bed, seized me by the nape of the neck and dashed me down on the floor. The sound of my fall woke my sister and brother-in-law who slept in a room below, and they ran to my door.

Norton locked it, and stood over me, declaring no one should enter. I could not speak – I only moaned. My brother-in-law burst the door open, and carried me down stairs. I had a swelling on the side of my head for days afterwards and the shock made my sister exceedingly ill.'[7] The Blackwoods left London a day or two later and Caroline and George settled into an uneasy and silent truce. She buried herself in her work as a distraction from her miserable marriage and drunken and difficult husband. Writing furiously, singing her songs in contralto, scratching away at the lyrics, every guinea she earned went into her husband's pocket. George was ahead of his time: not for him the notion that a wife should not earn money; he was happy for her to earn as much as she could. On the day she married him everything Caroline owned – her clothes, jewellery, cosmetics and underwear, the letters she received and each penny she inherited or earned, including her father's pension – legally became his.

Caroline grew increasingly vocal about politics. She was enormously proud of her grandfather, who had given up his career as a dramatist for an equally dramatic career in the House of Commons. Sheridan's rhetorical skills and his love of being centre stage meant his speeches in Parliament could be brilliant and epic in content, delivery and length. By the time of her marriage there was already a wealth of published material on Richard Brinsley Sheridan in the form of memoirs, letters and biographical sketches, and Caroline and her siblings were acquiring a celebrity of their own as the descendants of their colourful grandfather.

Letters and notes flew backwards and forwards from Storey's Gate to Great George Street and Hampton Court Palace about George's bad behaviour, meanness and laziness. One evening George, drinking and smoking, watched Caroline write a letter. Feeling excluded by the Sheridans' closeness and ignored by his wife, whom he thought should be giving him her undivided attention, he picked another quarrel, saying that from the expression on her face he knew she was complaining about him. Boldly she agreed, and said that she 'could seldom do anything else'. He snatched away the letter and told her to stop writing. So she started another, but 'after watching and smoking a few moments he rose, took one of the allumettes [matches] she had placed for his cigar, lit it, poured some of the spirit which stood by him over her writing materials, and in a moment set the whole ablaze'.[8]

George's aim was to 'teach her not to brave him', a lesson she refused to learn. He did not subdue her by his unpleasant behaviour, rather the reverse. Doing the social round of young marrieds, Caroline took her revenge, demonstrating her boredom and disillusionment, teasing and mimicking him. It was not a contest of equals: he was not up to her quick wit and repartee and he knew it. She also flirted with every man in her circle, unmarried or married. This made her plenty of female enemies. Not everyone enjoyed her skittishness, especially not mothers looking to marry off their daughters. Caroline diverted the attention of eligible society bachelors.

George's feelings for Caroline were mixed: he now realised that in marrying this clever beauty he had taken on more than he had bargained for, but he was still captivated by her looks, which were the talk of the town. Letters written in 1830 by the actress Fanny Kemble, daughter of the actor-manager of the Covent Garden Theatre Charles Kemble and niece of that great star of the stage Mrs Sarah Siddons, give an idea of the hopelessness George felt. Fanny was only a year younger than Caroline and 'deeply interested' in her, calling her 'a splendid creature', revering her 'blinding beauty', her flair for comedy and the recklessness of her wit. William Cavendish, sixth Duke of Devonshire, eighteen years older than her and the big Whig of all the Whigs, a 'connoisseur of all beautiful things', especially women, was one of Caroline's band of admirers. It was quite usual for men in Whig circles to openly admire someone's wife to the point of seduction, which must have added to George Norton's misery and rage. But Caroline enjoyed the attention too much to take George's feelings into account.[9]

Throughout the initial year of her marriage Caroline worked on her first book, *The Sorrows of Rosalie,* a collection of poems heavily influenced by Lord Byron, which she dedicated to Lord Holland, Henry Richard Fox, a politician and man of letters, whose Holland House was one of the centres of political and literary society in Europe.[10] Although published anonymously at the end of 1828 it was soon attributed to 'Mrs George Norton, wife of the Member for Guildford and daughter of the late Thomas Sheridan'. True to the appetite of the day for tragic tales, *Rosalie* is an epic story of an innocent girl who falls madly in love with a handsome aristocrat, elopes, is abandoned by him, finds herself pregnant, and goes to London to try to win back his affection. Finding him married, she flees to the country, gets ill, goes back to London to look for him again, discovers that her lover has gone abroad, and is so desperate she snatches a jewel from a lady's dress to buy food for the child. Sent to prison, where the baby dies, religion is her only comfort. 'Wild was my laugh – Oh! heartless and unkind! / Thou suffer! mayst though never feel like me! / Yes, give thy vows of passion to the wind; / Heaven heard them, though to man unknown they be; / Heaven sees me shunned by all, betrayed by thee; / Lured from the happy home where once I smiled; / Heaven hears my moan of hopeless agony – / Heaven hears thee scorn thy young and innocent child – / Heaven sees us stand e'en now, beguiler and beguiled.'

The Times thought the poems good for someone so young: 'there are some passages which are beautiful and full of true poetical feeling'; her 'versification was skilful and easy . . . the manner in which the subject is treated is highly skilful and forcible'. But the anonymous reviewer disliked the 'ill-chosen' subject matter and felt her talents should have been deployed in a more worthy area, criticising the 'sickliness in the sentiment which is probably the result of inexperience, but which is nevertheless an offence against good taste'. But the writer felt that Mrs Norton showed great promise: 'the authoress possesses feelings and genius of a very extraordinary kind'. *The Sorrows of Rosalie* sold well and went into several editions. Caroline had worked hard on the two hundred stanzas and it was a good result for a twenty-year-old's first foray into print.[11] George's bank account reaped the reward.

On 10 July 1829 the Nortons' first child was born at Storey's Gate. *The Sorrows of Rosalie* had paid for the expenses of the birth. Fletcher Cavendish Charles Conyers Norton was a frail baby, who would always be delicate. Ambitious for a literary career, Caroline Norton was at work on her next collection of poems, and confident enough to ask her publisher for five hundred pounds for the novel she was planning. During that first autumn of her son's life she and George seemed to get on better. As she juggled her careers as wife, mother and author, a new story was emerging in the press. The newspapers were reporting on the vivid personal life of William Lamb, who had recently succeeded his father as Lord Melbourne, a man who would have a profound effect on the lives of the family living at 2 Storey's Gate. He was handsome, clever and louche. By birth a Whig, Melbourne was born in 1779, four years after Caroline's father. His hero was Caroline's grandfather.

William Melbourne was his mother's second son, quite probably not his father's child, and became heir to the Lamb estate and title when his elder brother died in 1805. Educated at Eton and Trinity College, Cambridge, he was dabbling in the law and seemed to be wandering through life in a casual way when his brother died unexpectedly. His mother groomed him for a career in politics, manoeuvring William into a seat in Parliament, where he proved clever, cynical, lazy and indecisive, not qualities which immediately recommended him for high office.[12]

In June 1805 William Lamb married Lady Caroline Ponsonby, who was as volatile as a keg of gunpowder. She was the daughter of Harriet Duncannon, Lady Bessborough, a woman with whom Caroline's grandfather had been in a muddle of love and mad infatuation for years. On one memorable occasion Sheridan had got so drunk and desperate that she was ignoring him that he crawled across a ballroom floor and nibbled her ankles. In front of everyone. The Lambs' new marriage looked handsome but it was a painful disaster. Portraits show a pretty vulnerable girl, but she was more than that. She was a keen autodidact, having spent years in Europe on the Grand Tour with her parents. She felt under-educated, read widely and wrote too. She was also a tomboy. She had a son, Augustus, born in August 1807, who was severely afflicted by epilepsy, which in those days could only be treated by sedation. A girl born in 1809 died within a few days. That year she declared herself a convert to feminism after reading Mary Wollstonecraft's *Vindication of the Rights of Woman.* [13]

Unable or unwilling to have any more of their own, the Lambs adopted a number of children. Despite his casual exterior, William enjoyed being a disciplinarian and whipped the children when they misbehaved, as he had been whipped at Eton, where he had enjoyed the experience, believing that it would have been 'better if his tutor had flogged him more'.[14] But even in morally relaxed Whig circles Caroline's unconventional behaviour caused disapproval. Her most outrageous fling was with Lord Byron in 1812–13, an experience which led her to label him 'mad, bad and dangerous to know'. A string of wild stories, some of which were true, attached themselves to her like barnacles to the bottom of a ship: once she had emerged naked out of a soup tureen. Melbourne looked on in despair, and was persuaded by his family to legally separate from her in 1825. By then her behaviour had become so difficult that she had for some years been cut by their social circle. The badly disabled Augustus was looked after by minders, while she rattled about the Lamb country houses, Melbourne Hall in Derbyshire, and Brocket Hall in Hertfordshire, drunk. She was cared for by nurses from Bedlam, and became ill with heart disease. She died at the family's London house in Whitehall in January 1828.

William, by now Lord Melbourne, was thus free of his unhappy marriage. For two years before Caroline's death he had been having an affair with Elizabeth La Touche, Lady Branden, a Dublin hostess whom he met while there on government business. In May 1829 Lord Branden, a barrister and clergyman, found their correspondence and told his wife that he would 'overlook the offence if she will exert with Mr Lamb to procure him a bishopric'. When Lady Branden refused he started proceedings against Melbourne for criminal conversation with his wife. The case was dismissed for lack of evidence when the main witnesses did not turn up to court, and the cuckolded husband was paid off, but the affair had to end.[15] Melbourne should not risk another scandal if he was to have a credible career in politics.

The first picture that survives of Caroline is from 1830 and is by John Hayter, whose brother George would paint her some years later. The chalk and pastel drawing was engraved as a print and used to publicise her new book *The Undying One, And Other Poems*. This time the author was 'Mrs Norton' and her beauty was used to sell the book. Her hair is piled high in the Grecian way, braids curled around her head. The perfect eyebrows draw attention to her famously dark penetrating gaze, while the neckline of her gown is low but modest, revealing pale flesh. She is seated and leans against the arm of a sofa holding a book, gazing into the distance beyond the artist's easel. She is a lady of the neoclassical world.[16] John Hayter called the portrait *La Poetessa,* and exhibited it in 1832, drawing warm praise from *The Times,* which thought it a 'very excellent one of Mrs George Norton . . . and one of the very best of this artist's productions for its likeness was very striking and its execution admirable'.[17] Caroline dedicated the book to Adelaide, Duchess of Clarence, whose husband became William IV when George IV died in June 1830. She knew the royal couple, who lived at Bushy House in Bushy Park, near her childhood home at Hampton Court Palace.[18] As at this time married women had no identity in law – it was subsumed into that of her husband when they married – George acted as her agent. He signed the contract with Colburn and Bentley of New Burlington Street, who, on the back of the success of *The Sorrows of Rosalie,* were happy to publish her again. As well as her portrait as frontispiece, there was a biographical sketch. To this George took exception, insisting that the proofs be amended: 'Mr Norton is also anxious it should be clearly explained that I was <u>more</u> than sixteen when he proposed, as he conceives his dignity somewhat affected by paying his addresses to one "almost a child".'[19] There was a haggle over terms and extra monies if the book went into a third edition. Driven by financial self-interest and mindful of Colburn's reputation for unscrupulousness, George Norton dictated a polite but firm letter for Caroline to send to Bentley, who was an easier man to deal with.[20]

The title poem in *The Undying One* tells the story of the wandering Jew. It was a curious subject for Caroline Norton to have chosen. Her first biographer, Jane Gray Perkins, is dismissive: writing in 1909 she was scornful of the 'threadbare theme and its hackneyed subject'. The other poems in the collection included some songs, and with the long lens of hindsight, 'My Heart Is Like A Withered Nut!' cries out for a biographical interpretation. Caroline was only twenty-two years old. The opening verse yearned: 'My heart is like a withered nut / Rattling within its hollow shell; / You cannot ope my breast and put / Any thing fresh with it to dwell. / The hopes and dreams that filled it when / Life's spring of glory met my view, / Are gone! And ne'er with joy or pain / That shrunken heart shall dwell anew.'[21]

The Athenaeum was impressed with *The Undying One,* and its review praised the work's 'extraordinary power' and highly promising author. It was an ambitious piece: 'there is a forceful daring about it which stamps it as the production of no ordinary pen'. The thinking behind it was 'profound' and there was a 'rich profusion of imagery and a lofty dignity of sentiment'. The reviewer concluded hyperbolically that Caroline's 'nervous energy of description was to be found only in the highest productions of modern genius'.[22] Mrs Norton's precocious talent promised much.

On 10 June 1830, three weeks after receiving a proposal of marriage, Georgiana Jane Sheridan, known as Georgy and perhaps the most ravishing of the Sheridan girls, was married to Edward Adolphus St Maur, Lord Seymour, heir of the eleventh Duke of Somerset. This was the best of Mrs Sheridan's efforts. Not only did the bride and groom genuinely like each other, but Lord Seymour was 'very clever and good' – and rich, with an ancient pedigree. This was a man the Sheridans hoped would be a protector and a source of patronage. The groom's family was said to have mixed feelings about the match: his father, who was 'very kind', had no objection, nor did his three sisters, but others were not so happy. There was a whiff of sour grapes in the air among Georgy's acquaintances, who were 'rabid and frantic at my daring to do such a thing. They turned round after congratulating Mama and said, "Good heavens! Is Lord Seymour mad! What a fool", with other pleasing intimations of their good wishes.' Georgy's renowned beauty – 'large deep blue or violet eyes and black hair, perfect features and a complexion of lilies and roses' – was all very well, but cash and property were better, even to a family of great wealth. *The Times* was dazzled by the damsel, purring: 'the beauty and talents of this lady have drawn a high prize in the matrimonial lottery, and not a whit higher than they deserved'.[23]

The groom was born in 1804 and so was five years older than his bride. Georgy's elder sister Helen called him 'the kindest brother-in-law that was ever invented'. Seymour was educated at Eton and Christ Church, Oxford, and left in 1823 without a degree. He travelled to Russia and eastern Europe, and in the year of his marriage embarked on a political career.[24]

A special licence had been needed from the Archbishop of Canterbury so that the wedding could take place in the Grosvenor Place home of Fanny and Sir James Graham. Fanny had looked after Georgy and Brinsley, Caroline and Tommy when their parents were at the Cape. For the last eleven years Graham, a wealthy and politically ambitious man, had been head of the Sheridan family.[25] Born in 1792, he was tall and handsome. Harriette Wilson, the most famous courtesan of her day, called him 'a very Apollo in form', a form which she well knew. Tom Sheridan had had his moments with Miss Wilson before he eloped with the sister of the woman who would become James Graham's wife.[26]

In 1812 Graham wangled himself the post of private secretary to Lord William Bentinck, commander-in-chief of the British army in Sicily, and did well on a secret diplomatic mission to

Italy. When he married Fanny Callander at St Marylebone Church in 1819 he was the Member of Parliament for Hull. In 1820 Graham retired from politics when he lost his seat and for six years improved the twenty-five-thousand-acre Netherby estate in Cumberland, which had been neglected, investing in new roads and drainage and increasing the profitability of the land he farmed and rented to tenants. Graham and Fanny, their three sons and three daughters lived in Cumberland; he had inherited the estate and the baronetcy when his father died in 1824. Two years later he was back in the House of Commons as the MP for Carlisle. He was still ambitious for high office. When he and Fanny hosted the wedding ceremony for Georgy, he was only five months away from being appointed first lord of the Admiralty.

Because of the shyness of the groom the 'very merry' wedding ceremony was only attended by the bride and groom's close family: his parents, sisters and brother, Mrs Sheridan and aunt Georgiana, Caroline Norton and Helen Blackwood (in 'white satin and pearl ornaments' and escorted by their husbands), and their brothers Tommy, Frank and Charlie. Georgy wore a plain white satin gown, diamond brooch and earrings and a 'magnificent blonde veil thrown over her head, so large that it nearly reached her feet'. The men and women dined separately before the couple were married in the drawing room, which was 'arranged as a chapel for the occasion'. If Disraeli's dazzled description of Georgy is only half true the bride must have looked wonderful: 'anything so splendid I never gazed upon . . . Clusters of dark hair, the most brilliant complexion, the contour of the face is perfectly ideal.'[27] When the ceremony was complete the bride and groom left for their honeymoon in Wimbledon; soon after that two hundred guests arrived to celebrate their nuptials. Georgy's new home in the country was at Maiden Bradley in Wiltshire. Their London address was 18 Spring Gardens, across St James's Park from Caroline.

Two weeks after the wedding George Norton's political career stalled, never to be revived, and his new brother-in-law, Lord Seymour, began his. King George IV died on 26 June 1830 and was succeeded by the Duke of Clarence, as William IV. According to newly-wed Georgy, the old king was not much missed: 'everyone seems glad he is gone. I believe there never was such a king, who, without being actively wicked and tyrannical, was so little regretted as him.' As was customary when a monarch died a general election took place, and Seymour became the Whig Member of Parliament for Okehampton while George Norton lost his seat as the Tory Member for Guildford. This was bad news for Caroline. George Norton insisted that he had been the most popular candidate, that the winner was hated and that those who had voted against him had done so with tears in their eyes. While Caroline had never expected great things of George in the House of Commons, she knew the impact it would have on their marriage: 'it is something lost – one of the opportunities of life slipped through one's fingers'.[28] In the short term the loss of his seat meant she would have to spend even longer with her ghastly Scottish in-laws. Caroline who was in Edinburgh would not be able to return to London until early November, and there was a risk they would stay for Christmas – which his parliamentary duties had made impossible in the past – a prospect which filled her with dread. Lord Grantley was determined to get the seat back for his brother. He wanted George and Caroline to live in a cottage on the Wonersh estate (for which they would have to pay rent they could not afford) and woo back the voters who had clearly taken leave of their senses and voted him out of what had been a family seat.

In an angry letter to Georgy about the prospect of living in

Surrey Caroline revealed the tension within her marriage, her poor relations with Lady Grantley and the viperish atmosphere of the Grantleys' own marriage. George, who had to be grateful for any crumbs his brother condescended to drop him, went along with the Wonersh idea, sarcastically insisting that Caroline's brain was that of a butterfly, her mind a blank canvas: 'I am the sort of person to be interested about anything, that I shall easily change my delight in society for pride and pleasure in my dairy.' Crucially, George thought the move would be good for his health, and his career in politics was still salvageable. Caroline had reason to think that her odious brother-in-law was causing mischief in her marriage: 'I earnestly hope that the plan will not be feasible . . . I can only tell you that Lady Grantley says I shall never come there again, and will not speak to Norton. I think Grantley hopes that I am fool enough to refuse to live with Norton in the country, and that a separation would leave Norton once more a tool in his hands. He underrates my wisdom.'[29] For now she and George and their young son Fletcher remained in London, in the bosom of her family and friends.

Before the news was confirmed that George's seat was lost, Caroline had met Fanny Kemble for the first time at a dinner party in July 1830, an encounter the actress had been looking forward to eagerly. Fanny had heard many unpleasant things about Caroline – 'a too formidable ally to be challenged lightly' – but was pleasantly surprised and impressed, finding her charismatic and 'a splendid creature, nobly endowed in every way'. Kemble sounds as if she travelled too close to the sun: 'I feel deeply interested in her; not precisely with the interest inspired by loving or even liking, but with that feeling of admiring solicitude with which one must regard one so gifted, so tempted, and in such a position as hers.'[30]

At the end of August 1830 *The Undying One* was puffed by

an anonymous reviewer in an advertisement her publishers had taken in *The Times*. Her career as a poet was on track, and praise for her work was a respite from the gruesome Grantleys. 'Mrs Norton has fully entitled herself to rank among the real poets of the day. There are passages in this book in which may be found every quality required for the production of high poetry – namely, depth of feeling, force and freedom of thought, vigour and vitality of imagination, fancy imagery and eloquence.'[31]

The Sheridans were a tightly knit family. Their letters are affectionate, funny, sometimes illustrated with sketches, and show that they really liked each other. Getting a position at the Madras office of the East India Company was a good opportunity for the eldest son Brinsley, otherwise he might not have left. Their letters would be passed around or posted on and read aloud over and over and discussed. The youngest Sheridan, Charlie, aged thirteen, wrote to his sister Georgy in 1830 in immaculate handwriting from Mr Walton's school in Church Street, Hampton. He had recently attended her wedding and he was very fond of his new brother Lord Seymour, as he called him, and was looking forward to many hunting and shooting jaunts with him. Seymour was friendlier and more appealing than his sister Carry's husband, grumpy George. The shooting was fraught with danger, as his letter revealed. He begged his sister, 'Do not tell what I am now going to disclose to you. First, I just tell you that I have disposed of my gun as it turned out "a rotten affair" . . . it had an awkward trick of going off without being touched as the lock was a bad one and the barrel was not burnished so that if it burst it was sure to brush some one.'[32]

Charlie then shared his 'second secret', a recent near-fatal accident, which he was afraid would 'only make her fidgety'. While out duck shooting with his school pals Edward and Algernon, his gun went off accidentally, 'struck me in the breast' and nearly sent him toppling into the river, where the gun ended up but not before putting 'five shots into Edward, two in the knees'. The pellets 'were all picked out by a needle except one which the doctor said he might get out or let it stay in'. Luckily Edward was not 'the least bit hurt as it hardly drew blood . . . but think what might have happened'. Undaunted by the turn of events, Edward and Algy carried on shooting while Charlie fished the gun out with an eel spear and went to the gunsmith from whom he had bought it and sold it back to him for ten shillings less than he had paid 'as it was a good deal damaged'. He had no need to replace it; his school was awash with fire-arms. There were seven guns the thirteen-year-old could borrow if he happened to want one.

As 1830 drew to a close Caroline could look back with some personal and professional satisfaction. Her son Fletcher had survived his first year, during which simple infections and ailments killed many children; more editions of *The Undying One* were in the press; artists were asking her to sit for them; and her sister had married a man they all liked. Although George had lost his seat she had managed to avoid going to live at Wonersh near the Grantleys.[33]

Caroline's two younger brothers emerged into adulthood in the early 1830s. Frank, who was sixteen, had recently left Eton. His elegant handwriting is mature and was an important asset; 'a good hand' was the sign of a gentleman and one of the skills required for a career in the diplomatic service. It sloped when excited, lurched confidently across the page, telling tales of Frank's first skirmishes in the ballrooms. In February 1831 Frank took the first step on his career ladder when he was appointed a third-class clerk at the Admiralty, a position his great uncle Sir James Graham, first lord of the Admiralty, would have had no difficulty getting for him.[34]

Frank and the other clerks lived in at the Admiralty but his love of going out for long walks at night caused problems, so he moved into a friend's rooms in nearby Warwick Street, between Pall Mall and Whitehall, and helped himself to the contents of the wine cellar which his friend's parents had thoughtfully restocked. Frank threw himself into salon life with abandon, a trait that would be a constant of his relatively short life. One evening, when he 'was elated with champagne' he proposed to an heiress who was 'pretty with a most excellent disposition' and had a dowry of sixty thousand pounds, to whom 'I had just been introduced and never seen before. She was delighted with my appearance, and I said she had good taste . . . she laughed very much, so did I . . . but it all ended in her going away with her old mother whose heart I won by asking her to dance and then begging her pardon and saying that I took her for her daughter whose hand I affectionately squeezed as she got into the carriage.'

That was the last Frank saw of his pretty heiress. Frank's letters to Georgy reveal his contempt for George Norton, of whom he saw nothing but heard that he 'goes about as usual with his tongue loaded with improbabilities, seated upon his black charger which gives him the appearance of not '"Death on the pale horse" but "the pale ass upon death".'[35]

Caroline and George Norton met Lord Melbourne early in 1831, when he was home secretary, soon casting him in the role of benefactor, patron and friend. George Norton, with no great family fortune to his name, was looking for a position. The loss of his seat at Guildford was compounded when he was no longer required as a commissioner for bankrupts – a job his mother-in-law had helped secure for him – when that office was reorganised. George, a barrister but not keen to practise, asked his wife Caroline to coax their new and powerful friend into finding him a well paid and undemanding position. In April 1831 Lord Melbourne obliged by appointing Norton one of two magistrates for Whitechapel at the court in Lambeth Street in Aldgate in the East End, where he earned a generous salary of a thousand pounds a year.

Unusually for the Nortons' place in society, the income Caroline earned was the bedrock of the family finances. George Norton was irked by this affront to his *amour propre,* riven by resentment at being the second son and felt no compunction in exerting pressure on his wife to cultivate Lord Melbourne for more favours. During 1831 Caroline Norton's friendship with Lord Melbourne quickly developed. Their outings to the theatre and parties were gossiped about, while George's new position kept him busier than he liked: three days a week he travelled from Westminster to the heart of the poorest community in London to hear cases brought before him by the new police service. George was overqualified for the position – magistrates were only required to know the basic common law – it was the salary he needed. His jurisdiction included some of the roughest and toughest streets in the capital: it ran from the Tower stairs on the River Thames north along the boundary of the City and then east to Bow, then back down to the river at East India Dock, Ratcliff Highway and the Hermitage Basin. The title and role gave him gravitas, a quality he craved.

One evening Fanny Kemble saw Mrs Norton and Lord Melbourne at the salon of Lady Dacre, a playwright, sculptress and society hostess. Fanny was dazzled by Caroline – 'Mrs Norton was there, more entertaining and blindingly beautiful than ever' – and passed on her brother's 'desperate love' to her, but Caroline could only offer 'deadly scorn'. Giddy with the world of fashion, and out and about with a famous masher, she was unwise to be so high-handed when given a compliment. Her head may have been turned by having much artistic attention: there was a new print of her tinkling teacups, sitting underneath a portrait of her grandfather Sherry, by Daniel

Maclise, entitled *The Author of The Undying One*. Melbourne, smooth as always, asked to be introduced to the pretty actress. Fanny Kemble was taken by the older man's 'face, voice and manner'. He asked her to dine with him the following week.[36]

George Norton's new position sweetened the bitter taste of losing his seat at Guildford, but when the parliamentary seats were reorganised it was won by his younger brother Charles. Sibling rivalry seems to have been endemic in their fractious family and George was livid at being snubbed by the electorate and then sickened to see his younger swashbuckling brother voted in by the same folk. His special talent was to take things personally. At the end of May 1831 the usually penny-pinching Lord Grantley celebrated Charles's success with a *fête champêtre*, hiring barges to take seven hundred of Guildford's voters and their wives, who wore Tory blue ribands, from the town to the grounds at Wonersh. Accompanied by a band, they dined on an 'elegant cold collation consisting of every delicacy of the season', and there was a 'brilliant display of fireworks'. Lord and Lady Grantley were on their best behaviour that day: 'Nothing could exceed the amiable urbanity of the noble host and hostess in whose magnificent establishment may verily be found true baronial splendour.'[37] Caroline and George were not there: they had the perfect excuse. Caroline's first play, *The Gypsy Father*, was performed on the same evening at Covent Garden Theatre. They sat and watched it from a box with her sister Georgy and her husband Lord Somerset.

Fanny Kemble went to see the new melodrama at her father's theatre, and perhaps resenting Caroline's recent carelessness about her brother's feelings, slated it: 'What a terrible piece! What atrocious situations and ferocious circumstances! tinkering, starving, hanging.' Accusing Caroline of pandering to the public's taste, she conceded, 'But . . . she's in the right; she has given the public what they desire, given them what they like.

Of course it made one cry horribly.'[38] Mindful of how tight the margins were and that if *The Gypsy Father* was well received her own family would benefit financially, the actor-manager's daughter scanned the theatre and noted that the pit and galleries had empty seats but that the dress circle and boxes had been 'full of fine folk'. The great and the good had come to see if Sheridan's granddaughter could write for the stage, and they were not all as disappointed as Fanny.

The Gypsy Father was a florid tear-jerker which *The Times* believed displayed merit of 'a distinguished kind'. The reviewer acknowledged the evident lack of experience of the dramatist and also made the intriguing remark that some of the problems had been due to 'the mischievous practices which prevail behind the scene rather than to the author'. A soldier returns home from the wars to find his father and family have left the village, ashamed of their destitution, while the young girl he expected to marry has been adopted by her long-lost father who has turned out to be a wealthy man. The young man goes in search of his parents and siblings, who have been taken in by a band of Gypsies. Everyone is broken and starving; there is a fight and the soldier's mother accidentally stabs her husband and is carted off to prison. It gets worse and worse: the children have to eat nettles and cabbage stalks. For Fanny Kemble it was like a chapter out of the *Newgate Calendar*.[39]

While there were clearly problems with the story, *The Times* believed Mrs Norton 'has decided talents for this kind of composition' and criticised the actor playing the returning soldier: 'It is a great misfortune that he cannot be induced to play in a more subdued style and to walk and talk something in the manner of other human beings.' Among the gloom and doom of the piece there were comic scenes which were felt to be Caroline's best work: they were 'so well-managed and written with such liveliness of spirit that we cannot help thinking that the authoress's forte lies more decidedly that way than any other'. But despite 'the piece being very well received throughout and often very loudly applauded' it only had a short run.[40]

Caroline's literary ambition was burgeoning. Her songs and poems had been well received and provided a good income, now she had reason to feel encouraged by her first outing as a playwright. She was pregnant with their second child, whose birth was expected in November. Then George got both of them into trouble with the press, the muck-raking and facetious newspaper *John Bull* filling many column inches in its campaign against him, and by association Caroline, for wrongly putting the term Honourable in front of their names. George had helped himself to the honorific, and Caroline got dragged into the mess when her name appeared as the Honourable Mrs Norton. Theodore Hook, the editor of *John Bull*, exposed this snobbish affectation – or fraud – with great glee. George's elder brother was a Right Honourable and a Lord, but none of the other Norton siblings was entitled to the prefix because their father did not have a title. In the summer of 1831, canvassed by Lord Melbourne, William IV granted a patent for George and his brothers Charles and James, and sisters Grace, Caroline, Mary Eleanor and Augusta, entitling them to put 'Hon.' in front of their names. Caroline had asked her 'dear Lord' to help and he 'had been very kind about it' and had done so, another good turn done for George – and his family, who with the exception of Charles detested her.[41] However galling it may have been for George to rely on his wife's friendship with the older man, he had to be grateful to Melbourne for the favours and 'his kind hints to which I assure you have not been thrown away upon one who worships "the shadow of your shoetyes"'.[42]

During the summer the Nortons had work done to their house in Storey's Gate: the nursery at the top of the house was decorated to look 'less like an attic'. The smell of the paint drove Caroline to send two-year-old Fletcher and his nurse Mrs Moore by steam packet from London Bridge to Margate, where she would join them. Her letter to Mrs Moore from London shows Caroline was keen to get away: 'I am so poisoned here that if I do not get a mouthful of fresh air my little November baboon will be born with a green face.' The letter discusses her husband's controlling behaviour and penny-pinching ways with their servant. Even though he recently bought himself a cabriolet with the proceeds of *her* literary earnings, she is willing to share a bed with Mrs Moore in Margate to save money. It was not unusual for the mistress of a house to sleep with one of her female servants if there were no male servants on the premises to protect the house from burglars when the master was away. In this case it was all about George Norton's cheese-paring ways. 'Mr Norton still intends coming on Monday but as he returns on Wednesday I think an hotel would be as cheap as lodgings, unless the person you are with could let us have a little bedroom and sitting-room for two nights, which is hardly worthwhile. Perhaps Mr Norton will let me stay one week at Ramsgate: in that case, if we had a little sitting-room I could sleep with you, if your bed was a good size; or if they had a room with a single bed for <u>me</u>, we might eat our meals there, and have no sitting-room. Pray, dear old woman, ask about and get something low: I am sure if it is <u>cheap</u> Mr Norton will let me stay the week.'[43]

During July and August, the fifth and sixth months of her pregnancy, Caroline stayed with her sister Georgy on her country estate at Maiden Bradley in Wiltshire. The flurry of letters between her and Lord Melbourne reveals an intimacy between them which suggests a love affair was in the making, if not already made. Her tone is hardly that of the grand-daughter of his old friend Sherry, rather that of an infatuated young woman, proprietory and jealous of a thirteen-year-old girl called Susan whom Melbourne and his late wife had adopted. There are letters which brim with society gossip, when it seems that Caroline does not intend referring to Susan (whom she calls a child although at the age of thirteen she was about to become a young woman), but she cannot help slipping in a mention at the end. At times Mrs Norton sounds impertinent and interfering, insisting that Melbourne should help Susan become a governess because that is the only profession which would provide her with an income 'from her own exertions . . . among her own sex as <u>a lady</u>'. It would also give the girl a home and protection, which are vital for a respectable female suddenly on her own in the world, 'which I do not see how she is otherwise to obtain'. There was another solution which Caroline could have promoted – that Melbourne fulfil the obligations of a parent and provide his adopted daughter with a home – but Caroline does not recommend this as a plan: she sounds anxious to remove the girl from his orbit as quickly as can be arranged.

At other times Caroline expresses motherly concern at how Susan has been used as a toy which Melbourne has tired of and now considers a burden. Caroline's emotions were clearly confused: on the one hand she was unhappy about the attention Melbourne was giving to Susan's future, on the other, as the mother of a young child with another on the way, she was critical, accusing him of having 'domesticated her as <u>a plaything</u> in your house, you consulted your own caprice or that of Lady Caroline, and not the good of the child'. Her maternal instincts drew her to take an interest in Susan and even give her a home. 'You are annoyed and surprised at finding that you must provide for a future in which you have no personal interest, and merely because in a rash moment you let a little thing in a coral necklace and sash run about your drawing room years ago. You have done a good and generous action <u>if</u> it is persisted in; you have indulged a selfish and childish caprice if you are now wearily turning it over in your mind, in what way you can rid yourself of a tiresome responsibility. Send her to some good school as a half-boarder – let her be educated as a governess – and I will promise never to lose sight of her. If I have daughters she might be with me if she liked it hereafter. If there is anything which seems harsh to you in all I have said you will forgive it . . . Farewell dearest lord, don't be angry with me for my impatience on the subject of your protégée.'[44]

One day Caroline wrote George a letter which started off pleasantly, then scolded him for the 'little scrawl' he had sent her and concluded with a description of two disturbing dreams she had had the night before whose meaning seems obvious. She almost confesses that she is not a loyal wife: 'I dreamed last night that you were dying, and two old maids told you stories of me.' The old women told her she could not visit George, but she rushed into the room and found that they had lied, and that 'you were dying for my company, and then . . . as I was sitting by you explaining, I saw you grow quite unconscious and die'. She woke in floods of tears. Her rest at Maiden Bradley was troubled: the previous night she dreamed that her unborn baby had drowned: 'I saw him float away and no one would attend to me because I was mad!' Overwrought, she asked her husband to come and protect her from her 'horrid dreams' but he was not able to visit for another four weeks.

Down in sleepy Wiltshire, away from London salon society and with few distractions other than her younger sister's pet lamb and aviary, Caroline was bored and fed up with having her day organised for her. She complained that the only time she had to herself was when 'after tea I am allowed a quiet hour while the young couple caress one another'. Caroline became upset when she did not hear from Melbourne for three days. Her letters had to travel from Wiltshire to London by mail coach, and since Lord Melbourne was home secretary with affairs of state to attend to, it is remarkable that he was able to find time to write back to her so quickly. Having had to wait for his reply to her bossy advice about Susan, the sight of his handwriting excited Caroline. She wrote back immediately on 4 August 1831, relieved to hear from him again and grateful not to be admonished for her tone: spilling her emotions onto the page, the faster she wrote the loopier her letters became: 'my heart misgave me that my epistle had not met with the indulgence I had half hoped for it'. She was fearful that she had overstepped the mark, and agonised in a lather of insecurity, 'perhaps it is the feeling of inequality between us, more than the way in which you receive my tirades, which makes me always feel as soon as my letter is in the postman's hand as if it were crammed with impertinences'. She confessed to him she scolded herself for her letters, calling herself an 'ass' and asking rhetorically: 'why write two pages of disagreeable import for the sake of a child you never saw and whose destiny you cannot alter?' She was unable to accept that she had been completely in the wrong to write to him in the way that she did: 'Yet some of what I said was true, was it not? And if I mistake you sometimes, I do at least implicitly believe your contradictions.' This was a twenty-three-year-old married woman and the mother of a small son with another child due in three months, writing to a man considered one of the most eligible in the country, with a well-earned reputation as a rake, one of the most senior politicians in the government and old enough to be her father.

While Caroline's letters to Lord Melbourne do not mention any physical relationship – in an age of insecure post and prying messengers it is unlikely they would have made this mistake – the intensity of the only letters to survive and her very personal tone would not have been appreciated by George Norton.

Melbourne's letters to her were far more important to Caroline than they should have been, and certainly more important than George's; they bulked too large in her life to be the letters of a simple friend. Caroline's desperation to hear from him and the warmth of her letters are highly suggestive.

The correspondence throws light on what it was like to have Lord Grantley as a brother-in-law. His behaviour reveals a greedy man who was as happy to cheat his younger brother as he was to pull a fast one on his pushy new sister. When George was a newly qualified barrister his valuable mare, which had been hunted hard and gone lame, was given to Lord Grantley on the understanding that the next foal she had was to be George's, but bred at his brother's expense. A bay colt with black legs was born at Markenfield, their Yorkshire estate near Ripon, and turned out 'exceedingly well'. George gave the colt, now two years old, to Caroline as a wedding present, and Grantley and his grooms would send news of the horse's progress. However, when Caroline and George asked about the horse in the spring of 1830, they were told by Grantley that it was not ready to be ridden. The following spring a groom told George that Caroline's colt had been sold for sixty guineas, and Grantley had tried to bribe him to say that it had been shot. So appalled was the groom by his employer's behaviour that despite being a long-standing servant of the family who had known the Nortons since they were boys, he refused. The family had been in an uproar ever since: 'there has been nothing but swearing, quarrelling, discoveries and lie after lie in the nobleman's house'. George Norton was 'highly offended' and Grantley tried to 'coax him into quietness' by offering him a couple of hounds', a present he knew his brother was anxious to have to impress Lord Seymour. But George stood up to his brother and refused the hounds.

On 7 August 1831 Caroline sent a note to Melbourne, this

time suggesting that he 'change little Susan's name'. She plunged into another unhelpful argument: 'However, God knows, poor little thing, I do not wish to persuade you into adding anything to the discomfort of her life. Only tell me what she is to be and what you will call her and I will never speak to you in the imperative mood again.' It is surprising that Caroline did not seem to understand that the less she said about Susan the better. Her theatrical behaviour in company masked a young woman who was more immature than her wittiness suggested. A man with Melbourne's experience would have had no difficulty in seeing her heart being worn hopelessly on her sleeve. There was no need to read between the lines; her emotions were laid down and laid bare. Caroline ended her note to him in an odd way: 'I beg leave to mention that the young lady whom you so kindly promise to take for a wife, will be born in November.'

A day later Caroline was joined by her husband at Maiden Bradley. Her letters continued and she lost no time in mocking George Norton's clumsy behaviour and inadequate manners. To make up for the loss of her colt, Melbourne offered to give her a bay filly from his stables at Brocket Hall. Despite Norton's expressed worship of Melbourne's shoelaces, George was unhappy at the home secretary's role in their family and how much they owed him, so Caroline was nervous about asking her husband if she could accept Melbourne's offer: 'I will ask Norton when he comes in (if he has had good sport . . . I hope he will not be farouche [fierce, sullen] about it'. Melbourne asked her how much she missed him and was affected by his absence. Unconvincingly, she tried to regain her equilibrium: 'My Lord, absence makes no difference with me: your letters do because they are the pleasantest I get. Strike the balance in your own favour and endeavour to feel humble and modest.' But her attempt to appear detached was undermined by her final remark: 'who do you call on of a morning?'

Three days later Caroline was able to report that George had agreed to her accepting Melbourne's filly: 'so high is his opinion of your personal merit that I might take <u>anything</u> from you'. And she had another favour to ask. Recently an unfinished painting of her grandmother holding her father in her arms had come to light and Caroline asked Melbourne to verify that the woman in the painting was indeed her grandmother. He was able to confirm that the picture was of Tom and his mother, and had been painted in the studio of Ozias Humphrey, a friend of William Blake and George Romney. She bought it for ten guineas and gave it to her mother.

By the third week of August Caroline had family with her and her spirits lifted; her letters to Melbourne were more measured and reflective. Her son Fletcher was there but unwell, and her brother Charlie had arrived to accompany George chasing hares with Seymour's pack of beagles. She made an interesting response to a teasing remark Melbourne made about her vanity, which reveals what it was like to grow up as the least conventionally pretty of three girls whose reputation for good looks defined them. Caroline had not quite turned from an ugly duckling into a beautiful swan, but there is a hint of this in her meditation on her looks. 'I do not think myself <u>enormously</u> vain: there is a boundary to a fault when one is conscious of it: but what you say respecting the suddenness of any desirable acquisition turning one's head, I have often been pleased when told by my friends how much vainer I was than Georgy who was twice as handsome. People whose beauty is a familiar thing to their ears from childhood, might as well be vain of it as being able to read and write. In all events you need not fear personal vanity ruining me <u>now</u>, as I have always the pleasing reflection to recur to, that I have not in spite of the change of opinion among my friends on the score of my looks, obtained what I wished – perhaps

I should say what I <u>expected</u> when I first began to look in the glass with satisfaction.'

With the subject of Susan's future dropped, who Melbourne was seeing was a cause of Caroline's concern. In this context it would have been reasonable for him to remind her, and he probably did, that she was married and he was a widower. She insisted, 'it is only when I am entirely left to my own conjectures that I grow anxious'. As long as she knew he was busy with 'graver matters', all was well, and at Melbourne going to spend Saturday at Brocket Hall, his Hertfordshire home, she felt easy, or so she said: 'this I hope you will continue to tell me'.

Caroline and Melbourne swapped stories of their childhoods. Caroline did not share his enthusiasm for corporal punishment: she 'bit the fingers of the whipper and rushed to repeat my crime which proves it was good for you . . . and very bad for me'. She could not recall 'a single instance in which I was subdued by harshness'. As the Nortons' marriage began to lurch from one crisis to another, George's beatings of Caroline would have the opposite effect.

The last letter Caroline wrote to Lord Melbourne from Maiden Bradley that summer reveals her putting a brave face on her marriage to George Norton. She may not have married the man she would have wished given a free choice, but at least she had been spared 'living and dying a lonely old maid [which] was the only misfortune I ever particularly dreaded'. She tries to sound content with her lot in life: 'I like to be coaxed and petted and made much of . . . give my children doses of rhubarb and to correspond with noblemen who direct [write] to me'. Caroline felt at ease with her social superiors, and dropped in a criticism of the snobbery of Melbourne's circle of family and friends: 'I am amply content to be <u>Mistress</u> N, even without the <u>Hon'ble</u> and have even a pleasure in feeling when I am in company with your proud ones, that little as I am, I am satisfied as the best of them, perhaps more so – that I wish for nobody's place or lot in preferment to my own, and know that they can take nothing from me, or humble me in any way. At least I have never been humbled yet.'

Caroline was philosophical about the circumstances in which she found herself: 'My Lord, I am contented.' Rumours about their 'acquaintanceship' had been rife since they were seen together in public. Caroline knew of the gossip about them, was untroubled by it and told him with uncharacteristic sarcasm, 'I am quite willing to believe that I am wonderfully benefited by it, and at any rate it is a great pleasure to me.' A remark Melbourne had made to her in his most recent letter provoked a barb: 'Defend yourself with that mixture of mendacious eloquence and assurance which is so striking a feature of your mind.'

At the end of August the Nortons returned to London having heard that they had been robbed: a man working for them had stolen some Sheridan and Norton silver plate and a woollen dress Caroline had bought for the baby. They learned that the workman 'was the greatest rascal unhung' who had been refused a post as a policeman because of his 'bad character'. George Norton had hired the scoundrel, not an endorsement of the shrewdness to be hoped for in a magistrate.[45]

In the autumn of 1831 both Caroline's husband and her 'dearest Lord', home secretary in the Whig government, were caught up in the social unrest which had erupted around the country in the demand for reform of the electoral franchise. In 1831 only 3.2 per cent of the total population of sixteen million in England and Wales could vote for their Member of Parliament.[46] Those who lived in the English and Welsh counties and paid forty shillings land tax a year on their freehold property could vote; in the boroughs the vote was restricted to men who paid poor rates, or were freemen, or freeholders. The electoral system was open to corruption, with a cabal of powerful aristocrats effectively buying parliamentary seats and influencing voters to vote for their own man. For many years elections and electioneering had provided material for cartoonists like Rowlandson and Gillray.

For the Tories the demand to widen the franchise and clean up the voting system was a grumbling ache which refused to go away. Ideologically they opposed changes to the status quo and were against electoral reform since the existing system suited their (largely landed) vested interests. But by 1830 they could not say any more that the country was at risk from revolutionary France. Moreover, a new breed of Tory, whose fortunes derived from industry, commerce or banking rather than country estates, was emerging. These men still deferred to their presumed social superiors but were at least as wealthy as them, and some senior Tories were now reluctantly reconciled to moderate reform of the franchise.[47]

The Whigs, who wanted to extend the franchise, were certainly not in favour of granting the vote to every male adult. Their belief was that owning property conferred the right to citizenship, and that property owners had a vested interest in maintaining the stability of the country. If the bourgeoisie had the vote they would use it wisely; the danger lay in giving it to those without property, as they had no stake in society. To the Whigs, owners of substantial property would have leisure to take politics seriously and be educated enough to engage with the process thoughtfully. Men of means could also not be bribed and were therefore independent. In 1830 the Whigs, many of whom were significant landowners, were back in government after years in the political wilderness and were pushing for reform within their own ideological framework.[48]

On 7 November Caroline wrote to her sister Georgy conveying the drama of national politics being played out in the intimacy of her own drawing room in Storey's Gate. Norton was one of nature's Tories; his family even more so. Lord Melbourne had little appetite for parliamentary reform, a lukewarm pragmatist when it came to his party's ambition to pass a 'great reform act'. His job was to ensure that the peace was kept and law and order maintained, and this is where he was most active, rather than canvassing for change. Since 1830, when he had been appointed, his reluctance to act when others called for decisiveness had earned him a reputation for laziness. He had nearly lost his job in September for his casual approach, and it was only the lobbying of his friend and ally Lord Holland which had saved his ministerial skin: 'a dislike to meddling legislation and his careless nonchalant manner might give him the character of an indolent man . . . but those who had business with the office did not find him so'.

Melbourne's stance derived from his Whiggish belief that governments should always act legally, and what was not illegal, however troublesome, had to be tolerated. He knew that the government could only do so much during disturbances because its resources were limited and harsh tactics often only made matters worse. Melbourne preferred social unrest to be dealt with by local magistrates and lord lieutenants, who knew their population better than militias sent to deal with incidents. His Whiggish distaste for repressive government, especially at times of social upheaval, did not mean that he took a lenient approach, more a pragmatic one. When the situation in the country threatened to become unstable in the latter part of 1831 and the first half of 1832, his approach toughened. For instance, George Norton's younger brother Captain Charles Norton was dispatched with troops to deal with riotous pro-reformers in Bristol.[49]

Caroline's personality and her family pedigree as a grand-daughter of Sheridan drew her to the cause of reform like iron filings to a magnet. To her husband and his family's intense annoyance she was an outspoken advocate of reform of the franchise. Caroline was an instinctive reformer who had become a supporter of Catholic emancipation in 1829. She believed the franchise to be unjust and open to corruption. Her mother told her of her father's several failed attempts to become an MP, hoping to achieve some reform. In 1831 Caroline again spoke out, frustrated that the Great Reform Bill which had been passed in September in the House of Commons, was then rejected by the House of Lords.

Seven days away from giving birth to her second child, and miles away from sleepy Maiden Bradley, she was delighted to be at the centre of things, reporting on the comings and goings in her own home and in Downing Street. She told Georgy how she had shared some disturbing intelligence about the current unrest with Fatty, her new pet name for Melbourne. The news would have been concerning to anyone else, but he took it in his stride: he 'thrives, only yawns a little more than usual on his long days'. While she sat at her desk writing to her sister, George Norton was working on his day off because 'of the expected row', enrolling special constables from the 'most respectable local inhabitants' to keep law and order in Whitechapel. So many policemen were being diverted to deal with the three thousand working men rumoured to be armed with wooden staves and due to gather on White House Fields in Islington that night, that more constables were needed. In the afternoon Melbourne met a delegation of the organisers to warn them that if the meeting went ahead it would be regarded as 'seditious and highly treasonable' and the ringleaders risked execution. The meeting was called off. A few stragglers turned up but no demonstration took place. Thriving on the drama of the moment, Caroline put herself centre stage, suggesting she had an active role: 'nevertheless we think we have taken such measures that no great riot will take place'.

George Norton felt that his career was going well. Without a parliamentary seat he had played no part in the debate; instead he clattered off to Whitechapel in his new cabriolet, bustled about his office, a big fish in a little pond, caught up in the political ferment at grass-roots level. A possible case of 'burking', named after the murderous activities of the Edinburgh bodysnatchers Burke and Hare, on his patch came to his attention. George referred the matter to a higher court, which resulted in the execution of a thirty-eight-year-old woman for the murder and probable sale of the body of her elderly female lodger to 'resurrection men.' The demand for dead bodies from anatomists provided lucrative work for characters prepared to watch cemeteries for funerals and dig up fresh bodies. The old lady's granddaughter had been to several police stations and been laughed at until she put her concerns to George Norton, who took her seriously.[50] Lord Seymour scoffed at George's role in the case, but Caroline was proud of him and happy to bask in the praise which came his way: 'it has been a great feather in our cap, and done Norton a great deal of good, both in making him a punctual, enthusiastic and painstaking magistrate and getting shoals of compliments from people in authority'.[51]

On 14 November 1831 the couple's second son, Thomas Brinsley Norton, was born. He was 'very dark with long thick hair and a perfect beauty'.[52] The day before she went into labour Caroline wrote a note to Pricey, her sister Helen's husband, before he sailed for India, asking him to take a letter to her brother Brinsley in Madras. She was still concerned about Fletcher's health: 'my boy has given me both disappointment and anxiety by a recurrence of his old attacks on his lungs . . . we have by Herbert's [their doctor] desire put him into high dresses to guard his chest completely from the cold'. Caroline remarked on the affection that Royal Navy ships inspired in those whose family and friends served on them. She reported that many people had told her of the 'beauty and good sailing' of Pricey's ship the *Imogene*: 'I feel as if she was one of the family, and you know we are all proud of our beauty.'[53]

In January 1832 George's eccentric sister Augusta came to stay with them and remained for more than three months. She was a disruptive and demanding semi-invalid: her embarrassingly masculine looks and dress, and outspoken political opinions of the Ultra Tory persuasion were the cause of furious rows. Caroline could not stand her and refused to take her about in polite society, but George threatened to immobilise their cabriolet if Augusta did not go with her. So Caroline had to endure painful evenings with her sister-in-law expressing her hostility to the proposed reform bill to Caroline's Whig friends and relations, who were lobbying on its behalf. There was tension at Storey's Gate as Caroline juggled a sickly son, a two-month-old baby, the need to write for money and a house guest who reported her to George for every imagined slight. Norton was caught between his sister, who constantly tried to play on his affections, and his confident wife, who was not minded to kowtow. On her arrival from Edinburgh Augusta heard that a new book, *The Summer Fete, A Poem, With Songs and Music* by the well-known Irish writer Tom Moore, was dedicated to Caroline. Augusta, who had had a few articles published and fancied herself a poet, did not enjoy all the attention her rival was getting from the literary world.[54]

In the spring of 1832, as mistress of the house, Caroline advertised for three new servants. She wanted a cook – a 'respectable young person' who had worked as a kitchen maid in a 'nobleman or gentleman's family' – and a maid who could help in the nursery. The Nortons could not afford a trained cook and certainly not a French cook – only the best households could – so Caroline tried to make do with someone who had worked in a grander house than theirs. A manservant was also wanted, but they could not afford a butler or footman, rather an all-purpose indoor servant who could also act as valet to George.[55]

Augusta Norton left London in April, Caroline's sworn enemy; her hostility would prove to be a further serious complication in the Nortons' marriage. There was something unhinged about Augusta's dislike of her sister. She had worked herself into a frenzy when Caroline expressed her views on electoral reform. For her part, Caroline derived pleasure at annoying Augusta. The Great Reform Bill proved disastrous to their relationship, and the damage it caused would affect Caroline for the rest of her life. William Augusta Ann Norton would prove to be not just an odd sister, but a formidable foe.

On 1 May 1832 Caroline's brother Frank, aged seventeen, left third-class clerking for ever when he resigned his position at the Admiralty after fifteen months to become secretary to the Earl of Mulgrave, the newly appointed governor of Jamaica.[56] This was an important step up the career ladder, helped again by his great-uncle Sir James Graham. The Sheridans had known the Mulgraves for a long time; the earl's father had been a pall-bearer at their grandfather's funeral in 1816. Frank's new boss was the handsome and curly-haired Constantine Henry Phipps, second Earl of Mulgrave and later Marquess of Normanby. Frank was fortunate to work for a likeable man who was 'eager, gay and good-humoured'. Frank remained in his service for seven years, ending up in Dublin. Up to now Frank had led a sheltered life; he was unprepared for the bloody changes he saw in Jamaica – a slave rebellion and the execution of the ring-leaders, then the abolition of slavery in 1833.[57]

The Great Reform Act was won. The bill was passed on

4 June 1832 in the House of Lords by a majority of 106 to 22; the fifteen-month struggle was over. Caroline and her circle of supporters had won; George Norton and his family had lost. The qualification for the vote widened and the electorate increased by just under half to 4.7 per cent of the population; parliamentary seats were redistributed, and some were abolished.[58]

There was cholera in London that year; George's position as magistrate brought this unpleasant fact close to home. At work in Whitechapel, three miles downriver from Storey's Gate, he was confronted by the horror of what was unfolding. By the end of 1832 thousands of Londoners would die of the disease, the cause of which was still a mystery. Many thought it was caused by 'miasma' – bad vapours. The highly infectious disease, which produced diarrhoea and racking bouts of vomiting, was a new plague which had first arrived in England the previous autumn at the port of Sunderland on ships from the Baltic, and then spread to London on colliers bringing coal from the north-east of England. It was a fact of life and a significant cause of death until its cause, the contamination of drinking water by human waste, was discovered by John Snow in Soho in 1864. The diarist Charles Greville noted that the government's preoccupation with electoral reform had left London unprepared for the arrival of a disease that could have been contained if the quarantine laws had been applied to ships coming to London from places where cholera had already established itself.

In July George Norton was visited in Lambeth Street by Mr Kelly, 'a medical gentleman', who described in detail the misery of people suffering from cholera a short walk away from his office in Cartwright Street. Men, women and children huddled together without food or clothing; young strong men were dying of the disease in a few hours. Kelly asked the magistrate for 'a few pounds to alleviate the extreme misery', that piles of 'filth' (human excrement) in the neighbourhood be removed and that houses, courts and alleys should be whitewashed to try and check the spread of the disease. The beadle of the parish of Whitechapel was also present and showed the harsh face of local politics when he dismissed Kelly's concerns and rejected his pleas for help, telling him that Cartwright Street was 'inhabited by the very lowest order of Irish who congregated from all parts of the town, in consequence of their not paying any rent . . . that they were only a pack of low Irish and therefore the parish could do nothing for them'. Norton and his fellow magistrate Mr Walker listened, but told Mr Kelly that Cartwright Street was not within their jurisdiction, but that of the vestry of Aldgate. Mr Walker said that they 'did not wish to interfere in the local jurisdiction and advised Mr Kelly to apply to the magistrate of that office'. By the end of the epidemic there had been more than seven thousand deaths in the capital.[59]

In August the Nortons took their three-year-old son Fletcher, sometimes called Spencer or Penny within the family, leaving baby Brinsley (whom Caroline called her 'abandoned chicken') with her mother at Hampton Court Palace, and travelled to Scotland, where Caroline spent most of September at Rossie Priory, Inchture, Perthshire. It was a grand house filled with Roman antiquities excavated and collected by Lord Kinnaird, after whose father Charles Kinnaird Caroline's brother Charlie was named. En route they stayed with George's eldest sister, tricky and truculent Grace, and her husband Sir Neil Menzies on Loch Rannoch. After the briefest of visits to her 'ungracious host', Caroline left George behind to shoot to his heart's content and took Fletcher to stay with 'kinder friends of her own', the Kinnairds. At Rossie Priory she dashed off a dutiful letter to George, emphasising the wholesomeness of her stay: 'I fear this will be but a hurried line, for they do run about so all day in the open air that time slips away till we dress for dinner. Penny is very well indeed, and I have bought some flannel at Dundee to wrap him in. I have not heard again of Baby.' Knowing that Norton was safely stalking the moors and fishing the loch, she urged him to 'come back darling, I am wishing for you . . . flinging beech-nuts at one another's head is all we do; and very good sport it is'.[60]

Caroline's letters to Lord Melbourne were different: long, gossipy and flirtatious. She was bored on her own and pretended to be shocked by the behaviour of her fellow guests, but Melbourne was too old and wise not to realise that he was being manipulated. He was still unable to conceal his irritation: 'it is evident to me that you are running your rigs', a quaint phrase for her flirty behaviour. Replying, she told him it was not a place where the Bible was read; champagne dinners turned into sing-songs, and generous nightcaps of whisky rounded off every evening. She hoped he had received her last letter 'in a good humour' and was not angry 'at my objecting to your not letting me run my rigs'. She agreed with his sly remark that the 'Scotch air' was bad for her, but insisted that it was even worse for the young men of the party, who had 'gone frantic'. A recent 'adventure' she had 'has sobered her enthusiasm for country houses'.

One evening Caroline was reading in bed in the early hours of the morning when 'little' Charles Ossulston appeared in her bedroom looking like a 'corsair' and refused to leave. Charles was the sixth Earl of Tankerville, two years younger than Caroline. The way she described the sexually charged and histrionic scenes at Rossie in her letters to Melbourne, and her outrage at the gall of the arrogant young generation of earls and barons, who assumed her availability for a holiday romance, was in the style of a popular novel. Her accounts were clearly intended to amuse, but also to inform Melbourne that she was the object of men's desire and he was not the only man interested in her.

Apparently she admonished the young man for 'being such a fool as to suppose that any woman would give herself to you at the end of four days merely because there was no other in the house for you to make love to'. Undaunted by her response the young lord 'threw himself into a chair and remained panting'. Caroline knew she had to get him out. If it was known that Ossulston had spent the night in her room her life and marriage would be in tatters: 'I could almost laugh, both at the obstinacy you show and you expecting me to run the chance of losing my home, my children and my reputation, in order to give you a night's amusement.' Caroline offered to keep Ossulston's nocturnal visit a secret from her jealous husband, promised to behave towards him 'exactly as if it had never happened' and reminded him that 'adultery is a crime and not a recreation'. He accused her of coarseness, but when she reminded Ossulston how much her husband liked him 'and would think you the last person in the house capable of what you are doing' he burst into tears and 'agreed he was a scoundrel'. After that evening, she told Melbourne, she always bolted her door.[61]

Some days later Caroline wrote a franker, bitchier letter to her brother Brinsley, who had recently returned to England from Madras. It included more high jinks than the carefully worded letters she had written to her 'adored Fatty'. Evidently, George's continued absence and the drinking, late nights and high living were taking their toll. It was only six months since her second son had been born and she was 'not yet well . . . I have almost constant pain in my side.' Caroline felt languid and did not dress until one o'clock in the afternoon; dinner was served at two and she worried she might have gout. At three she would go riding for three hours and then walk for an hour, which left little time for work and correspondence.

When Caroline was in London her two boys were cared for by servants, which left her days free to be filled with the important tasks of earning money by writing and keeping in daily contact with family and friends. Writing by day, she would socialise in the evening, and end the day's work with another stint at her desk until the early hours, working by candlelight or oil lamp. Caroline frequently made copies of her more important letters to send on to several family members. Mrs Norton's life was wholly consumed by scratching words on paper, her closest companion her dip-pen.

Even on holiday in Scotland Caroline dashed off letters to her family and edited *La Belle Assemblée and Court Magazine*, a publication launched in the summer of 1832, but her time was being squeezed by the relentless partying expected by her host and companions. Fortunately Caroline's brothers and sisters were such a talented bunch that she regularly obtained contributions from them, such as poems from Helen and descriptions of life in Jamaica from Frank. She also included poems and essays by her late father and grandfather. Fanny Kemble's work appeared, and Caroline published a piece by a new friend, the author of *Frankenstein*, Mary Shelley. In June she had announced a new work of her own, *The Coquette*, which was eventually published in 1835.

At Rossie Caroline made a new friend, Lady Augusta Baring, daughter of the Earl of Cardigan, and took delight in dismantling some of her strait-laced ways. Augusta had wed Major Henry Bingham Baring, whose father was a banker and gambler, in the same year that Caroline married George Norton. She was nine years older than Caroline but had led a more sheltered life than naughty Mrs Norton. Lady Augusta was 'particularly good, strict and virtuous and pious to a degree . . . cheerful and good natured', and Caroline's greatest pleasure was to sing her 'drinking songs . . . she likes my sinful ways and improves rapidly under my tuition'. Then there was a newcomer to the party, the fascinating Mrs Heneage, who had 'blue almost purple wicked eyes and dark hair and petite figure' and was '*tres coquette*'. She 'pretends to be so very young and innocent and to understand so little that I thought I had stumbled upon a little bride of seventeen'. Mrs Heneage had bewitched Lord Edward Thynne, a son of the Marquess of Bath, a 'handsome, gentleman-like sweet-natured' fellow, who was there with his newish bride, who 'pined for her lord', while Mr Heneage, 'a little scamp of a guardsman' had paired off with Lady Augusta. Caroline, who liked Major Baring 'excessively' because he was 'clever and odd' and returned her affections, also flirted with a rich wag called Edward Montagu, Lord Rokeby, an 'arch villain' whose amusing '*trop libertine*' anecdotes she enjoyed. For Caroline the fun and games were due to end with the arrival of her husband, who was due on 19 September.[62]

George was not good in such louche circles: he preferred stalking and shooting every stag and bird in sight to hanging around drawing rooms polishing his epigrams and paying compliments to other men's wives. Caroline told Melbourne what happened on George's first evening at Rossie. The conversation was witty and daring, and Caroline was having a good time, 'mixing in the conversation', but Norton took offence at something Lord Edward said and asked for an explanation, which Thynne 'frowned down'. But George could not let the matter rest, and when they went to bed worked himself up into one of his jealous rages and interrogated Caroline about the meaning of the remark. She tried to calm him down, saying what a 'civil, gentleman-like and kind-hearted' man Lord Thynne was, helpfully reminding George his lordship was a 'capable shot'. But Norton stormed out of the room, determined to have satisfaction. There was a great hue and cry as Caroline raised the alarm, terrified that George would call

Thynne out for a duel. The women shrieked and hoped Norton would not shoot him, and Caroline was ashamed to have been the cause of all the trouble. The men could not find Norton and Thynne, and everyone feared there would be a duel the next morning. Eventually the two men reappeared and the duel was averted, although they 'hated each other like poison'. The next day the party mood had evaporated. Lord Kinnaird got the women to tell their men to behave. The general opinion was that George was a fool. Mr Heneage stopped sitting on Lady Augusta Baring's knee, and Mrs Heneage had to extricate herself from Lord Edward's arms. Caroline's popularity with the ladies recovered; they enjoyed her stories and company too much to blame her for long. The women noted that she 'took as much pain to amuse them as to please the men which is saying a good deal in my favour'. She ended her letter to 'dear Fatty' by giving expression to her own jealousy, saying she was 'vexed' that he was 'anxious' about an old lover, Lady Branden.[63]

The longer Caroline stayed in Scotland the tetchier the mood and tone of the letters between Melbourne and herself became. Her letter of 29 September shows how much their separation made them miss each other and raised suspicions of what the other was doing while they were apart. Four years and many letters later, when their lives and his career came close to collapse, their insistence that they had always been just friends, never lovers, is open to question.

Now Melbourne was 'vexed' because she accused him of taking no notice of her. He had not replied immediately to three letters she had written. Caroline responded, 'I would not give you a moment's vexation for the world.' She was grateful to him for 'scribbling to me when you have so little time to spare'. Because he always affected a relaxed demeanour she sometimes forgot that he was the home secretary. She lightened the mood and changed the subject, delighted at her success in having avoided the horror of George and herself escorting his older sister Caroline to Madeira for her health. She made a quick visit to Edinburgh and arranged for George's unmarried brother James, a young clergyman, to take his sister on the two-month trip.

Mrs Norton's oldest rival, Lady Branden, who had been widowed in Ireland in the spring, was never far from Caroline's fretful thoughts, and she could not stop herself reproaching Melbourne for being 'a little cross with <u>me</u> because Lady Branden had not written'. He had reacted to her story of Norton's 'skirmish' with Lord Thynne with a man-of-the-world air of having seen the trouble coming a mile off. Some of the guests had gone, and she was getting ready to leave Scotland to make her way home to London, calling at Chillingham Castle, the Northumberland home of fellow guests, the Tankervilles, on the way. She poured her heart out to him in the last letter from Rossie. 'Dearest Lord, do not be angry with me if I say that it is selfish to be discontented with me for being amused here – you talk of my romping and flirting and forgetting everything else. I have not forgotten anything. I am sure your name is always on my lips and there is hardly anything they can say, or do, or look, that does not bring me back to some of your opinions or expressions. If I could always be with you – if you were with me in any country house you would be <u>the one person</u> to talk to. I <u>cannot</u> be with you always, and therefore I amuse myself as I can or rather I <u>amuse</u> them for they come and coax me out of my room if I attempt to write there. In all your letters there is some dissatisfied expression. Are <u>you</u> then never amused in your society? It vexes me that you should write these sentences. I can assure you I would much rather sit by your sofa in South Street [his home] than be <u>Queen of the Revels</u> here. You don't believe me and yet it is true. God bless you.'[64]

During the winter of 1832 and spring of 1833 the Nortons entertained a great deal at Storey's Gate. Caroline was the driving force: socially and professionally ambitious, she worked hard to make their newly redecorated drawing room a salon for her family and growing circle of smart friends. The novelist not yet politician Benjamin Disraeli, author of *Vivian Grey*, was a frequent visitor and loved being in the presence of Caroline and her sisters, basking in the witty beauty of the 'Three Graces'. He thought the Sheridans 'the handsomest family in the world.' Caroline would often sing and do 'everything that was delightful'. While she could never be one of those powerful Whig hostesses who dabbled seriously in politics, due to her lack of a title and wealth, Caroline used her brains, sexy singing voice and good looks to put herself in the spotlight in her own salon, which celebrated poetry, song and witty repartee. George was never the social butterfly his wife was, but he was ready to enjoy any favours or patronage that came his way from her friendship with Melbourne or anyone else, and consistently encouraged her relationship with a man with a reputation for dallying with other men's wives. Norton allowed a portrait of Lord Melbourne to sit on a drawing-room table, encouraged his daily visits, turned a blind eye to the blizzard of notes that went backwards and forwards and would walk her to Melbourne's house in South Street. There were times when he would not let her family see her when she was entertaining Melbourne, who was his ultimate boss.[65]

George did not always handle himself well at their dinner parties and sometimes let himself down. One evening, perhaps irritated with Disraeli, who openly admired his wife, George patronised him by insisting that he try a particular wine, insisting that he had probably never tasted anything so good. When Disraeli agreed it was good, George boasted that he had wine 'twenty times as good in my cellar'. Years later, Caroline's sister

Helen remembered her 'insufferable' brother-in-law's behaviour, delighting in Disraeli's put-down: 'But my dear fellow, this is quite good enough for such *canaille* [rabble] as you have got today.' Everyone at the table 'saw that the remark was intended as a slap for Mr Norton' except him, who was 'too obtuse to feel it'.[66]

It is clear that George was becoming increasingly resentful of his clever and attractive wife. There are many examples of George verbally lashing out at her. He had a notoriously short fuse and was capable of acts of extraordinary pettiness. In the first weeks of 1833, when she was newly pregnant with their third child, Caroline was at breakfast when Norton came into the room and told her to get out of her seat as he wanted to sit there and look out of the window into the park. She told him she was not feeling well and that he should 'have come down earlier if he had any fancy or choice about places'. No more was said, 'then Mr Norton deliberately took the tea kettle, and set it down on my hand', scalding it. She ran to the nursery and sent a maid to call for a surgeon to dress the wound which was 'bound up and useless for days'. While this was going on George sat down in her place, ate his breakfast and went out 'without one word of apology or enquiry'.[67]

Caroline was sure the child would be a girl and told her sister Georgy she intended naming her Susan, because it is 'poesy'. This is an interesting choice of name given the correspondence about Melbourne's adopted thirteen-year-old daughter. Caroline sent her sister a book from Melbourne, 'the lord of my love', and instructed her not to write and thank him because her other sister Helen had written to Melbourne but forgotten to mark the envelope 'private'. It was opened by his secretary, 'a grave and religious man', who was scandalised by its contents and shocked by Helen addressing the home secretary as 'Melly' and signing off 'your Nelly'.[68]

In January sixteen-year-old Charlie, the youngest Sheridan, started his career like his brother Frank by becoming a third-class clerk at the Admiralty.[69] Meanwhile, their uncle Sir James Graham was taken up with Caroline's financial affairs. The Nortons lived beyond their means and were short of money. The value of the income George Norton had brought to the marriage had fallen by two thirds in the six years they had been together, and they had had to borrow from uncle Charles Sheridan to pay for their trip to Scotland. In February George pestered Sir James, one of the trustees of their marriage settlement, to authorise him to borrow fifteen hundred pounds in a bond against the trust. Although the matter was between her husband and Sir James, Caroline also got involved: embarrassed at having to borrow money from her uncle Charles she was grateful for his help when he was 'in the midst of so many important occupations'. She also expressed concern about the wisdom of the loan: 'I should be sorry to find anything went wrong with the little Norton has to leave them.' After consultations with his solicitors, and mindful of what a tricky fellow his niece's husband was, Graham refused the request: 'I am afraid this may occasion some annoyance and inconvenience to Norton'. A distinct air of mistrust about how Norton and his brother Grantley conduct their affairs pervades the correspondence dealing with this matter.[70]

In the spring of 1833 two novels, *Aims and Ends* and *Oonagh Lynch,* were published anonymously and later translated into French. The author's identity was soon revealed as Caroline Norton's mother. Her last book about forgers had upset readers because 'it claimed attention to distresses too mean for sympathy, and characters too degraded for compassion'. Her publisher Edward Bull took advertising space for this new work to point out that the author had been advised by friends that her new book 'required more aristocratic affliction' to

interest the novel-reading public. *The Times* reviewer guessed
it was from a 'female pen' but noticed its 'acuteness and vigour
of a male understanding' as well as the 'depth of feeling
peculiar to a woman'. *Aims and Ends* dealt with 'that one
great scheme of life's lottery – marriage' of which Mrs Sheridan
had many years of experience to draw. It was funny and had
wide appeal, and 'a quiet and sarcastic humour' ran throughout.
Sarcasm was a Sheridan strength and weakness, gaining them
many friends and enemies. *Oonagh Lynch* was a wild romantic
tale of disappointed love with a parade of colourful characters,
but the inclusion of 'a contemptible bigot' was criticised:
'people of fashion in a certain Tory clique may sympathize
with this fanatical tyrant' but others 'of all parties and all
ranks despise him'. Perhaps Mrs Sheridan's dealings with the
Nortons had given her this character so much disliked by
the unnamed reviewer.[71]

Frank Sheridan wrote to his mother – 'Muddles' – from Jamaica.
He had started a magazine, but owing to the unpopularity of
Lord Mulgrave's regime had lost many subscribers – the reason
he gave for losing money he could ill afford and which might
have been spent paying off his creditors in London. Mulgrave
was deeply disliked by the planters and slave owners as he had
been tasked with the dismantling of slavery on the island. To
the intense annoyance of the planters, in August 1833 the Slavery
Abolition Act was passed and became law the following year.
Lord Mulgrave was 'so bullied and badgered here – there are
so many villains and such a scarcity of anything like society
here, he is heartily sick of Jamaica' that he asked the prime
minister, Lord Grey, for a post back in England.[72] Frank said
that they would be back in England in a year, and that Mulgrave
had promised if he got into office 'he would give me a situation
under him'. In Jamaica Lord Mulgrave spent more than his
salary for very little reward, 'entertaining those who betray and

bully him in the papers', but they were managing to make the most of it by being 'very jolly and sociable'.

In 1833 Caroline became the editor of *The English Annual,* a glossy coffee-table book of its day. Filled with engravings of grand people and places, poetry and bits of prose, it was intended for an aristocratic readership, and Mrs Norton was working hard to finish it for the Christmas market, ahead of the birth of her third child. One evening the Nortons had a cataclysmic row at dinner, just weeks before the baby was due. It had started in the usual niggling way and escalated. Weary of the familiar cycle of arguments and the violent conclusions, Caroline left the table to go and do some work, and not wanting to be disturbed locked one of the doors in the dining room, and herself into the drawing room. George left by the other door, stomped upstairs to find her and broke the door open. When he saw Caroline's maid, he ordered her out of the room. Caroline told her to stay, saying she was afraid of being left alone with him. He upturned her writing table, blew out the candle and broke it into pieces. He seemed to calm down and ordered the maid to light another candle, but when he saw that Caroline was unperturbed by his 'extraordinary exhibition', got into another rage and took hold of her with great force. This was the worst he had ever been. He pushed her out of the room, and if the maid had not grabbed her would have thrown her down the stairs. She escaped to the nursery, where she slept with the two boys. The next day she was too ill to leave the house but told her family what had happened. Led by her brother-in-law Lord Seymour, they demanded that George put into writing a promise to improve his behaviour.[73]

On 26 August 1833 Caroline gave birth to a 'fine little boy', who was christened William Charles Chapple Norton: named after their esteemed friend and patron Lord Melbourne, and in memory of George's grandmother Grace Chapple, who had had such a trying life with John Wallop. It was a difficult birth, and it took more than six weeks for her to recover sufficiently to be able to travel to fashionable Worthing for some bracing sea air. She went with her uncle Charles, the three children and a couple of servants. They went riding and visited the theatre, but she found the place deadly dull: 'there are only sick people – women and children here'. Caroline was nervous about her marital troubles. She had been bullied more than she wanted to admit and now feared Norton and his family and how they might treat her.

Mrs Norton was enchanted by 'Too-too', telling her sister Georgy that he looked like their father and was 'destined to be the beauty of the family'. The 'little tadpole' was 'fair and girlish looking', with dark grey eyes, long eyelashes and long straight eyebrows 'as thin and light as spider threads in the grass'. He was a sickly baby, given to bouts of colic, 'and screams to a degree that quite worries the life out of me'. She hoped he would get 'jollier' when she herself got stronger, and sat 'in dread of it going into fits, it turns so blue round the mouth, and so cold on its forehead'. In Worthing Caroline was still far from well: 'little do you know how ill your sister has been, or how black and sallow she had grown and little did I myself ever think that I could be so weak and uncomfortable as I am'.

While Caroline was at Worthing, George Norton was staying with his sister Grace and her husband Sir Neil Menzies at Loch Rannoch, sending her 'an exact description of the looks of the sisters of his tribe'. Knowing how much they disliked her, Caroline must have wondered what he had told them about the recent row and her family's response. George had only given Caroline thirty pounds for the trip to Worthing, and as it had cost her twenty-two pounds to get there, she was already out of funds. Assuming her well-heeled uncle

Charles would pay whatever was needed, George had sent her off financially embarrassed.[74]

In early December George and Caroline went to stay with the Duke of Richmond at Goodwood in Sussex. On the morning of the journey she found her husband crouched over his desk calculating the cost of repairs needed to their carriage. They argued all the way there about money. George refused to pay for any refreshments, and Caroline told her mother she was 'starved, so I paid the extras'. The roads were heavy with mud and ice, and progress was tediously slow. They missed the dinner provided by their host because of 'a little accident. One of the postillions was thrown, and they stopped to bleed the horse; the man was as nearly killed as possible; the wheel went over his hand and the carriage was stopped just in time to spare his head. It made me nervous as we kept backing into the ditch all the time on very frosty grass.' Norton then left Caroline and the three boys to go off to perform the not very onerous duties of recorder of Guildford.

Although Caroline knew the other guests – many were literary friends and Whigs – the strain of a new baby and life with George meant she did not write the usual gossipy letters which she knew her mother and sister enjoyed. To her the party seemed 'supereminently dull . . . there is a stiffness, a punctuality, a shyness about everyone in the house which makes me think of the fairy tale in which the air froze the words'. Three-month-old Too-too had managed the journey surprisingly well and had not yet 'taken cold', but the damp lowered her spirits: 'my hands shake with the cold . . . and my head aches like ten'. Georgy invited Caroline and the children to Maiden Bradley for a few days, but Caroline was unable to let her know as 'I must await many decisions.' George was in Guildford, and if he declined to give his permission she would not be able to go. Uncle Charles Sheridan offered to come with her and share the travelling expenses, but the situation was awkward. Unless George 'gave his leave' and doled out some money, she could not go to Wiltshire. As his magistrates' duties meant that he could not leave London again that year, he was unable to join her, and he seemed unlikely to finance a trip to stay with Lord Seymour, with whom he had taken issue about the family's recent interference in their marital dispute.[75]

Before the year was out Frank wrote from Jamaica to his uncle at the Admiralty in his unofficial role as government spy. He and Lord Mulgrave had toured the island 'explaining the real state of things to the rejoicing niggers'.[76] Assiduous Mulgrave had managed to neutralise the threat of a general strike promised for the new year, although for the 'first signs of disturbance' there were regular troops stationed in detachments all over the island. The governor was weak after a recent attack of 'the horrible [yellow] fever' but was working 'indefatigably night and day to ensure the peaceable settlement of the great question [abolition]'.[77]

In the spring of 1834, under pressure from George, Caroline sent a begging letter with her new poem, 'The Ruined Laird', to Lady Holland, Elizabeth Vassall Fox. She and her husband, Henry Richard Fox, third Baron Holland, were the first couple of Whig society and wielded enormous influence in politics and literature. Caroline knew this grand couple well through her parents and her grandfather, and her Sheridan ancestry guaranteed a place in their circle. With the best address book in London, if anyone could make something happen it was the Hollands. Caroline was 'very anxious just now' and was looking for another job for George, who 'had long been hoping' for the post of chief magistrate at Bow Street court. If he got it she believed it would net him four hundred pounds a year in addition to the salary he earned as magistrate for Whitechapel and would lead to a seat in Parliament. Norton had been hoping to get the job when the incumbent, Sir Frederick Roe, resigned, which was expected when Mr Adair, a relation from whom Roe hoped to inherit, died. Caroline wrote to the Hollands, 'As Mr Adair is dead therefore we expect to hear that Sir Frederick Roe has resigned immediately.' The position was in Lord Melbourne's gift, and Caroline had asked for it for George when it was vacant in 1832, but her petition had been 'in vain'. She flattered Lady Holland, pleading: 'I know . . . that if <u>you</u> once felt an interest in this you would carry your point.'

Could Lady Holland persuade Lord Brougham, who was lord chancellor, to appoint Norton to the position? The difficulty was that Brougham was 'strongly <u>opposed</u> to us and dislikes Norton on account of a quarrel he had with Lord Grantley long ago'. Melbourne, who was prepared to support Norton, did not want to be attacked in the press for favouritism, so preferred Brougham to make the appointment. Caroline told Lady Holland, 'you have great influence over him' and asked her to urge Brougham to overlook 'a few disagreeable sentences' which had stoked the row between him and her brother-in-law, which were 'a light evil compared with the benefit' her husband would bring to the role.

The Norton estate in Scotland had been so badly managed that for the past two years Caroline and George only had George's magistrate's salary and Caroline's literary earnings to live on. For many such an income would have been ample, but the Honourable Nortons were mixing with people who were far richer than they were. Whig society was an expensive place to frequent; they had to look and play the part and they were struggling. Unless his elder brother died unexpectedly, there was no prospect of an inheritance in the near future and even that was contingent on Grantley remaining childless. The only Sheridan who could afford to live the Whig lifestyle was Caroline's youngest sister Georgy, Lady Seymour. 'The job is therefore a greater object than ever to us, and the 400 a year would make a material difference to people whose income is only <u>twice</u> that sum. I know I ought to apologise for this tedious letter, and for so boldly requesting assistance from one on whom I have no claim – but I cannot help hoping that you will speak for us. I think persons accustomed to affluence, rarely (if ever) comprehend the <u>real</u> miseries of a very small income. They see that you have no diamonds and no carriage, and think no more about it. They do not know what it is to see a man's temper rapidly souring under difficulties he has neither means to avert, or strength of mind to bear – to see one's children's birth a matter of regret and grumbling instead of joy – and to feel amidst all the discomfort and suffering which <u>precedes</u> the birth, that it requires all the patience that man is master of not to show irritation at the <u>cause</u> of your discomfort.'

Caroline told Lady Holland how the embarrassments suffered by 'The Ruined Laird' of her poem were inspired by her own suffering, but in the end nothing came of her letter. Sir Frederick Roe did not resign from office until 1839, by which time every-thing had changed irrevocably.[78]

In the summer of 1834 Frank Sheridan returned to England from Jamaica with the Mulgraves on HMS *Pallas*. Lord Mulgrave's work was done; he was looking out for his next post. Lord Melbourne, who two weeks earlier had become prime minister (Lord Grey had 'resigned in a huff' over Irish affairs), appointed him lord privy seal on 30 July.[79] Frank remained in Mulgrave's service and went with him to Dublin in 1835, when he was appointed lord lieutenant of Ireland.[80]

Caroline's family now invited the couple to accompany them on a three-month tour of Ghent, Antwerp and Cologne, cruising down the Rhine and staying with King Leopold in Brussels on the way home. They clearly felt obliged to invite George, but he refused to go, insisting that Caroline and the children accompany him when he went shooting at the Menzies, in August, as he always did. At the last minute Norton relented and agreed they could accept the invitation, but only if Caroline agreed to pay the expenses. Caroline's sister Georgy and husband Lord Seymour, sister Helen, whose husband was at sea, and elder brother Brinsley set off with the Nortons in August leaving all the children behind.[81]

Caroline had to raise the money for the trip and tried to sell a new poem to John Murray, son of the founder of the firm which had published Jane Austen, Lord Byron and Walter Scott. George's miserly behaviour reduced her to offering the poem and other shorter pieces for a hundred pounds. She told Murray in a letter that she would take less: 'I would willingly give you the manuscript <u>without</u> the last mentioned condition if you would undertake the publication.' She asked for a meeting the next day, when her husband would be free to accompany her, wives not being allowed to make contracts on their own. In her letters to Murray Caroline makes the surprising admission that perhaps in the past she had overrated the value of her work so he had declined to publish it, and thanked him for his past critiques, which she had found so helpful. But John Murray was out of town, and they did not have a meeting. He replied that he was 'gratified and not a little proud of your flattery and skilfully-penned note' and went on a charm offensive of his own. He did not know if he should be sad or glad to have missed the date of her proposed visit, 'confident as I am that however rigid my rules are, upon the subject of publication', if she had been present he could not have resisted 'any request of Mrs Norton'. John Murray did not publish the poem.[82]

Somehow or other the money was raised, but they had a miserable time. The obvious unhappiness of the Norton's marriage blighted the atmosphere as they bustled on and off boats and heaved themselves in and out of carriages. George hated travelling, especially abroad, did not have a smattering of any foreign language and was a dreadful companion, always complaining, becoming ill and insisting Caroline look after him. He proved to be as much of a handful as the three boys under the age of five they had left at home. He became lame at Aix-la-Chapelle and the others left Caroline behind to look after him, continuing on their merry way until the Nortons caught them up. Seeing the happiness of others highlighted her own feelings: 'seeing every one in such capital spirits . . . always makes me sadder and crosser'.[83] Caroline's letters to them poste restante were so miserable that her brother Brinsley returned to Aix to keep her company while George rested.

They then set off on the next leg of the journey. The Nortons were travelling in a cramped and stuffy carriage on their own when Caroline complained that the smoke from George's hookah was making her feel ill. He refused to put it out so Caroline grabbed the pipe from his mouth and threw it out of the window. At this point they were travelling slowly uphill; George clambered out, retrieved the pipe, climbed back in and 'came back to repay her for her loss of temper by a savage onslaught which left the marks of his fingers on her throat, and from which she with difficulty escaped by slipping out of the half-closed door of the carriage to run after the others and entreat some of her family to travel with them and protect her from further ill-usage'.[84]

This was the end of any pretence of friendly relations between George and his Sheridan in-laws. Caroline travelled with her family to Paris pleading illness, and George was left to make his own way there. Caroline was used to his abuse and she had been anxious to forget about the time he had tried to push her down the stairs a month before their third child was born. Now she forgave him for this latest attack and even apologised in a letter to Paris, signing off 'your ever affectionate Car. You can't think how I reproach myself at your being ill; it makes me quite unhappy; but it shall never happen again your remorseful wife promises you faithfully. You are a good kind husband in the long run, and don't believe me when I say harsh things to you. Glad to make friends and happy to see you at Paris, and forgive me!'

They all met up in Paris in November, where the three sisters caused a stir. There they heard the disappointing news that Lord Melbourne was no longer prime minister, since the Whig government had been dismissed by the King on 16 November 1834, and a new Tory administration, nominally headed by the Duke of Wellington but in reality led by Sir Robert Peel, took over.

While Caroline was abroad, she took obvious delight writing to a Royal Horse Guards officer, William Francis Cowper, three years younger than her. He had a young face 'and a roué heart'; his mother was Lord Melbourne's sister, and his father Peter Leopold Cowper, fifth Earl of Cowper, although William was rumoured to be the illegitimate son of Henry John Temple, third Viscount Palmerston, whom his mother married in 1839, two years after her husband died. As soon as they met, Mrs Norton gave him a pet name, Willoughby, and struck up an easy, flirty correspondence, at once consolidating her links with Melbourne and making him jealous. She teasingly called Willoughby her nephew and signed herself his aunt. There was gossip that he was in love with her. The letters allowed Caroline to pretend that her life was better than it was. With her circle of friends and her clever pen, she could escape from the life to which she was legally bound. The young man sent her poetry, which she thought was a 'little rough', so she suggested they correct the proofs when he was next in London: 'there is no doubt you will improve under my fostering care'.[85]

Writing from Paris she told Willoughby about some of the places she had visited, how tottery the people were in the spa towns, the smelliness of the waters they gulped down and the dreary conversations: 'everybody asked their friends how they were; and every body told <u>me</u> when they were better, and when they were worse; I <u>very nearly</u> swore at them'. She told him she was 'fidgetty' with Paris, wanting to get back to London, revealed that she was missing his uncle, Lord Melbourne, and wondered if Cowper was 'in high spirits at Panshanger [the home of the family] with 'the virtuous Stanhope and the virgin Eden'. Caroline was being sarcastic in describing the wife of Philip Henry Stanhope, Catherine Lucy, as virtuous. Catherine had been Lord Melbourne's brother Frederick's mistress and had the sharpest tongue in any drawing room. Queen Victoria called her a 'very amusing, clever and agreeable woman', but Lady Holland, more worldly-wise than the young queen, said Catherine was 'very amusing, gay and original, <u>not of the best polish</u>, but still very sprightly'. Emily Eden was another impressive young woman Caroline identified as a rival. She was witty and interested in politics, just the sort of woman Melbourne liked and needed, and Caroline was jealous. To Caroline's despair she had to share Melbourne with Emily Eden, as confidante and companion, from 1832 until Emily went to live in India in 1835.

In mid-December Mr and Mrs Norton left the family party in Paris and returned for Caroline and their three sons to spend Christmas at Hampton Court Palace with Mrs Sheridan. George did not go with them to Hampton. Her letters to him were friendly and chatty, full of the endearing remarks and snuffles of their sons, and trying hard to play happy families. 'Let me wish you a happy new year and many of them, dear "Geordie", in quietness and comfort at home, and what prosperity may chance abroad . . . Mamma begs you to drink melted gum from

Arabia in all your drinks.' Two publishers drove out from London to discuss future projects and also brought the maddening news that a certain Mr Bull had compiled his own version of her book *English Annual* and was selling it in Paris. A lawsuit loomed. 'I have sent for a copy, and expressed the utmost indignation.' Feeling that the stormy waters of their marriage had calmed, Caroline even told Mr Norton – perhaps unwisely given Geordie's vast reserves of resentment – that one of her visitors had been 'struck with my personal charms and beauty' and had asked her to sit for an artist to help publicise *The Book of Beauty*, which she was currently editing. Also, she wrote, Lord Melbourne had sent her a copy of a new book which proved that Mary Magdalene was the most virtuous of her sex: 'I am very curious to see it proved.'[86]

At the start of 1835 Caroline busied herself producing two books of ballads with her sister Helen and Augusta Cowell, a musician. The songs were dedicated to two old family friends of the Sheridans, the Duke of Devonshire and Lady Jersey. Miss Cowell lived with her widowed mother and her banker brother, John Welsford Cowell, near Hyde Park, and was seven years older than Caroline, a spinster and an innocent in life. 'The Fairy Bell', 'They Bid Me Forget', 'The Mother's Lament', 'The Lord I Love', 'I Do Not Love Thee' and 'The Merry Lark' were sentimental songs for a thriving music market. Keen to acknowledge the skill of 'my dearest Cowellina', Caroline nevertheless wanted to keep her own melody intact in response to Augusta's suggested changes. Not wishing to seem conceited she remarked self-deprecatingly, '"Conceit will enter the heart of even a pig," as my Irish nurse told Fletcher yesterday,' and thanked her for her patient good nature.[87]

Lurking in the wings of Caroline Norton's drama were two men, Benjamin Robert Haydon and Edward John Trelawny, who now entered her life and added to the havoc of what turned out to be an histrionic year. Haydon was an artist whose infatuation with her would sorely test Caroline's patience, and that of Mrs Haydon too. Edward Trelawny looked like a corsair, a Byronic creation, and he was just that. The men's passionate interest in her, driven by their self-dramatising personalities, was another distraction in a year full of demanding distractions.

In March 1835 Benjamin Haydon exhibited a painting, *Cassandra Predicting the Death of Agamemnon*, at the British Artists' Society in Suffolk Street off Pall Mall. Cassandra's head was recognisably that of Mrs Norton, but critics remarked that it looked to have been painted hurriedly. *The Times* said there was a problem with her mouth, which was 'no more like than was flattering to the model', and 'more pains might have been properly bestowed upon the finishing of a picture of such pretensions as this'.[88] Drama and muddle were central to this artist's life.

Benjamin Robert Haydon, born in Plymouth in 1786, was in his mid-forties when he became part of the Norton circle, attracted, to his long-suffering wife Mary's despair, to the beauty of Caroline and her sisters. His father was a printer, publisher and bookseller. Haydon described himself as a child as 'excessively self-willed and passionate': he loved performing for his school chums, painted obsessively and gave lectures to himself. His father apprenticed him as an accountant to the family firm, but the intense and headstrong boy was determined to become an artist. In 1804 he arrived in London to study anatomy, his aim to emulate the man he most admired, Sir Joshua Reynolds, and became a student of Henry Fuseli, keeper of the Royal Academy. Haydon settled in London and started to make a name for himself as a painter of historical subjects on epic-size canvasses.

In 1821 he married Mary Cawrse Hyman, the pretty widow of a Devonport jeweller. She was ten years younger than Haydon and had two young sons. Haydon had met the Hymans in 1816 shortly before Mr Hyman died, and was immediately smitten, growing 'more and more inextricably enraptured'. For him she had 'the simplicity of a child, the passion of an Italian woman, joined to the tenderness and fidelity of an English one'. Before Hyman died Benjamin Haydon started stalking his wife. He paid a neighbour half a crown to watch for her to leave her home. Mary Hyman rejected his advances and after her husband's death kept Haydon at arm's length until she eventually relented and agreed to marry him. Hyman had settled an annual income on her of fifty-two pounds, the interest on a thousand pounds, a useful sum but not large. The day after their wedding Haydon was arrested for debt. Mary may not have realised quite how patient she would have to be to cope with her husband's mood swings; his erratic earnings since some paintings took him several years to finish; the frequent rows with his most supportive friends and patrons; his debts (he was declared bankrupt in 1823 and imprisoned in 1823, 1827, 1830 and 1836), which he carried with him for the rest of his life; and the birth and death of five of their eight children from tuberculosis between 1831 and 1836.[89]

Benjamin Haydon was a close friend of some of the great men of his day: the poets John Keats and William Wordsworth, writer and critic Leigh Hunt, and writer William Hazlitt. The year before he met Caroline he had been given the prestigious commission of capturing the moment in paint when the Whigs gathered at the Guildhall to celebrate the passing of the Great Reform Act. He also painted a portrait of Caroline's uncle Sir James Graham. In the summer of 1833 Haydon was introduced to Caroline Norton's salon and invited to Storey's Gate, where Disraeli and Lord Melbourne were guests. More than once Haydon went to the theatre with Caroline and Melbourne.

Haydon's diaries, a million words, are unguarded in every

sense of the word, brimming with details of his trembling crush on Caroline and his tormented guilt about how his wife would feel if she knew the depth of his regard for Mrs Norton. The object of his devotion was 'to women provokingly handsome . . . like a bit of Greek sculpture just breaking into life' while 'her grand majesty of beauty is sublime'. The diaries detail accounts of their many meetings. He confesses 'when I am with her I am confused. When I am absent I do nothing but muse, and think how much more agreeable I might have been. Then I think what I didn't do, then what I did, then what I ought to have done, and then I whistle and feel my heart ache, then take up my brush, put it down, curse the ugly faces I am obliged to paint, think of her.'90

One evening he called at Storey's Gate hoping to sketch her. 'She came down déshabillé, like a Sybil who had not put her hair in order.' He fantasised that 'the love of Mrs Norton would be a rage' and confessed when he saw her his heart 'swells to bursting', happy that she 'was spinning her web to catch me into a sketching!' although there is no evidence that Caroline lavished more attention on Haydon than good manners and her flirty personality dictated. Haydon enjoyed seeing the jealousy of other men who witnessed moments when she seemed to single him out, and refused to accept that he read too much significance into her acts of kindness to him. He became a nuisance, often calling unannounced. As well as spending time with her, he was fascinated by George's tales of the sensational cases that came before him. More than once Mrs Norton offered him a lift in her carriage. He tried to convince himself that he had his feelings under control, mindful that when a fashionable lady like Caroline 'says she is in love she only means she admires, and would have no objection to admit a man to her train of adorers', but though he knew the rules of the game, he did not believe they applied to him. His volatile personality read too much into her behaviour: he was sure Caroline reciprocated his feelings because he wanted her to. In June 1833 he dropped in at Storey's Gate. 'Mrs Norton was dressing for the Queen's Ball. She took me with her in the carriage, leaving half a dozen fellows, saying unutterable things. I went off of course almost cheering. I had a great mind to say "Hip!"'

Six days later Haydon's wife had a daughter, whom he named after two of the Sheridan sisters, Jane Georgiana Caroline Elizabeth Sarah Seymour Haydon. In 1835 the girl with so many names died of convulsions before her second birthday. Ten days later Mary Haydon gave birth to a son, who was named Newton after their patient landlord.[91]

In the days leading up to the birth of Caroline's third son, William, in August 1833, she and Haydon had a row after he blurted out his feelings: 'I roused her pride by telling her I loved her, but that there could be no hope in innocence . . . this angered her.' He was no longer invited to Storey's Gate. Haydon and his wife were having a dreadful time: almost all of their children were sickly, four-year-old Harry had recently died, and they were mired in debt. Benjamin confessed the depth of his feelings for Mrs Norton to his wife, who told him that she trusted his 'good faith' – at least that is what is recorded in his diary.

In 1834 Haydon started work on *Predicting the Death of Agamemnon* and asked Caroline to sit for the head of Cassandra, writing that if she refused his request his family would be 'ruined'. The previous year he had told Caroline provokingly that 'Men of Fashion' said she was 'merciless and unforgiving, passionless and cold and cruel and vengeful' and that he hoped she would prove them mistaken. Perhaps more concerned for his wife and children's fate than Haydon's wounded pride, Caroline Norton agreed to sit for him but pointed out: 'those who know me, know them [these criticisms] to be false and those who do not know me are welcome to their <u>conjectures</u> of what my disposition may be'. She was cool with Haydon and too busy to sit as often as he demanded, and his unrequited love bubbled to the surface again. He wrote in his diary of his hope that by seeing her 'I shall vanquish my intense passion . . . by absence it only grew worse.'

Reading the entry, Mary Haydon learned that he was still infatuated with the Sheridan sisters, and his passion for Caroline was as strong as ever. This came at a time when she was having to pawn their children's clothes and her best gown to make ends meet. Haydon denied the obvious interpretation of what he had written, saying it was only the work of his imagination and as soon as the painting was completed everything would be resolved. But Mary was extremely angry and insisted on seeing Mrs Norton, who said that nothing improper had taken place. She told Mary that 'nothing like <u>connection</u> could take place from the nature of a <u>complaint</u> she was subject to'. From this time on Caroline Norton became the target of two very confused and vengeful people. In 1835, when the *Cassandra* painting received indifferent reviews and Caroline's head came in for pointed remarks, it reminded Mary Haydon of the woman she loathed, feelings she communicated to her children, who took a bust their father had of Caroline into the street and 'dashed it all to pieces'.[92]

Caroline had to continue writing and earning to keep all the strands of her life together. Around this time she was so hard up that she had to borrow money from William Cowper, Melbourne's nephew.[93] In the middle of April 1835 Lord Melbourne became the prime minister of a new Whig government and Willoughby left the army when he was appointed his uncle's private secretary at Downing Street. This was useful for Caroline, who liked to keep tabs on Melbourne's movements. She offered to take Willoughby to visit her mother, first turning him into a 'beau for the benefit of the Hampton Court virgins'.

A literary acquaintance was Mary Shelley, whose mother, Mary Wollstonecraft, had published *A Vindication of the Rights of Woman* in 1792 and been abused as 'a hyena in petticoats'. Mary Wollstonecraft had died giving birth to her daughter. Mary Shelley was the widow of Percy Bysshe Shelley, the most romantic of the Romantics, who had drowned in a storm at sea off Italy in 1822. Caroline was fascinated by the life Mary had led and the world she came from, and admired Mary's close friend Lord Byron's poetry.

Mary Shelley asked Caroline to help her secure a pension for her father William Godwin and her stepmother, who had fallen on hard times. Caroline wrote to Melbourne, who rather than agreeing straightaway asked that Mrs Shelley write to him directly. Caroline assured Mary that she had done as much as she could and was confident of a good result: 'do not suppose that any worries of my own would ever prevent me doing what I could for <u>anyone</u>, far less for you, of whom tho' <u>I know</u> comparatively little and I have <u>heard</u> and <u>thought</u> a great deal'. She was sure that a personal petition to Melbourne would do the trick, praising Mary's 'winning frankness whose manner would please him, as I remember it enchanted me'. Their joint endeavours were successful and Mrs Godwin was granted a small pension.

In May Caroline's brother Frank left London for Dublin Castle to take up his position with Lord Mulgrave, and Mrs Norton's *The Wife* and *Woman's Reward*, were published. Confident in their success, Messrs Sanders and Otley paid her three hundred pounds for the manuscripts. They discussed women's powerlessness in marriage and men's abuse of domestic authority, and drew heavily on her own life. The eponymous wife was Susan Dalrymple, a beautiful young woman married to a man she did not love who behaved as jealously as George Norton. An older female cousin of his comes to live with them and causes much mischief, a character drawn from Caroline's recent encounters with Augusta Norton and George's cousin Margaret Vaughan. *Woman's Reward* is the story of the devotion of Mary, a young woman whose dying father asks her to care for her unlovely brother Lionel. This character has some of George Norton's traits and behaves as he had on their recent trip to Europe. Lionel was 'wretched and restless', obsessing and haggling over the cost of everything and 'always abusing the last hotel-keeper and swearing against the bore of a long journey'. Caroline did not just use her husband as the villain throughout the novel, she also gave Mary some traits of which she herself was accused: vanity, a sharp tongue and a cutting wit. The book was well reviewed. She had described society 'with all the delicate and minute analytic powers which belong to the woman of genius', 'Mrs Norton has touched with a master-hand our sweetest and noblest sympathies,' 'We recommend it for its exquisite sentiment and sound appreciation of nature.' But sales were disappointing.[94]

There was a breakdown in the Norton marriage in 1835: 'early in the summer, the quarrel, which divided him from my family for ever' took place. There was a violent scene. Caroline was in the latter stages of her fourth pregnancy – the baby was due in the autumn – and, strongly encouraged by her family, she took the momentous step of leaving her husband. She went back to him and had a miscarriage at the end of July. A notice in *The Times* announced, 'Mrs Norton has been dangerously ill, but we are happy to say is now convalescent.'[95]

In 1835 Brinsley Sheridan succumbed to the family habit of running away with beautiful young women and eloped with twenty-year-old Marcia Maria Grant, marrying her on 17 May at Gretna Green. When her father, Sir Colquhoun Grant, found out, there was the most enormous hullabaloo. In his prime the seventy-year-old general had not been a man to tangle with lightly: when he was fifty he had five horses killed underneath him at Waterloo. Previously he had been wounded leading his regiment during the recapture of the Cape of Good Hope from the Dutch in 1806, and served with distinction in Spain. Knighted and showered with honours, after he retired from the army he became a groom of the bedchamber to the Duke of Cumberland. Grant had been a Member of Parliament but his constituency disappeared in the Great Reform Act. In 1833 he inherited a vast amount of money and land at Frampton in Dorset from his friend Francis John Browne, whose wealthy niece he had wisely married. A widower, Marcia was his only child.[96] She was born in London in the year of Waterloo and would inherit a fortune.

Sir Colquhoun knew Brinsley Sheridan was hovering, and nervous about leaving his daughter on her own at Frampton while he was away in Poole trying to get elected to Parliament, put her in the care of Sir Robert MacFarlane, her guardian in the event of her father's death. Marcia gave MacFarlane the slip, arranged to borrow a carriage and ran away with the tall, dark and handsome Brinsley. Horrified to find her gone, MacFarlane sent a note to Colquhoun Grant, who dashed to Dover thinking the couple had fled to France, while MacFarlane travelled to London to question Brinsley's sister Lady Seymour, who refused to see him. MacFarlane barged his way into her drawing room to find there Brinsley's mother, Mrs Sheridan, herself an eloper, his sister Helen Blackwood, and George and Caroline Norton and a couple of friends. Sir Robert demanded to know where Marcia was and what the family's role in the affair had been. It was just like one of their grandfather's comedies of manners.

Sir Colquhoun Grant then accused the Sheridan sisters and

two of their husbands of being accessories in the drama, and issued a writ ordering Brinsley to appear at the Court of Chancery, charged with the serious offence of abducting a minor. Meanwhile the couple were honeymooning on Sir James Graham's estate in Cumberland. Grant wanted 'satisfaction' in the matter from Lord Seymour and George Norton. He had been brought up in the world of duelling and for him this was the natural solution, although duels were now illegal. A newspaper of the day wrote of Caroline, Georgiana and Helen's role, 'were the laws of witchcraft still enforced in England, these beautiful sisters would stand a chance of being burned at the stake'. Fashionable folk were said to be wondering if a spell had been cast on the heiress.[97] The heated correspondence between Grant and Seymour and Norton appeared in *The Times* in full.

Grant laid his emotions bare, unafraid to describe his feelings of loss for a daughter who had been spirited away by a ne'er-do-well without a penny to his name. The Grants were red-blooded soldiers, whereas his new son-in-law's grandfather had made his name with his pen, writing stage plays. Grant was furious with George Norton, accusing him of being 'deeply involved in the disgraceful plot that has been fatal to my pride and happiness' and also dismayed because, as Norton was a magistrate, he 'might be prevented from taking that course . . . that would be most congenial to my wounded feelings'. Grant accused Norton of dereliction of his duty as a magistrate: 'for had its duties been your care, or ever once occurred to you, I should not now have to mourn an affliction, which if it does not carry me to the grave, must embitter the rest of my life'.

Norton was also lambasted for his loss of authority as a husband. When Sir Robert MacFarlane asked Caroline who had abducted Marcia, she refused to say. Grant insisted that both Norton and Seymour had sanctioned their wives' conduct when they had been 'honour bound' to overrule them and had thus been 'participators in this most dishonourable conduct'. Grant's words were carefully chosen: 'honour' and 'gentleman' were intended to embarrass and humiliate them into action. 'I will not hazard the world's reproach by asking of you that satisfaction which, I am told you might officially decline, but I take it upon myself to tell you that your behaviour has been disgraceful to you as a magistrate and a gentleman, and you have so identified yourself with this nefarious proceeding as to make yourself unworthy of either title.'

George denied any role in the elopement, explaining that his presence at Spring Gardens when MacFarlane appeared was a coincidence: he had called to collect his wife to take her to Lansdowne House, the Berkeley Square home of the Whig politician Lord Lansdowne, and it was only at this time that he had learned of the elopement. The satirical press reported that Caroline had not visited Lansdowne House that evening but Melbourne House, the London home of Lord Melbourne's family, and that George had lied about her destination to avoid adding to the gossip about his wife's relationship with the prime minister. George said the plot had been hatched by the young couple and that no one else had been involved, and insisted on his 'honour as a gentleman, I was not present at the elopement, and knew not of it until many hours after it had taken place'. In deference to the old warhorse's feelings Norton wrote, 'I am the last person to provoke a duel' but that if Grant did not do him the justice of retracting the accusation 'on you the responsibility of any ulterior measures that may result from it must rest'. In order for George to keep his character as a gentleman, he was prepared to waive his duties as a magistrate: 'I would not for a moment suffer it to shield me from any personal responsibility.' Eventually Grant accepted George's pleas of ignorance and retracted his accusation, but Norton was affronted by the attempt to impugn his honour.[98]

Lord Seymour's letter from the angry old man described his 'agony of mind'. It had taken Colquhoun Grant some time to calm down and 'command my reason sufficiently to enable me to examine the full circumstances of the foul transaction', but Marcia was the 'last solace of his life' and had been 'torn' from him by a 'train of artifice disgraceful as it is cruel'. MacFarlane had asked Lady Seymour what role she had taken in the affair and she had refused to answer his question, a sure sign of guilt to Grant, who demanded to know what role they had both played. Seymour asked for a meeting so that he could 'remove the erroneous impression . . . with regard to the share that Lady Seymour had taken in the matter' and insisted he had been ignorant of what had happened. Grant's reply suggested Lord Seymour had fallen down in his duty as a husband by not preventing his wife from taking actions that risked bringing dishonour to the family name, and he rejected his lordship's offer of a meeting. The old general and the young lord met in a field near Hampstead, 'where they exchanged shots, but without effect'. Pistols were flourished and discharged into the air, no blood was shed, and honour was satisfied, whereupon George Bentinck, younger son of the fourth Duke of Portland and Lord Seymour's second, announced that his lordship was ready to explain 'various circumstances connected with the affair which would probably much alter [Grant's] opinion respecting it.'[99] The choleric general was soon to be reconciled with his naughty daughter and her new husband, who returned from the Continent, to where they had fled during the uproar.

We do not know what role Caroline and her sisters played in the elopement, but it is likely they provided moral support and material help to the young couple on their dash to Scotland, a place which they knew and loved. It was the kind of romantic adventure the Three Graces enjoyed. The cloak-and-dagger drama was the stuff of their childhood love of romantic tales and happy outcomes. Perhaps taken aback by the strength of Marcia's father's feelings, they did not divulge their roles. Fearful of being charged with conspiracy the Sheridan sisters and their spouses denied any involvement and were relieved when the matter was happily resolved. Marcia was a splendid new sister who happened to be extremely wealthy.

This affair was one cause of the monumental rift between George and Caroline Norton in 1835. Given his previous difficulties with his in-laws, George did not believe them when they said they had known nothing of the elopement. The anger he felt at being caught up in the scandal was vented on Caroline, who was six months pregnant. Of all the parties involved, she paid the highest price. Her newly married and newly wealthy brother Brinsley was now also able to help her. He wrote to Norton saying that it was 'not to be thought that any brother would permit his sister to receive the treatment she did'. George's tone to Bentinck was conciliatory and accorded him the respect which the son of a duke was entitled to, but the reality of the situation was somewhat different: 'I said to Brinsley Sheridan last night I am willing and ready to make every sacrifice in <u>my power</u> to Mrs Norton when she returns to my house.' 'My house' is indicative: Caroline now had no house of her own to go back to, as the marital home was no longer hers to share. Striking a reasonable and considerate tone about money, Norton 'should be very unwilling that any question of pecuniary affairs should prevent Mrs Norton seeing the children'. He had William, their youngest, who was less than two years old, with him in London and agreed he could be taken to see his mother at 9 Grosvenor Square, the home of Brinsley and his new bride, but only in the presence of his nurse. Six-year-old Fletcher and four-year-old Brinsley were 'in the country'. The letter ended by offering Caroline the possibility of seeing the two older boys by the end of the week, but only if 'she will so far acquiesce to my plans'.[100]

At this time no matter how dangerous the circumstances which drove a wife to leave her husband and children or take temporary refuge, she had no right to be allowed to see her children again until they were twenty-one. Like her, the children were her husband's chattels and his to dispose of as he wished until they reached the age of majority. It was unthinkable for a mother to be given automatic access to, let alone custody of, her children. In law the only parent a child had was the father. George Norton knew the law. He was negotiating from a position of strength; Caroline could not have been in a weaker position. In Brinsley and Lord Seymour she only had moral support and money to pay for legal advice.

Behind the scenes George Norton's brother Lord Grantley gathered a team of family friends, all powerful men, determined to bring Caroline to heel and back to Storey's Gate by refusing to allow her to see her children. Caroline's anguished letter to Willoughby shows her being manoeuvred and manipulated. 'No one can help me – but I feel your kindness in offering to do so. I am not in the hands of my weak and violent husband. I am in those of Lord Grantley, Lord Wynford, and Sir W. Follett. I cannot enter into a long explanation of <u>why</u> those names promise me the worst they can do, because I am ill and worn out and it would serve no end, but when they have done their worst, they will find, miraculous as it may appear to them, that of the woman they think vain and vicious, <u>they already know all there is to tell</u> – that there is no <u>discovery to be made</u>, which may crush me and give them a base triumph and that incredible as they naturally deem the fact, I have been for eight years the "faithful wife" of Mr Norton. They have begun too soon – they should have waited three or four years longer.'

Caroline denies having a physical relationship with anyone

other than her husband, although throwing open the possibility that she might have succumbed in the near future. Although there is no proof that she and Lord Melbourne had a sexual relationship, the content and tone of her letters to him from 1831 reveal a level of intimacy which suggests that some kind of sexual relations were being enjoyed. It is reasonable to suppose that if George read those letters he would have drawn the same conclusion – that criminal conversation had taken place. Caroline's letters to Melbourne are those of a woman missing a man with whom she is in love: they read like adultery. Letters were not secure so Caroline had to avoid any suggestion that she had been an unfaithful wife. With men like Grantley, Wynford and Follett involved (the prosecutors of Lord Melbourne in the trial he endured a year later), she had to be careful. While she was unafraid to call George weak and violent, she had to hold the line that she had not been sexually incontinent.

She asked William Cowper to 'speak <u>slightly</u> if you <u>do</u> speak of this matter' and advised him that he would help her a great deal by saying that the quarrel was likely to end in 'my going home again for such a termination is still on the cards (as far as it is good for my <u>reputation</u>)'. Her heart had been 'numbed' by Norton withholding her 'merry little children' from her: 'nothing can comfort me, nor can any thing be a further vexation to me while <u>they</u> are kept from me'.[101] When Caroline told her family she felt she had to return to her husband, they sent Bentinck to arrange the conditions which they insisted Norton had to abide by. George pledged to treat her well, and wrote to her begging her not to let her family come between them, and then also wrote to the family 'in the extremest and most exaggerated terms of submission'. Norton said he was glad they had 'avenged me [Caroline] and scorned him' and promised to treat her 'kindly for the future'. Her family were unhappy about her decision and would have read his letters to her sceptically.

Caroline fell for the promises and abject apologies and went back. She insisted George's letters 'were impossible to read without being touched . . . in spite of past deceiving, past broken promises, past ill-usage – in spite of advice from every friend she had and to "hold firm" and not return', she did.

George Norton said that no words could describe his remorse and promised that if he could not make her happy they could 'quietly and rationally separate' and he would tell the world that she was not to blame. He begged her 'by all that was dear and holy' to grant him 'complete' forgiveness, a real pardon, which she should 'write the moment she received his letter and seal it and send it by the post and not let anyone see it, for fear they should advise against it'. If Brinsley and Seymour had read that particular exercise in manipulation they would certainly have prevented her from falling for his emotional blackmail. George told Caroline she would never 'repent of this; you shall not – you shall not' and begged her not to 'crush' him. He appealed to a woman who was on her knees: 'I go on my knees to you! Have pity – have compassion on me.' Caroline Norton pitied a pitiless man and went back to him.[102]

Within two days of her return, life with George Norton was back to normal. There was another row and further blows, and Caroline became ill and lost the child due to 'the agitation and misery to which I had been exposed'. Despite the miscarriage George behaved 'with the utmost harshness and neglect', and abandoned Caroline to go shooting in Scotland with his family. He left no money and Brinsley was obliged to settle the doctor's account, which George had refused to do. Caroline's lack of funds was galling since her new book, the unfortunately titled *The Coquette and other Tales and Sketches in Prose and Verse*, was published at the end of August. But during Caroline's convalescence there were ongoing legal wrangles with the publisher of her new work.

However there was good news for her brother Brinsley: Sir Colquhoun Grant was reconciled to his daughter's hasty marriage and his son-in-law, and in the middle of September they travelled together from their house in Grosvenor Square to the estate at Frampton. Unfortunately Grant died a few days before Christmas of 'dropsy of the chest', although *The Times* reported that Marcia and Brinsley were with him and 'tended him with assiduity and affection.'[103]

During the autumn of 1835 Caroline's attention was drawn to Mary Shelley's friend Edward John Trelawny, a darkly handsome adventurer sixteen years older than her, who leaped off the pages of an adventure book and into her life. He had known Byron and Shelley (the latter and Trelawny were born in the same year) and been part of their bohemian circle. Trelawny's biography was the stuff of legend and some of it was only legend: his version was often the only one, and much of it cannot be corroborated. He had lived several lives before he met the lovely Mrs Norton.

Edward Trelawny was born in London in 1792 into a family of Cornish forebears who had fought at Agincourt and battled the Spanish Armada – in the stories he often told. His father had been a lieutenant colonel in the Coldstream Guards and a Member of Parliament, and inherited money from a rich cousin in 1798. Edward's colourful autobiography, published anonymously in 1831 with significant help from the widowed Mary Shelley (whom he asked to marry the same year), *Adventures of a Younger Son*, contains shocking reminiscences. Trelawny disliked his father, whom he called an 'oafish brute', and when he was five years old, persuaded his elder brother to help him slowly torture and kill their father's pet, a clip-winged raven. The brothers were sent to boarding school in Bristol, where his father told the headmaster Edward was 'savage, incorrigible! Sir he will come to the gallows, if you do not scourge the devil out of him.' He was frequently flogged, attacked the headmaster and half-strangled the man who flogged him, and tried to burn the school down. He was expelled and joined the navy in 1805 aged thirteen, and then spent six years going round the world, visiting Mauritius, India, Ceylon, Cape Horn and St Helena. In Java in 1811 Trelawny acquired the raffish scar on his face from a musket ball. There was a violence in him and an inability to conform, and his naval career stalled at midshipman. His frequent assaults on officers meant that he was passed round the navy like a parcel. Trelawny was invalided out in 1812 with a small pension, but lived on an allowance of three hundred pounds a year, not generous for a wealthy father.[104]

In 1813, when Edward Trelawny was twenty-one, he married Caroline Addison, the daughter of an East India merchant. The marriage lasted three years, ending in tears of joy for her and public humiliation for him. The Trelawnys lived in Denham, where their first child, Julia, was born, and then moved to Bristol, where Mrs Trelawny became pregnant with her second child.[105] During the summer of 1816 Trelawny's marriage disappeared in front of his eyes, and he did not even know it. Caroline, who was five months pregnant, fell in love with a fellow lodger, Captain Thomas Coleman of the 98th Regiment of Foot, a much older man and an invalid attended by three doctors, who was often 'indisposed' and always travelled by carriage when he left the house. Their landlady, Mrs Prout, peeped through the half-open blind in his bedroom and saw 'Mrs Trelawny reclining on the sofa on the left arm of Captain Coleman whilst his right hand was thrust into her bosom and he was kissing her'. A servant had seen Coleman pull his pantaloons down and the couple have 'carnal knowledge of each other's bodies', and remarked how 'tumbled' the captain's sheets often were. Mrs Prout confronted Mrs Trelawny, who denied everything, then admitted it, got down on her knees and begged her not to tell her husband, saying her life was in the landlady's hands. Mrs Prout insisted that the Trelawnys left immediately, making the excuse that the house needed redecorating. In July they went to live in Bath, where their second daughter, Eliza, was born in October. But the Trelawny marriage was in trouble, although Edward did not know about his wife's lover. In December their landlady could not stand the bad relations between her new tenants any longer and asked them to leave. Caroline took her chance and eloped with Captain Coleman and the baby to France.

In 1817 Trelawny's solicitor, Mr Physick, visited Mrs Prout, who supplied him with the evidence his client needed to sue Captain Coleman for criminal conversation with his wife and for damages of five hundred pounds and costs. Trelawny's name and the shame of being cuckolded, and the tawdry details of his wife betraying him for someone older and often 'indisposed' were in the public eye for two years until the middle of 1819, when the House of Lords granted Trelawny his divorce by Act of Parliament, with damages and costs.[106]

Trelawny now made his escape from England, travelling around Europe and becoming infatuated with Lord Byron and Percy Shelley, whom he met in Pisa in 1822. He attached himself to them, insinuating his way into their lives. The poets and their women liked him and fell for his butch charm, although Byron saw through many of the yarns he told with such vigour, shrewdly remarking that 'Trelawny could not even to save his life tell the truth.' Trelawny liked Shelley more than Byron and shared his views; Shelley's story chimed with Trelawny's own stormy childhood, his failed naval and marital careers.

Trelawny then found himself at the centre of the biggest drama in the story of the Byron and Shelley circle. Disastrously, Shelley allowed Trelawny, although he was not a qualified shipwright, to design his new vessel, *Don Juan*, which sank in a storm off Livorno on 8 July 1822. Trelawny scoured the coast for ten days before he found the badly decomposed bodies of Shelley, their friend Edward Elleker Williams and the boat boy Charles Vivian at Viareggio. He buried the bodies in quicklime before he went to tell Mary Shelley the bad news. On 14 August they all gathered on the beach and Trelawny exhumed the bodies, which were cremated the next day. Byron was too shocked to watch the scene that then unfolded. As Shelley's body burned, Trelawny pulled the poet's heart from the flames and handed it to his widow, Mary. Trelawny's reputation was sealed.[107]

Trelawny had Shelley's ashes buried in Rome, comforted the circle of heartbroken ladies and went with Bryon to Greece in 1823 to help the Greeks in their war of independence, where his impatience for action caused them to fall out. Trelawny was hungry for a good fight and dashed off to the mainland to help the Greek struggle there. He also bought fifteen women in Athens for a harem. The men who fought alongside him marvelled at his toughness and his love of their cause. When he heard that Byron had died at Missolonghi in 1824, Trelawny again took it upon himself to be funeral director, so was disappointed that the body was sent back to England. Trelawny then rubbished Byron's memory and the role he had played in the war. He married Terzitsa, the thirteen-year-old sister of a Greek warlord with whom he had fought, and in the summer of 1825 was again shot in the face. Even though his mouth and jaw were shattered he refused all medical treatment and, amazingly, recovered. In 1826 his child bride herself had a child and when she became pregnant again left him to live in a convent. The baby died and for the second time Trelawny was divorced by his wife. In 1828 the wounded warrior returned to England and asked Mary Shelley and her stepsister Claire Clairmont to marry him. They both refused.

After spending three years in America trying to make his mark, Trelawny again returned to England in the early part of 1835, causing a stir wherever he went: those scarred and rugged looks and the terrifying tales of hair-raising escapades set many ladies' hearts a-tremble. Fanny Kemble met him for the first time while she was acting in America, admired him but was also wary of this wild creature whose 'countenance was habitually serene and occasionally sweet in its expression, but sometimes with the fierceness of a wild beast'. Trelawny's movements and speech were 'slow and indolently gentle, his voice very low and musical, and his utterance deliberate and rather hesitating'. He looked and played the part of the Byronic hero perfectly: 'he was very tall and powerfully made, and altogether looked like a hero of the wild life of adventure'.[108]

Known breathlessly as the Corsair Trelawny, he cut a dash in London drawing rooms. His gaze was piercing, his attitude 'ferocious': 'he is a ruffian-looking man, with wild moustache, shaggy eyebrows, and orbs beneath them that have the gimlet property beyond any I have ever encountered'.[109] Benjamin Haydon met him at the end of 1835, was impressed with his connection to Lord Byron and thought him 'a fine animal'. He soaked up Trelawny's tales of his dashing past and hung on his every word: 'This must be the man that breathed the air of the Pampas, hunted the buffalo in the Prairies and fought for Greek liberty amidst the mountains of Greece, and swam torrents in pursuit of a beaten enemy.' But Haydon subsequently became disillusioned with Trelawny.[110] It cannot have helped that it was only a matter of time before Trelawny met Caroline Norton, who was a new friend of Mrs Shelley. She knew Trelawny too well to become romantically involved with him, and graciously said she was too old for him.

Trelawny was enchanted with Caroline Norton, and she

reciprocated the feeling. Mary Shelley confided to Trelawny that she too was attracted to Mrs Norton and may have even been at one time a little bit in love with her. 'I do not wonder at your not being able to deny yourself the pleasure of Mrs Norton's society. I never saw a woman I thought so fascinating. Had I been a man I should certainly have fallen in love with her; as a woman, ten years ago, I should have been spellbound, and had she taken the trouble, she might have wound me round her little finger. Ten years ago I was so ready to give myself away, and being afraid of men, I was apt to get "tousy-mousy" for women: experience and suffering have altered all that. I am more wrapt up in myself, my own feelings, disasters and prospects for Percy [her son].'

Despite being attracted to Mrs Norton Mary Shelley was also wary of the 'witticisms that glide from her lips'. She admired how Caroline flushed and blushed, and her complexion, which 'is so variable', being drawn to the way 'her blood which ebbs and flows, mounting as she speaks, to her neck and temples . . . gives a peculiar attraction to her conversation, not to speak of fine eyes and brows'. Knowing how indiscreet he was, Mary warned Trelawny, 'Now do not in your silly way show her what I say. She is despite all talents and sweetness, a London lady . . . well do I know the London *ton*.'[III]

In the middle of October Caroline Norton took her children to Brighton for three weeks 'to get better' and wrote a frank letter to her mother. About Trelawny, her feelings were complicated and ambiguous. Almost bewitched by him, she was also trying to be sensible and not the impulsive creature of the past. She was disappointed that the chance for 'intimacy' – which at that time could mean a close friendship as well as an affair – had gone. Putting on a brave face, she announced that he intended visiting Muddles at Hampton Court Palace, confiding, 'I fear my intimacy with Trelawny is past praying for, but I think you will like him too . . . I know he sounds handsome, but he is not: indeed, sometimes when I look at his haggard and fiercely sullen face, I think him the ugliest beast I ever saw . . . and he is the hunchiest man that ever looked like a gentleman – and the growliest, and the least complimentary knight who ever sat among women and the kindest to children and his hand is long, and his grasp fierce, whether it be friend or foe.'

Caroline Norton's letter shows her feelings careering all over the place: she realises that she should not be interested in Trelawny, but she cannot help it. Caroline and her mother were both writers, lovers of language and the expression of intense emotion. These were risky thoughts to put on paper if they fell into the wrong hands.

Caroline's pet name for Trelawny was Wolf or Tame Wolf. She may have believed that she had tamed him, but wolves cannot be domesticated, and this craggy-faced shaggy creature of nature was no exception, although she wrote to Trelawny wishing that he would settle down in one place, indeed become homely. Their conversations thrilled her and took her to places she had only read about: listening to his stories Caroline felt that she had sailed all over the world with Trelawny 'in an open boat'. Despite all their imaginary adventures she told her mother she had 'neither been drowned, ravished or sold on the coast of Barbary'. Caroline admitted she was 'in hopes he has sowed his wild oats'. But unless she wanted to have a romance with Trelawny it is hard to see why she should concern herself. She drew a pen-and-ink sketch of him for her mother, urging her to hold it up against the candlelight to get 'a very good idea of this worthy man'.

While they were in Brighton Caroline, Fletcher and Brinsley spent time with Trelawny, who sailed along the coast from Dover, where he was visiting his mother. He took them for a sail in his boat to Worthing. It was a happy day: to Caroline's sons he must have seemed like a pirate. Trelawny taught four-year-old Brinsley how to raise and lower the sails: 'his miniature strength, pulling at the ropes, made me die with laughter'. When she and the boys returned to London, Norton was not at home. Although he knew they would be arriving, he had arranged to go out for the evening and had not ordered any food to be prepared. When George returned at one o'clock in the morning 'he bowed to me, asked after my health, and disappeared'. At breakfast he was as sullen as ever and dined out that evening. Caroline could not cope with his coldness and made the disturbing remark of the abused wife that she preferred 'to be beat, even by him' than to be ignored. It was so unpleasant at Storey's Gate Caroline wanted to go back to Hampton Court Palace and asked her mother to 'pull out a few of your bosom feathers, and smooth a corner of "the nest" for me that I will come to you the day after tomorrow to stay a week'. Remembering Trelawny's wish to visit Hampton Court may have been another incentive to see her mother for a few days.[112]

Caroline wrote to her sister Georgy about her time in Brighton. Away from George she had been 'very happy and frisky', enjoyed not having to worry about saying 'with your leave', or 'by your leave' and had the freedom to have prawns at breakfast if she wanted and invite her friends round to 'tea and smiles'. Her leisure time was mostly spent with 'villainous but satisfactory Trelawny'.[113]

In October Caroline wrote to her Tame Wolf a nagging letter. She reminded him of his years of freedom when Trelawny was a 'sea-gull and rested in the black clouds instead of having a home', and told him it was time to sober down. The sooner he did it, the more 'gracious' it would be, and she invited him to imagine the very un-Trelawny state of being incapacitated by age and gout in a few years' time. Caroline also said he needed to settle down emotionally and that Trelawny was 'so fond of being loved . . . you can't go on inspiring <u>passions</u> all your life, or at all events you can't go on feeling them; and even if you could do both there is a peace and rest and confidence in a <u>home love</u>'. Love was very much on Caroline's mind: trapped in a loveless marriage and unable to recollect her own father, who had been dead nearly twenty years, she was sure that if he had lived she would 'never have loved any man as well'.

Caroline was keen to make Trelawny a part of her life and mentioned the imminent arrival in England of Zella, his ten-year-old daughter born to his child bride Terzitsa. Caroline dared to dream that she might play a part in Zella's upbringing and help with the 'transplanted rose'. Caroline was not sure she believed in Zella's existence and may have wondered if he was a fantasist: 'whether she is coming or nor, or whether there is such a being in existence – whether existing, she is anything to you – are all doubts and dreams to me'. Caroline was broody for a daughter and sounds sad when she confesses, 'I want a little girl, and hope it is all <u>real</u> and <u>true</u>.'[114]

Mrs Norton would have liked Trelawny to accompany her and a party of family and friends to see the sixty-year-old and portly Charles Kemble play Hamlet at Covent Garden Theatre. But Trelawny was in Dover. The great tragedian must have been nervous before the curtain went up, having endured the previous evening one of the worst nights of his long career. A boisterous gallery behaved so badly that Kemble had to have order restored by the theatre manager.[115] The gallery did not 'govern their roaring throats' and were so obstreperous and noisy that the first act 'was performed in a dumb show'. Eventually a man leaped from one of the boxes onto the stage, and ran across it to find Mr Wallack, the manager, who was able to quieten the crowd down. Kemble continued, a 'little ruffled by the storm', but managed to deliver his soliloquies with 'more than usual feeling and impressiveness'.

The same day that Caroline Norton was writing this letter to Trelawny, her husband was one of the two magistrates who heard the shocking tale of Charles Billings and Joseph Newbury, privates in the 2nd Battalion of the 1st Regiment of the Guards, stationed at the Tower of London. Newbury was charged with kicking Catherine Ware, a pregnant intoxicated woman, in the stomach outside the Brown Bear public house in Leman Street. She was described as 'an unfortunate female', a kindly meant term for a prostitute. Some days later 'under the greatest bodily suffering', battered and bruised, Ware was able to come to court and give her account to Magistrates Norton and Walker. Ware said that one of the men kicked her 'in the lower abdomen in so brutal a manner she was deprived of her senses for some minutes'. A witness, a 'respectable tradesman', added details, describing how a row which had started in the pub spilled onto the pavement outside. He saw Ware hit Joseph Newbury twice, and 'he . . . gave her a most violent kick in the front part of her person'. The witness was surprised that men present at the scene did nothing to help her.

Norton and Walker severely censured Newbury's 'brutal conduct' and convicted him of assault, giving him the option of being fined forty shillings (now two hundred pounds) or spending one month in prison. The magistrates said they also expected the army to punish the men for being drunk away from their quarters; otherwise they would have fined Newbury five pounds with the option of two months in gaol. Charles Billings was not charged with any offence. The punishment appears unduly lenient, but this kind of attack took place not only in the poorest neighbourhoods; it also happened in the bedrooms and drawing rooms of Westminster. If George Norton had been charged with his recent assault on his wife, the last of which had caused her to miscarry, he too might have been treated less severely than we expect.[116]

The Norton family had bad news in the middle of November: George's youngest brother, Charles Francis Norton, died in Canada on 27 October from 'drinking cold water whilst over-heated in the pursuit of moose deer'. He may have died of pneumonia, which had a high mortality rate before the twentieth-century invention of antibiotics.[117] Charles, more or less the same age as Caroline, was the only Norton to like her, and when he died she lost a sincere friend and her only ally in that tricky family. He had been acting as assistant military secretary to his father-in-law, Sir Colin Campbell, the governor of Nova Scotia. His widow was left with two small children, the younger only five months old. That autumn Caroline took every oppor-tunity to spend time away from her husband in London. She was in Eastbourne when she heard this news, which made her 'melancholy'. Back in London 'every room puts me in mind of him and my heart sinks'.

So sad that Charles had died, Caroline wrote to Trelawny about how much her husband's brother had meant to her, a retort to his trite remark that 'sudden intimacies were as good as those of long-standing'. Caroline shared some of her dearest memories. She remembered the sound of Charles's bugle calling from the side of the lake when she went boating, and his 'cordial and kindly voice'. She treasured the memory of his 'childlike and frank laugh' and how he had 'made me feel an affection untinctured by passion or vanity and who defended me against the pride and insult even of <u>his own people</u>'. Loyal and sweet Charles had made the time she had to spend with her in-laws in Scotland bearable. They sang ballads together as they boated, and when she was thrown from her pony, he carried her through the streams and over the hills when she was 'bruised, wretched and laughed at by everyone else in the party'.[118]

As the most difficult year of her eight-year marriage drew to a close, Caroline heard the good news from Dublin that her brother Frank had been appointed gentleman to the bedchamber of his boss, Lord Mulgrave. Frank's fortunes were to be tied up with the helpful Mulgrave until 1839. Caroline's friend and recently widowed sister-in-law Maria Campbell Norton joined the Mulgrave family when she was married to his lordship's younger brother Edmund Phipps in 1838, binding the two families closer.[119]

Caroline arranged to spend Christmas with the children, but without George, at Maiden Bradley, her sister's home in Wiltshire. Norton was more eager than ever to please his rich relation Margaret Vaughan. She was besotted with him, and he spent much of his spare time with her. She was very wealthy, owned several grand houses in the most fashionable part of London and estates in Yorkshire, and lived in splendour at 1 Lower Berkeley Street, off Manchester Square. She may have done some will-dangling because Caroline had to play second fiddle to what Miss Vaughan liked and did not like. George's financial problems were one of the reasons he spent so much time charming her and putting her wishes and opinions above those of his wife. Caroline, who had contributed so much to their finances with her writing, now knew how low their funds were. She found out that when their marriage settlement was drawn up in 1827 Lord Grantley's lawyers had deceived her mother into thinking her new son-in-law's annual income was greater than it was. As prolific and high-earning as Caroline had been throughout their marriage, what she made was never enough because George's salary did not make up for the income promised by the estate that was not there. Miss Vaughan, who did not like her young, beautiful and jumped-up relation, therefore exercised considerable influence over the Nortons' personal affairs. Caroline again found herself snubbed and excluded by a weak husband and another odious in-law.

While they were at Maiden Bradley, Caroline's eldest son

Fletcher caught scarlatina, a mild form of scarlet fever, so they stayed longer than she had planned. Two days before the year ended Edward Trelawny appeared out of the blue. Caroline was out when he called and he left her a 'harsh and bitter note'. Trelawny was cross that she had not been at his beck and call. He seemed to resent her family and parental responsibilities, and she felt she had to respond with an appeasing note: 'You think I am too glad to go [to London] – but that is because you don't wear chains and so don't know that the weight and clank of them wear one out.'[120]

Frank and Charlie Sheridan were both unwell. This marked the start of their failing health, plagued by tuberculosis until they died in the 1840s. Charlie was still a clerk at the Admiralty and had been spitting blood – which his family tried to explain by saying his coughing fits had 'broken a blood vessel' – but had recovered for the time being. In his quarters at the Vice Regal Lodge in Dublin Frank had been coughing for six weeks and had months of illness before he was well again, until the next episode. The damp Irish climate was one of the worst for one with a weakness of the chest.[121]

In 1835 Caroline's marriage had disintegrated. She had left home, but because she felt bereft without her children had gone back, and then it got far worse. The violence which had started in 1827 had resumed, even though George had promised her family it would stop. And she had lost a baby. They began to lead separate lives. Caroline spent more time away from Storey's Gate – at Brighton, Eastbourne, Wiltshire, anywhere but London. Miss Vaughan's influence was on the rise, and within her own marriage Caroline's power was almost gone. Her fraught friendship with the artist Benjamin Haydon had been resolved awkwardly, and the egocentric Trelawny was a new cuckoo trying to climb into her nest. Her work was published and admired, but although she was earning money she had no access to it. As prime minister, Lord Melbourne had been forced into unaccustomed busy-ness, while his nephew and private secretary Willoughby and Caroline had become close friends, forging a vital link between her and the man she cared for above all others.

IV

1836: 'Norty Mrs Norton'

A superb lump of flesh
Sydney Smith

Caroline and her sons stayed for a month at Maiden Bradley until the third week of January 1836, on her doctor's orders. Short dark days looking out at the bleak landscape lowered her mood. There was no avoiding going back to London and George. Her brother and his wife Marcia were at the start of a happy marriage: Grant had left them with an income of nine thousand pounds a year (now three quarters of a million pounds) and his siblings called Brinsley Croesus. He played the role of squire at Frampton Court, a 'modern mansion' overlooking rolling parkland. Caroline's sister Helen was happily married to Pricey and besotted with their ten-year-old Freddy; Georgy and Lord Seymour were as giggly as ever, with two daughters and a son. Frank and Charlie Sheridan's health was causing concern, but their doctors made reassuring noises about them making a full recovery. All around her people were happy, but she was depressed, anxious about her marriage and her intense relationship with Lord Melbourne.

Caroline wrote to Trelawny on 4 January, in response to his hectoring note that he had a 'great deal more feeling' than her.

Wearily she stood her ground, insisting he was mistaken to 'think that he had more feelings than others' because he was 'ungovernable and impetuous', and she reprimanded him: 'outward indulgence of feeling is no proof of its existence in one's heart more strongly than another – it is a proof of carelessness of forms and sometimes disregard of the feelings of others'. Caroline clearly attempted to end this strange interlude she had been indulging herself in. 'You do not comprehend me – and perhaps I do not understand you – there is a gulf between us. Strangers we met and strangers, in spite of all, we still are. I feel it continually when we are discussing some point of opinion, or when I could express myself on matters of feeling. My heart shrieks under some cold checking touch, and my words are frozen with a confused mingling of distrust and weariness – there is nothing left in me worth loving, nor is there any chance of me loving again.'[1]

Without naming Melbourne, she confessed the importance and durability of the feelings she had for him. Caroline admitted that her 'warmest and least selfish thoughts' for Melbourne were an 'affection' which started in 1831, the year they met. She conceded that there had been 'more pain than pleasure' in that affection. Sounding beaten by her circumstances she admitted that she was 'wasted and worn and sick and suspicious and sad and a woman of the world'.

Caroline was angry about the manner in which Trelawny wrote to her, his proprietorial attitude to her thoughts and conduct, and made it clear he was no longer part of her life: 'what have you to do with my career, or I with yours?' She agreed that Trelawny could baffle or bamboozle his way out of trouble, but warned him there was a limit to the power his 'wild energy, animal strength and vehemence of passion' could exert over 'thought, soul and heart'. Caroline disliked him writing to her as if she was a 'young and trusting girl and you were my lover', and the way he threw 'chains around a shadow and think to bind it'. Having vented her anger, she posted 'this disagreeable letter' unsigned.

An influential and helpful man emerged as a prominent figure in Caroline's correspondence from January 1836. Edward Ellice was something of a father figure – although Ellice and her father had little in common – becoming a rock at a time when she needed one to cling to. Born in London in 1783 he was widely known as Old Bear Ellice because of the fortune his family had made in the Canadian fur trade. He was instrumental in getting the Great Reform Act through Parliament and in May 1836 would be a founder of the Reform Club. Ellice was the first man from the merchant class to hold a position in government: in 1833 he became secretary at war, and had a seat in the Whig cabinet under Melbourne's premiership until December 1834. He was a political ally of Caroline's uncle, Sir James Graham, first lord of the Admiralty, until Ellice resigned in 1834. He was out of office when she wrote to him at his home at 14 Carlton House Terrace in the early days of 1836 and confided her problems to him.

Ellice's grandfather had built the family trading business in North America, Canada and the West Indies; his father made even more money by investing heavily in the fur trade in Canada. Edward was educated at Winchester, graduated from Marischal College in Aberdeen and worked in the family business in Canada in 1803 for two years until his father died. He returned to England in 1805; his marriage to the sister of Earl Grey in 1809 took him to the heart of Whig politics, and via his brother-in-law Sir Samuel Whitbread he met Caroline's grandfather Richard Brinsley Sheridan during the rebuilding of Drury Lane Theatre. For forty years he was the Member of Parliament for Coventry. Earl Grey appointed him joint secretary to the Treasury and a government whip when he became prime minister in 1830.[2] Bear Ellice was a good man to have on your side. The Ultra Tory Nortons disliked his politics, but knew they were dealing with a powerful man. Ellice was a Whig *éminence grise* and entrusted with important negotiations with foreign powers in an unofficial capacity on the government's behalf.

On 6 January Caroline replied to a letter Bear had written and apologised for the long gap in her correspondence. Groping for the right words, she sounded melancholic and hopeless: 'I do not myself know, as the maids say "What has come over me" and I believe the next thing you will hear of me is that I have taken to <u>drinking</u>.' She told him how she would sit with her hands in front of her 'looking at the rain drops on the window and begin to think I must have lost my soul when I was ill last summer' – referring to the miscarriage and all that had preceded it. It was an honest letter to a kind man who had helped her by lending money without a quibble. In a roundabout way, she solicited his opinion about whether she should 'part with my "good man"'. The Nortons' marital situation was at a 'standstill'; her mother, who was 'strict in her notions', was exerting pressure on Caroline not to end the marriage, saying it would 'break her heart' if she did. Mrs Sheridan had arranged the match, got her into the sorry situation she was in, and may have considered it a slight on her judgement and shaming to the whole family if her daughter brought the marriage to an end. Caroline told Ellice that she had 'lost her looks' and was certain that he would be sorry to see her. Her female contemporaries who did not know her husband thought he was a 'model of mien' and that she was a 'profligate hussy', and these misconceptions made her feel unable to deal with her own affairs. She was bored by her own misery, and the dreary landscape: 'nothing is more ugly than the country'.[3]

Caroline Norton aged twenty-three at home in Storey's Gate.
This 1830 sketch by John Hayter was an engraving for the frontispiece for her
new book *The Undying One*. Four years after her marriage to George Norton
she had two sons and was a celebrated poet and songwriter.

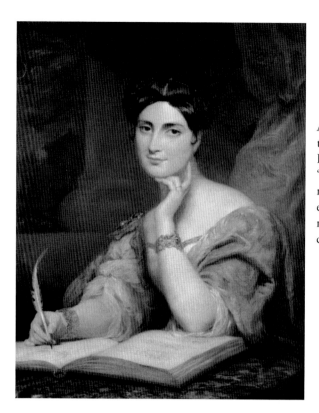

A luscious portrait commissioned by the Duke of Devonshire. The actress Fanny Kemble was dazzled by her: 'Caroline Norton looks as if she wer made of precious stones, diamonds, emeralds, rubies and sapphires; she i radiant with beauty… a splendid creature, nobly endowed in every wa

Turtle Doves in the Bird Cage Walk. Caroline and Melbourne are caricatured as lovebirds perched on the balcony of the Norton house. At the trial much would be made of Lord Melbourne's frequent visits to Mrs Norton on his way home from Downing Street to his house on the other side of St James's Park.

THE CRIM-CON GAZETTE

No. 12. SATURDAY, NOVEMBER 10, 1838. PRICE TWO PENCE

PRINTED AND PUBLISHED BY GEORGE HUCKLEBRIDGE, NO. 2, CHARLES STREET, HATTON GARDEN, MIDDLESEX.

The Regency equivalent of tabloid journalism, the *Gazette* titillated its readers with details of criminal conversation – 'crim con' – trials for adultery. Transcripts of evidence appeared in the broadsheets and would be cherry-picked by the *Crim Con Gazette* for the sauciest material, here seen through the keyhole by a servant.

The woeful state of e Norton's marriage and Aelbourne's patronage of her cuckolded husband provided irresistible material for the press.

LOVE WITHOUT RISK.

Painted in the year of the trial, William Lamb, Viscount Melbourne, was the most important m[...]
in Caroline's life and the cause of her greatest pleasure and pain. Fanny Kemble noted his appea[...]
'The most charming of debonair men ... after dinner I sat for some time opposite a large crimso[...]
coloured ottoman on which Lord Melbourne reclined, surrounded by the three Sheridan sisters[...]
A more remarkable collection of comely creatures, I think, could hardly be seen.'

Fletcher Norton, 3rd Lord Grantley, painted by his father-in-law
Sir William Beechey in 1825, wearing his Waterloo medal. For years
the Ultra Tory Grantley pulled his brother George's strings. He persuaded
George to accuse his political enemy, the Whig Prime Minister,
Lord Melbourne, of 'criminal conversation' with Caroline.

Georgiana Zornlin's 1825 portrait of the artist Benjamin Robert Haydon who was obsessed with Caroline Norton to the despair of his long-suffering wife. Mrs Haydon joined in with her husband's efforts to blacken Caroline's name.

Edward John Trelawny was a handsome and histrionic presence in Caroline Norton's troubled life in the 1830s. She became infatuated with the six-feet tall, weather-beaten, snaggle-toothed adventurer and teller of tall tales, but wearied of his emotional demands. In 1839 he retired from society to live a vegetarian and teetotal life, without underwear or overcoats. When he died in 1881 his ashes were buried next to Shelley's in Rome.

Caroline Eliz.th S. Norton

Engraved from a drawing by Landseer with whom Caroline was said to be romantically linked, this picture was used as the frontispiece of Caroline's book *The Dream and Other Poems*, published in 1840.

This picture was painted about the time of the death of her nine-year-old son William, who died after a fall from his horse. Septicaemia set in and William died before Caroline could see him.

Meanwhile Trelawny preferred to be the one to break relationships and responded to Caroline's unsigned letter. There was a spat on paper between them before she left Wiltshire to return to London. Trelawny tried to make her jealous by mentioning a young lady he was courting, but Caroline would have none of it and told him it was time he acted his age: 'I always catch myself talking to you as if <u>you</u> were the <u>younger</u> of us two, whereas in <u>years</u>, whatever may be the hopes of those who wish to push me off the stage, I fear you have <u>at least</u> fifteen years the start of me.' Telling him she was not capricious but a loyal friend, Caroline wrote that her friendship was not unconditional, but only offered on the understanding that Trelawny did not abuse her family – whom he resented because of the time she spent with them instead of him.[4]

While she was in Wiltshire George Norton wrote to Caroline more than once asking her to lobby Lord Melbourne and Lord John Russell, the home secretary, to give a friend of his the co-magistracy of Lambeth Street court. George's colleague, Mr Walker, was resigning. He was confident of success and praised Melbourne's 'kindness on many occasions'. George also wrote to Melbourne, pestering him so much that the latter wrote to Caroline complaining about her husband's behaviour. Two months later Norton's friend was not appointed, and George's anger triggered another row.

In the meantime Brinsley invited Caroline and the boys, but not George, to spend Easter with all the Sheridans at Frampton. This snub was the beginning of the end of the Norton marriage. Brinsley would not back down and George refused to let Caroline take the children if he was not invited. On 23 March, a week before Easter, Caroline wrote a distraught note to Edward Ellice from Hampton Court Palace revealing that he was helping her cope with events as they unravelled by acting as a conduit for her correspondence with Lord Melbourne. At this stage in the

Nortons' dispute Melbourne was keeping a careful distance but was 'not against' her leaving George, saying that 'it will not affect <u>him</u>'. Unable 'to write from faintness and headaches', Caroline asked Ellice to tell Melbourne that she had received his last note. She also asked Ellice to let her know, presumably by having someone watch Storey's Gate, when George returned, perhaps from his brother's at Wonersh in Surrey, and she promised to tell Ellice what she planned to do before she acted. She signed off the note, 'God bless you for you are <u>most kind to me and I will never forget it</u>.'[5]

George Norton was already at Storey's Gate on the day Caroline wrote this. At the same time as he received Caroline's note Ellice got a pushy letter from George asking him to procure a 'small office at £2–300 a year to hold in conjunction with my police office'. There had been some correspondence between them in which Ellice had suggested George take a job abroad. By calling upon him in this way Norton was assuming an unwarranted level of friendship with Edward Ellice. George was prepared to consider anything as his magistracy was not onerous: 'I have plenty of time to spare from my police duties.' He asked for a position 'about the Court – in short anything in London'. He was also prepared to swap his position as magistrate for 'something in the Post Office or Stamps' at the same salary. George needed to earn more money to pay off the debts incurred because of the mismanagement of his trustees; money worries drove him to take liberties with his wife's influential friends and gave his rich cousin Miss Vaughan too much say in the Nortons' unravelling private lives.[6]

On 28 March, the day before Caroline was due to leave London with the children for Dorset, the storm broke. George Norton's recent violence and broken promises meant that under no circumstances would Brinsley have him in his house that Easter. George had confided in Margaret Vaughan, and she made the situation worse, making disparaging remarks about Caroline's 'ways'. Twenty-five years older than George, she had promised to bequeath him something in her will, and he felt obliged to pay attention to her views. She persuaded him to make a stand. Miss Vaughan's advice was perhaps coloured by her own experience. Her parents had separated when she was small; she had been brought up by her father's family, and contact with her mother was intermittent.[7]

Edward Ellice was unwilling to do anything for George, and this had made him 'exceedingly cross'. In the days leading up to the planned day of departure for Dorset George was biding his time and never intended to let Caroline take the children. Lord Melbourne had called at Storey's Gate on the afternoon of 28 March to say goodbye to her, but she was out shopping with Charles Norton's widow Maria and Maria's elder brother Fitzroy Campbell. Melbourne was chatting to George when she returned and witnessed the Nortons' discussion about her plans for the next day. She was to leave for the country at seven o'clock in the morning. George told Caroline that Miss Vaughan had visited him that afternoon and reported her saying that she 'hoped I was not going to take her <u>little favourite</u> [Fletcher] out of town in such bad weather'. Caroline snapped back that Miss Vaughan 'being an old maid, need not teach <u>me</u> a mother's duty', and was 'always meddling'. The family doctor had ordered Fletcher to the country for his health after his recent bout of scarlatina. George asked Caroline to delay the trip for four days until Saturday but Caroline refused: her depression at being in Wiltshire at Christmas had turned into joy at the prospect of being in 'the cool green country, unmolested, with my little ones'. Melbourne and the others left and Caroline went to get ready to go out. The Nortons had separate dinner engagements, she with Lady Mary Fox, and he with Sir Frederick Adair Roe, magistrate at Bow Street court.

She had a 'sulky' five minutes with him when he told her it would be the last time she would be permitted to accept a dinner invitation 'singly'. He 'desired' her to meet him at Raggett's Hotel in Piccadilly, to say goodbye to the Campbells before they left for Scotland the next day. Caroline and George had been invited to a party that evening at Mrs Leicester Stanhope's, wife of Colonel Stanhope, an army officer and Graecophile who had fought in the Greek War of Independence and brought Lord Byron's body home from Missolonghi. In 1831 he had married Elizabeth Green, an heiress half his age.[8]

Caroline arrived at Raggett's and spent twenty minutes with the Campbells, but George was not there so she suggested that she and Fitzroy Campbell return to Lady Mary Fox's to see if George turned up there and then go on to the Stanhopes, where she was sure he would find them. Fitzroy Campbell reminded Caroline that George's engagement was 'a male dinner' and 'ten to one he's too drunk to come so if we are to go let us go'. Caroline and Fitzroy, a good-looking guards officer the same age as her, piled into a carriage but then saw George and a friend walking towards them. Norton got into the carriage with them and a quarrel started immediately. George admonished her: 'What a damned fool you are, not to do as I bid you.' He then took exception to Fitzroy piping up: "Why my good fellow we waited till half past eleven" and started in earnest: 'We waited – what do you mean by we? How are my wife and you, we? I dare say you were both of you very glad to go on without me. You're a damned rascal and she's a cursed coquette.'

This was the tinder that sparked the flame which ended in the Court of Common Pleas in Westminster in June. George was drunk and continued to be rude to his brother-in-law, whom he assumed was flirting with his wife. Caroline tried to calm things down as they continued to the Stanhopes. She dreaded going home and stayed there as long as she could. George glowered in the corner, his mood made worse by the unexpected presence of Trelawny, with whom she 'conversed feebly and stupidly', and 'my beauty MacNeill', another of her admirers. Eventually they left the party and got into the carriage. George lost his temper, drunk and eaten up with jealousy of Fitzroy, who only a week ago had accompanied Caroline on a social engagement so that he could 'take care' of her. She burst into tears. 'Well, it is the last night of this most wretched life. God knows if I was naturally so profligate I have not <u>spirits</u> enough for "love-making" now! Tomorrow I am gone! and it shall be long before you see me back again at Storey's Gate!' There was a silence for a while and then he said, 'I think I have a way still to govern <u>you</u> my lady, – you may go to the devil if you like but you go <u>alone</u>'.

When they arrived home after midnight George told the footman that none of the children was to be allowed to leave London the next day and started to climb the stairs. Caroline then ordered the same servant to take a message to Lord Seymour in Spring Gardens at seven o'clock the following morning that she wanted to speak to him before he left London for Wiltshire. George 'turned fiercely round' and told the footman that he and all the other servants of the house were to ignore any orders that his mistress gave them. The Nortons went their separate ways to bed.

After a sleepless night, Caroline went to see Seymour at eight the next morning and told him what had happened. He advised her that she could either stand up to George by giving orders to the servants in the usual way, or wait until George had gone to his office and then leave London with the children as planned. The Seymours had to leave London and could not wait to see how the situation developed, so she went to Raggett's to ask Fitzroy Campbell to come home with her. Caroline told him of

George's suspicions about the nature of their friendship and about his 'attractiveness in my eyes'. When they arrived at Spring Gardens she sent a message to her footman, who returned to tell her that George had put all the children in a coach and sent them to a secret location.

After a 'stormy scene', Campbell managed to bribe from the coachmen and servants for information that the boys had been taken to Haike's Hotel in Duke Street, and then to Miss Vaughan's house at 1 Lower Berkeley Street. Caroline went there and had a furious row with the meddlesome woman, who denied knowing where the children were. 'I think I should have <u>strangled</u> her' if Fitzroy Campbell had not walked into the room with the news that he had found out where the boys were being held. Caroline and Campbell drove to the office of a Mr Martin Jacinthe Knapp, a house agent who looked after Margaret Vaughan's properties in London, and confronted him. Knapp showed Caroline his client's written authority and also a note from George Norton to Vaughan saying that the children were 'to be kept' from their mother '<u>by any means they chose to employ</u>'.

Caroline was on the verge of collapse. It had taken four hours to find her children; Fletcher was ill, and she was afraid that her husband would be unkind to his second son Brin, whom he 'always snubs and ill uses'. Caroline became 'perfectly frantic and sat threatening and sobbing in the office'. She shouted and screamed at people who came in and made 'wild and vehement appeals, begging them to help her'. Knapp called the police to remove her, which had the effect of calming her down. Caroline begged the agent to let her see the children and also pleaded for permission to write to her boys' physician to find out how Fletcher was 'after being dragged about in a damp hackney coach all day, recovering from a sore throat after the scarlatina' but was refused.

Fitzroy Campbell, who had left to ask a magistrate to intervene on the grounds that the children's father had not given them to Knapp but Miss Vaughan, now returned with bad news, and Caroline left without seeing her children or saying goodbye to them. They had been in the room above where she was and would have heard everything: 'I could hear their little feet running over my head while I sat sobbing below, only the ceiling between us and I not able to get to them!'

Caroline next heard that the boys had been sent to Lord Grantley, who 'hated her and was keeping them at Wonersh to spite her'. The children's nursemaid was forbidden to write to her, and the only conduit of information she had was secret notes from her footman – he had been ordered not to communicate with his mistress in any way – who also gleaned snippets of information from Lord Grantley's servants. The footman was upset at the harshness which had been 'dealt to a lady who never dealt it to others'. Perhaps the most distressing intelligence that came from Caroline's loyal servants was the news that George and his brother had interrogated Brinsley about their time in Eastbourne and their mother's conduct with Trelawny. Dejected, she asked Bear Ellice, 'where is the heart of a man who could try to make his own innocent child prove its mother's shame'.[9]

Caroline left London for Frampton for Easter and wrote an emotional letter to Lord Melbourne, her handwriting becoming ever more scrawly, her pen losing control, like her temper, as it gouged the surface of the paper. Not bothering with the courtesy of 'My Dear Lord', she screamed across the page to him, 'He has taken my children from me!' George had picked 'a quarrel over nothing' as a pretext for banning the children from going to Dorset. She told Melbourne, 'if they keep me away from my boys I shall go mad'. She had not stopped crying for days but now was able to make plans as to how she might see them:

'I have done weeping now and we will see whose wit will carry them furthest.' But Caroline was on her own, bereft of her children and the man to whom she was pouring out her feelings. 'I cannot write any more – write to me – there is more comfort in a word of yours or a look than in all that other people can do. I wish I had never had children – pain and agony for the first moments of their life – dread and anxiety for their uncertain future – and now all to be a blank.' Caroline signed off saying she was 'very miserable', but before she posted the letter she added a postscript with news of a troubling development.

The Nortons' footman wrote to say that George had been interrogating him and the other servants about her behaviour when he was not at home – if he had noted 'any familiarity on Fitzroy Campbell's part, or any other gentlemen who come to the house'. Her servant's note was 'most respectful and well-intentioned' but she was appalled at the direction in which her husband's enquiries were heading, and afraid: 'The disgrace of this will kill me and my boys.' She did have the loyalty of the servants at Storey's Gate, 'who hate him, so they will all write and tell me what is done'. The footman was prepared to be dismissed rather than answer questions which were 'so disagreeable, and dishonourable' to her that he refused to answer them and told Norton 'you may turn me away if you like'.[10]

There were two stages in the collapse of the Norton marriage in 1836. Initially George took the children away to punish her for her defying him at various times during the day and evening of 28 March. Caroline knew that when he was defeated, especially in front of others, he always believed the blame lay elsewhere, never with him, so he cast around for another man to hold responsible and proceeded on that basis, taking the breakdown into the second stage: allowing his thoughts to be poisoned by the insinuations and political ambitions of others.

As the details of the situation leaked out, encountering some opprobrium for what he had done, George looked for a means of justifying his extraordinary actions and set about smearing Caroline's reputation.

Norton broke open his wife's desk and rifled through her papers looking for incriminating material. He tried to find evidence of an adulterous relationship between her and Fitzroy Campbell but there was nothing to find. He discovered an 1828 letter from Lord Mulgrave, her brother Frank's boss in Jamaica and now Dublin, which was romantic but hardly the love letter he was desperate to find. Urged on by Miss Vaughan and Lord Grantley, George opened any letters addressed to her, scoured through all her belongings and bribed Fitzroy Campbell's servant to steal all his letters at the Guards' Club.

By 4 April the situation had progressed. Caroline wrote a resigned note to Lord Melbourne: 'I am worn out with pondering on my affairs and with wondering why this sudden <u>crash</u> has come upon me.' She missed her children so badly that she was prepared to go back to her husband. The possibility of divorce had been raised by the Nortons and she was waiting to hear the legal opinion of George's lawyer Sir William Follett, who was the solicitor general.

Caroline asked the Reverend Barlow, the vicar at Duke Street, to discuss the situation with her husband. She believed George might respond to Barlow as he considered himself a religious man. The vicar was a good choice as a mediator: he was more or less the same age as George and had been a married man since 1824. The Reverend Barlow was used to managing delicate situations, and Caroline thought he might succeed, as George was 'entirely guided by others . . . my foes', and none of them would 'ever countenance any terms she proposed'.[11]

If George agreed to her coming back she would go home

unconditionally. She acknowledged the possibility of it being unbearable and having to leave again but with the benefit of bitter experience knew she would have to 'pave and prepare the way for that step' rather than walking out on the spur of the moment as she had in the past. If she went home and obeyed the rules and then was forced to leave, she would be able to say that she had left for reasons other than 'for this man or that man'. Most importantly, she would be with her children 'without a struggle and I shall baffle those who have planned all this against me'.

If George refused to have her back, she would be 'deprived utterly of my poor boys' and be forced to sue him for alimony. If this happened she planned on behaving as if she had accepted her fate and would 'acquiesce <u>apparently</u>' but secretly write to various friends abroad to see if they would help – for instance, ask King Leopold of Belgium to enquire if his wife would accept Caroline at Court in Brussels. If the Belgians agreed she would abduct the children and take them to Belgium, and if Leopold was unwilling she would take them to live in Italy or Germany. A third possibility which occurred to her was that George would take 'a middle course', giving her an allowance, allowing her to have the children but dictating where she and the children lived. Given his previous behaviour and attitude to money, this seemed unlikely.

Caroline was twenty-seven. On 4 April she wrote to Melbourne, keeping him in her life and needy of his counsel: 'If you advise me in any way on these points, pray do. No one knows how I have suffered, or the chilled, cold quietness with which I am now writing.' If she abducted the children the world would be scandalised, Caroline would be frozen out by everyone she knew, and only her family would write to her. But her greatest fear was to lose Melbourne: I regret . . . that <u>you</u> will find perhaps someone as willing to devote her time and thought to you, and more able to entertain you. This is a <u>triste</u> ending at seven and twenty.'

Caroline told Melbourne she could not help smiling a 'bitter smile, bewildered at how a man who had been "mad to marry me at eighteen" turned me out of his house nine years afterwards and inflicts vengeance as bitterly as he can, by taking away the children . . . of that long-desired union and cursing me through them'. She did not mention having left him once and having announced her intention of doing so again, her sometimes provoking behaviour, mimicking him in company and flirting with rich, powerful men.

Writing about the way the balance of power and feeling in their relationship had changed, Caroline hinted at suicide: 'here I am, appealing to you (with a mournful conviction of my own folly) to <u>try</u> and feel as much for me as you did when you "<u>could not think what had become of me because I had not written to you for three days</u>". Well, well, it is all a folly perhaps – only I cannot think what spell is on my life that it should finish me so much sooner than others . . . if I could make my peace with God it would be as well to die <u>now</u> as to wait.'[12]

Melbourne replied to her letter as soon as he received it, but it was hardly the response she wanted. The man who had been at the centre of her life for the past five years pulled back from her, as he had to. The prime minister could not be seen to be the cause of the breakdown of the Norton marriage or risk being cited in another criminal conversation case. Caroline might have anticipated this, but isolated, depressed and worried, she surely did not enjoy being told to calm down. 'I hardly know what to write to you, or what comfort to offer you. You know as well as I do, that the best course is to keep yourself tranquil, and not to give way to feelings of passion, which God knows, are too natural to be easily resisted. This conduct on his part seems perfectly unaccountable. You cannot have better or more affectionate advisers than you have with you on the spot, who are well acquainted with the circumstances of the case and with the characters of those with whom you have to deal. You know that I have always counselled you to bear everything and remain to the last. I thought it for the best. I am afraid it is no longer possible.'[13]

Two days later Caroline wrote impatiently to Dear Wolf asking him to return her books and sketchbooks as he had promised. She was rumoured to have run away with Trelawny; others speculated it was with Lord Seymour. Mrs Norton was accused of so much bad behaviour, 'it is no wonder if I feel a little fatigued with all I am supposed to have done as the poor little wax figures melted by witches of olden times caused them to wither and waste'. She asked Wolf to go on a gossip offensive on her behalf and tell anyone who would listen that she was at her brother's house with her mother and Lord and Lady Seymour having a long-planned holiday.[14]

A few days later Caroline wrote to Augusta Cowell explaining why she had not written the lyrics to a piece they were working on: 'you are too true a little friend to keep putting off with a feeble excuse'. She learned that Margaret Vaughan's malign influence had started earlier than she had realised. During that ill-starred European holiday with her family George had received anonymous letters about Caroline at Aix-la-Chapelle – where he was ill and insisting that Caroline nurse him – which had been sent by the vexatious Vaughan. In effect poison-pen letters, they told tales of her adultery, which George did not confront her about at the time but had blown up about in the wake of Brinsley's elopement. To Augusta, Caroline referred to the miscarriage as having made her 'as ill as it was possible to be and live'. She was 'so unhappy' she could not write any more but would do so when all was settled 'whether we are reconciled or part as my friends wish, but I do not'.[15]

Caroline's letters had some effect on Melbourne, who was chastened by her remarks and felt obliged to offer her some support: 'You describe me very truly when you say that I am always more annoyed that there is a row than sorry for the person engaged upon it. But, after all, you know you can count on me.'[16]

The Reverend Barlow visited Caroline at Frampton. The curate was 'very kind' and took a letter to read out to George in London. But before her meeting with Barlow, Caroline had heard of a new twist: Mr Norton had been persuaded by Lord Grantley that Lord Melbourne had been her lover. She managed to keep her composure with the clergyman, not mentioning the prime minister's name or making any reference to this latest development in her open letter to George, feeling it best 'to the last possible minute to <u>appear</u> ignorant of this new accusation'.

By 10 April 1836 Melbourne had become another of the many problems in the Norton marriage. His name was in the newspapers and would remain so for months to come; his efforts to keep Caroline married to George had failed and he was now embroiled. Melbourne's talent for staying aloof was no match for the determination of Lord Grantley and the Ultra Tories, who wanted to bring him and the Whig government down and were prepared to manipulate George Norton to bring this about. Melbourne confided that he had been concerned for some time about that 'folly and violence which might lead to any absurdity or any injustice'. There was an I-told-you-so quality to Melbourne's 10 April letter to Caroline. Reminding her that she knew his opinions on marriage so well it was unnecessary for him to repeat them, he then repeated them, and seemed to lay the blame for her difficulties at her door. 'I have always told you that a woman should never part from her husband whilst she can remain with him. This is generally the case; particularly so in a case such as yours, that is in the case of a young, handsome woman of lively imagination, fond of company and conversation, and whose celebrity and superiority has necessarily created many enemies. Depend upon it, if a reconciliation is feasible there can be no doubt of the prudence of it.'

Melbourne also put more distance between them, knowing that if his letter fell into the wrong hands, he had to be seen to be saying the right things and certainly not as an active agent in Caroline's marital troubles.[17] Meanwhile his as family, friends and political allies looked on in horror at the disaster that loomed, having feared it for the past five years.

Caroline was embarrassed and seemed to accept his rebuke in another letter to Melbourne: 'I recoil from this burning disgrace with an agony which is perhaps a triumph to those who inflict it, but I will yet hope it may not be – I will hope to the last.' She still seemed to think that through Barlow the scandal could still be averted. She clung to the belief that George was 'most unwilling himself to bring you forward' and told Melbourne, 'for the present suppose us to be on the point of reconciliation'. Resigned that she could not see Melbourne, she prayed that he would not be ill and that he would remember her kindly.[18]

In the last week of April Caroline went to live at Brinsley's Mayfair house. All her clothes and papers and possessions were under lock and key at her own home, from which she had been banished and where her eldest son Fletcher was staying with his father.[19] In a letter to Melbourne Caroline reported on the Reverend Barlow's two visits. George had refused to read her letter or allow the clergyman to read it out to him. Barlow told her that her husband had behaved like 'an ungovernable child'. He had 'foamed and stamped and rambled from one accusation to another so that it was impossible to make out what he wanted, or who he meant to attack'.

Barlow felt that Norton had not made any of the decisions which were driving the rumours, and was sure that her husband did not believe Caroline was guilty of adultery. George had told Barlow that he was 'unable to back out because of his lawyers'. Caroline's uncle Sir James Graham had also been to see George, who told him he intended marrying again and would keep the children. Barlow informed Norton that Caroline would resist a divorce 'by every means in her power', and that such action would only bring 'disgrace' on both of them. He told his irate parishioner that Caroline would 'rather starve as his wife' all her life than 'leave him free to give a step-mother to my children'.

Caroline's brother and uncle were consulting the best lawyers to see how best to proceed and how they could get a firmer grip on what Norton and his people were likely to do next. The pressure of being less than a mile from her son and the speed with which her troubles were escalating sent Caroline into a tailspin of exhaustion, and despite her brave fighting talk to Barlow had undermined any confidence she had for a battle with George. Caroline wrote to Melbourne that she felt utterly in Norton's power and was 'vexed and frightened' about her children. She dreaded them being looked after by the Grantleys, who were 'capable of any treatment towards them'. Worn out with crying and lack of sleep, 'my heart sinks and chills at seeing how little I am to <u>you</u>'. Knowing that making him feel guilty about what she was going through might annoy him, she tried to explain calmly how hurt she felt: 'I know you <u>don't</u> want to vex <u>me</u> but every circumstance of this affair . . . seems doubled for me.' She was facing up to the possibility of being a childless mother and disgraced wife because of her 'supposed power to charm strangers'. Caroline did not want to 'torment him', but her message to Melbourne was clear when she said that 'worse women had been better stood by'.[20]

Whatever plans Caroline and her family considered, the last thing Lord Melbourne wanted was for Norton to bring an action against him in pursuit of a divorce. For both their sakes, and especially his, the only advice he could give was that Caroline should resist the divorce and return to the marital home: 'If for the sake of your children, you think you can endure to return to him, you will certainly act most wisely and prudently for yourself in doing so.' Melbourne's reply to her outpouring of feelings was to offer the most trite advice it was possible to suggest, that she should keep cheerful and not get too upset.[21]

Caroline's response to his unhelpful advice was swift, bitter and desolate in tone. Now that she was in London, the words she wrote in Mayfair could have reached him at Downing Street before the wax on the seal was set. Despite Melbourne's previous assurance of support, he had been closing down the lines of communication between them: 'you need not fear my writing to you if you think it commits you. I struggle to think of all the fortuitous circumstances that make your position seem of more consequence than mine.' Lord Melbourne was doing what anyone in his position might have done, which was to withdraw until the brouhaha had died down, but that was painful to a woman who had no idea when or indeed whether she would see her children again. Caroline had the support of her wealthy brother Brinsley, Lord Seymour and uncle James Graham, or her position would have been doubly dire; now she may have lost another loved one, her dear Lord Melbourne. To his horror, she arrived unannounced at Downing Street. 'I will not deny that among all the bitterness of this hour, what sinks me most is the thought of you – of the expression of your eye the day I saw you at Downing Street – the shrinking from me and my burdensome and embarrassing distress. God forgive you! For I do believe no one, young or old, ever loved another better than

I have loved you . . . I look forward with satisfaction . . . to seeing you <u>defend</u> the action (if that cruel coward brings one) to the utmost of your power. I <u>trust</u> to your doing your best to clear yourself from the imputation of having loved me enough to be rash enough to commit yourself for me . . . I will do nothing foolish or indiscreet, depend on it, either way it is all a blank to me. I don't care much how it ends. I have always the knowledge that you will be afraid to see as much of me – perhaps afraid to see me <u>at all</u>. I have always the memory of how you <u>received me that day</u> and I have the conviction that I have no further power than he <u>allows</u> me over my boys. <u>You</u> and they were my interests in life. No <u>future</u> can ever wipe out the <u>past</u>, nor <u>renew</u> it.'

Caroline promised not to write to Melbourne again as he seemed to 'dread' it, and apologised for being a 'vexation' and 'embarrassment' to him. She ended her letter saying that she would 'willingly have devoted my life to add to the comfort of yours' and hoped he would think of her 'with something of the gnawing pain I now think of you'. Caroline warned him that Norton, led by his lawyers, refused to meet the lawyers Brinsley had appointed, and ended pointedly that their mutual friends the Lansdownes, Henry Petty-Fitzmaurice and his wife Lady Louisa, had been 'most kind' to her.[22]

In May Caroline left her brother's house in Mayfair to live with her mother at Hampton Court Palace. Trelawny told Caroline a bit of gossip she already knew: that George had a mistress, a 'Mrs Reed', but that he did not know her address. Apparently Fitzroy Campbell knew it but had left London; Caroline asked Trelawny to try and find out where she lived. She was astonished by George's 'insolence' and his 'inquisition' into her conduct when he had a mistress, and there had been others. At this time there was uncertainty about whether George would take legal proceedings against Melbourne, although

Caroline hoped that he would not as he knew how 'fatal it would be to himself as well as me'. She did not want to make any 'public recriminations about his mistress' unless she had to: 'No woman was <u>benefited</u> by any attempt <u>publicly</u> to right herself. It always goes against the <u>woman</u>'. Caroline wanted a legal separation by mutual consent from George and care of the children; she dared not go down the route of counter-accusation. She was hopeful that Norton would abandon 'the mad idea' of divorcing her, but knew that if he did not she would have to defend the action and reveal the truth of her marriage, and then 'open warfare' would break out. 'If once I prove in a court of justice all I <u>can</u> prove, of the man who vowed 'to love and protect me', we are for life open, bitter and irreconcilable enemies and of course he inflicts the only vengeance in his power, by keeping my children. I know as well as anyone else, that do what he will, Mr Norton <u>cannot</u> divorce me – even if he procure witnesses willing enough to perjure themselves . . . The proceedings in a Court of Justice <u>must</u> ruin a woman's reputation and my great object is to avert that and to delay till the last moment open warfare.'

Caroline was being advised by 'the best legal advice it is possible to procure' thanks to the generosity of Brinsley. George too had powerful legal advisers who were studying the situation forensically. Norton's legal team had no more legitimate moves to make at this stage, but knowing 'her impatience and suffering' hoped that Caroline would play into their hands by seeking the protection of one of her lovers. However, Caroline wisely decided to 'wait among my own people, and under my brother's guidance and protection' resist the divorce. Her children's future was 'dearer to me than my <u>own</u> and I will suffer more than Mr Norton thinks I can before I leave him free to give <u>them a stepmother</u> and to inflict on them all the capricious violence and mean tyranny which has been my mean penance for the tenure of what is called "my position in society"'.

Caroline was prepared to lose her status as a wife to be able to breathe 'freely' in her own house, and if she got the children she would be 'infinitely happier'. Trelawny, in typical Wolf style, suggested she steal her boys and he offered to help in the risky venture. She told him she would wait and keep the 'wild and desperate plans which haunt me as I sit alone . . . locked in my heart and brain' until other avenues were exhausted. Caroline had regretted not having a daughter but was now glad that she had been denied that wish, remembering the prayer of a Red Indian woman in a William Cowper novel: 'Let not my child be a girl for very sad is the lot of women.'[23]

Caroline's relations with Lord Melbourne stabilised; it was in their mutual interest to keep lines of communication open and exchange intelligence as it was gathered. On 6 May Caroline wrote him a note to say that Norton was still uncertain how best to proceed and who to cite in any action he might take. She had learned from uncle Charles Sheridan that Norton had sent for a former servant, and interrogated him about her 'acquaintances' and had come up with the preposterous notion that when she was a young girl she had behaved incorrectly with Prince Leopold of Belgium. This news, though galling, she felt was a sign that they were at a standstill; she thought the Norton family's 'investigations' were over.[24]

On 11 May Caroline heard from Melbourne that he was ill, and Lord Seymour also noted how much he was 'suffering'. On the same day the diarist Charles Greville wrote of the 'great talk' about 'Melbourne's affair with Mrs Norton which if it be not quashed by a handsome *douceur* to Norton will be inconvenient'.[25] Melbourne had difficulties of his own at home. His son Augustus, who was the same age as Mrs Norton, was still affected by epilepsy and lived much of the time in

South Street. Augustus' difficulties meant that if he outlived his father he would be unable to inherit the title, which would pass to either Melbourne's brother Fred or a nephew. Melbourne's younger sister Lady Cowper was canvassing against Caroline. The wife of Earl Cowper, she was a powerful opponent, a formidable Whig hostess. She had married the dull and complacent Cowper in 1805, and as soon as her first child, a son, was born, became the mistress (and eventual wife) of the politician Henry John Temple, third Viscount Palmerston. The first of the four children she had with Palmerston was born in 1808, the year Caroline was born. Her marriage to Cowper remained intact until he obliged his wife and lover by dying in 1837.[26]

Lady Cowper was a notorious meddler in her brothers' affairs, especially Lord Melbourne's, and had further complicated his troubled marriage with Lady Caroline Lamb. Augustus' epilepsy meant that it was not in Lady Cowper's interest for Melbourne to remarry and have any more sons; she wanted their younger brother Frederick or her own son to inherit the title. When Caroline heard of Emily's 'worldy brazen-ness', sending Palmerston to discuss Melbourne's difficulties with the Sheridan family, she was incensed and asked Edward Ellice to visit her at Hampton Court Palace. 'I shall go mad if something is not done. Pray come to me. It comforts me even if there is no more to be done. I never will believe Melbourne capable of baseness – his whole life disproves it . . . I know he is timid, vacillating, what they will, but not ungenerous . . . Bring word how he is.'[27]

It was common knowledge that Caroline's husband was playing a dangerous game of politics masquerading as hurt feelings. From the middle of May 1836 newspapers like *The Satirist* and *The Age* started slyly to feature schoolboyish ditties, the tiniest bombshells, and drip-feed readers with the latest 'news'.

The Tories were 'so eager for power' that they had 'induced Norton – he is a fool – "as gross as ignorance made drunk" to put himself in their hands'. Edward Trelawny gossiped to a friend that they spread malicious reports incriminating Lord Melbourne and Mrs Norton 'politically as well as in the other way.'[28]

In the third week of May 1836 it was confirmed that George Norton was suing Lord Melbourne for criminal conversation with his wife. For over a year the colourful publisher of *The Satirist*, Barnard Gregory, had been seeking information about Lord Melbourne's friendship with the Nortons. Since launching his newspaper in 1831 Gregory had had several encounters with the libel laws, being convicted in 1832 and 1833 and fined hundreds of pounds and costs, only narrowly avoiding prison, which came later.[29]

In yards of newspaper columns, and cartoons which went on sale in print sellers' and stationers' shops, the Nortons and Lord Melbourne were getting unwelcome attention from all over the country. The stupid-looking horned goat and the man who could not get his hat on because of his horns – the sign of being cuckolded – were easily identified as George Norton. Melbourne's family surname of Lamb was a gift for the cartoonists: he became Lambkin beseeching the rapt attention of the pretty shepherdess Mrs Norton.[30]

On 29 May 1836 *The Satirist* remarked that George Norton had known for a long time of 'the intimacy subsisting between his Lady and Lord Melbourne'. Smugly, the newspaper congratulated itself for having 'in a friendly way apprised him of it'. The anonymous reporter suggested that now Norton had roused himself to take the situation in hand he might consider suing the Duke of Devonshire, who had commissioned the colourful half-portrait of Caroline by George Hayter in 1832 which still hangs at Chatsworth House in Derbyshire, as well as Edward Trelawny and Thomas Slingsby Duncombe, a Whig politician held to be the best-dressed Member of Parliament and a compulsive gambler and ladies' man. There were one or two others 'whose attentions have in turn assumed a very questionable shape and who are all eyeing the reputation of being equally culpable with the noble offender'. Citing these names Gregory was again sailing close to libel, but nobody took any action.[31] Now the rumours were out in the world, in black and white, Caroline's reputation as a coquette was burgeoning, and any hope of her being seen as a loving mother was fading by the day.

By the last weekend in May the tone of reporting in the satirical press was harsher about Caroline, whom *The Satirist* called 'the unblushing one'. The paper puffed the claim for damages to twenty thousand pounds (it was half that) and declared, 'we have heard that <u>one farthing</u> would be about a reasonable sum of damages' as compensation for Melbourne taking 'possession' and having 'peaceable enjoyment for having <u>loan</u> of the offending lady'. A verse entitled 'Conservative Trick' alerted readers to who was behind all the fuss – Barnard's favourite foes: 'The Tories, base corrupted slaves, / On Norton fix – a specious drift – / To oust Lord Melbourne, what, the knaves, / Take this advantage of a shift.'

Apparently Caroline had been spotted with a new 'liaison' at the flower show at Surrey Zoological Gardens at Kennington earlier in the week – Sir Francis 'Goose' Goodricke, a Conservative Member of Parliament – who was seen to 'play the monkey to her'. The article sketched a ludicrous scene in which Caroline is portrayed as a hussy, quoting the poem she is supposed to have composed in the hearing of *The Satirist* reporter, who is presumably lurking among the blooms: 'How like this flow'r, so lonely in the sun / Which closes all its charms, when day is done, / Art thou fair Norton! Graceful, slender, sweet! / In thy full bloom all woman's beauties meet. / Poor simple man! to think I'm like the flow'r / Expanding all its charms at such an hour! / T'is known to all – a few have had a sight – / My charms I love to show best at midnight.'

The Satirist ended its smear against Caroline with the outrageous suggestion that she was conniving with her husband to extort damages from Lord Melbourne, blackening her character further. 'Mrs Norton we all know is most accomplished in the art of design of which the match got up between her brother and Miss Grant furnishes indisputable evidence but bad as she may be, it is to be hoped, for the honour of her sex, that her conduct stands clear of impeachment in this instance and that she has no participation whatever in the project of extortion.'[32]

During the three weeks leading up to the trial, now set for Wednesday 22 June, Caroline stayed at her brother's house in Grosvenor Square or at Hill's Hotel in Spring Gardens, as advised by her lawyers. Knowing that Melbourne was annoyed and Lady Cowper was lobbying madly against her, it was an unpleasant interlude. Caroline picked up her pen and worked when she was able, as well as dealing with her vast correspondence concerning the case. Though she was at the heart of the affair, as a married woman she was prohibited from appearing in court in her own defence. To be able to give the jury and the public a better impression of herself was denied her. Her Sheridan ability to perform and her talent for eloquence would have served her well, but this was a stage Caroline could not appear on.

While many of her acquaintances, and even friends, would have cut her if she had ventured out into polite society, she did not lose all support. Kind words from Augusta Cowell and her mother moved Caroline and she asked her co-writer to think well of her when she heard gossip: 'I do not ask you to speak for me aloud but to say to yourself "let me think that some of these tales must be false, for I know that others are!"' Caroline also revealed to Cowell that 'her heart was fairly broken'; she wished she had died in 1829 when she had been recovering from the birth of her eldest child, that she might be lying 'moulding to dust in the churchyard, lying close to the cheerful widows' at Long Ditton.[33] The sad note sent Miss Cowell scurrying round to Grosvenor Square to see her.

On 9 June, the solicitor managing Melbourne's defence called on Caroline at her brother's house and asked her impertinent and intrusive questions to which she took great exception. She dashed off a letter to Melbourne. He had anticipated the hurt it would cause and been reluctant to sanction it, but thought that it would be 'for the best'. Years of experience had left him with a low opinion of lawyers, who all seemed to Melbourne to have the same manner: 'hard, cold, incredulous, distrustful, sarcastic, sneering'. In answer to Caroline's suggestion that he was 'unfeeling' Melbourne revealed the depth of his feelings since hearing that Norton was proceeding against him. Suffering 'more intensely than I ever did in my life', he had not eaten or slept. He assured her he was not worried about his own character 'because as you say the imputation against me is as nothing'. Unflustered about his position as prime minister and the political impact of what might happen, he was concerned about what the consequences of his 'indiscretion may bring upon' those who were dependent on him for their careers. Melbourne maintained that his real concern was for Caroline: 'The real and principal object of my anxiety and solicitude is you, and the situation in which you have been so unjustly placed by the circumstances which have taken place.'[34]

On 12 June, with the trial less than two weeks away, *The Satirist*'s coverage was scurrilous. An article titled 'The Nun

Norton' linked her present plight with her rackety father and grandfather and asserted that the 'whole family of Sheridans had a disposition opposite to prudery'. The author of the piece had no sympathy for 'poor' George Norton, who had been sent so many 'curious communications on the subject' saying he had surely known his wife-to-be was on 'the free and easy list'. Feigning sympathy for the hapless husband, a poem called 'The End of Life', sniggered that Norton's marriage could be the end of him: 'Tom Duncombe joked on Norton's state / Thus bound by matrimonial fate. / In union so divine. / "Wedlock's the end of life," he cried. / "It is indeed," poor Norton cried, / "Twill be the end of mine."'[35]

Leading up to the trial, Caroline was quietly confident of the outcome, boosted by her lawyers' opinion that George would lose. There was always the matter of how Norton would react to a defeat, but for her there was a more pressing concern: her relationship with Melbourne. She found him cold and distant, and apprehensive of what she might or might not do.

Caroline spent the three days before the trial at Hill's Hotel writing letters to Miss Cowell, Trelawny, but mostly Melbourne. On Tuesday afternoon (21 June, the day before the trial) she returned to her mother at Hampton Court Palace. There were new salacious stories about her paying calls on men in other houses. The waves of slander were irritating, but the only opinion she cared about was that of her children. A not guilty verdict for Melbourne would mean a not guilty verdict for her too, vital if her sons were not to 'grow up believing in their mother's shame'. Because of the 'harsh and unjust' position she was in, Caroline could only refute salacious gossip in notes and letters to her lawyers and because she was not one of the parties cited in the action – even though her reputation was being destroyed by it – her lawyers were not allowed to produce any evidence in her defence. There was one consolation: everyone was sure the trial would last no longer than a day. She asked Augusta Cowell to 'remember me that day when you pray I solemnly assure you I am innocent'.[36]

On 19 June had Caroline defied Melbourne's wish that she make no attempt to see him, and turned up at his residence at South Street. An awkward scene ensued. Caroline veered between breezy confidence about the trial verdict and fear of what might happen and the consequences. At her hotel she would 'fret and fidget' most of her waking hours and try to write her way out of trouble. We do not know what happened when she was shown into Melbourne's drawing room, but two letters she sent him the next day describe a painful visit and being asked to leave. 'I am sure when you reflect on all my conduct to you, you <u>cannot</u> think otherwise than that I have been most willing to consider <u>myself</u> <u>last</u> and you <u>first</u> – you <u>cannot</u> <u>look</u> back upon our intimacy and say that you have any reproach to make me. For *this* reason you should be willing to bear with me now – you should try and repress any impatience you feel at being mixed up in my affairs . . . I especially told my uncle and friends who were settling the matter for me, that the moment <u>your</u> name was brought forward (if it should so happen) they should give up <u>everything</u> and take what terms Norton pleased rather than vex <u>you</u>.'

Caroline was distressed to think he may have believed stories about the other men who were supposed to have been in her life, and was anxious to put his mind at rest. 'You <u>might</u> also consider that the <u>only</u> <u>reason</u> why your name has at length been resorted to, is because (tho' lawyers enemies have worked incessantly for three weeks) they find it <u>impossible</u> to prove familiarity of manner with <u>any</u> <u>other</u> <u>men</u>. If you knew all the struggle it was to go to you at all – all the pain it was to say it to you – all the <u>hopelessness</u> with which I set out – your manner would have been kinder than it was'.

She had called at her own house on the way back to Hill's Hotel and learned something materially useful from the servants – the name of an ex-employee (John Fluke) who was going to be called as a witness, whom Caroline knew could be proved to be 'utterly unworthy of credit'. She passed this on to Melbourne for his lawyers. As upsetting as her ejection from his house had been, Caroline was not done with her feelings for Melbourne; they were too deep for that. Hoping he would still write to her, she asked him to imagine her life being finished at twenty-eight: 'let the thought give you that patience with me which fancy and passion cannot – and be kind to me – since you are not intending that I should be a sufferer does not prevent my suffering'.[37]

On Monday 20 June, two days before the trial, she wrote to Melbourne filled with regret that their relationship was at an end. It is the first of many letters from an abandoned lover. The chain of letters she now wrote to him, starting with this one, makes a nonsense of the denials she and Melbourne made about the nature of their friendship and her protestation of innocence to Augusta Cowell just two days before. 'If <u>every friend I have, knelt to me to persuade me to a different line</u> – I would do whatever you asked or bid me to do. I merely repeat my strong impression that you have ceased to feel the affection for me which you did. I will do anything on earth that <u>voluntary exertion </u>or sacrifice can enable me to do, and that <u>instantly and without demur</u> – it does not depend on voluntary exertion how one <u>feels</u>. I wish it did, for my sake, not for yours!'

Raking over his love life, she felt that she was being as badly treated as her predecessors and berated herself for having a woman's vanity, 'which always leads them to think their own an individual and peculiar case, and that they are to be treated better than their neighbours'. Caroline felt misled into a 'painful struggle of hope and fear, instead of quietly taking my place in <u>the</u> <u>past</u> with your wife, Mrs Lamb and Lady Branden'.[38]

The day before the trial Caroline's uncle Sir James Graham was perturbed that he had 'not heard a syllable' from Lord Melbourne, as promised. He asked Caroline to write to him to break the silence, as Melbourne was unwilling 'to force himself <u>uninvited</u> upon you although it is now the day before the trial'. The 'universal opinion' was that Melbourne would succeed, and one of Norton's lawyers 'let out as much to the clerk who repeated it to my lawyer'. In the letter which Caroline sent to Melbourne the morning of the trial she revealed the extra-ordinary plan that he had suggested that if Norton lost the case. Melbourne 'could arrange to "come to terms" . . . I forget the exact expression . . . that he [Norton] should "take me back" '. This is a shocking revelation about the power of patriarchy and the powerlessness of women in nineteenth-century Britain: after every ugly twist and nasty turn she had been through – at Norton's instigation – Melbourne had the arrogance to assume that he could glue them back together again as if they were broken ornaments, and that she and her estranged husband would go along with his scheme.

Caroline dropped a bomb, rejecting Melbourne's scheme in favour of one of her own. She told him that she intended divorcing Norton and had already taken the best legal advice that Norton's birthplace, Edinburgh, could offer, and would do so in Scotland.[39] If Norton lost the case, she planned to start proceedings, and all the papers were 'ready for the purpose'. Caroline now took control of her life, reminding Melbourne that even if he did approach Norton via his attorneys with his scheme, 'it will not bind me to him in any way to come to terms with him'. Her message was clear: if Norton loses, keep out of my marital business. Caroline admonished Melbourne with confidence and an overdue recovery of her spirit and poise: 'I thought I had better tell you this as you generally <u>act first</u>, and <u>then</u> let me know what has been done'. The female servant who delivered this letter and paperwork was told to wait for Melbourne's reply as to what Caroline should tell Sir James Graham, or a reply could be sent by messenger to arrive before she left her hotel at three o'clock that afternoon to go to Hampton Court Palace. She ended the letter with a chilly 'I hope you are quite well now.'[40]

A few hours later Caroline's mood had changed. She wrote a love letter to Melbourne that was calmer, and took some blame for her failed marriage. Accepting that her connection with Melbourne was over, she did not want to 'reproach' him or give him 'pain', but expressed her disappointment at him having 'shrunk' from her as she would 'not have been any burden or trouble to you . . . under any circumstances'. In a spasm of self-reproach, she wrote, 'the fault is in <u>me</u> – I do not <u>attach</u> people'. Caroline had been a good wife to her husband – 'I was of great service and great comfort to him' – and she praised herself for nursing him when he was ill: 'I nursed him devotedly at a time when many young married women could have shown great displeasure and resentment.' However, George Norton's violence towards her showed that there was a serious disparity in their feelings for each other: 'no man ever admired me <u>more</u> or loved me <u>less</u> . . . he thought me beautiful and full of talent but I did not <u>attach</u> him'.

The letter then broke into a declaration of love. Her husband was incapable of feeling kindness towards her, the kind of love she might have earned from Melbourne, 'but you! I was no service or comfort to you because I have never been in a position to render either – but my life has been divided . . . into the days I saw you and the days I did not – nothing else seemed of importance but you; your opinions, even your fancies (for you have had them) have been laws to me'. Caroline remembered meeting Melbourne when she was only twenty-two and how she was flattered by his interest in her. Urbane, handsome, he was an older man with a plentiful supply of the aphrodisiac of power: 'when you first visited me, I thought merrily and carelessly about you'. Melbourne had been everything her husband was not. The only virtue Caroline now felt in leaving for Hampton Court was that she was rid of the 'restless feeling' of 'being so near you and may not see you'.[41]

Caroline also wrote to Trelawny before she left, asking him to 'guard me like a true friend'. He was said to be one of her lovers and some suggested there was a flakiness about him which made his help unsettling. 'They may say what they will, I know you will do your best. There is a want of generosity in all that has been done by me which makes me sick. I may have been foolish – I may have been romanced too much for their cold and clipped winged society, but believe me no attempt they can ever make will prove me to have been vicious.'[42]

Caroline wrote to Miss Cowell the same day. She hoped that once the trial was over her friends 'need not be ashamed of assisting and supporting me' and that she would not ask her for help 'if I was a guilty woman'. Having lost 'all for a shadow', it was a 'deep and heavy vexation' to Caroline to see the high price that some had to pay for knowing her. Her 'poor little friend' Sophia Armstrong had become entangled in the wreckage of the Norton marriage. Such a situation could damage a young lady's reputation and perhaps marriageability. Colonel Armstrong, an Irish-born army officer, tried to stop his daughter being subpoenaed as a witness at the trial but failed.[43]

Throughout the day of the trial Caroline received messages about what was being said about her at Westminster Hall, men arriving on horseback with news. She wrote with a shaky hand to Brinsley about how one of the lawyers, Mr Jennings, had been 'delicate and earnest throughout' and had shown 'all the feeling and attention I could have expected if he had been an old friend'. But having to hear the 'coarseness of the details' of some of the evidence drove her 'quite wild'. Wishing to 'seem in as good spirits as I could to the poor worn mother', Caroline and Mrs Sheridan went for a carriage ride in Richmond Park as the nerve-racking day dragged on. Caroline was irked by Melbourne's irritation with her and bitter about Norton 'trying to grind me all he could by the filthiness of the evidence'. A not guilty verdict was what everyone, with the exception of Lord Grantley and George Norton, confidently predicted, but Caroline was concerned what effect the lurid details presented as evidence might have on her sons, and she desperately hoped that 'years of prudence may make this great and burning disgrace pass away'.[44]

Judge Charles Kendal Bushe, solicitor general of Ireland from 1805 to 1822, in 1836 lord chief justice of the King's Bench, was strolling through Westminster on the night of the trial, and found himself in Storey's Gate in front of the Nortons' house. He was standing there thinking about 'the dramatic events of the day' when he felt a hand on his shoulder. To his surprise the hand belonged to Lord Melbourne, who gave him a 'rogueish look and said "What does this mean, Mr Solicitor?"'[45] Melbourne was taking his usual route home from Downing Street across St James's Park.

Melbourne's victory was the strongest acquittal of Caroline that the law could deliver. The defence had been presented in a 'gentlemanly tone', and in such cases the lady's character was determined more by 'the mode of defence than the charge brought'. Caroline's brother and Lord Seymour were satisfied with the strategy adopted by Melbourne's team. Norton's people had done everything they could to 'harass, sting and humiliate' her; Seymour felt they had been 'most vindictive and unmanly', as many of the lurid details they gave in court were unnecessary to their case. But Lord Grantley's presence in court to 'encourage his witnesses had worked against their cause'; the jury and public had not liked his behaviour or general manner.

Charles Dickens wrote to his friend the publisher John Macrone on Thursday evening about their proposed visit to Bedlam Asylum, remarking, 'Norton v. Melbourne has played the devil with me.'[46] The trial, which had titillated the public's imagination for months, was over so suddenly that it left everyone hungry for more. A sixpenny souvenir of the 'Extraordinary Trial!, with a portrait and memoir of the Honourable Mrs Norton' was published within twenty-four hours of the verdict.

At Hampton Court Palace the reality of the verdict was sinking in, and Caroline sent a series of thank-you letters. To Miss Cowell and her mama she was grateful: 'I shall never forget any kindness that has been shown to me at this fearful time.'[47] When she wrote to the worldly Mary Shelley, a woman who knew about the vicissitudes of life and the scorch of the public's disapproval, she was blunt: 'it is impossible not to feel bitterly the disgusting details of that unhappy trial . . . a woman is made a helpless wretch by these laws of men, or she would be allowed a *defence*, a counsel, in such an hour'. To count for nothing 'in a trial which decided one's fate for life, is hard'. Three days after the trial Caroline had no idea if she would be allowed to see her children, whom she had not set eyes on for three months.[48]

Seymour, who had been in court to hear the cheers when the verdict was announced, could see how Caroline was 'overcome and hurt by all the horrors which were deposed against her' but was confident she would bounce back once the newspapers lost interest in the 'horrible details' of the story. Seymour, Sir James Graham and the lawyers decided they would not pursue 'the brute' Norton on her behalf for separate maintenance as he was 'ruined' and could not pay.

Lord Melbourne should have been pleased with the outcome and grateful for the warm cross-party and royal support, but instead took to his bed in a fit of depression. It seemed that Whig and Tory rakes alike heaved a collective sigh that one of their own had won such a potentially disastrous action. One of Melbourne's chief political opponents, the Duke of Wellington, congratulated him on escaping 'the low and foul conspiracy'. William IV, who had plenty of dirty laundry of his own and ten illegitimate children with the actress Mrs Jordan, was delighted with Melbourne's victory, believing that if his prime minister had been found unfit for office, then he himself would 'not be fit to be king'.[49]

The Times editorial on the verdict laid the blame on Lord Melbourne, and as a Tory newspaper, scorned the view of many other newspapers that he had been the victim of politics rather than his own vanity. In order to mount a further attack on Melbourne *The Times* sprang to the defence of 'the lady', writing that she had been put in an impossible situation by her husband and the man whose favour he sought. 'If he demanded as the price of it that Mrs Norton, a beautiful and clever woman of twenty-seven years of age, should be subjected for whole hours of every day to the twaddling gossip of a vain man of fifty-eight, it would, we think, have been difficult to have resisted the payments so exacted for his Lordship's service to her husband.'

The editorial maintained that a man of Melbourne's age and experience, holding the most important office of state, should have known better than to have exposed Caroline to the possibility of scandal by 'eccentric visits'. Melbourne might have behaved better towards the daughter of an old friend of his, and not encouraged her to 'disregard the usages of society to neglect the duties of a wife and mother for such conversation as an elderly idle statesman could afford'. This was at odds with the truth, as Caroline had enjoyed their affair for five years and was bereft now that it was ending.[50]

The Tory attempts to bring down Melbourne and the Whig government had fallen flat on its face, and the personification of that failure was George Norton. A poem called 'The Sad Disaster' in the *Satirist* chuckled at his failure to prove what was widely felt to be true, that the defendant had got away with it:

> We've lately had some precious sport on,
> About the simple noodle, NORTON;
> But sadly did poor NORTON'S luck hold,
> He could not prove himself a cuckold.
> We fancy now we hear him chatter,
> And swear it is a grievous matter.
> But noodle NORTON, can you tell us,
> You know we are inquiring fellows,
> What is the use of all this pother,
> To fix the charge on one or t'other?
> To take such pains is really grieving,
> To prove what all the world's believing.[51]

Both the *Satirist* and the *Age* went to town about Norton's evidence, which had been given by 'discarded and characterless servants', two 'strumpets' and a drunken coachman. The fact that Norton had not resigned his position as a magistrate was held to be further proof of the contemptible character of the man. (He kept this position for thirty-six years until he retired in 1867.)

On 26 June 1836 Caroline wrote to her husband about seeing the children. She told him she wanted to send their eldest, Fletcher, to Mr Walton's school at Hampton, where her brothers Frank and Charlie had gone, and then share 'such portion of the holidays as suits you'. Brinsley and William, who were five and three, should live with her. The youngest was too young to be without her, and she wanted to teach Brinsley herself because of his speech impediment. Her greatest concern was her 'wish to know how to shape my future plans as regards the children. You cannot doubt but that any wish or regulation of yours respecting them will be faithfully attended to, and that they will be sent to you <u>when</u> and <u>where</u> you please. I merely wish to have these first years of their lives at my disposal, seeing that much of their future well-being, whether as regards the exercise of their talents or the guidance of their dispositions, <u>must</u> depend on a mother's care and instruction of their infancy.'

Caroline was negotiating from a false belief in the strength of her rights as a mother and her own legal position. Her remarks would have gone down badly with the Nortons. She boldly asserted her rights as a mother and demanded the right to fulfil them. She had taken 'great pains' with their eldest son, who was very intelligent and 'well instructed for his age' and asked that George would not deprive her of 'the POWER of fulfilling one of the great duties of my life and the affection of those little beings, to whom the agony of their birth, and the anxiety for their future, makes every mother think her claim so strong'. She assured him that despite everything the boys would never hear from her 'anything that may interfere with the respect or affection which a father claims from his children'. While they were with her she would not forget that 'it is of <u>your</u> children that I have the charge'. It might have taken a degree of calm she did not feel to tell Norton that 'your relations and connexions are also theirs, and they are inseparably bound to those who bear your name in common with themselves'. The only obstacle, she pointed out, to her fulfilling her responsibilities, was them <u>being forcibly withheld from me</u>'.[52]

Caroline was naive to think that George would agree to her wishes concerning the children. Although he had lost the case he had their sons. Less than a week after the trial Norton's lawyers were playing with her by sending a letter to kindly Charles Jennings saying that her wardrobe of clothes had been sold. It was a hoax: they had not, although they did sell them later. Caroline wrote to Brinsley, 'my hand shakes so . . . my mind misgives me they will make another struggle to destroy me'. There was also news that Miss Vaughan had been saying defamatory things about her to the Cowells. The Nortons were determined to undermine all of Caroline's friendships, in this case her professional partnership with the musician.[53]

A letter was printed in *The Times* from Sir William Follett's lawyers denying he had any involvement with events leading up to the trial. His name had been mentioned in the post-mortem but he 'refused to take any responsibility on any account of a cause with which I had no concern'. Although not a blood relation of the Nortons, he was an executor of their late father's will, a trustee of his property and a guardian to George and his brothers and sisters. George Norton had told Sir James Graham in April that he had consulted Sir William, the solicitor general, who had 'seen all the evidence and who advised him to proceed with the action'.[54]

In the light of Follett's denial of any pre-trial role, Lord Seymour realised that this last remark was another of 'the wretch Norton's bold falsehoods'. Brinsley and Seymour were optimistic about public reaction to the verdict but there was still work to do. The next step was to 'invalidate all the evidence of misconduct' in order to restore Caroline's reputation, and they were considering bringing a case against Eliza Gibson for perjury, who had accused her mistress of 'acts of misconduct' in 1833 at a time when she had just given birth to her third child and was ill in bed. Follett's letter prompted Caroline's family to consider what Norton might do next. They learned that if he tried to divorce her in the Ecclesiastical Court he would have to pay the expenses upfront and Caroline's legal fees as well;

Sir James Graham estimated it would cost Norton at least eighteen hundred pounds, so they doubted he would. Seymour was happy with the continuing newspaper reporting of the case, which seemed to be going Caroline's way: 'none can speak of Norton except with contempt'.[55]

A week after the trial there was a new print of Caroline Norton on sale, engraved from a portrait, now lost, by the artist and architect Edmund Thomas Parris, who had a reputation for portraying the beauties of the day.[56] A new edition of her book *The Coquette* was available in the first week of July. At the end of the month Caroline left her mother to live in London with her uncle, the bachelor and lover of all things Greek, Charles Brinsley Sheridan, who had taken a lease on 16 Green Street, a few steps from Hyde Park. Socially it would have been impossible for a woman in Caroline's situation to live on her own. The only women to live alone were courtesans. There was much toing and froing with her lawyers as they wrestled with Norton over her seeing the children and his resolute refusal to pay for items a husband was obliged to provide. There were the enquiries about the possibility of a 'Scotch divorce'.

Caroline was preoccupied with her feelings about the loss of Lord Melbourne. She was unable to write to him for some days after the trial 'because I was ill and weary and it brings a choking sense in my throat and a pain to my heart every time I sit down to address you'. Caroline vowed 'never to feel the same for anyone else'. She would not be 'the sufferer again for any love or trust I am likely to bestow on any human being'. Melbourne was relieved to read that her legal team had abandoned the plan to prosecute Eliza Gibson for perjury. Caroline would have had to give evidence but was in no mood to step into the witness box and 'gratify the spite of Lord Grantley'. Melbourne did not want his role in Caroline's life reprised in the newspapers.

Caroline loathed the loss of the small degree of independence she had enjoyed as the wife of George Norton. Brinsley was 'very anxious' to help her in every way and had rescued her from what would have been a terrible emotional and financial mess, but she recognised that 'throwing the burden of my distress on him and Uncle [Graham] I have lost my free agency in some measure'. In a letter to Melbourne in the middle of a paragraph about other news Caroline blurted out her pain at him keeping her at arm's length, his cold scolding letters to her and how she is 'very low and unhappy'. Caroline had no news of her sons, and her spy at Storey's Gate, the footman John Fitness, had left. For a Scotch divorce her lawyers would have to prove George Norton's adultery to get a result in twelve months, or wait four years to get a divorce on the grounds of her desertion.[57]

Caroline now heard from her sister-in-law, the widowed Maria Campbell Norton, that on 28 June George's sixty-year-old mother and his gaggle of sisters, including the awful Augusta, had left Edinburgh and travelled south. Caroline was sure they were on their way to London 'to take away my poor boys back to Scotland'. What she had previously failed to take account of was that George might seek revenge for his defeat and humiliation by depriving her of what she wanted the most.[58]

Caroline received a letter from Lord Melbourne which angered her by taking a 'majestic tone' because he was 'now safe from all risk and sitting in triumph' in his house in South Street. He had taken exception to Caroline writing that she could have published his letters to her, taking it as a threat that she would do so. Smarting she went on the attack: 'You are the cause of this blight upon my life – the cause of this public ribaldry and exposure in every way – the cause of all the filth and insult. I say considering all this, there is hardly a man in earth who would not have written a kind word when the trial was over and asked how I was . . . I hope I shall not live time enough.

I have spit blood twice, for two or three days at a time this last fortnight, and I am so weak I can scarcely stand.'

A bright red bloodstain on a handkerchief, towel or pillow-case was a sign of consumption. Caroline lived another forty years and had recurrences of the symptom but did not die of tuberculosis. She may have had a mild episode of tuberculosis which went into remission, or bronchiectasis, another lung disorder.[59] Caroline's father had had a strong constitution and was himself cited in a criminal conversation case, then wasted away and died of tuberculosis ten years later. Caroline wrote, 'I shall go too and relieve you of your fears of committing yourself to a correspondence with me.' She continued her most impassioned letter, 'In what capacity do you wish to be consulted – as a friend? Have you written as a friend? Have you shown a friend's feeling? Have you shown a friend's indulgence? Have you shown a friend's sympathy? . . . What have I ever done to you that you should grind me too? Have you always so preserved the inequality of age and understanding between us, that you should talk to me like God delivering the tablets of law to Moses? Can you give me back my children? Can you make all that shame pass away which has been the penalty for the amusement of your idle hours? Can you undo the curse that is on me?'

Caroline promised not to show Melbourne's letters to anyone for them to judge him by or to see on 'how much or how little of your temporary regard I cast my youth's hopes away'. Despite the public denials, it is clear that she saw herself as an abandoned lover: 'others (perhaps as unhappy) have preceded me – others as unhappy may succeed me – but no one either in the past or the future will have loved you more earnestly, more completely and may I say more steadily than the woman whose threat of passion you pretend to fear and who has been made to appear a painted prostitute in a Public Court before a jury of Englishmen. Pray do not write harshly, pray do not! I had rather be forgotten, I have not deserved it, and it kills me.'[60]

Because George Norton left no papers all the inside details of their unhappy marriage are from Caroline's point of view. There are few traces of George in their joint papers, and he always gives the worst account of himself; there are no extant paintings of him, but many portraits in words as an unattractive and aggressive man. His work as a magistrate is mentioned in *The Times* in their weekly reports of the cases he heard in Whitechapel. Sometimes he comes across in a kindly light, capable of making humane decisions, at other times not. Some of the human dramas involved in cases he heard during the last six months of 1836 bore some resemblance to his own difficulties.

On 11 July 1836 Magistrate Norton heard the story of Sarah, 'a decent-looking' woman married to a blind man. She told Mr Norton that they had 'a most uncomfortable life in consequence of his jealousy of her'. Sarah came to see Norton proposing to swear a 'solemn oath that she was faithful to him', but her husband rejected her offer saying he had grounds to be jealous. Their new lodger, a young man called Tom, had told the husband that he could have his wife 'whenever he liked', and Sarah had agreed with him. The blind man asked George if that was 'not enough to excite suspicion', but his wife said that she had been joking. George Norton refused to administer the oath, remarked that the wife's conduct was 'highly censurable' and told the couple they had to resolve their differences the best way they could. They left the room, 'the wife leading the husband'.[61]

Caroline Norton wrote to Lord Melbourne again on 13 July. She could not cut the thread that was stretching and fraying between them. Their letters were addressed in the care of loyal friends. The last time she had seen him was when Caroline called on him unannounced and he had asked her to leave. She acknowledged how they had grown apart and took some of the blame: 'The difference between us is that you never wrote a kind sentence and I wrote too many unkind ones and often the reflection of the thoughts of others than of my own.' Although Melbourne had told her that they could not see each other again, Caroline coaxed, 'you might write more at length but I don't press it'. By the end of her letter her mood had plummeted and she gave in to despair: 'from my soul I most earnestly wish I was in my grave . . . the purpose and spirit of my life is gone and I can do nothing'.[62]

On 15 July Caroline received a letter written by Norton's solicitor about seeing her sons. It was combative rather than helpful, telling her she could see the children to satisfy herself they were being well cared for, but that her husband would have no truck with her ignoring his rights in law: they were his children and his alone. Norton would bring the eldest two to London from Wonersh in a week's time, and she could see them at his solicitor's chambers. George was pompously implacable about his status as a father: 'whether access or not, and the quantum of it, shall be entirely within my own breast in all future time to determine. This is a most sacred trust, which a sense of duty forbids me to divest myself of.'[63]

The children were her hostages to fortune. Five days after she received his offer, after consultation with her family and their attorneys, she rejected the offer 'however bitter it may be'. She refused to see them in the office of the legal team who had collected the evidence, examined the witnesses and conducted proceedings at the trial, which if Melbourne had been found guilty would have been the first stage in her being divorced. As she had been found innocent of adultery, she asked why her children were being withheld from her, when even the hostile witnesses had said what a 'careful and devoted mother' she was. Caroline accepted the fact that Norton had the law on his side but pointed out that it worked only as far as she would agree to accept it, and she refused to see the children in conditions which she felt would always associate her in their minds with 'secrecy and shame . . . I would submit never again to behold them till they were of an age to visit me without asking permission of another human being.'

Even though George was liable for her debts, desperate to see her boys, Caroline had offered to make a contribution towards paying them off (with Brinsley's help) but now withdrew the offer until she was 'satisfied respecting my children' and her possessions were returned. George threatened several times to sell her jewels and clothes, the gifts her family had given her on their marriage, her father's books and presents from friends to settle them. She called his bluff, saying that if her children were kept from her 'all else is trivial and indifferent'. Caroline said she would have helped her husband financially, as she had always done, and painted a picture of the nine years she had been married to him somewhat differently to that presented in court three and a half weeks earlier. 'I have been accustomed to assist him; the life represented by false witnesses as so frivolously employed, was a life of incessant occupation; I have written day after day, and night after night, without intermission; I have provided for myself by means of literary engagements; I provided for my children by means of my literary engagements; I assisted Mr Norton by means of my literary engagements; and I am still willing to do so – for my children, but not to buy back from my husband my clothes and trinkets.'

The third area of contention between the Nortons was the question of the terms of their legal separation, to which George would only agree if he was freed from all financial liabilities regarding paying her maintenance and responsibility for her debts.

Caroline wrote that she would not discuss anything with her husband's legal representatives other than access to her children. She refused to move from this position and allow other issues to obfuscate her central demand. George Norton was trying to thwart her, to undermine her career by keeping her manuscripts and papers and threatening to sell off all her possessions, so that all she had were the clothes she was wearing when she had left at the end of March. 'They may bereave me of my beloved boys (since the law allows it), they may drive me mad, or wear me into my grave by the slow torture of that greatest of sorrows; but while I have control of my reason, and strength to guide a pen, I will sign nothing, do nothing, listen to nothing, which has reference to any other subject till it is decided what intercourse is to be allowed me with my children.'[64]

Caroline used carefully chosen friends to conduct something of a public relations campaign, giving some permission to copy the letters she wrote to them and the letters she received from her husband's attorneys, and circulate them to their friends and useful acquaintances. Years of writing to deadlines proved useful, and Caroline wrote clear and cogent letters to clarify the position she was taking with regard to seeing her children and exposing George's hypocrisy. Augusta Cowell was one of her conduits to the wider world. Caroline warned Augusta to be careful to whom she sent copies, as 'long and sad experience had made me involuntarily distrustful . . . although I have no reason to dread even my enemies should they see them'. She summarised her position neatly, pointing out that even if she had been found guilty of adultery her husband's position was harsh, and that if George thought she was guilty, which his behaviour suggested, 'why does he keep the magistracy which was alleged to be the bribe for his wife's misconduct?'[65]

Through his attorneys Currie and Woodgate, George offered Caroline an annual allowance of a hundred and fifty pounds.

In order to reopen negotiations to see the children she felt she had no alternative but to accept this paltry sum, believing that if she and her brother took any action concerning money her husband's 'past bitterness and implacability lead me to . . . expect that he would then seek doubly to punish me . . . and would not allow me to see the children at all!' George's annual income at this time was twelve hundred pounds a year with the annual rent on their home three hundred pounds, so he was left with three quarters of his income on which to live. He also tried to keep the annual interest on the fifty-seven pounds annual pension left to her by her father, but as it could not be drawn without her signature she was hopeful of keeping that for herself. Caroline's financial position was dire: she had no 'furniture, plate or linen' or funds (other than loans from her family) to rent furnished lodgings, or pay servants, estimating that she needed three to four hundred pounds a year to live on 'which is what any other man would have offered'.

The financial wranglings were tedious and convoluted. She confessed to her brother 'darling Brin' that she cried all night but had put on her 'cork jacket' and felt more 'buoyant' when she received a letter from him. To try to speed matters up she warned Brin that Norton would drag the bargaining out to cause the maximum annoyance and distress to her, and exasperate them into agreeing to a poor deal.[66]

Caroline wrote under cover of her sister Georgy's seal to Melbourne. He had embargoed meetings and letters, which she found hard: 'after being in the habit of hearing from you or seeing you so constantly, it gives me a feeling as if you were dead and adds one needless misery to what I am enduring'. She told him he owed her the kindness of a letter after she had taken so much trouble trying to keep his name out of George's recent action: 'I have behaved with little selfishness to you dear Lord – I have not deserved it from you.'[67]

This time Melbourne replied to her, under secret cover, revealing a fuller awareness of what a difficult opponent George Norton had been, but irritation that she had failed to anticipate her husband's ability to behave badly. Melbourne urged Caroline not to write to Norton and his lawyers so frequently: 'it elates him and encourages him to persevere in his brutality' and admonished: 'you ought to know him better than I do, and must do so'. He snapped, 'You seem to be hardly aware what a gnome he is, how perfectly earthly and bestial. He is possessed of a devil, the meanest and basest fiend that disgraces the infernal regions. In my opinion he has made this whole matter subservient to his pecuniary interests; he has got money from it.'[68]

By the end of July Caroline was living mostly at 16 Green Street, sharing the lease with her uncle Charles. Caroline's mother was not completely sure of her daughter's innocence in the case and had urged her to be honest with Brinsley and Lord Seymour, who were working hard to salvage her reputation. She was 'vexed' by her mother's lack of trust: 'I knew she disbelieved me all along.'

In London Caroline was able to hear about what was going on in her home from servants there who were loyal to her and willing to risk dismissal. A shocked maid told Caroline her husband had kept her desk when 'he ought to have thrown it into the fire if he really thought those things about you'. Servants also told her that George had asked all of his household if they noticed any resemblance between five-year-old Brinsley and Lord Melbourne. Caroline feared George would treat Brin badly, behaving like a character by the popular novelist Mrs Gore, who 'keeps the child out of revenge but yet believes it another's and ill uses it till it dies'. George interrogated Brin about her, threatening to lock him up in a dark room for a week. Their eldest son, who was seven, was taken to be questioned at the office of Currie and Woodgate in Lincoln's Inn. She also heard that George was irked that his youngest son was called William and was now insisting that he be known by his second name, Charles. Caroline begged to see or hear from Melbourne: 'God knows with your way of thinking when I shall see you again. Send me a line.'[69]

On 24 July Melbourne responded positively, practically and emotionally: he gave his opinion on the financial war she and her lawyers were bogged down in and acknowledged her money troubles. His letter was generous in its intent and revealed the depth of feelings he had for her. 'I have never mentioned money to you; and I hardly like to do it now; your feelings have been so galled that they have naturally become very sore and sensitive that I knew how you might take it. I have had at times a great mind to send you some, but I feared to do so. As I trust we are now on terms of confidential and affectionate friendship, I venture to say, that you have nothing to do but express a wish, and it shall be instantly complied with. I miss you. I miss your society and conversation every day at the hours at which I was accustomed to enjoy them; and when you say that your place can be easily supplied you indulge in a little vanity and self-conceit. You know well enough there is no one who can fill your place.'[70]

An irritating reminder from Caroline's recent past resurfaced after the trial: during the first week of August she was pestered by the Haydons, Benjamin and his wife Mary, for the return of the overwrought and compromising letters he had written to her. They had panicked that he might be the next victim of George Norton's litigiousness. Caroline refused to return them and Haydon fired off an histrionic letter accusing her of having 'a diseased appetite to flirt without heart and intrigue without meaning' and liking to 'torture Men and lacerate the feelings of their wives'. Haydon even wrote to Melbourne

accusing Caroline Norton of bringing 'misery into every family
... evil following her beauty like a shadow'.[71] The letter was
ignored.

Number 16 Green Street is not far from Storey's Gate, and
Caroline heard that the boys were in London, which she was
sure meant they would be taken to Scotland with the Nortons
in August. She kept her old home under surveillance and followed
the children twice when they went out with their nursemaid to
St James's Park. She spoke to her eldest son Fletcher 'seriously
... it was a great comfort to me' and explained as best she
could 'how matters stood between her and their father'. He
handed her a crumpled letter he had in his pocket which he
had written to her but none of the servants dared post. 'He was
so dear and listened so attentively to everything I said to him.
It was a melancholy satisfaction to have had this interview. I
know he will never forget me. Poor little fellow, I never saw
anything more affectionate and intelligent than he was! Let them
do all they can about the children, I will undo in two hours
what they shall have laboured to do for ten years – I have a
power beyond brute force to swing them round again, back to
their old moorings.'[72]

When Miss Vaughan heard what had happened she insisted
on taking the children out in her carriage to prevent Caroline
talking to them. One day when Caroline saw Norton leave the
house she knocked on the door, marched past the footman and
managed to see the children for a few minutes before being
asked to leave. A few days later she tried again, but this time
the footman, afraid for his job, shut the door in her face.[73]

Caroline heard that the boys were due to sail to Scotland
and asked her doctor to write a note to her husband 'begging
to be allowed to see them to say goodbye'. She received no
reply. Even though she was unwell – 'I am so ill today I can
scarcely move' – on Wednesday 17 August she left her sickbed

and made her way to the docks. Learning that they were sailing from St Katherine's Dock on the SS *Royal William*, she waited on the quayside for several hours watching all the passengers embark, but the children did not appear. She eventually learned from the steward of the *Royal William*, who made enquiries on her behalf, that they were travelling on the SS *Dundee*, which was moored at Wapping, but she missed them. In the afternoon Fletcher, Brinsley and Charles and their uncle Lord Grantley boarded the *Dundee* at Hore's Steam Wharf at Wapping and sailed for Edinburgh.[74] Caroline dreaded them going to her sister-in-law Lady Menzies, 'that most masculine of Scotch women', who ran a comfortless house at Rannoch Lodge in the Highlands and by all accounts was a brute. Her fears were not misplaced: they stayed with George's 'haughty and intemperate sister'. Caroline wrote to her sons and later learned that Grace had flogged Fletcher for reading Caroline's letter 'to impress on his memory that he was not to receive letters from me'. When five-year-old Brinsley needed to be 'corrected' he was stripped naked, tied to a bedpost and chastised with a riding whip.[75]

At the end of August Caroline heard that her husband had sold all her books, clothes and jewellery. Her manuscripts too were lost, including one she was working on which was worth five hundred pounds. George also sold a bust of her 'to an utter stranger' who rented Storey's Gate when he moved out later in the year. Caroline spent some time with her sister Helen at Bookham Lodge, Cobham in Surrey, trying to write, as she was 'utterly dependent on the bounty of my family'. There was still the matter of what George would do with her family 'trinkets' such as the picture of her father. 'Burning with anxiety' to pay back Brinsley, Caroline started work on a novel hoping it might be ready for January, but the continuing correspondence with lawyers and friends meant that creative energies were in short supply. Every day was a new challenge: 'one day I feel brisk and inspired, and the next languid, and ready to hang myself; but I think and hope I shall persevere'.[76]

Caroline brooded about going to Scotland but it was not a journey to be undertaken lightly. While she was considering her next step there was an altercation by letter with Trelawny, who had been steady during her crisis but was feeling possessive about her friendship with his friend Mary Shelley. As in the past, Caroline had to pull back from his intense and demanding friendship in case she was destroyed by it. 'Whatever disappointment there may have been or you may fancy there has been in your acquaintance with me, has depended on yourself. But for two things (with my disposition to romance and admiration for all your talent) you might have been a hero of chivalry in my eyes – as it is you are a clever man, and I firmly believe a kind-hearted one . . . I sail along on my calm lovely moonlight sea of imagination, seeing everything by a sweet false light – making false estimate of everyone's character – brightening and silvering up things to my own fancy, and lo! one of your dark "realities" runs me down like a heavy black brig which I had not been on the look out for.'[77]

When Trelawny received her letter he fired off a florid one to Mary Shelley, selectively quoting parts of Caroline's letter, clearly aroused by the woman, her words and the power she had over him. 'The darts from those eyes are still rankling in my body; yet it is a pleasing pain. The wound of the scorpion is healed by applying the scorpion to the wound. Is she not a glorious being? Is she not dazzling? There is an enchantment in all her ways. Talk of the divine power of music, why, she is all melody, and poetry, and beauty and harmony.'[78]

At the end of September things were at a standstill: Norton had offered Caroline a deed of separation but only if she accepted a hundred and fifty pounds a year, and there was no mention of the children. Dr Stephen Lushington, Whig Member of Parliament for Tower Hamlets and a judge with experience of negotiating matrimonial disputes, had been appointed to deal with Lord Wynford, Norton's godfather and string-puller. In 1816 Lushington had secured Lady Byron's separation from her husband and successfully defended Queen Caroline in 1820 when George IV tried to divorce her. He was a forceful and effective speaker in the House of Commons and sympathetic to the interests of women, believing that the law placed them at a disadvantage. He made it clear to Lord Wynford that no 'treaty or proposal' would be listened to unless it contained 'a satisfactory arrangement with respect to the children'.[79]

Caroline now went out into the world with family members to prove she had no reason to lock herself away from society. She 'laughed restlessly . . . to prove mortification and sorrow could not reach me' but sometimes could not cope and left parties. She found herself unable to answer polite enquiries and afraid of 'the sneering smiles'.[80] In the middle of October she wrote a pious and penitent letter to her uncle Thomas Le Fanu, Dean of Emly in Limerick, saying she was sure God had inflicted on her the trouble she was in 'to awaken her from the dream of worldliness and vanity in which my heart was engaged' and 'that the injustice of Man was punishing her for other sins'. Caroline said her quarrel with Norton was not about jealousy. She and Melbourne had had 'six years of the utmost intimacy', which was sanctioned by her husband; rather the trial had been triggered by her brother Brinsley, who was 'hurt and revolted' by George's violence. She wrote that Brinsley's efforts to protect her and his refusal to invite George to Frampton at Easter had started the war between her and the Nortons.[81]

By the end of October Norton's attorneys had reduced their offer by seven pounds to a hundred and forty-three pounds a year, and factoring in the annual interest on her father's pension, this would give her an annual income of two hundred pounds. Once again there was no mention of the children. Currie and Woodgate also announced that their client planned to serve notices on all tradesmen who dealt with Caroline that he 'has made her an allowance amply sufficient to her needs' and that he was no longer liable for her debts. Caroline's letters to her lawyers were indignant at the absence of any reference to the children, and restated her position that nothing would be agreed without an arrangement which included her seeing the children. While they were still married George was liable for her debts, although having notices served on the tradesmen would be 'disagreeable and doubtless there will be mortification and impertinence to endure, these things are light in comparison with what I have already borne'. She refused to be bullied into settling.[82]

Caroline accepted that there was an argument for her sons to be in the care of their father when they were older, but not at the ages of three, five and seven. It was a 'harsh and unjust law which enables a man to take such young children from the care of their mother'.[83] Caroline's thoughts were turning in a direction familiar to readers of the works of Mary Shelley's mother, Mary Wollstonecraft. 'A woman has apparently no individual destiny. She is the property of those on whom she may reflect discredit or otherwise. If I succeed I hope my success will be a satisfaction and triumph to "my people" for nothing will ever be a matter of triumph or satisfaction to me again'.[84]

Caroline was taken aback when Currie and Woodgate suddenly announced that she could see her sons at her brother's house in Grosvenor Square for half an hour in the presence of witnesses: 'two vulgar, curious women'. It was traumatic. She was desperate for more time, but the women bundled the children out of the door.[85] The day after her meeting with the children Caroline wrote to her lawyers saying that on no account would she agree to anyone, even Dr Lushington, arranging to see her boys in the presence of others. 'I would rather not see my children <u>at all</u> than see them as I did in Grosvenor Square . . . the women took them away before I was sufficiently collected to speak to them . . . That visit was no pleasure to me, on the contrary, a great and bitter pain at the time, and the cause of severe indisposition afterwards. I never desire such a visit to be repeated and have been urged by all my friends who saw what I then suffered, not to expose myself to that pain again.'

Caroline would agree to seeing her children for a portion of the year, and suggested the winter months as in Scotland these were too harsh for their 'delicate chests'. She also wanted them for half of their holidays when they were at school. But she refused to see them for odd hours and half-hours. Caroline promised that she had never tried 'to prejudice her children against their father or his relations' and she accepted that the day would come for her sons 'to consider and decide for themselves'. Nor did she dispute the legal authority of their father, 'but as I am the only competent judge of the effect on my health and feelings of the miserable terms on which it is proposed I see them, so I am the only person who can decide in the matter'.[86]

On 21 November Caroline heard that Miss Vaughan had died. The words 'she is dead' made Caroline feel as if 'a veil of ice had fallen on me'. A rich old woman who was a giver to many causes, but malign, miserly and cruel to Caroline, Margaret Vaughan's death was one of the few bits of good news she had heard all year. Caroline often wanted 'to do something, I scarcely cared what, to punish that cruel woman'.[87] George Norton inherited her Yorkshire estates including Kettlethorpe Hall, a handsome family house built in the 1720s near Wakefield, and an annual income of two thousand pounds. Caroline was adamant that the dynamic of that relationship had been George's venality and Miss Vaughan's malevolence: 'it was for money that he sacrificed home and home comforts'.[88]

At the beginning of December 1836 George Norton moved out of Storey's Gate and took up residence at Lord Grantley's house at 10 Wilton Place. Edward Ellice wrote to him offering to help settle things between him and Caroline, but his offer was firmly refused. George's offers of the 'utmost concession my sense of duty permits me to make' had been rejected. Mr Norton said he did not regret bringing the action against Lord Melbourne: 'In the most painful circumstances in which I was placed I could not have acted otherwise.' Snubbing Ellice, he sent out a warning to Caroline that he would keep his children and 'bring them up with the strictures which I know their dearest interest requires and those interests shall not suffer for anything I may have to endure'. George Norton insisted he had acted to save his wife from herself. 'My endeavours to save the mother of my children from further exposure are fruitless. She is determined to drag herself yet more before the public and I yield to a necessity by which my utmost exertions have failed to avert.'[89]

A few days after the trial, when George had left for the office, Caroline's brother Charlie talked his way into the house and took a handful of papers, including a poem, from her desk; this was the only work she ever managed to retrieve. John Murray agreed to publish *A Cry From the Factories*, for sound commercial reasons: it was topical and timely. Because of her notoriety and her concern that she might be accused of 'meddling' in something she did not understand, her name did not appear anywhere in the book, which went on sale in time for Christmas.

Not her best work, heavy-going and strongly influenced by Lord Byron's stanza style, the poem dealt with child labour in factories. The long hours and dangerous and unhealthy working conditions had been exposed in Parliament by Anthony Ashley-Cooper, the seventh Earl of Shaftesbury, who had campaigned for children and young people to work no more than ten hours a day. His campaign had led to a royal commission into factory conditions and the passing of the Factory Act of 1833. In the face of opposition from factory owners and other vested interests, not all of Shaftesbury's recommendations were adopted, but it was an important step. *A Cry From the Factories* was dedicated to Ashley, who was married to Melbourne's niece Lady Cowper.[90] 'Ever a toiling *child* doth make us sad; / 'Tis an unnatural and mournful sight, / Because we feel their smiles should be so glad, / Because we know their eyes should be so bright. / What is it, then, when, tasked beyond their might, / They labour all the day for others' gain, / Nay, trespass on the still and pleasant night, / While uncompleted hours of toil remain? / Poor little FACTORY SLAVES – for YOU these lines complain!'

Caroline had more projects, which she told Mary Shelley about. She decided to write two pamphlets to expose the unfairness of the law relating to mothers' claims to the custody of their infant children and a comparative study of the English and Scottish divorce laws. 'I think there is too much fear of publishing about women – it is reckoned such a crime to be accused and a disgrace that they wish nothing better than to hide themselves and say no more about it. I think it is high time that the law was known at least, among the "weaker" sex, which gives us no right to one's own flesh and blood.'[91]

When Edward Ellice forwarded George's letter to him Caroline was badly shaken. Norton's hypocrisy infuriated her, and in her reply Caroline let a chink of light into the dark atmosphere that had pervaded her marriage. Caroline recalled the mood of many evenings when Mr and Mrs Norton were alone together, his 'half-drunken jests on his own safety from disgrace and my safety from any love on Melbourne's part'.[92]

On Christmas Day 1836 she was at Maiden Bradley with Georgy and her brood, feeling 'so truly broken' that she was a miserable guest. She was absorbed in writing the text for her 'Observations' pamphlet, wrestling with the intricacies and, to her, illogicalities of the law, and her unnamed 'stupid publishers', who were jittery about some of the content. Even though Norton had lost his case, his appetite for the law made the firm nervous of being sued for libel.[93]

Consider what next to do.

V

A Large Black Slug in
a Damp Wood

A woman is made a helpless wretch by these laws of men.
Caroline Norton to Mary Shelley

In the cold dark days of February 1837 Caroline Norton
spent two weeks confined to her sofa in London 'spitting
blood'. She wrote in despair to her collaborator 'dear
Cowellina' that she was 'very, very ill . . . I am worn out and
killed by this man's dogged cruelty'. No one was 'so base and
cruel or so unrelenting' as George Norton. Caroline was frightened of a consumptive death: 'soon I shall be past all he can
do to me', and her 'restless misery', which she had 'so long
endured', would be over. She was sinking under a gloomy cloud:
'all my elasticity of spirit cannot help me'.[1]

Caroline had spent the previous month at Maiden Bradley
with blinding headaches. Dealing with Norton's 'dogged spite',
her new year's resolution was 'if they won't give my children
back to me, I will take them as soon as ever this spring is gone
by'. Caroline hoped 'to God that nothing will happen to make
this year as black as the last'.[2] Across the Irish Sea, her free-
spirited brother Frank, with a few officers of the garrison, hired
the Amateur Theatre in Dublin to perform for charity. He was
Hamlet in a parody of the play which was 'broad and ridiculous

in the extreme but full of point and humour'.[3] For his next career Frank fancied performing in Parliament. He put out feelers to his wealthy sister Georgy about finding him a seat in the House of Commons and financing an election campaign.

Frustrated by Norton's tactics and with the aid of her pamphlet 'Observations on the Natural Claims of a Mother to the Custody of her Children As Affected by the Common Law Rights of the Father' (1837), Caroline started her assault on Parliament. Abraham Hayward, an essayist and lawyer who practised as a special pleader with chambers in the Temple, canvassed on Caroline's behalf with the help of Mr Serjeant Talfourd to introduce a bill into the House of Commons which would give judges the power to order that either of the parents should have access to children under twelve. She did not know the genial Talfourd personally but was aware of how well he had defended Lord Melbourne nine months earlier. She felt Talfourd was an excellent choice to raise this controversial subject in the House of Commons: 'I could not choose a man whose talents and good feeling and weight with the House would give a better chance of success.'[4] The first reading in the House of Commons was announced for the end of April.

There had been 'so much worry and dispute about prosecutable passages' in the pamphlet, her publishers had taken fright, and she borrowed the money to have it printed privately. Mary Shelley had been helpful: 'I improved the passages materially by your observations on what we permitted to women, or rather excused in women when they received any rudeness.' Of a later draft Caroline worried that Mary might think it 'weak'. Caroline would have liked to have been more hard-hitting in her prose, but was advised by her sister Georgy that she should have 'the appearance of calmness and fairness'. Caroline did not feel calm but had 'struck out many passages which my sister called my "callow wrestling bits"'.

Researching and writing was draining: 'I never felt so fagged in my life.'

Caroline's emotional and intellectual development had matured with a sharper feminist focus. Her remarks to Mary Shelley reveal a woman whose personal experiences had brought her to a clearer understanding of the invidious position of women and their unequal and unacknowledged rights. 'Does it not provoke you some times to think how "in vain" the gift of genius is for a woman? How so far from binding her more closely to the admiration and love of her fellow creatures, it does in effect create that gulf across which no one passes? . . . I have been interrupted by letters which by recalling to me all that is real and grating in my position, and obliging me to answer lawyers etc. and cut short that which is pleasant – which is writing to you!'[5]

Caroline's brother Brinsley worried about the 'indelicacy' of her appeal to the public in publishing the pamphlet. Before he left for Paris he had only read the proofs of the case studies she had included of various mothers' battles to see their children and had not seen what she had written about George's role. He fretted that no matter how carefully she worded her remarks about him, Norton would take it badly: 'I dread, I really dread it drawing forth a counter-statement from Mr Norton' and that George would print his own pamphlet, not to contradict her points but to 'make public a series of accusations (true or false, it matters not) that must injure you and make your position more disagreeable than it is at present'. The pamphlet gave George Norton – her 'bitterest enemy' – the opportunity to criticise her behaviour during the marriage and 'exaggerate into a crime every little impudence you have committed'. Brinsley was aware how easily Caroline's flightiness could alienate the conservative newspaper-reading public. Although her view was that her husband was 'universally despised' and that no one would take a counter-attack seriously, her brother was more worldly, and knew how negatively she was viewed in some circles. Brinsley begged her to 'be most cautious about what you say about Mr Norton . . . pray let me read it. Be assured, I will be most happy to meet your wishes.' Brinsley's last words before he left for Paris were nervous: 'For pity's sake take care of what you are about to do.'[6]

The Sheridan family were uneasy about Caroline's friendship with Mary Shelley. In 1818 Mary's first novel *Frankenstein* was published anonymously to serious critical acclaim; initially reviewers thought it was by a man as it was said to be the work of 'a masculine mind'. Her unconventional past with Percy Bysshe Shelley was a problem for some, although she was regarded as a gifted writer of romances, becoming one of the best-known authors of the period. Caroline Norton and Mary Shelley were fond of each other. Mary had a seventeen-year-old son, Percy Florence, whom she doted on. Three other children had died, and she had had a miscarriage that nearly killed her. Caroline was consoled by her and flattered by the friendship and moral support of the older, clever woman. Shelley admired Norton 'excessively, and I think I could love her infinitely, but I shall take very great care not to press myself. I know what her relations think of me.'[7]

What Lord Melbourne felt about Caroline always disturbed her emotional equilibrium. On 6 March, after a long gap in their letters, she wrote to him after he had visited her at Green Street, an event which did not go well. In their short time together there were harsh words and stormy behaviour: 'don't be provoked with me! I know I asked for it myself and made up my mind to do so before you came – but now, somehow it weighs upon me. It has haunted me all night, and I have a paid-off, cast-off feeling. At present I feel as if I had voluntarily raised one more distance-post between us.'

Melbourne had accepted her invitation but everything between them had changed. Caroline feared he thought her 'more forward than I should be' and that she had 'done exactly the things' she should not. Melbourne told Caroline it had been an 'impudence' for her to go to his house in South Street, so she exasperatedly quoted verbatim one of his many invitations to her: '"I have been in despair today at not seeing you but I know it is a long way and a difficult operation – if you <u>can</u> continue to call, the later the better, as a number of people come to me for one reason or another." '

Caroline admitted she may have gone to his house when he did not want her there, but when she noticed his irritation she would stop calling and Melbourne would become 'anxious and miss me for a few days'. Caroline summed up her feelings: 'It breaks my whole life not seeing you, and you come unwillingly, to satisfy me and yet I am the younger and should have been the likelier to alter.' She could not resist asking him to visit her on his fifty-ninth birthday on 15 March.[8] Melbourne was too worldly, experienced and casual for her, perhaps careless with his words. As a wordsmith Caroline was scrupulous in the way she deployed language; she hinted he was not. Melbourne, as a politician, worked with the spoken word in a different way.

On 11 March 1837 Caroline heard that her youngest son, 'her baby', had had an accident and went immediately to see George at his office in Whitechapel. She 'remonstrated' with him at his 'barbarity' at keeping her children away from her, not letting her know how they were and keeping their location a secret. He asked her to put it all into writing, which she did. George replied that he refused to speak to her lawyers or her brother Brinsley – an attempt to undermine the position of the men around her – and insisted on communicating with her directly. He also asked her to sign a solemn pledge that she would not abduct the boys and agreed to 'see them in the manner I shall think expedient and best, and I shall hasten every arrangement which may be necessary to enable your seeing them in the shortest possible time'. Knowing how Caroline felt about being told when she could see her own children, this was an offer he knew she would not accept. He offered her a crumb: 'Let me assure you, the children are quite well, and by all accounts so much grown, that we [meaning she] shall hardly know them.' Manipulatively, he underlined 'Carry' (once his pet name for Caroline) in 'it will be a sad parting from little Carry', which also happened to be the name of the nursemaid who had been looking after them for a year.[9]

George's most recent plan was that the two youngest boys could go and live with Caroline her but only if 'Miss C' lodged there too. Alternatively they would be allowed to live with Miss C at her own residence, and Caroline would be given the same 'liberty' to visit them there as George would have. Caroline had been prepared to consider this, but his promises were too vague and she would not sign any paperwork: 'no one knows better than yourself the degree and strength of that temptation; but I have to consider that I am binding myself for our mutual lives and it is not a short-sighted pining affection which shall make me pass a promise I might after-wards be tempted to break'. She rebuked George for his concern that the boys would be sad to part from 'their pretty little companion', flabbergasted that he had made such an insensitive remark to their mother, who had only seen them briefly in the most upsetting circumstances for a few minutes during the last twelve months.[10]

Mr and Mrs Norton were at an impasse. George repeated his 'hope' that the children would eventually be permitted to live with her but then reiterated old conditions which he knew she would not accept. On 15 March a new condition was added, his insistence he be satisfied about 'the certainty of their being brought up with the strictness I require'. If everything were agreed, the payment of her annual maintenance would be contingent on Caroline's 'conduct' and his ability to pay. George tried to bully her into making an 'immediate settlement otherwise those legal steps must be resumed'.[11]

Caroline rejected his proposal but was prepared to accept the intrusion of a young woman whom he had 'casually known for a year' into her children's life and 'suffer' the 'most undeserved insult' that the lady was 'fitter to rear them than their mother'. Her new offer was that the boys should live with Miss C for the next three months and that she herself would have unlimited access to them during that time 'except in the case of such obstacles <u>as shall be beforehand named</u>, in order that they may be avoided'. After three months Caroline should have the children to live with her with or without the superintendence of Miss C 'as may be the pleasure of their father', and thereafter they should live 'under their mother's roof as their home' except when they were with their Norton relatives. If these terms were accepted for the next three years, Caroline would agree to accept her maintenance, newly increased to two hundred pounds a year.[12] George rejected her plan.

Ten days after her last letter to Lord Melbourne (he presumably had not visited her on his birthday) Caroline wrote to him, wryly rather than histrionically. She could never resist prodding him in the chest with her verbal fan and delivering a tap to his shins with her satin slipper. She repeated her sister Georgy's remarks that 'men have no real feeling' and that 'in love they are kind, and when that noble feeling has burnt out, they are brutes'. Caroline wrote that once men were out of lust a woman's power had gone: 'Like iron, they are only malleable in a state of fusion; you can't <u>bend</u> a cooled man.' She reminded him of the good old days, when Melbourne used to write to her and worry that at his age he 'could not replace an object of unceasing and anxious interest'. He would write, 'I was very melancholy all yesterday after your departure. I knew I should feel it a great deal, but did not think I should feel it as much as I do.' Caroline rejoiced in reminding him how malleable he had been then, when he could be 'nailed to the threshold to keep away ill luck' like a horseshoe. Someone, she hinted, had rekindled his forge: 'a fine bright bar of iron – a poker, resolutely stirring up a fire on other people's houses, and only warming the tip of his own cold nose in the blaze'. Caroline rattled off the names of several fires Melbourne was warming himself beside: all beautiful and mostly the wives of powerful men. She heard he had the buoyancy of a boy and the 'carelessness of a greyhound – the only dog besides yourself who cannot attach himself to any <u>one person</u> but to the cushion where he habitually rests and the house where he is accustomed to be fed'. Caroline wrote that she would not trouble him any more if she could find another man who was literate and who did not 'carry a comb and a box of pink lip-salve in his coat pocket', but she could not. Disliking his 'shuffling about' their shared social circle and feeling that he was trying to 'outwit her', she asserted that this would be the last note she would write to him, which may have come as something of a relief. The prime minister was being scolded like a dog and accused of being fickle.[13]

Caroline heard no more from her husband for two months. The first reading of Talfourd's bill was due in April. Furious that Melbourne had not replied to her intemperate note, Caroline sent another, claiming 'there is not a human being . . . who does not join in denouncing as heartless and cold-blooded the manner in which you parade yourself among my acknowledged and open foes, and who do not wonder at it'. Caroline told him she was beginning to listen to others' low opinion of him. Around this time Melbourne's tolerance was at a low ebb and he blamed her for making him ill. Hearing he was spending time with Lady Stanhope and how Mrs James Fox-Lane held dinners for him maddened her: 'how you sit among my foes and make them your friends, they know they may act as they please and you will not resent it'. Caroline even brought up Lady Branden, conscious that she had been recently widowed and might yet snap him up. 'If you could stab me instead of only making my heart ache – but while I breathe, it shall not be well. I looked to you for protection – for kindness – for sympathy. I perceive nothing but shrinking and a vague desire to be rid of me all together.' It would take little, she threatened, to 'make me utterly careless of what may be the effect of my own destiny or that of others' and little to 'make me careless of disgrace, ruin or life itself'. Everybody seemed to be urging her to be quiet, but that 'would not do . . . You will drive me mad and for my madness you may thank yourself.'[14]

Aided and abetted by Lord Grantley, George Norton took advertising space in several newspapers on 30 March denouncing his wife, to which her brother Brinsley responded. Norton had broken the rules of polite society and gone public with their troubles, and Brinsley Sheridan felt he had no choice to refute the lies being told about his sister, defend her tattered reputation and refute the slanders about himself. He denied that Caroline had voluntarily left her home and children, and told readers that she had visited him at Easter 1836 with her husband's knowledge because Norton's 'conduct had rendered him obnoxious to the other members of the family'. Caroline had been forced to stay away from her home because of the 'gross and unjustifiable measures pursued towards her'. Brinsley had also been assailed by 'every species of outrage and injury' directed at him by his brother-in-law and reminded readers that recently Mr Norton had asked his wife to go back to him.[15]

While Caroline waited for responses to her pamphlet and for

Talfourd to introduce his Infant Custody Bill, she returned to her hobby of pouring out her love to Lord Melbourne and simultaneously reproaching him. Many times she threatened this would be her last letter, but there was always another, and another. In April she suggested that if he was afraid of what society might say if he visited her on his own, he might bring Edward Ellice as a chaperone. 'I feel that I <u>have</u> a claim upon you, tho' . . . there seems very little willingness to admit it. I think it is not presuming very much on that claim, to propose you pay <u>one</u> visit . . . considering that for some years I sat waiting, as my principal object, for your more <u>voluntary</u> calls. There is no woman who has not appeared to take it for granted I have seen you – most believe you came to Lord Seymour's after the trial to "wish me joy". I did wish to see you anywhere – anyhow – perhaps even without being able to speak to you – anything to <u>see you again</u>.'[16]

Fearful of a scene, tears and drama, and embarrassed to be caught between her broken-hearted disappointment and his sister Lady Cowper's hostile opinion of her, Melbourne did nothing at first. Caroline was surrounded by her family and visited by a handful of friends, whereas Melbourne was living the life of an eligible bachelor of a certain age and also prime minister. Caroline saw Melbourne's sister as a powerful enemy and her biggest obstacle. She was bored, frustrated and abandoned. 'I am sorry to be nothing to you. I thought it would all come right in the end. I am sorry to be nothing . . . when my family ask you to dinner etc. you will go if you can (you need not be afraid of meeting me there that will be taken care of) as it is necessary for my reputation that the two families should <u>appear</u> to treat the whole thing as a vision and a lie . . . I hope that in time the six years last past will fade from my memory, as they do more easily from yours, and I hope you will not find any other woman who is more willing to "suggest Annoyances" or more fiendish and diabolical indisposition. I thought to the last I might have depended on you. Adieu.'[17]

Melbourne finally went to see her accompanied by Edward Ellice. Deeply grateful for the visit, she regretted her insistence: 'I hope you do not think the worse of me. I hope not.' Caroline shared her worries about her son Brinsley – 'there is so much ill-feeling about him, so much wilful misconstruction' – whom George Norton had insisted was Melbourne's child and what the implications might be for the boy if her husband persisted in his belief. Caroline was 'much the happier' for having seen Melbourne, and his presence had made the room 'seem more cheerful – it makes things seem less irrevocably wrecked round me'. She was sorry that she had criticised his family and hoped not to write 'bitterly' about them again. Unable to help herself, she asked him to pay her another call 'when the fine summer weather comes and you are not obliged to drive such a short distance in your carriage'.[18]

Mr Serjeant Talfourd's Infant Custody Bill was read for the first time in the House of Commons on 25 April 1837, the second reading being scheduled for 24 May. On 19 May Caroline Norton received an extraordinary overture from her recalcitrant husband. Mr Norton was sure they could 'adjust their differences' themselves and suggested they meet alone to 'make a last attempt to obviate extremities'. George proposed they get together later that day at half past five at number 1 Lower Berkeley Street, the London home of the late Miss Vaughan. He advised Caroline that the house was empty except for one servant. She did not reply – she may not have received the note – so George sent it again. When further time passed he sent another note to her asking to meet him instead at the house he had taken at 10 Wilton Place.

Caroline went to Wilton Place and had a long emotional 'interview' with him. George asked her to return to him and 'forget the past', insisting that he had been 'hurried on' to act when he had been 'sore and angry', and that others had persuaded him to launch the case against Lord Melbourne. He deeply regretted it and asked Caroline to promise she would go with him and the boys to Kettlethorpe Hall, which he had inherited from Miss Vaughan, in the autumn. Meanwhile she could see them every day. George also asked her to write him a letter which he could show to Lord Grantley, who was the 'chief obstacle to all arrangements' and 'very bitter' against her. Caroline found her estranged husband 'very kind in manner' and agreed to all he proposed as she was 'quite worn out'. George told her the children were in Scotland. Caroline wrote to him as instructed, 'You do me injustice in thinking that it possible that the liberty of seeing my children would be attended with results which might make you repent having allowed it; I give you my <u>most solemn pledge</u>, that under no circumstances will I seize or detain the children, if you will bring them up from Scotland, and arrange some plan for my access to them, <u>not inconsistent with my feelings and respectability as a mother.</u> I am sure when you see how my health is breaking, and when you consider that, as my medical attendants can testify, my illness is the result of the daily anxiety and fretting, you will not interpose any further delay between me and my only comfort . . . I have not seen my uncle or any relations, nor shall I do so till I hear from you; but I am sure Sir J. Graham or Capt. Blackwood would guarantee the pledge I have given, should you consider any guarantee necessary beyond my own solemn promise.'[19]

The next day George Norton ('Your Poor Old Worn-Out Geordie') sent Caroline ('My Carry') another note telling her that his brother was 'opposed to <u>everything</u>' but that he wanted 'to take her to his heart again; we must not sacrifice the children'. He asked her to write directly to Grantley, care of the

Talbot Hotel at 39 Green Street. Duplicitously, George suggested Caroline tell Grantley that he had not responded to her letter, say that she did not know how to interpret his silence and ask Grantley to intercede on her behalf. George warned Caroline 'not to submit too much' in her letter, and urged her to request a meeting with himself the next morning at the Talbot Hotel as he and Grantley were due to leave for Wonersh at noon.

George reported that his brother had advised him that if he allowed Caroline to see the children 'I had better take you home at once', and if he agreed to giving Grantley 'full power to act he will settle everything in a month'. George warned Caroline that his brother was 'most hostile and ready to take advantage of any "line" given him' and begged her to be cautious in her words and to meet his brother the next day if she thought it advisable. Her husband wrote at the bottom of his note, 'Grantley is most difficult to manage.'[20]

Caroline wondered at the meaning of this sudden burst of correspondence attempting a reconciliation. She was suspicious of George's motives and Grantley's real role in the new development. Norton's advice to Caroline comes across as a dangerous piece of double-dealing.

Three days later, on 23 May, the day before Talfourd's bill was due its second reading, George returned to London and asked Caroline to visit him at Wilton Place that evening. He was solicitous: 'if it is not irksome, or does not make you ill it is the best mode of our meeting'. Things had gone well with his brother – 'everything prospers' – but George made a point of not offering her dinner, saying he would be home at six and telling her she 'had better dine first'. Feeble-sounding and perhaps bullied, George had abdicated all authority to his elder brother, which worried Caroline. George Norton explained his own impotence: 'it is essential that he should sanction our arrangements – indeed I do not see any other mode by which my family and friends could be reconciled to them'. Since coming back to London, George had written to Wonersh to hasten his brother's return: 'so anxious am I to shorten the duration of your anxiety to see the children'. But Grantley remained absent and nothing could be settled.[21]

On 24 May Mr Serjeant Talfourd announced that he was postponing the second reading for two weeks, so it would now take place on 7 June. This had to do with what were being called the Norton Negotiations. Caroline's painful separation from her children had been the catalyst for the framing of the bill, and her 'Observations' pamphlet had provided Talfourd with helpful information and case studies to add to his own professional expertise. She was such a powerful figure in the wings that until she was fully focused and behind what he was doing he was afraid the bill's passage into law would be compromised. One must wonder if Norton and Grantley's actions at this time were an attempt to distract her attention from the bill. A great deal of her time was spent analysing George's letters and replying.

On 29 May George wrote that the situation was delicate and changing: 'this must be the last letter I can write to you under present circumstances'. He admitted that he had taken the 'opinions and advice of a discreet friend' whom he had not previously consulted. This friend, never named, thought her 'guilty of great impropriety of conduct', but also that she had 'heart and feeling, which if left free to act, will conduct you to peace and happiness'. George donned his martyred, magnanimous hat and offered to give her another chance: 'if reasonable ground be only afforded by your present conduct that such trial may prove successful'.

George insisted that she give up all power to him and his brother. He wrote sanctimoniously, laced with the threat of 'revolting exposures' if 'amicable arrangement does not take the place of hostile proceedings'. He was proposing two possible outcomes: that she was 'restored' to him, their children and his society, or alternatively to her children only. The first option was to live a life that reversed the past, implying that she would have to change her ways and mind her words and behaviour. George suggested that if she preferred to have her children only, she must see his brother 'and express to him your entire trust in, and submission to your husband' and 'confidently leave it to me to make every arrangement for your seeing the children, your allowance'. Norton urged her to tell Grantley that she wanted to prove her innocence to him. George left mention of her debts to the end and then reminded her that he could only pay off five hundred pounds.

Norton said that as soon as those matters he had outlined had been arranged and she surrendered all power to him and his brother, Caroline should go to see the children in Scotland. Fletcher's delicate health required him to remain in the pure air of the Highlands rather than being in London. Caroline could visit them immediately; George could not go until September, making the 'sacrifice' of letting her see them first. He even recommended transport arrangements: her health being what it was, she should travel by the shortest route, to Dundee on the 'very best steam-vessels that sail'. Mindful that 'the line' he had 'chalked out will require sacrifices on both sides' (but mostly from her), he hoped that love of the children and 'contrition for the past' would enable the Nortons to compromise.[22]

Caroline replied immediately. She had kept her family informed of recent developments, which had been given urgency by Norton's knowledge of her pamphlet and Talfourd's bill. Caroline made it clear to George, and thereby Grantley, that she had a team of people behind her including her brother Brinsley. Knowing how poisonous the feelings her brother and husband had for each other, Brinsley had not been referred to until now. Caroline said she was happy to see the children but only at George's mother's house in Edinburgh and not his sister Grace's home at Castle Menzies.[23] The next morning, 30 May, George sent a hurt response, 'sorry' that she distrusted his advice, which he assured her was 'dictated by prudence and was honestly and sincerely given'. He included an extract from a letter from the children's physician in Scotland, who advised against them being moved 'from the Highland air' to London 'at this hot season'. Norton did not care for the tone of her latest letter, which he said was 'at variance with the feelings of honour and trust on which I had hoped we were acting, and should continue to act until we had conquered the difficulties of our present situation'. The presence of her brother in her letter had clearly rankled. George's strategy was to seem to be reasonable and apparently see things from her point of view, but then to lay down his wishes in the most unflinching terms. He concluded by drawing a line which he told her he would not cross. 'Those I have to contend against are I fear, little understood by you – perhaps yours are not fully appreciated by me – but I feel certain they are only to be overcome by the most unbounded confidence in each other; a confidence that will not admit of the participation of a third party, EVEN OF A BROTHER. Trusting that your note of last night was written amidst the excitements of the world, and that your heart had no share in it, believe me your affectionate George Chapple Norton.'

In a postscript George gave himself a pat on the back for being brave by breaking the agreement Grantley had insisted on, in writing to Caroline without his knowledge. Norton expected her similarly to exclude Brinsley from the negotiations. He then said that their letters would have to stop until she had been to see his brother.[24]

Either George Norton was utterly confused and a victim of Grantley's bullying, or he and his brother were playing a cruel game with her by raising her hopes and then dashing them, always changing the conditions of reconciliation. Caroline was indignant. She noted the remarkable change of tone in his last letter, exposing his servility to Grantley and his sister at Castle Menzies. She was especially cross that Norton had proposed she travel four hundred miles to Grace, who 'never much liked or treated me kindly, to see the children whom, five days ago you solemnly promised should come here to ME'. Caroline took a sarcastic swipe at him, saying that she did not think so badly of him as to believe that he had 'angled for me with the bait of that promise'. She could have no trust in any of his proposals, 'which shift and waver every day'. The contradictions in his letter would be 'ludicrous if they were not so bitter'. Caroline asked how George could have offered to take her back to his heart unless he believed in her innocence, and yet he threatened to 'bring forward revolting tales' against her. 'It does amaze me that any human being should have the heart so to play upon the affection and sorrow of another as you do upon mine! This is the second time I have vainly trusted that you will recall my children. You promised it most heartily; you explained your plans most fully; and how am I to believe anything again. I can give you no worse reproach than this: I really <u>did</u> believe you – I really <u>did</u> think you were sending for the boys, and against all others could say, to warn me not to hope.'[25]

At eight o'clock that night George dashed off a note asking her to visit him at Wilton Place that evening or the next morning so that he could convince her he had 'but one object – our peace and the welfare of the children'. He wanted to 'satisfy her' that 'all my plans are devised to comfort not to "torture" you; that there has been no thought or care for myself – all has been for you and them'. At the end of an exhausting day, marshalling her feelings on paper, she showed her reply to Brinsley before she sent a servant to deliver it to

Norton. She told Augusta Cowell, 'all was once more expectation and hope'.[26]

On 1 June Caroline received a bizarre letter from George. Annoyed at being pestered by Caroline's dressmaker, 'that impudent-faced Miss M', he told his wife to pay the bill herself out of the money he had recently deposited in her account. The most important news was that he had written to his sister that the boys should be sent to London and would be accompanied by his mother. He then went on to describe what he had bought from the auction of Miss Vaughan's possessions, an odd thing to tell Caroline, who had hated her. George's boasts about the bargains he picked up before the dealers arrived reveal his coarseness and lack of tact. His letter took a sinister turn at the end, when he imagined a conversation between himself and Caroline, using evidence at a recent trial at the Old Bailey. James Greenacre, a cabinetmaker, had been hanged for the murder of his fiancée Hannah Brown, a washerwoman, whom he had killed for her dowry, depositing bits of her dismembered body around London. George Norton signed himself 'your affectionate intended, Greenacre'. Caroline humoured him in this unpleasant running joke.[27]

Caroline received a bunch of carnations from Lord Melbourne. The flowers took her back to their shared past – 'it was like meeting an old companion after years'. They were the first flowers she had received that year. She sat down and cried before she was composed enough to put them in vases.[28]

It was now two weeks since George had asked Caroline to see Lord Grantley, who was a week late arriving from Wonersh, and still the delays continued. Caroline gave George short shrift over his excited plans for furnishing their new home at 10 Wilton Place, which he promised would be 'the most comfortable and elegant little place in London'. It was thoughtless: she had very little furniture, not even a dining table, in the house she shared with her uncle Charles. Tired of his talk of curtains and chairs, she was 'hungry' for her children.[29]

The next day, 4 June, George continued to nag her about Miss M's dressmaking bill, though he knew that it was in the hands of lawyers and Caroline could do nothing about it. He sounded hurt that her brother Brinsley had not paid it, implying that George and Brinsley had a cordial relationship, which was at odds with the truth. He ended his letter by advising Caroline to get rid of her share of the lease of her home in Green Street, and dangled the possibility that at the beginning of August she could take the boys to Ramsgate for a month and that they would go as a family to Kettlethorpe Hall for a holiday in September.[30]

Shortly before 7 June, the day the Infant Custody Bill was due for its second reading, Talfourd postponed it for another two weeks; it had again been compromised by letters between the Nortons. It would have taken considerable steel on Caroline's part to ignore George's offer to let her see the children and instead direct all her energies towards the bill.

On 7 June George returned from Guildford, where he was recorder, and talked to his brother about Caroline and the children. Grantley promised to write to her. In a letter George wrote to Caroline the same day he linked the alleged imminent arrival of the children with her paying the debts for which he was legally liable. 'I have sent for the children absolutely, you had better assist me in the meantime, in arranging how the debts are to be paid, and the creditors who are very clamorous (pray instead of allowing your servants to send them to me at present, keep them quiet for a short time), satisfied.'

George Norton was confident that they would be reunited as a family and was keen to present himself as the prime mover, asking her bizarrely – in the light of his ongoing tussles over paying her dressmaker's bill – what her allowance should be until 'I trust we shall be happily, safely and comfortably reunited.' George's communications were mercurial, next sending news that his brother was keen to draw up a deed of separation. It was all so confusing, possibly deliberately so, and Caroline could not predict what might happen next. To underline his eagerness to restore familial harmony George returned to the soft furnishings and decor at Kettlethorpe Hall, telling Caroline how much Spitalfields silk he had bought for curtains and his plans to decorate: scarlet curtains and scarlet leather chairs in the black-oak-panelled dining room, pale blue silk curtains and crimson damask chairs for the drawing room. He intended furnishing their home with some of Miss Vaughan's bits of furniture he had picked up cheap at the recent sale.[31]

Caroline was weary, having not heard from Lord Grantley as promised. As soon as she read George's letter she reminded him for the umpteenth time that until the boys were in London neither she nor Brinsley would discuss anything. She could not resist pouring some scorn on his home improvement plans, asking him not to put blue in the drawing room, considering it 'most unlucky' as it was the colour of the Storey's Gate furniture, and saying that the black-panelled dining room sounded like the Spanish Inquisition.[32]

At eight o'clock that same evening George sent a servant with his response. He wilfully persisted in his stubborn plan that she could only see the boys if she intervened on his behalf with Miss M, persuading her to suspend her action against him. Norton accused his wife and her family of colluding with the dressmaker. If this proved to be the case, he told her, he would end their dialogue and deal through his lawyers, and 'things must resume their old course again'. He also accused her of getting her tradesmen to bring more 'threatening actions' against him. He offered to pay her five hundred pounds a year including the annual interest on the fifty-seven-pound pension her father left her, which as her husband he claimed in his income port-folio; in return she was to 'indemnify him from all the debts incurred', to stop all actions and settle her own bills. If she agreed then things 'may go well, if not they will go to the devil'. If Caroline did not accept these conditions, she would not be seeing her children at her house or anywhere else. George was ratcheting up the emotional temperature, asking that she deal with him 'amicably and render me every assistance instead of opposition, else I shall give the whole matter up in despair'.[33]

Caroline responded in her strongest letter yet. It is an extra-ordinary tour de force of cogency, chilling and calm, telling George how during the past year and a quarter since she had seen her sons she had 'wept, stormed, struggled and prayed to God and man to get them back again'. Caroline scorned his self-pity: 'no one felt for ME'. She had to rely on others to help her cope with her heartache, and he had the temerity to be impatient, attempting to coerce her into agreeing to his condi-tions without having seen the boys. Caroline reminded him that he had been the one to renew their dialogue and that after three weeks there was still no sign of the children: 'no one but myself believes they are coming'. If he was afraid to take his sons from his sister, she would go to court and warned him that his corres-pondence to her would be very damaging: 'I do not fear it and your own cruel letters would show at once the gross and cruel injustice of the whole proceeding.' If he closed down their lines of communication and returned to 'their old course again', she warned him that it would be the end of her personal commu-nication with him as there would be no point in continuing. 'You sent for me, offered to take me back, offered to send for the boys, and now you write on money matters, as if the chil-dren's coming were to be bought by me! For God's sake George, think well of what you are doing; they advised you ill once to an action at law; they may advise you worse now.'[34]

That same day Caroline wrote to Lord Melbourne of her conviction that Norton was insane. Melbourne had little idea of 'the shuffling, the tyranny, the cunning' with which she had to contend. She wrote that even the heart of someone of so sunny a disposition as his would become 'lead' if he had to deal with George's letters.[35]

Predictably, Caroline's threat to make Norton's letters to her public elicited a hostile response. If she promised to keep his letters to her confidential, he would send for the children, he said. If she did not, George threatened legal action. If they did not quickly settle their affairs there would be 'revolting exposures'; he would authorise an advertisement about her in the newspapers, and he and his lawyers would do everything in their power 'to prove that <u>no</u> access be allowed'.[36]

On 9 June, eleven days before Talfourd's Bill was due for its second reading, Caroline still had hopes of seeing the boys and forced herself to keep communications open with George. She reiterated that she was the only person in her circle who believed the children were on their way and reminded George of what she had suffered at the hands of him and his family. 'I cannot close this letter without saying that I do think you ought to be more anxious to make me amends for the admitted injustice of that trial than for any other earthly point! You continue to write as if you had some plea for withholding the children, though the only plea (and that an insufficient one for so cruel a separation) is gone! All you or your family could do can never make amends for the public shame I have suffered, or the year of alienation from my boys'.[37]

Three days later, on 12 June, George wrote to 'my dearest Carry' that he 'half expected' his mother and sisters to arrive in London with their sons that day. But there was a problem: Grantley had apparently flown into a rage when he heard George had 'been forced into a compromise with Miss M' and was saying that Caroline had not done enough to stop the dress-maker's action to recover the money owed. His brother insisted George give him carte blanche to act with regard 'to the children and everything else', and when George said he would not do so, Grantley told him that he 'washed his hands of the whole concern'. Unless something was done to appease Grantley and assure him of 'the honesty of her intentions', George warned, 'the results may be very injurious to the children and myself'. Norton urged Caroline to go to Wilton Place that morning to see his brother, instructing her to say that she had heard Grantley was in town but not to mention that George had put her up to visiting him. George assured Caroline that he had kept all 'their private arrangements and understanding a profound secret'. He warned her not to mention that she knew the boys were on their way and asked her to trust him when he said he would bring the boys to Green Street 'as soon as I possibly can'. George's plotting came to nothing as Caroline was too ill to see Grantley.[38]

Later that night George sent her a note saying that the children were in London and 'in good health and spirits'. He had collected them from the steam packet at Blackwall and would send them to her at eleven o'clock the next morning for the day. He hoped she would be pleased with how they looked and how much they had grown; they did not 'speak so much with the accent as they did when they first went to the Highlands'.[39]

George honoured his commitment, and the children spent 13 June with her, but the following day he wrote to say that Grantley had flounced out of the negotiations: apparently his brother was as displeased with George's conduct as he was with Caroline's. George used this as a ploy to bounce Caroline into agreeing to his latest set of contradictory proposals. All thoughts of her returning to him as his wife had evaporated; instead George suggested that they sign a deed of separation 'whenever either of us may call upon the other to do so'. He would give her an annual allowance of four hundred pounds paid quarterly if she gave him a guarantee that he would not be liable for any future debts. If she gave him 'her best assistance' with the creditors, he would pay them off 'as speedily as I can'. George saved a condition about seeing her sons to the last. He told Caroline he had not 'the slightest objection' to giving her a written promise – 'so long as your conduct CONTINUES IRREPROACHABLE you shall have honourable and sufficient access to them; and you will find that, so long as it is such, I shall have pleasure and satisfaction in consulting you in everything that may interest their welfare'.[40]

Caroline was in no mood to be compliant. Shocked at her five-year-old son's health, she repeated her wish to bring up her young children. 'I do not dispute your people's intention to take the best care of my children which circumstances would admit . . . and I do not hesitate to say that you are wronging your poor boys as much as you are wronging me by depriving me of the power of performing a mother's duty towards them, and leaving them to the care of others less interested in their welfare.'

Caroline welcomed the news that Grantley was no longer involved in their discussions but knew that her husband's behaviour was driven by his fear of being disinherited by his elder brother. She suggested they sign a deed of separation straight away and sort out the financial arrangements and custody of the children. Caroline was concerned about Brinsley's health, which required 'immediate medical advice', and believed that all three boys needed 'care'. She asked George to be allowed to have them immediately and not wait until August, when she was to take them to Ramsgate. 'I feel, after again reading through all of your letters, that our children are somehow made a means of barter and bargain between us, and therefore I say bluntly give me my boys, and I will give you every assistance in my power; continue our painful separation, and I must depend only on the proposed legal arrangements . . . I am miserable when I think of the boys – but I will say no more. I have clearly and decidedly explained myself, and you must be fair and frank, and do either one thing or the other.'

Caroline asked George to look at Brinsley when he was undressed.[41] The next day she thanked Lord Melbourne for the flowers he had sent, which arrived when the children were with her. Although George had promised a visit from them every day, she was mistrustful of her husband: 'there is such shuffling and changing and such an evident desire to outwit me and get me nailed about money and all besides is his own will and pleasure that I do not yet feel assured or comfortable about them'. In general her sons looked 'tolerably well', but Brin had 'grown more nervous and is a perfect skeleton and appears to be growing crooked'. Her youngest, who was three, was 'the sharpest little fellow you ever saw, and speaks as fluently as I do'. The boys were happy to see their mother but did not understand why they had to leave in the evening. Caroline felt sad at the time she had lost, regretful that her youngest was no longer the 'fat fair baby' he used to be. She sounds drained and gloomy about the future and the likely battle ahead with George. 'I feel much the same weariness of heart that one does when watching by a sick-bed: everything very cold, very dim, and very silent and the clock ticking very loud.'[42]

George dismissed Caroline's concerns about Brin's health. He had examined the boy three times and could not 'discern any cause for anxiety'. Norton insisted on keeping them under his own roof but would allow them to be taken to Ramsgate before August – but only if she agreed with the 'reasonable proposals I have made, and that you are sincere in your so often-repeated promises . . . that every possible facility should be given me in adjusting our matters'. George had no objection to Brin being examined by Sir Benjamin Brodie, who had been George IV's personal doctor and was sergeant surgeon to William IV.[43] Norton's postscript took issue with her accusation that he had used the children as a bargaining tool: as their fortunes would ultimately be affected by his finances, Mr Norton felt he had 'every right to obtain such adjustment by every means' in his power.

On 16 June Caroline again took issue with George's obsessive pursuit of a guarantee against any debt she incurred: 'weary of these long vague letters which lead to nothing', Caroline reiterated that she was not asking to see her sons once or twice, but wanted a binding agreement that she would be able to see them all her life. Her position, that if Norton promised she would not 'have to endure any separation from my boys' she would guarantee him from future debt, remained unchanged.[44] George replied by reminding her of her 'conduct', which had to be 'as such as I can approve'. This was the only way Caroline would be granted 'abundant and continued access' to the children. George assured her that he 'cared little for her written acquiescence'; rather it would be 'a grand point for me' in dealing with the feelings and opinions of Grantley (who had re-entered the fray) and 'others who are connected with me'.

Caroline fired back, 'I cannot bear it!' Furiously, she wrote that if he wanted anything done, he had to send the children to her straight away, and if 'you want to drive me mad, you must just keep them and let them suffer by it'. She railed at his weakness in the face of Grantley – 'he is a bad model for faith to be copied from' – and despaired of George's cowardice: 'I wish you would free yourself from the fear you are in of offending him.' She reminded George that he had initiated the dialogue they were engaged in and the face-to-face meetings and letters. Caroline tried to shame George by saying that if he was so scared of his brother and sisters they should sign a deed of separation and have done with it. As for the boys' seaside holiday, she was ready to take them a month earlier to Ramsgate on 30 June, which Sir Benjamin Brodie said was the best thing to do. She asked George to stop writing about paying creditors without settling her access to the children.[45]

On 18 June, three days before Talfourd was due to outline his bill in the House of Commons, George wrote to his wife, saying that he was so upset by her report of Brodie's opinion of Brin's health that he had written to ask the doctor to put it in writing. This sounded to Caroline as if he was questioning her word, hinting that she was exaggerating her son's frail state for her own ends.[46]

In the early hours of the morning of 20 June William IV died of complications after a severe asthma attack at Windsor Castle, the day before the twice-delayed bill was due to be read. A few hours later Lord Melbourne had his first meeting with the new monarch, Victoria, and was told by the diminutive eighteen-year-old that he was to carry on as prime minister. Victoria recorded her first impressions of him in her diary: 'he is a very straightforward, honest, clever and good man'.[47] Talfourd withdrew his Infant Custody Bill from parliamentary business that session because it was a 'subject of great delicacy and importance' and he was 'not entirely satisfied with its working details'.[48]

The children were allowed to visit Caroline each day, and on once occasion Brin, 'who was very unwell', asked to stay with her that night as his father was out of town. Although her 'heart ached for the little creature who was crying and appealing, and to whom it was utterly impossible to explain', she 'dared not offend' George by keeping him. She took her sons back in the carriage to Wilton Place and was soothing Brin outside when her sister-in-law Caroline came to the door, insulted her and shouted at the little boy. Caroline lost her temper with George's sister: 'my answers were extremely passionate'. The next day

Caroline sent a carriage for her children but it returned empty, and she was told the boys would not be coming any more. After the scene at the door her sister-in-law had summoned George from Wonersh, and he was there when Caroline went round to see what was going on. She tried to push her way into Wilton Place but was kept out by George and his sister and came away 'much bruised'.

Caroline next heard that the boys had been taken to Lord Grantley's house, where they all caught measles. The letter she sent to their nursemaid asking after them was sent back to her by George's brother with no reply, and she decided to go to Guildford to see them for herself. Fortunately Grantley was out, and she managed to gain access to the nursery. She was sitting with Brin on her knee when Grantley marched into the room and ordered her out of his house. 'He pulled and shook me fiercely by the arm; I said I would indict him for assault if he was so violent with me. He let me go and called to his servants. Two men came. His butler and he took hold of the sick boy on my knee by his arms and legs; my arm was round him; I was afraid they would break his limbs; I made no struggle on that account, I let them do what they would; they took him from me; the other children ran screaming away.' Grantley ordered the servants to lock the children away and Caroline was ejected from the house. She returned to London and was confined to her bed for much of July. News of her 'escapade' got into the newspapers.[49]

The situation was grave. All direct contact between Mr and Mrs Norton was ended, and George's legal team was threatening to take out an advertisement in the newspapers and go public about their private affairs. Caroline's attorneys, led by Charles Jennings, briefed a special pleader of 'great ability' called John Unthank, of King's Bench Walk in the Temple, for his opinion on the liability of George Norton for her debts. Unthank considered that as she had been driven from her home by her husband's accusations and not been commanded to return, and because he had not arranged an allowance 'sufficiently ample' for her 'station in life', the creditors who had supported her with their goods were in fact creditors of his. It was suggested that if her brother Brinsley was willing to authorise the creditors to supply her, he could then bring an action for payment against George.[50]

Caroline remained in London during August, caught in the familiar situation of waiting to respond to lawyers' correspondence. Boldly she went to the hotel where George's mother and spinster sisters were staying in London prior to sailing back to Edinburgh. Interested to 'see their mood' and hoping that Mrs Norton would have some sympathy for her plight, she was disappointed but not surprised to find them 'all alike'. Not only were they vehemently opposed to George's attempts at reconciliation, they were outraged that she had refused to go back to him – 'the principal reproach they hurled at me was my daring to say I would not return' – and they informed Caroline that the only way she would ever see her children again was if she did go back to her husband.

In August Charles Dickens wrote to his friend the singer and actress Madame Henrietta Sala that he would be 'exceedingly happy to know Mrs Norton'. He had been unable to attend Madame Sala's soirée to which Caroline had been invited. This was the second time he had failed to meet her. Dickens knew Caroline's uncle Charles Sheridan and was hoping that this acquaintance would smooth the way to meeting his niece. The author was having a success with his serial *The Pickwick Papers*, selling forty thousand copies a month. Having been a court reporter at the 1836 trial, he had drawn on the sly and pompous characters he had seen in court that day for an episode, published in March 1837, describing the case of Bardell vs Pickwick.

Dickens asked Madame Sala to put in a good word: 'Please tell Mrs Norton from me that I am a most unceremonious person, and most anxious to have the pleasure of her acquaintance'. He would be delighted to call on her 'if she will communicate the when and where'. In their family backgrounds Dickens and the Sheridans may have been closer than they realised.[51]

At the end of August Caroline's sons were to be taken back to Scotland, and she considered 'a last desperate attempt' to snatch the two youngest, Brin and Charles, and take them abroad 'from whence I am well convinced I could make better terms with [my husband] than anywhere else'.[52] Nothing came of this plan.

On the 31st Caroline Norton and her lawyers received a copy of the advertisement George's lawyers were threatening to place in *The Times* and other leading newspapers. In this one-sided version of events George described how his wife had left him, her family and her home, how he had provided her with an allowance considered by his legal advisers to be 'ample and liberal' and how she had refused to accept it and had run up debts in his name. Norton now announced that he was not liable for any debt she had contracted since the day she left him, 30 March 1836, or any future debt, and that she had no authority to deal with anyone on his credit.[53] It was a bitter attack, but Caroline's position remained unchanged: 'I will not enter into any terms of separation that do not include access to my children who form the only point of interest to <u>me</u> in this matter.' Caroline was bullish in her determination to let the courts decide about her debts and whether they were extravagant for her 'rank and position'. News of the advertisement did not deter her from going that evening to the Haymarket Theatre with Mary Shelley to see *The Irish Ambassador* and *The Nervous Man and the Man of Nerve*.[54]

On 5 September the advertisement appeared in *The Times*.

Caroline's brother Brinsley authorised Jennings and Bolton to respond to it by sending a letter to the editor, which was published a week later. 'The whole of it is false,' it said, but no further details would be divulged as 'the case will shortly appear before a court of justice'.[55] Choreographing the Sheridan response from his estate in Dorset, Caroline's brother hoped that they could nip in the bud any more trouble from Norton's 'cruel advertisement' and show their opponents that his sister's case was in 'good hands'. Brinsley Sheridan, whose honour was at stake, wrote to Charles Jennings, 'I would not enter into any correspondence with a man that is used to swear lie after lie and permit his cowardly and false assertions to remain uncontradicted would only injure the cause and character of my word.'[56]

Caroline passed on to her brother news of George's current behaviour as relayed to her by a servant. 'It is such a grinding insult to us all, he thinks himself so secure in his ill usage of me. At this moment I do not even know where my children are and when you think of those "Dear Carry" and . . . "devoted Greenacre" it really makes me mad and just now when I am so ill . . . It is high time Norton was shown up, he is in a state of triumph such as you can scarcely believe since the children disappeared. He has been giving drunken dinner parties <u>every evening</u> and swearing he will <u>bring me to his feet</u>. He is gone quite mad – he wants someone to show him he can be proved a beast.'[57]

On 19 September Caroline went to stay for a month with her uncle Charles, who was holidaying at Tenby in south Wales.[58] It took her twenty-three hours to get there by mail carriage and steamer. Mrs Gore, her worldly novelist friend, advised Caroline not to trouble herself about any stories that appeared in the newspapers, assuring Caroline that she herself would never respond: 'even if they were to say I had murdered my father'.

Caroline enjoyed hearing that George had been castigated in the *Globe* for 'descending to the means employed by mechanics and small tradesmen to avoid his wife's debts'. She went sea-bathing and sketching, hoping to get better from her 'painful cough' and shrug off her melancholic mood: 'I strongly resemble a large black slug in a damp wood.'

Caroline was back in London at the end of October, when the action against George regarding his liability for her debts and maintenance was due to be heard. Charles Jennings was 'sanguine' about their success, guessing Norton would take fright at the thought of more legal expense, and give up the children 'by way of economy'. The only good news from the Norton camp was that Grantley had been very ill, and in what sounds like a case of wishful thinking, Caroline predicted, 'I think two or three years should see him out.'[59]

The night Caroline arrived at Tenby her uncle went to meet her off the steam packet, lost his footing and fell off the pier into the sea. Charles could swim and was soon rescued but 'it was a frightful accident to occur and terrified me very much'.[60] Charles sounds accident-prone. Although he was only fourteen years older than her, Caroline writes of him as if he was much older: one day he went out with a friend in a 'jaunting' carriage and was pitched onto his face and 'loosened his front teeth'. Apart from Charles' scrapes, she had a quiet time, although she was troubled by insomnia, it became too cold to bathe in the sea and there was a creeping calm-before-the-storm mood. Caroline had more time than usual to read the newspapers and learn about Lord Melbourne's latest project, the new queen. There is a hint of jealousy: he seems to be 'roofed over from life at Windsor Castle', and too busy to write to her in wind-swept Wales.[61]

Well before the hearing George returned some of her manuscripts to avoid any accusation that he had prevented her earning money. His lawyers then proposed that Sir William Follett 'shall settle everything between us', which her legal team rejected outright. It was settled that the sides should agree on a referee (anyone except Follett), and if that did not work then the case would be heard in December. Perhaps weary and wanting to avoid 'renewed slanders', Caroline came round to Brinsley's point of view – that it was better to get terms which would allow her to enjoy her 'children's society' and a decent income without going to court. Mindful of how much 'her tedious and time-consuming affairs' had cost her brother in trouble and expense – 'God bless you dear. I am sorry to be so perpetually tiresome' – she was hopeful that with the threat of hostile publicity and mounting legal bills, George 'must either pay or fight it out, or give up the children'. She promised Brinsley that if she got her children she would never trouble him again.[62]

December was creeping closer. Caroline was house-hunting, and took the lease on a house where she could live, perhaps with her sons for some of the year, in Bolton Street, Mayfair. She reported with pleasure to her sister Helen how much her 'tormentor' was rattled by their tactics whereby he was unable to 'sting' her any more without hurting himself. Caroline wrote Helen a wry impression of her life: she had a cough and cold and spent most evenings by the fire 'like a flower on the desert sand', all her spare pennies spent on caps and pink ribbons 'to keep my ears warm'.

Although her lawyers were negotiating for more maintenance, she was prepared to accept less than had been offered. 'God knows I worked hard enough to help him and them at home – no lawyer's clerk could have worked harder – in the midst of all my "fashionable amusements"'. And although the correspondence with George had been stressful, she was delighted to have his bundle of letters to threaten him with. Caroline knew George dared not go to court and listen to them being read aloud. In the build-up to December her lawyers were pressing for her to have the boys to live with her for six months of the year, and she was quietly confident that they would be successful. There was ample evidence of George showing little interest in them – he had hardly seen them in the last two years – and Caroline knew this fact would look well for her and bad for their father.[63]

It was agreed (against Brinsley's wishes) that John Bayley, the barrister son of the judge and legal writer Sir John Bayley who had represented George at the criminal conversation trial, act as an arbitrator between Mr and Mrs Norton. Bayley only agreed to accept the 'delicate role' if both parties agreed to abide by any decision he made.[64] Norton warned Bayley, 'you will not be met with that honesty of purpose which we would wish for and expect. The people we have to deal with are tricky, worldly and revengeful' and accused Caroline of 'playing fast and loose with us all'. George was actually describing himself and his own behaviour: 'if you can bring them to reason and better feelings, it will be next to a miracle'. He assured Bayley that whatever terms 'you think right to accede to will be cheerfully and confidently accepted by myself and all the members of my family'.[65]

Considering his father had been on Norton's legal team at the previous trial and he himself was her husband's chief legal adviser, John Bayley was surprised that Caroline accepted him as arbitrator. Bayley thought Caroline vain and frivolous. Although his father had lost the case, Bayley believed she had committed adultery with Lord Melbourne, she was only motivated to get a bigger allowance so that 'she might dash about to fashionable parties', and her attempts to get the children back were driven by a concern to rescue her reputation. Before George contacted Caroline that summer Bayley had advised him 'to resist most strenuously every attempt' to give her any access to the boys and advised him that no court would allow her to have the children while their father was alive and forbade it.

However, on 29 November John Bayley visited Caroline at her new home, 24 Bolton Street, and during the two-hour meeting she made an excellent impression. 'I found Mrs Norton anxious only on one point, and nearly heart-broken about it; namely the restoration of her children. She treated her pecuniary affairs as a matter of perfect indifference, and left me to arrange them as I thought fit. I found her husband, on the contrary, anxious only about the pecuniary part of the arrangement, and so obviously making the love of the mother for her offspring a means of barter and bargain, that I wrote to him I could be no party to any arrangements which made money the price of Mrs Norton's fair and honourable access to her children.'

Bayley learned that Norton's account of Caroline's expenses and extravagance was untrue, and read the letters he had written confessing 'gross personal violence'. In spite of all Mrs Norton had been through, he found her 'tractable', 'reasonable' and 'very forbearing indeed in her expression towards him'. Caroline insisted that she wanted to be 'at peace' with George for the sake of her children. The barrister cannot have had the highest personal regard for his client: he had heard from his father that when they lost the criminal conversation case Norton had blamed everyone but himself, saying his advisers had forced him to bring the action. Now Bayley saw at first hand how George's wife's refusal to go back to him had been caused by his spiteful behaviour. Bayley read the Greenacre letters George had written to her with 'amazement' and knew, unlike Brinsley Sheridan, that had she been his sister he would have had no hesitation in publishing them.

Before Bayley met Caroline, Norton had confided in him that he believed she had not committed adultery with Melbourne. Meeting her, Bayley had an epiphany, saw how cruelly she had been treated and became convinced there 'was no earthly reason' why the children were being withheld from her.[66] When the meeting was over Bayley wrote to Norton saying he had found his wife 'extremely reasonable in her conversation' and told him that the children should be returned to London immediately. 'You can command their presence and no real friend of yours would stand in their way.' Bayley expected Norton to send for them right away, if he did not do so he would be 'very much disappointed'. George replied to Bayley, 'I fear, and am certain, the goodness of your heart deceives you as to the character of Mrs N,' but agreed to ask for the boys to be sent down on the SS *Dundee* in six days' time. In a letter to his sister Grace, Norton wrote, 'I beg you will let no impediment stand in the way of as speedy an execution of my wish as can be contrived.' Bayley corrected parts of George's letter in his presence and took the trouble to post the letter himself.[67]

For Caroline the meeting with Bayley was a great success: it went well because she held her nerve and kept her anger against George under control. She then wrote to John Bayley, warning him that George would revoke his letter in the same post, and asked him to 'be with him as much as possible . . . I am so fearful he will refuse you the power to act and take the arrangement out of your hands . . . ask all who know him how difficult he is to bind.'[68] The next day Caroline wrote to her brother, 'I have seduced Norton's referee – he seems a most kind and honourable gentleman,' saying she was in a fever, excited and trepidatious. She had heard reports that Bayley was a 'thorough gentleman', felt empathy with a man who had two sons of his own, and was desperate that he would succeed where she had failed: 'God grant it for if this goes by I may as well hang myself.'[69]

After this first meeting with Caroline Norton, John Bayley thought everything was settled: all she wanted was the right to see her children. He wrote to her the day after and told her not to doubt that her will would prevail: 'What I have said should be done will be done. You shall have "Deeds Not Words".' He also promised to retrieve her account books, a 'pocket book' and jewellery from Norton. During his meeting with Mrs Norton he had liked her so much that in a gesture of friendship and solidarity, and unafraid of her scandalous reputation, he asked if his wife Charlotte might pay a call on her.[70]

On 2 December Norton saw how independent his personally nominated arbitrator was, and interpreted it as Bayley turning against him. He had not enjoyed writing to his sister for the immediate return of the children, and he point-blank refused to return Caroline's pocket book and jewels. Bayley was taken aback by his client's disregard for the terms of his arbitration, and wrote to George, 'My present position toward Mrs Norton and yourself appears to me so awful, that I deem it necessary to bring it once more fully before you, that I may not be ship-wrecked on the quicksands of wavering and distrust whilst endeavouring to make safely to harbour . . . You repeatedly assured me by word of mouth and in the presence of your solicitor, and since by letter, that any arrangement I thought fit to make, or any terms I agreed to, should meet with the entire concurrence and approbation of yourself and your family.'

Bayley was angry at the turn of events, saying that while fault lay on both sides he believed that Caroline had 'suffered an irreparable injury'. He did not agree with George that Caroline was not to be trusted, that she was 'wholly in the wrong, and he was wholly in the right'. The new conditions and restrictions Norton wanted to impose on Caroline before she could see her children were, Bayley felt, 'unnecessary and disgraceful'. Bayley urged George to 'make his path as easy and as straightforward as you can', which was a forlorn hope.[71] John Bayley could have walked away from the task and saved himself a great deal of trouble, but his empathy for a maligned mother at the hands of a devious man made him persist, and he reassured Caroline, against her intuition and ten years' experience of marriage and victimhood, that he would succeed in getting her children for at least some part of the year. On 2 December Caroline wrote a confident letter to Mary Shelley: 'My affairs are I think really ending well. There has been no end of worry and lies, but I trust all is now settled or settling.'[72]

Unfortunately, that same day Bayley received another dissembling note from Norton which sent the temperature of their correspondence soaring. Confirming his worst doubts, Bayley told George that the letter proved that his 'wavering and distrust beyond a possibility of a doubt are confirmed'. Later that evening, when Norton visited Bayley at his chambers in the Temple, they rowed. Bayley resigned his role as arbitrator when Norton again refused to be bound by the written authority he had given him.[73] In an extraordinary development, the barrister's wife Charlotte, moved by Caroline's plight, intervened to try and talk George round, speaking to him as a mother on another mother's behalf, but it was 'water poured upon sand.'[74]

For the rest of December George dangled the possibility in front of Caroline that she might be able to be with her sons at Christmas, the first she would have spent with them since 1835. But the day before the boys were due to arrive in London Norton announced he was keeping them in Scotland – clearly they had not set foot on the SS *Dundee* as she had been led to believe – and they would enjoy the 'Scotch festivities'.[75]

In despair and frustration Mrs Bayley retired from the fray while her husband re-entered, motivated by his feelings of outrage on Caroline's behalf. One day he would seem to be making progress, and then the parameters of the discourse would change and everything was thrown up in the air and he was back to square one. George made his final offer on 11 December; it was more barefaced in its effrontery than anything else he had proposed to date. Before she saw the children Caroline would have to sign a deed of separation; her annual allowance would be agreed by a mediator of his choosing; Caroline would have to 'arrange' to pay her own debts; George would not be liable for her future debts; he was in charge of the boys' education, choosing their schools and appointing their governesses; Fletcher was to go away to an unnamed school, while the youngest two, Brin and Charles, were to live at Kettlethorpe Hall until they went to school, except when they were with their mother; her visits to Fletcher at school were to be determined by George; the children could spend half their holidays with their mother 'so long as it was convenient and proper for them to come home for their holidays'; Sir James Clark was to be their doctor and Caroline was to have no say in the appointment of any other 'medical man'; the boys were to be dressed as their father provided and there were to be no changes in their clothing or diet unless he gave his permission; and the mediators were to have the power 'to moderate or altogether restrict Mrs Norton's access to their children, should her conduct render such steps necessary'. All future decisions about them were for George and him alone.[76] This offer was so outrageously bad that Caroline and Bayley rejected it outright, as George knew they would.

In a last-gasp attempt to blacken her character, George pretended he had found new evidence, waving around three old letters which Caroline had supposedly written years before: the real one was to her sister Helen (she did not deny that their letters to each other were 'playful') about the propriety of eloping to Italy; the others were obvious forgeries about her making 'appointments' with an unnamed person, and telling her children that their father wanted one of them to die so that he would have one less to keep.[77]

On the last two days of the year letters passed between John Bayley in London and Caroline Norton in Frampton, Dorset. His were filled with anger and pain at his failure to get her children back for her: 'I am grieved almost beyond the power of expression . . . if the devil is not with him, there is no such spirit.' Ashamed for human nature 'when I see a woman so cruelly treated by a man, and that man her husband', the kindly Bayley urged Caroline 'never to think of trouble or expense on my account' and assured her that he would do everything he could to see her 'righted'.[78] Caroline's letter to Bayley was stoical: she was happy in her 'misery' that after two years' 'incessant calumny' her husband's position was such that he had been forced 'to walk back to the shadows with which he began', desperately trying to convince even those people who were her enemies that she had no claim to her children.[79]

John Bayley now realised that he had been manipulated from the outset. George, dominated by his brother Grantley, had never intended sending the children to England. During the whole of December quantities of ink were spilled, quills were resharpened, clerks and servants zig-zagged across London from Mayfair to the Temple and Knightsbridge and back again, wrestling with the many-headed hydra that was George Norton. But an agreement for Caroline to see the children was never an even remote possibility. Bayley had been hoodwinked and Caroline had been right. Immediately after Bayley got George to write to his sister Grace on 30 November, George had written a second letter, countermanding his instruction to send the children down from Scotland. When Bayley discovered this he was appalled: 'Mr Norton was base enough to write a second letter, unknown to me, to forbid their coming.' Learning of Norton's 'treachery and breach of faith', Bayley resigned as arbitrator and 'remonstrated in severe terms with him and my intercourse with him ceased'. The gallant barrister son of a famous judge, whose father's team had dragged Caroline's name through the mud eighteen months ago, swapped sides.[80]

VI

The Infant Custody Act

Her conversation is pleasant and powerful . . . masculine without
being mannish.'
                    Charles Sumner meeting Caroline Norton, 1839

A t the beginning of 1838 Caroline's brother Frank was
back in London with debts of three thousand pounds
– now a quarter of a million. Brinsley and Frank knew
they had no right to expect their brothers-in-law, Lord Seymour
and Captain Price Blackwood, to help, but Brinsley made it
clear he was 'totally unable to do [Frank] any service alone'
without denying his wife many of the 'little comforts she has a
right to expect'. He suggested that the family make Frank sign
a written promise that he would 'neither bet, play or gamble
in any way'.[1]

Charles Jennings, already immersed in Caroline's affairs, was
called upon to clear up the 'awful mess'. On the rare occasions
Frank had returned to London he had kept a low profile to
avoid being imprisoned for debt. Frank Sheridan also had poor
form in the marriage stakes. No respectable family would countenance a match between their daughter and a young man with
buckets of charm but few prospects, no money and uncertain
health. In London, Frank was 'living the life of an owl for night

alone is safe to me', with his family standing security for him to borrow money to pay off his creditors. His mother, the now elderly Mrs Sheridan, had been managing his debts and appeasing his creditors, paying the most pressing bills, but her means were small and she had long since reached the limit of what she could do. Frank had got involved with a number of moneylenders, including Richard Keily of Cleveland Row, St James, who had loaned him almost a thousand pounds. Frank called him a 'd----d scoundrel', and was being charged 'sixty per cent interest doubled in six months'.[2]

Jennings was familiar with this kind of situation – 'unhappily for the young men of the present time these occurrences are very rife' – and was asked to find someone else, but he not find a 'stranger' who would lend money on personal security rather than raised against a mortgage. In an extraordinarily generous move Jennings offered to lend his own money and ask his own banker to help, secured by a bond guaranteed by his client, Lord Seymour and Helen's husband, Captain Blackwood.[3] Frank's sister Georgy, Lady Seymour, had serious reservations about the family getting involved in raising such a large sum of money. In an open letter to all family members, including Frank, she was 'most anxious' he was helped but also reluctant to be part of the arrangements; she could not see how Frank could pay back the interest let alone the principal. Moreover, if the Whig government fell he would be out of a job.[4]

Caroline's finances were also parlous and she too was in need of Brinsley's help. Caroline told Brinsley that she had run out of money and was having to send out for a 'pennyworth of potatoes and a half-a-pound of tea': 'I have not a farthing and even that shopping must soon cease.' She wanted his authorisation for certain tradesmen to supply her. Caroline had a butter man, a coal merchant, a milkman and a butcher – which was remarkable since George Norton's advertisement that he would not be liable for her debts. Some shopkeepers would not trust her and she was unable to find a chandler or grocer who would give her credit. (The chandler was important in the nineteenth-century home, making and selling candles.) Her servant Sophia, married to Frederick Burton, an usher at a police court, had not been paid since Caroline was locked out of her home in March 1836. Sophia was working for Caroline at Bolton Street, and would still be with her in the 1841 census, which shows the loyalty she inspired in her servants. Jennings recommended that Burton bring an action against George Norton for his wife's wages, alongside Brinsley Sheridan's action planned for February. Caroline told her brother that if she had peace of mind about the tradesmen and the prospect of Sophia's wages being paid, she would be able to get back to her desk and earn some money from writing for magazines, which with the songs she wrote with Augusta Cowell, were her sole livelihood.[5]

Caroline's focus needed to be directed towards the next parliamentary session, which would put her two-year battle to see her children in the public domain. Serjeant Talfourd was now due to reintroduce the Infant Custody Bill in May. To persuade Members of Parliament of its merits she wrote a new pamphlet, 'The Separation of Mother and Child By The Law Of Custody of Infants Considered'. To give the bill the greatest chance of success she published it anonymously, although many guessed she was the author. Caroline had been housebound, lying on a sofa at Bolton Street, trying to write during February, and at the beginning of March was 'very ill spitting blood'. An ominous sign for anyone, this would have been especially alarming to her considering the prevalence of consumption in the Sheridan family. However, Caroline did not develop the disease during her life, and this episode may have been the result of broken blood vessels in the throat caused by a persistent hacking cough accompanying a nasty chest infection.

Ever since Caroline had learned that a letter she had written to George had been opened by his 'housekeeper', whom Caroline suspected was his mistress, she was nervous about letters coming to her 'safely' and asked her family and close friends to send letters to her care of the Honourable William Cowper, Melbourne's nephew and secretary at Downing Street. Caroline Norton was not by nature cautious, and these requests at the ends of her letters show the insecurity of letter post.[6]

The content of Mrs Norton's pamphlet was as sharp and as clearly cut as a diamond, although she fretted that it might be 'too earnest and womanish'.[7] Eloquent, indignant and pithy, it unpicked the injustice of a mother's position when a marriage broke down. The law was made by men for men; women were at the mercy of its power. Her pamphlet was written from the head and the heart; only someone who had endured what she had could have written such a fine piece of personal and political polemic. Powerful and persuasive, it provided ample ammunition for those reasonable souls who supported her campaign.

Caroline Norton added an appendix of five case studies, from 1804 to the baffling judgment against Mrs Greenhill of 1835. The unwillingness of the Court of Chancery and the King's Bench to award mothers access to their children, even those with unblemished reputations, was indefensible. Mr Greenhill had had a mistress for several years whom he called Mrs Greenhill, lived openly with her for part of the year, and yet was awarded custody of his wife's three little daughters under six years of age. The law as it stood recognised that the father, however inappropriate and immoral his behaviour, had the right to custody of his children, whereas a mother did not.

Caroline Norton's pamphlet aimed to educate, raising consciousness about the injustice of the law. Her opening point was well-delivered. Many people assumed that upon the break-down of a marriage a mother had the custody of her children until they were seven years old, but this was not the case. Due to a 'curious anomaly in law' the mother of an illegitimate child did have custody, presumably because of the likelihood of the father being absent or a married man, but from the moment of their birth children born in marriage were the father's; a mother could not make a claim for custody as a wife had no separate legal existence.

The pamphlet went on to point out that a father who was legally separated from his wife could deny the mother access to her children; only he had any say in the way the children were brought up. He could appoint whoever he liked to look after them. If a mother refused to hand over her children, her husband could physically seize them. A mother might have to hand over her children to be brought up by a woman with whom her estranged husband had committed adultery. In Caroline Norton's view the law was despotic on one hand and impotent on the other. 'The fact of the wife being innocent and the husband guilty, or of the separation being an unwilling one on her part, does not alter his claim: the law has no power to order that a woman shall have even occasional access to her children, though she could prove that she was driven by violence from her husband's house, and that he had deserted her for a mistress. The father's right is absolute and paramount, and can no more be affected by the mother's claim, than if she had no existence.'

She described how the law had in effect surrendered its respon-sibility to the husband in a rocky marriage by giving him the incompatible roles of accuser and judge – a blatantly unreason-able situation because 'the one man in the world who is least likely to be able to judge his wife with the smallest particle of fairness or temperate feeling, and he is the man to whom the real judges of the land yield their right of protection, their intelligence of decision, their merciful consideration of individual wrong and their consistency in securing public justice'. Caroline underlined the hypocrisy of a country and legislature which paraded its loathing of oppression, where a master could be charged with assault if he struck one of his servants, and violent and offensive language were punishable: 'It is a strange and crying shame that the only despotic right an Englishman possesses is to wrong the mother of his children.'[8]

George Norton's name is not mentioned, but the details of the criminal conversation trial were still fresh in many people's minds. Readers knew that he hovered over every page and that Caroline's experience of his fickle and tyrannical behaviour would have informed her rhetoric from beginning to end. If George did indeed read it, he would have seethed to see his shabby behaviour exposed to underpin the demand for a legal change, which if successful would have constituted another defeat.

Not everyone in Caroline's family was happy about her trying to change the law. Her uncle Sir James Graham, the most senior family member, was a firm believer in the law as it stood. Caroline found it astonishing 'how even kind and good men narrow their minds on this subject'. It was a curious position to adopt for a man who knew well the dark side of her marriage. Graham was 'tender and indulgent in his home' but outspoken in his belief that 'the rights of husbands and fathers ought to be despotic', and she knew that 'many others take the same tone'.[9] Her uncle Charles, with whom she lived, was also 'very much against' her pamphlet being circulated.

In the weeks leading up to Talfourd's reintroduction of his bill, Caroline went out of town to stay with her sister Helen at Bookham Lodge in Surrey. She was anxious to maintain her friendship with William Cowper, her line of communication with Lord Melbourne, but felt the awkwardness between them.

Cowper's family disliked her, and she resented being treated coolly by them when they were invited to the same social gathering. On 10 March Cowper was thrown from his cabriolet, broke his leg and was laid up for ten weeks. She jokingly wrote she wanted to pay a call and lecture him on her pamphlet but was sure she would be thwarted by his 'sisters and careful watchers'.[10]

When Caroline returned to London, she lobbied politicians whom she hoped would support Talfourd's bill, at her home in Bolton Street. It was a dispiriting battle. 'No one knows, and no one cares, that is the fact . . . it is an unheard lamenting and an uneven struggle. The woman drops out of her place in society and her happiness at home, as the leaf drifts from the tree to the ground – no sound echoes it, and no eye follows it.'

The writer and independent radical Member of Parliament for St Ives in Huntingdon, Edward Bulwer-Lytton, went to see her to discuss the bill. At the meeting Caroline surprised herself, suddenly feeling shy and unable to pluck up the courage to ask him to read her pamphlet. Caroline was not sure how much sympathy he felt with the cause: 'I cannot feel at my ease with Bulwer, tho' I do with many men who I imagine to be greatly his superiors.'[11] The subject was close to his experience. Bulwer-Lytton and the clever Irish beauty Rosina Anne Wheeler, whose mother was an advocate of women's rights, had married six weeks after Caroline wed George in 1827. Like the Nortons' marriage, the Lyttons' ended badly. They quarrelled violently; Rosina was humiliated by his philandering and neglected while he pursued his writing and political career. In 1836 his lawyers drew up a deed of separation, citing 'incompatibility of temper'. When Caroline met him Bulwer-Lytton was allowing his wife to see her children, but that would end in 1838, when Rosina Lytton was denied access to her eight-year-old daughter and five-year-old son. Rosina was livid at being cast aside, resented having to live on an allowance of four hundred pounds a year and took up her pen to earn a living by writing, determined to make her estranged husband's life as miserable as she could by putting him into her novels, thinly veiled, ridiculous and hateful, for the next forty years.[12] Bulwer-Lytton himself wrote the line 'The pen is mightier than the sword.'

Meanwhile, Caroline's lawyers Charles Jennings and Frederick Thesiger (one of Melbourne's defence team in 1836) were putting together a case against George Norton, which was scheduled to be heard on 21 April. A Mr Emmett, who ran a livery stable in Bond Street and from whom Caroline had hired carriages and horses during 1837, was cooperating by suing Norton for her outstanding account. Caroline was nervous; the legal huffing, puffing and bluffing was to be tested. She asked Brinsley to come up: 'I do hope and trust that you will be in town . . . as it may be of consequence to me to have you at hand, to rebut any lie about my leaving my home.' She knew there was no way of avoiding bringing the case but hoped it was a 'stepping-stone to an immediate arrangement which it is evident would never have been come to without this'. Caroline was afraid that 'the more open the warfare, the more certain the keeping away of the children for ever'. She admitted to Brinsley, 'I have no ready money at all now.' She had been reduced to borrowing money from her youngest brother Charlie, whose finances were as chaotic as Frank's. Recently Caroline had steeled herself to go back into society, attending a soirée at the house of the Marquess of Lansdowne in Berkeley Square, which had gone well. The guests were 'very civil to me which was lucky as I was dreadfully nervous'. Relations within her social circle were slowly starting to thaw: 'the Sebastians asked me (which they did not do last year) but I was too ill to go'.[13]

In May George Norton took out another classified advertisement in *The Times*. This warned tradesmen that, as he had provided for his wife, as of 15 May he would 'not henceforth become or be liable for any debts or liabilities of any kind whatsoever . . . which she may contract or incur'.[14] It did not divert Caroline from concentrating on the second reading of Talfourd's Infant Custody Bill on 28 May. The speeches made against it exposed male prejudices about women who kicked against bad marriages. There was a widespread assumption that all women unhappy with their husbands were committing adultery and a fear that if the bill became law it would be impossible to prevent 'unchaste women' from getting access to their children. A blind eye was turned to the fact that under the law an adulterous father could take his children from an innocent and faithful wife and hand them over to his mistress. A recurring theme with those who spoke against the bill was the idea that if any concessions were made the most 'dreadful change' would follow – once-faithful and devoted wives and mothers would become a 'most dangerous menace to society'. However, in a low turnout of its six hundred and eighty-five Members, the bill passed its second reading in the House of Commons by ninety-one votes to seventeen, and was sent to the Lords for debate on 30 July.[15]

Mr Emmett's action against Norton was eventually heard in the Court of Exchequer on 21 June. From Mr Serjeant Bompas, said to be the inspiration for Dickens' Sergeant Buzfuz in *The Pickwick Papers*, the jury heard that Norton had only paid half of Emmett's bill of one hundred and forty-two pounds. Because she had no vehicle of her own, Mrs Norton had to hire horses and carriages, and this bill was for March to December 1837. Her doctor had advised Caroline to ride in the park because of her 'delicate health', and she had also hired riding horses from Mr Emmett. Bompas, who had been briefed by Jennings and Thesiger, reminded the (all-male) jury that the law was clear that a husband was bound to pay the debts his wife contracted, especially if she had been turned out of her home without the promise of any income 'even for the supply of necessaries'. Norton's lawyers emphasised the allowance he had made Caroline and the extravagant lifestyle she pursued, 'unsuited to her past', and listed other livery stables to which she owed money. Norton's legal team presented their client as a 'man of honour and a gentleman' being fleeced by a woman who had ignored his repeated offers to 'make some arrangement of their domestic matters'. The cross-examination of servants provided glimpses of the angry confrontations which had taken place: a coachman told the court how Norton had pushed his wife out of the front door at Wilton Place and would not let her back into the house.

Summing up, the judge, Lord Abinger, advised the jury that they were not required to speculate if Mrs Norton had committed adultery, and indeed pointedly directed them to bear in mind that she had not been exiled from her home for that reason. He reminded them that all they were required to decide was whether Mr Norton was 'liable for the contracts which his wife had entered into so long as they were for the supply of articles suitable, proper and reasonable to her rank and position in society' and if her expenditure was reasonable 'under the circumstances of the case'. The jury, most of whom would have been married men who prized frugality highly in a list of wifely virtues, took only ten minutes to decide that it was unreasonable expenditure and found in George Norton's favour. Caroline was not in court to hear the disappointing verdict.[16] She learned that Judge Abinger 'spoke confidently of his power to prevent' Talfourd's bill being carried into law.[17]

Before the bill was debated in the Lords in July Caroline wrote dozens of letters canvassing the support of those peers she knew personally or whose liberal principles would dispose them kindly to the legal changes the bill was designed to introduce. One of her targets was Lord Brougham. Born in 1778, Henry Peter Brougham was a barrister who had been lord chancellor for the first four years of the 1830s. His private life was somewhat untidy. He had had a fling with Lord Melbourne's wife Lady Caroline Lamb, and in 1819 married a widow who had two small children, a house in Mayfair and an income of fifteen hundred pounds a year. It was an unhappy marriage, his wife was out of her depth in his world, was rarely invited to host his dinner parties and became a reclusive hypochondriac. Like several other aristocrats and politicians Brougham then had an affair with Harriette Wilson (Caroline's father Tom also had a dalliance with her), which she blackmailed him with during the 1820s and 1830s. They had a daughter born in 1822. Brougham's wife's misery and mental fragility were well hidden.[18]

Caroline told Lord Brougham she greatly depended on him to help 'what I will not call my cause but the cause of all women' and 'hoped to God that something will be done. If those who strain the law to its present interpretation would but consider that it is only where a man is harsh, selfish or foolish that instances can arise of utter denial of the mother's claim, they might not be so ready to uphold the justice of the general rule. I will not bore you on paper – only if you can spare half an hour I will gladly take my chance of it.'

In their opposition to the bill the Nortons had a valuable political ally and family friend in Lord Wynford, William Draper Best, a key member of George's legal team in the 1836 case. Lord Wynford was circulating a pamphlet he had written against the bill, which characterised the struggle as a thinly veiled vendetta by Caroline and mentioned her by name. Caroline had gone to considerable trouble to keep herself out of the newspapers in the weeks leading up to the debate to give the bill the greatest chance of success. Wynford's pamphlet was a blatant attempt to smear the motives for the bill. Caroline saw it as 'the gratification of private spite' and a bid to frighten away reasonable support by creating prejudice on 'personal grounds'.[19]

When the bill was debated in the House of Lords nine peers voted for it and eleven against. Lord Brougham spoke at length against. It was a disappointment for Caroline to hear the arguments he used: 'It would open the door to such frightful changes in the whole of this country, and in the whole of the principles on which the law of husband and wife was founded.' Brougham also argued that the bill would not remedy any of the other disadvantages which existed in the law with regard to a woman's legal position in marriage. If the bill had become law this would have been an admission of the principle of the natural right of mothers to their children and a stepping stone to incremental change, a point not missed by Brougham and its other opponents. Referring to other concerns about women's rights in marriage could therefore be seen as a reasoned opposition rather than mere stubborn resistance to change. The most extravagant remarks made by Brougham came in his final objection to the bill. 'If there was any one thing which more than another tended to protect the sanctity of the marriage vow, it was the love and and affection which women bore to their children . . . What could have a more powerful tendency to make a wife faithful than the knowledge that infidelity on her part would sever her connexion with her offspring? . . . But would not this salutary influence against criminality be removed if the wife should be told, that by the short-sighted and one-sided humanity of their Lordships she might, when living apart from her husband, obtain access to her children?' Brougham's fears that the bill was a veiled attack on the institution of marriage and the patriarchal values on which society and the law had been constructed were widely shared beyond the House of Lords.[20]

Lord Wynford spoke when Brougham had finished. He blustered that the bill could only do 'a great deal of evil and produce no good': it would inflict hardship on husbands, families would be ruined by the costs of litigation, and a father's lawful and natural duty to educate his children would be undermined. Wynford questioned how a father's duties could be performed satisfactorily if his 'efforts were neutralised and counteracted by the influence of the wife'. As well as encouraging adultery, the 'morals of the younger generation would also be corrupted', said the seventy-year-old married judge, who had four daughters and six sons. In his 1845 obituary in the temperate language of the legal press he was described as 'a man of pleasure whose devotion to the opposite sex amounted to a controlling passion'.[21]

Although Caroline told him she was not 'hurt' by his words and actions, a letter to Lord Brougham from her in August accused him of hypocrisy and being 'inconsistent with and opposed to your general line since it is cast in support of oppression and injustice to persons in a helpless position'. She warned that if a mother's good conduct made no difference to custody and access to her children, then more women might seek divorce rather than legal separation and look forward to substituting 'real ties for the mockery and name of ties'. Caroline also warned Brougham that more women might abduct their children and take them abroad, as she had so often considered.[22]

On 4 August 1838 Caroline wrote to George Norton sounding exasperated with his determined self-deception. 'You must assiduously quote yourself and answer yourself – control yourself and justify your opinions to yourself for a little while longer – for the Devil of sitting up has been very potent with me and hath driven out the angel of early rising whose golden and sweet face is becoming, as it were, a dim memory and a thing recalled at times as the face of a friend long-departed.'[23]

A couple of weeks later she went to the Isle of Wight, staying in cheap lodgings in Ryde, a town of 'considerable celebrity as a fashionable watering-place'. Aristocratic families such as the Buckinghams, Spencers and Pelhams had handsome houses thereabouts.[24] However it was not her favourite spot on the island: 'there are no sands and cliffs and for bathing, one is ill off, having to drive nearly the length of the pier to reach the water'. But there were 'pretty drives and walks in the interior', which she planned doing when she felt 'brisker'. Caroline filled her days writing letters and taking lessons from a local water-colourist. Poignantly, she told her sister Georgy that her sitting room overlooked a nursery, and she could see the child, perhaps the same age as her youngest son, saying prayers before going to bed.[25]

When her holiday was over Caroline had to deal with the annoyance of a 'very long, very coarse and very violent attack upon' her in the Tory periodical the *British and Foreign Review*. Hiding behind anonymity, her enemies called Caroline a 'renowned agitatrice' who had written a pamphlet on sexual equality. She denied that she was a feminist or an advocate of full equal rights for women. 'I believe the beauty and devotion of a woman's character mainly to depend on the consciousness of her inferiority to man, and that the greatest suffering that a right-minded and pure-hearted woman can feel, is [being] unable to respect and look up to her husband. Had you read the pamphlet on the mother's claim, from which so many twisted and misquoted fragments are taken, you would have found in it no violence (although so much violence has been lavished upon me), nothing that militated against the religious duty a woman owes her husband; or the inferiority of the position she is intended to occupy; not a line that the purest woman who ever writhed under unmerited slander need have been ashamed of writing.'

Caroline's quarrel was with the law as it treated mothers separated from their children. She was trying to fulfil her role as a mother to her three sons but was being prevented from doing so by a husband whose position was protected by laws written by men, and upheld and enforced by the institutions they ran. She was outraged by the 'offensive innuendo' that she and Talfourd were lovers and that he had only become involved with the issue because of their sexual intimacy. Caroline insisted that the withdrawal of the bill in 1837 had nothing to do with her fruitless negotiations with her husband and that she was not pursuing a vendetta against him: 'if it pleased God to restore my children tomorrow, I should still feel the deepest anxiety for the success of that measure'. Her interest in the bill was not contingent on her own 'misfortunes' and 'would not end with them', and she would always believe that it was a 'gross injustice' for a mother to be denied access to a sick or dying child by his father, that a mistress could have the care of the children of a wronged wife and that the law was unwilling to solve the problem.

Caroline had correctly anticipated the reaction to her answering the article – she would be criticised for seeking publicity – but if she ignored it people would think it was true. She looked into the possibility of suing the periodical but learned that a woman was not allowed to sue for libel in her own name; such a case would have to be brought by her husband.[26]

Despite her disappointments Caroline Norton was able to resume songwriting with her friend Augusta Cowell and a new composer, Mrs Arkwright. For the first time since the spring of 1836 she felt less gloomy and more able to work. She usually dreaded going home after a visit to her family, but recently walking back into her house at Bolton Street 'did not make me cry, or bemoan myself for hours as has been my custom'. Caroline hoped that Madame Vestris, a daring singer and actress who had stormed the London stage in the 1820s with her enthusiasm for breeches (male) roles, would sing one of her new songs.[27]

But Caroline's health took a turn for the worse, and for much of October she was back on the Isle of Wight, this time with her friend Sophia Armstrong. They went on jaunts round the island, Caroline's mood lifted by her companion. She enjoyed it more than on her previous visit. Caroline called the Undercliff at Niton 'Paradise' and hired a canoe and two 'rather stout boatmen' to paddle her round Alum Bay while sketching the view from the sea. One day she and Sophia walked to 'the very point of the Needles and shivered, as the child of the lighthouse entertained me with an account of her father's death, he having fallen over into the sea'. One Sunday they went to church and heard an excellent sermon about divisions, quarrels, partings and deaths, borrowed it from the vicar to make a copy and sent it to George Norton. Caroline wrote to her mother that she would be puzzled by him to her 'life's end' and often wondered if he thought he was a good man, 'for no one would dare so much hypocrisy in religion or carry it on so constantly who did not somehow contrive to justify himself'. There were low moments which even Sophia and the extraordinary views could not ameliorate: 'I find myself tolerable company, except when I am in a fit of lowness, and then no one could talk me out of it. I begin to believe that one's health depends very much on one's mind.'[28] She admitted to her worried mother that her future seemed bleak and fraught with contention. 'If Norton would but give over this wearisome quarrel about nothing, and let me rest! If he would but see, that even he would be better for it, but I suppose we shall continue for the next twenty years . . . feeding lawyers, and maddening ourselves.'

Troubled with migraines, which affected her sight, she worried about the 'dull fogs and tradesmen's worries' she had to face when she got back. Caroline's top priority was to pay the seventy-one pounds George had been let off to Mr Emmett. Caroline confided in Georgy, who sent her sister some money, that she was 'getting weaker-minded by the day'. The weather turned stormy and her fragile optimism evaporated: 'in the morning I wish it were night, and at night, I say "would God it were morning" '. At the end of October she booked a seat in the mail coach and went to London.[29]

The *Crim Con Gazette* was a new twopenny periodical for lovers of lewd tittle-tattle in 1838. On the front page of the issue of 10 November was a drawing of Lord Melbourne and an outrageous account of his relationship with Mrs Norton. There is no evidence to prove that George and his family planted this story, but they would certainly have enjoyed reminding the reading public that the womaniser who was their prime minister, who enjoyed unrivalled access to Queen Victoria, a girl of nineteen, had been entangled with that pushy lady Mrs Norton who was behind a bill to allow separated wives to see their children. The editor accused Caroline of being aware of his 'amorous character'; that in her heart 'the reign of hymen was short indeed'. Soon after the Nortons were married 'an acquaintance with Melbourne' unloosed the connubial knot and she became 'open to the assaults of variety'. The *Crim Con Gazette* accused Mrs Norton of unleashing a storm of adjectives when asked to describe a 'modern husband. He is a snarling, crusty, sullen, forward, cross, gruff, moody, crabbed, snappish, tart, splenetic, surly, brutish, fierce, dry, morose, waspish, boorish, fretful, peevish, sulky, touchy, blustering, ill-natured, churlish, growling, maundering, stern, grating, frumpish, envious dog in a manger, who neither eats himself nor lets others eat.'[30]

Caroline spent Christmas at Frampton, returning to London before the year was over; she had been bruised by the defeat of the custody bill in the Lords but was ready to start again the following parliamentary session. Although Brin, his wife Marchy and Mrs Sheridan begged her to stay until the end of the year, she had work to do on her new pamphlet, *A Plain Letter to the Lord Chancellor on the Infant Custody Bill,* writing it under the pseudonym Pearce Stevenson, Esquire. The recipient of her epistolatory pamphlet was Charles Pepys, first Earl Cottenham, made lord chancellor by Lord Melbourne in 1836, who had refused to reappoint Lord Brougham to the most senior legal position in the country. A contemporary commented waspishly, 'Melbourne must have felt very much like a man who had parted company with his brilliant and capricious mistress and married his housekeeper.' Cottenham was an aloof and prickly man in public, mindful of the widespread view that he was a very ordinary man who have been over-promoted, and was keen to stand on his dignity. He was also a devoted father to his fifteen children. Caroline had great hopes for the new lord chancellor.[31]

The Times devoted two columns to the pamphlet on 23 January, although it did not wish 'to open a controversy on this very complicated subject'. The article only referred to the arguments for the measure but extracted a sizeable chunk of the narrative from the pamphlet concerning what the paper asserted to be 'the true story of the background to Mrs Norton's case'. *The Times* quoted the pamphlet contrasting 'the good luck of the defendant' (Melbourne) in the 1836 case with 'the unfortunate condition of the lady, who, if the verdict meant anything was equally acquitted'. For the first time Caroline Norton's side of the story was being told in the press. The details of her efforts to see her children and her husband's recalcitrance were now on public view, materially improving the chances of success for the Infant Custody Bill. Lord Melbourne's life indeed appeared to be charmed: he held the highest office in the land

and enjoyed unrivalled access to the Queen, with his own apartment at Windsor Castle. This was a source of resentment for
the Tory party and suited the editorial position of *The Times*,
a Tory paper.[32]

Caroline also lobbied publisher John Murray to speak up for
her and her cause. Nervous about the forthcoming parliamentary
session, she told him she needed all the help she could get for
her pamphlet to be read objectively: 'It is so easy to crush a
woman, especially one whose reputation has already been slandered . . . I entreat you to use your influence to prevent my
name which has grown to be only the watchword for insult and
cruel abuse from being any more alluded to.'[33] Caroline was
smarting from being described as 'something between a barn
actress and Mary Wollstonecraft' in an article in the *British and
Foreign Review* written by John Mitchell Kemble, brother of
Fanny Kemble. A precociously clever man – at Cambridge his
friends included Alfred Tennyson and William Thackeray –
Kemble was so talented he could not make up his mind whether
to be a mathematician, a radical politician or a barrister, or
become a clergyman, and he is remembered for his work as an
historian and philologist. He was a sportsman and both handsome and witty. It is curious that he persecuted Caroline, who
was a friend of his sister. Kemble had married a German profes-
sor's daughter in 1836, the year he unofficially took over his
father's role as examiner of plays. The Kembles had three children but divorced after eleven years, their marriage broken by
his drinking and her fondness for adultery.[34]

The identity of the author of the *Review* article confirmed,
Caroline went on the offensive. Hearing of plans to appoint
John Kemble examiner of plays in his own right, she wrote to
Lord Conyngham, a politician with a say in the appointment.
Describing the proposal as 'monstrous', she complained that
Kemble had 'written me down in a style so blackguard and

coarse that even his <u>friends</u> apologised for it'. It was absurd that a man who had called her in print a 'she-devil' and a 'she-beast' be given the role of censoring drama and the language of plays. Kemble had even written that the only reason Caroline had married was for sex – 'so that lust may exist where love does not'. Bewildered by the viciousness of the article, Caroline reminded Conyngham, perhaps unnecessarily, of her links to Lord Melbourne: 'I am sure he has too much generosity and kindness, even were I a <u>stranger</u> to him to wish it done, and I shall certainly send him the extracts from Mr Kemble's work.' She told him, 'the press is a heavy machine against our sex' and if its journalists were rewarded for their unbridled, slanderous work, the situation for women could only get worse. She had walked on 'hot ploughshares for three years', had refused many offers to sell her story to the press, but was resolute in her determination to emerge from 'the shadows'. 'I may be but a worm and they may cut me to pieces but they shall find that like the worm, every atom has life in it still, and if I have refused to turn their own follies against them, it has been out of respect to my own nature and not to them. The press of England will never rest, while it has such easy and careless supporters; "the press" has persuaded the common people that the higher orders are gamblers, infidels and tyrants as men, and Messalinas as women.' But despite her fighting talk, John Kemble was appointed examiner of plays in 1840, and the candidate for whom she lobbied hard, the Irish playwright Sheridan Knowles, was passed over.[35]

Her insecurities and feelings of isolation were expressed in her letters to 'Mr Willie' Cowper, at 10 Downing Street. Every time she saw him it might be the last: 'I know it is all folly and nervousness just now, but there is no one to care whether I am foolish or nervous now, unless you do.'[36] Each time Caroline wrote to Cowper there was the risk that the scar left by her relationship with his uncle would open up again. Remarks in the press about the closeness of Melbourne to the young Queen did not help. Everybody seemed to be being invited to be presented to Victoria except Caroline, and this rankled. To rebuild her life she needed to be presented at Court. Until that happened Caroline would remain in social limbo.

In February 1839 Lord Melbourne received a sheaf of anguished letters from Caroline. She reprised the broken-hearted and angry feelings of the abandoned lover of the summer of 1836. These were prompted by jealousy at the time he spent with other women, including Queen Victoria, and the snubs Caroline felt she received when she ventured beyond her immediate family circle. That the rebuffs came from women with whom Melbourne was on close terms made it hard for her to bear. Caroline accused him of having a long-standing affair with Lady Stanhope predating the 1836 trial, and another with her nineteen-year-old daughter Catherine, who was the same age as Caroline had been when she first met Melbourne. Catherine Stanhope was a celebrated beauty who was adored much as Caroline and her sisters had been ten years before. 'I think if your preference for Lady Stanhope was so very decided it is a pity you made such a useless needless wreck of my life, when you <u>had</u> a woman whose husband is quite contented it should be so – a liaison which suits your sister and your people much better than I. However there she is – make the most of her – credulity lasts a long time but it does not <u>come back again</u>.'

Caroline finished this letter to him with a threat and a flourish instead of a signature. She remarked ominously that he knew very well 'what folly' she was capable of 'for the sake of a preference' and wrote that he should have 'played true'. As he had not done so he was 'the last human being' who had any right to judge her, 'whose spring of evil rests with yourself and never showed till you woke it'.[37]

Another cross letter quickly followed, incredulous that her family had not been invited to join the new royal circle. Lord Seymour, a supporter of Melbourne and the holder of a government position, and his wife, Caroline's sister Georgy, had not been 'considered good enough company for Royalty and its attendants', whereas Lady Stanhope, whose husband 'dealt out abuse to you all and is a rank Tory', had dined several times at the Palace. The thought of Melbourne, the Queen and Lady Stanhope, who was Melbourne's brother's mistress as well as his own, having 'a little family reunion' provoked a rant. 'If you think I will bear it all for ever, you are mistaken. I have been blind – wilfully blind – but I will not be the only one to suffer – I will proclaim what this woman is, who is so fortunately protected and who sins without observation – the visits to you which in me were <u>crime</u> . . . Let her try and disprove it and many other small irregularities your own servants can testify to. You have treated me with the most selfish ingratitude – your hold over me never was fear of consequences, but a personal feeling, which it has been your good pleasure to insult and destroy.'

If Melbourne was not prepared to have her presented to the Queen – the implication being that she was 'not fit to associate with the ladies of the Court' – Caroline warned him that she would expose the 'injustice' of her exclusion and that the Queen had made a companion of Lady Stanhope, who some considered 'an unfit associate'. Feeling belittled, Caroline reminded Melbourne, 'there are few trodden on in this world who do not sting in return'.[38] By the end of February Caroline had not carried out her threat and offered him a last chance, saying it was 'now or never' before she went public with her 'account'. It is easy to forget – and sometimes perhaps Caroline did – that she was writing to the prime minister, who was also the guiding influence on a teenage monarch, but Caroline had to get herself presented to the Queen to stand a chance of picking up the pieces of her life prior to 1836. The last letter she wrote to him in February was two thousand words. Bleakly Caroline wrote how she struggled to find the words in her heart which 'may make you feel for me'. She regretted Melbourne's regard for her 'had faded and has been destroyed by other temptations and circumstances which have pleased, excited and occupied your mind' and reminded him how he had once written that he could never replace her when she went away for a couple of months.

Caroline railed against his explanation that the Queen could not receive her and do 'what is just' because 'it might call forth the abuse' of enemies of royalty in the press. She asked him if the Queen was the only person entitled to his protection: 'Is the abuse I endure nothing, are the paragraphs about me not worth thinking of? If you had the smallest real regard or manly spirit and courage to waste on my behalf, you would have said "My word is pledged . . . I will not tamely see a woman dragged down and trampled upon to bear the punishment which, if just, should be inflicted on <u>both</u> . . . I will not crawl to shore and leave and look round upon her drowning. I will stand upon my word for <u>her</u> as well as myself if <u>I</u> feel the stigma, the abuse, the dread of comment, what must it be like for her who has neither position, connection, nor influence to enable her to bear up against it, and who being a <u>woman</u> must be crushed by the tone of disbelief."'

Caroline had endured a two-pronged attack – her personal enemies had tried to turn her 'giddiness and youthfulness into a crime', and his political enemies had attacked her in order to get at Melbourne – and he had let the attacks on her go unchallenged. Caroline also laid some blame at his door for the appointment of Kemble as examiner of plays after the latter's vicious attack on her, when Melbourne might have urged

Lord Conyngham otherwise. 'Oh my God if it had been <u>you</u> that was helpless and <u>me</u> in power, how impossible it would have seemed to me to leave you to suffer, to make your worst foes my most familiar friends, to sit with them laughing and trifling through those scenes of gaiety from which you were exiled on my account and the exile from which was considered the stamp of degradation.'

Caroline's exclusion from Court was 'a badge of shame' which she would not bear; she had previously kept quiet in case her words damaged him. She accepted that exposure of her 'unjust' treatment would not get her what she wanted, but reason was overwhelmed by her wish for revenge: 'it is the next thing to justice and it is a just punishment on those who inflict it'. Fuelling Caroline's tirade was her desire for Melbourne to show 'A Plain Letter to the Lord Chancellor on the Infant Custody Bill' to the Queen and ask for her opinion. Saying she was saddened at having to write 'that which you do not like to read', she told Melbourne she loved him 'better than most things in this life, better, far better, God knows, than you ever did me – but not better than my whole life'. She begged him for compassion so that she did not lose her future as well as her children.[39]

In March Caroline had to focus on Serjeant Talfourd's third attempt to get the Infant Custody Bill onto the statute book. She wrote to Willie Cowper from Maiden Bradley, reminding him to read 'Pearce Stevenson' and to get others to do so too 'for friendship's sake'. However, an important ally in the Commons, 'kind, honest-hearted' Lord Clements, Member of Parliament for Leitrim, a contemporary of Brinsley, had died of pneumonia in Ireland. Disappointed that the bill did not go straight to the Lords, where it had failed last session, she was 'a good deal out of spirits'.

For such a creature of the town it was hard for Caroline to

spend so much time at Maiden Bradley, the Seymours' country seat. The house was surrounded by beautiful countryside, but the village itself was 'hideous' and lowered her mood. It had been home in the Middle Ages to a 'dreary convent of leprous maidens', and she felt it had not shaken off its 'unromantic origins'. The local people seemed 'sickly' and so did the thatched cottages where they lived, which were covered with a lichen which made them look diseased. In the day the village was deserted: instead of playing the children had to help their mothers spin and wind raw silk.

Cowper was now caught in the crossfire between Caroline and Melbourne. His recent letter had tried to reassure Caroline that his uncle was concerned about her, but she would have none of it: 'your uncle is not anxious about me – if he were, God knows I would have less need to be anxious about myself!' She was an all-or-nothing friend, she admitted, totally loyal to her close friends and equally 'vehement' about her enemies. Caroline was determined to have yet another go at bringing Melbourne back to her and slyly asked Cowper to intervene: 'I do not know that they [her efforts] would be bettered by any human exertion on my behalf, tho' of course I cannot but desire a struggle to be made.'[40] Mrs Norton sent Melbourne two dozen claret glasses on his sixtieth birthday, saying that she had ordered them some time ago before she knew they were to be 'such very distant acquaintances', and sent them with 'a sulky heart because of the dinners you will give to other people and I do not like to add your birthday to the many blank anniversaries I have had to keep this year'.[41]

When Caroline returned to London, George made another pretence of allowing her to see the children. A pattern emerged: ahead of the child custody issue being discussed in Parliament, there would be notes and letters, tears and protestations on his part; meetings would take place and possible access to her three little boys would be raised. George would then agree to pay all the debts which were his liability. The intention was to upset her and distract her from Parliament and Talfourd's best endeavours. She agreed to see George at his office in Whitechapel. The meeting lasted three hours and was arranged by a magistrate colleague, John Hardwick, a bachelor ten years older than George. Even a man of his experience, reputation for 'extreme certainty and courtesy of manner' and the 'inflexible uprightness of his judgements' could not persuade Norton to compromise from his long list of outlandish demands and conditions.[42]

George offered to let her have the children only if she engaged a female companion, a certain Miss Cole, with whom Caroline had attended the school near Wonersh where George had first spotted her fifteen years ago. When Caroline agreed immediately, he backtracked on his offer, saying that the boys should first live with Miss Cole and that they could each visit them there, and then she might be able to have them on her own. Caroline also agreed to this straight away. A meeting with Brinsley was mooted but he refused to meet George, saying he was out of town. Caroline explained this as carefully as she could, but George took it as badly as she anticipated, although she remained quietly 'sanguine that some settlement will be come to about the boys and soon'. She had prepared herself well for the meeting and took the initiative, saying that she was there 'to speak about my children'. Possibly because of the presence of Hardwick, George politely defended himself point by point; there was no acting the part of the outraged husband and he called her 'poor dear Carry'. His behaviour and demeanour seemed odd to Caroline: he did not seem 'rational – but anyone more utterly insane I never talked to except Lady Kirkwall', whose history was well known to the Commission of Lunacy.[43]

In the spring of 1839 a new barrister was given the job of wrestling with George Norton and his interfering family, and helping her work on Serjeant Talfourd's Infant Custody Bill. Nathaniel Ogle was a 'kind and generous friend' and an 'able advocate'. Describing herself as 'a crushed woman', Caroline made an emotional appeal to his bachelor gallantry. She flattered Ogle throughout her 'private and confidential' letters to him by praising his 'friendship and earnest zeal'.

Caroline also sent Ogle a sheet of notes taken by an unknown person in 1836 giving information about George which flatly contradicted his own version of events. The most remarkable note asserted that George had tried to 'borrow' fifteen hundred pounds from Melbourne three days before his final row with Caroline. Melbourne's refusal had helped trigger the chain of events which followed. Frequently, the note taker added, George's behaviour was so 'indelicate' that Lord Seymour was averse to his wife being in his company. Sounding like a pimp, George Norton had several times induced his wife to 'become familiar with men of rank to promote his own interests severely chiding her if she did not do so'. He had also compelled her 'to perform unnecessary and disgusting acts' for him. Desperate to avoid a duel with Sir Colquhoun Grant, who was a crack shot, George had lied to the elderly general about his knowledge of the elopement of Grant's daughter with Brinsley Sheridan. More than once George Bentinck, a family friend, had been sent to Storey's Gate to discuss George's 'indecent conduct' towards his wife.

Caroline instructed Ogle to be careful how he handled her marital difficulties: she refused to be party to any public condemnation of Norton. The line Ogle should adopt was that her husband had been guided and persuaded by others to take the actions he had as 'this was his own excuse to me'. Caroline had great confidence in Ogle, whom she addressed as 'genie of the lamp'. Magic would certainly be needed to overcome the obstacles likely to be thrown up by the 'dark gnome' Lord Brougham. She issued Ogle with instructions on how to lobby for the bill, the angles to take, what to cite in conversation and in letters and the speciousness of Brougham's red herrings, and also asked him to burn her letter when he had read it, a request he failed to obey.[44]

At Westminster in April and July the Infant Custody Bill was read, debated, sniped at by the old guard, who gave their arguments another airing, and passed into law. On 17 August 1839, alongside parliamentary decisions concerning prisons and prison discipline in Scotland, the police in London, and improving the navigation of the River Shannon in Ireland, the first piece of feminist legislation in Britain became law. The act's four clauses amounted to less than four hundred words but changed the legal status of mothers with good reputations for ever. If a wife was legally separated or divorced from her husband, and had not been found guilty of adultery in a criminal conversation case or in an ecclesiastical court, she was now entitled to have custody of her children up to the age of seven and periodic access thereafter. However, because a woman had to be wealthy enough to take her case to the Court of Chancery, few were able to benefit from the change in the law.[45]

Caroline might have hoped to take her youngest son Charles into her care as he was less than seven years old, and to have the legal right to see Brinsley and Fletcher, who were eight and ten respectively, but the act only applied to England, Wales and Ireland. While other women could benefit from the act she had worked for, the prospect of seeing her children was as remote as ever. However, she was not surprised. Nathaniel Ogle had opened negotiations with George at the end of July knowing that the bill would soon become law but found him 'unbending'. George refused to remove the boys from Scotland, where their 'morals, health and comfort were most strictly preserved'. Ogle was told to advise Caroline that she might be permitted to visit the boys in Scotland, but only if a third person was present; and if she demonstrated 'a spirit of conciliation and an altered mind' her husband might be 'disposed gradually to relax in his restrictions' and bring the boys to London and 'permit that intercourse which a mother ought to have with her children'. It would take more than Nathaniel Ogle to conjure up a solution to the problem of George Norton. Ogle told Norton that these conditions were a 'degradation' to which Caroline could not be expected to submit. Meanwhile George was determined not to offer her a penny more than four hundred pounds a year and refused to return her 'trinkets'. Ogle was pessimistic: 'You are to give way upon every subject and he is not to recede upon one; and it seems to me to be ridiculous to talk of conciliation upon such a footing. I fear that, as matters stand at present, there is little hope of any benefit resulting from the interposition of friends, at the same time I should be sorry to abandon the attempt, if there were the slightest probability of my being useful to you.'

The barrister found Norton 'vacillating and vexatious'. George had constantly excited Caroline's hopes only to dash them, and only made promises 'for the opportunity of breaking them'. It became clear to Ogle that George was weak, easily manipulated and not a 'free agent'. Ogle scorned this man who could not be a man – 'until he has the strength to break his leading-strings there can be no prospect of a permanent arrangement' – but could see that Norton still had a great regard for his wife, and she had a 'considerable influence' over him. Despite his generous inheritance from Margaret Vaughan, George still relied on his elder brother's largesse. Vulnerable to control by the dangling of wills and trusts, it seemed unlikely that he would act in Caroline's interest. Norton was also a barrister and knew his wife could do nothing about the children; he had several family homes in Scotland at his disposal, and the new English law, of which his wife had been the secret architect, could not touch him.[46]

In October, feeling 'very low in spirits', Caroline, Helen and her husband Pricey set off with their uncle Charles for a two-month holiday in the south of France and Italy. The warm sunshine, the azure sea and the scent of the wild flowers in Nice were restorative, making Caroline's 'lazy and flattened soul shake out its wings'. Despite appearing 'hideous', her face covered with mosquito bites that made her look as if she was recovering from the 'speckled monster' (as smallpox was then known), being nipped by a spider, stung by a wasp and falling into a pit of quicklime at Cannes and burning her foot, Caroline was happier. After France they travelled to Italy, ending up in Rome, visiting the places and antiquities they had only seen in oil paintings and architectural books. They also sailed past Lerici across the Gulf of Spezia and Caroline asked the boatmen to point out where Mary Shelley's husband had drowned twenty years before.[47]

Helen and Pricey returned to England, calling on the way at Baden-Baden to take the waters. Their son Fred, now thirteen years old, was at Eton, and Caroline wondered if her boys might also attend. She wrote to Helen from Rome asking after her health: 'How is your little frail body? Do the small bones still hang together, or are you mended with white silk, like the ivory skeletons in the chemist's shops?' She learned Italian in the mornings, saw the Colosseum by moonlight, mingled with some other English tourists and exchanged news of mutual friends – a Mrs Craven had lost her senses and was 'under restraint'. Of all the fates Caroline believed madness, 'to have one's soul out of one's keeping', the most melancholic.[48]

A few thousand miles restored some equilibrium to Caroline's correspondence with Lord Melbourne, although her emotions see-sawed in a December letter. She set off for the long journey home but had to return to Rome after her carriage overturned and was smashed to pieces. She was not badly hurt but was a 'good deal shook and frightened and my head has ached ever since'. Her uncle bought another one to get her to Florence and a port from which she would get a ship back to England. Caroline told Melbourne that while she was away she had received news about her mother, who had lost the sight in one eye and had a cataract in the other. There were plans for Mrs Sheridan to be operated on by the famous eye surgeon Benjamin Travers, president of the Royal Medical Chirurgical Society and for the past two years surgeon extraordinary to Queen Victoria. In 1839 the removal of the lens was not easy or straightforward. 'The needle can be passed through the cornea as it is less abundantly supplied with blood vessels and nerves and possesses less sensibility to pain and inflammation. In order to give the surgeon sufficient space to enable him to lacerate the capsule and cut up the lens, the iris should be previously dilated by freely rubbing over the eyebrows and the lids the extract of belladonna. The patient should then be placed on a low chair, the head supported against the breast of an assistant who at the same time elevates the eye lids with his fore and middle fingers. The surgeon should be seated on a more elevated chair – the lower lid of the patient should be depressed by the two fingers of his left hand, while he passes the needle through the cornea. Having reached the centre of the pupil, the needle is plunged through it, and the operation completed by dividing the lens into fragments and forcing a portion of them into the anterior chamber where they are more or less rapidly absorbed. This operation sometimes has to be repeated.' [49]

Caroline wrote to Melbourne that although she had enjoyed the sightseeing, art and antiquities, she was glad to leave Rome,

having found most of the English she met 'cold' in their dealings
with her. She also felt awkward with the 'puzzled curiosity of
the foreigners' as to her position. She had not chanced upon
any friends, rather 'just enough acquaintances to enable strangers to judge how it was the fashion to treat me in England
and act accordingly'. Caroline inserted remarks into her letter
which were bound to make Melbourne wince – she was clearly
not ready to drop her complaints. 'I am worse off than any
woman might be, because my name, and my family, and something in myself makes me an object of attention and curiosity
– and turns all that was a flattery into an insult . . . It is nothing
to the Queen or you that I should not be able to command the
company of one female companion while I have been here but
it is something to me when I come in after my sightseeing is
over and sit down by the fireside in my hotel, to feel that wherever I go, this shadow walks after me.'

She told Melbourne that she had seen something in a shop
of curiosities that would have interested him, a small black
cabinet inlaid with ivory etchings of birds, and 'to my astonishment your favourite subject of a woman whipping a child or a
nymph whipping Bacchus, or some such thing'. Caroline was
nervous about taking such a 'bad contraband joke' back to
England and having it seized at customs.[50]

The day before Christmas Caroline's dreary debt drama was
back. It was embarrassing to return home to another creditor's
case being heard in the Court of Queen's Bench. Mr Harvey of
Westminster Road, a carpet retailer, was suing George Norton
for an unpaid bill of fifty pounds for rugs and carpets he had
supplied to Caroline at Bolton Street in January 1838. The
presiding judge, Lord Denman, had supported the Infant
Custody Bill in the House of Lords, saying an 'alteration of a
sweeping character in the present law on this subject was absolutely necessary . . . for the prevention of the frightful injuries

to society which the present system gave birth to'. Denman advised the jury that a wife must be clothed and fed by her husband according to their rank in society, and there was no reason why she should not be furnished with 'necessaries' in the same way. As Norton had excluded his wife from the house without 'assigning any reason', he was prima facie liable, but only for goods supplied for the purpose of maintaining her in a 'reasonable manner according to her station in life'. Norton's heavyweight legal team, which included Sir William Follett, argued that he was not liable for this debt as she had not needed the rugs and carpets, and they were in fact for Charles Sheridan's use. The jury was clearly sympathetic to George Norton and did not bother to retire to consider its verdict but immediately found in his favour. Mr Harvey was still out of pocket; George had again wriggled out of his financial responsibilities; and Caroline's lawyers were no further forward in establishing his liability for her debts.[51]

Caroline spent Christmas Day in London alone, detained by having to proofread a new hundred-and-twenty-five-page pamphlet. Three days later she went to Maiden Bradley to spend New Year with the Seymours, nervous of being 'crunched on the rail-road'. Before she set off she heard that her brothers Frank and Charlie, who were both trying to forge new careers, were displaying symptoms of the dreaded consumption. Frank's job in Ireland had come to an end earlier that year when the Earl of Mulgrave was appointed secretary of war and the colonies, but Mulgrave got Frank a position as secretary and clerk of the council and remembrancer of the Court of Exchequer on Barbados. Also helped by patronage, twenty-two-year-old Charlie, after clerking for several years at the Admiralty, was starting in the diplomatic service in Bogotá in Colombia.[52]

In the snakes-and-ladders game of Caroline's life, she had inched her way up the ladder when the Infant Custody Bill was made law, but she was now back on the bottom rung. Her boys were in Scotland, where her law could not reach them, and she was stranded in a social wilderness until she was presented to the Queen – and facing more creditors.

the ladies would be very sea sick if they felt how often they trembled in the scale —

VII

Wrangling, Dangling and Death

I'm certainly dying – I shall soon be strangled, pray for me.
William Charles Norton aged nine

Caroline Norton suffered what her uncle described as hydrophobia when she heard that her boat from Calais could not dock at Dover and that she would have to go ashore in 'a little boat'. Nowadays this would be called a panic attack. She was in a nervous state as she returned home.[1] The first weeks of 1840 she spent in Brighton. Always afraid of any signs of blood in her sputum, she asked Sir Benjamin Brodie to examine her, and he assured her she was not consumptive.[2]

For some time Caroline had been looking forward to having what she called a love life, but that was impossible while her separation from Norton was still unresolved. She had to be without the whiff of any scandal if she was to see her children again. Caroline confided to 'dear Willie' Cowper that she was only two years older than her sister Georgy, but because of her social exclusion she had 'kept company with the old' and wanted to spend time 'being among the young, those who know the least of me, those of who I know least'.[3]

However, Caroline's rehabilitation into society was at last

under way. She was invited to a concert in February for the newly married Queen and Prince Albert hosted by the wife of the Marquess of Normanby. The professional singers were men; the female voices – 'sweet, quavery and nervous' – were supplied by her ladyship, her sisters and other ladies of the Court. After five years Caroline was back in the company of ladies, and in the same room as the Queen if not by her personal invitation.[4] Word had leaked from inner royal circles that now the Queen was married she had time to consider Caroline's position and might reverse the decision of her uncle, William IV, who had ruled that Mrs Norton should not be presented at Court again. William had been dead for three years. Caroline was hopeful that her moment had now come, and asked William Cowper for his help. 'I stand upon the King having had no right to make a rule against me, which is put in force against no other woman. I stand upon the Queen's having no right to do it – I stand upon your uncle having little right to leave a weak party involved <u>with him</u> to bear the punishment which both or neither should undergo . . . while the obstacle appears less, the hardship seems the greater, and the interference of any one who has influence over him more likely to succeed.'[5]

Caroline's spring was spent trying to secure access to her children by corresponding with her mercurial husband for the fifth year running, in the meantime attempting to earn some money by completing a new book of poems. George recycled some of his old demands and added a provocative final condition. He said that if he was 'legally secured' against her debts he would pay her four hundred pounds a year but only as long as he held his magistrate's office. Caroline had to promise 'with legal security' that she would 'not carry off or suffer any other person to carry off' the children 'from any place where they shall be placed by my direction'; to promise that she would not 'weaken or impair the respect or affection of the children for me or my family' or let anyone else do so; there was to be no interference 'in the slightest degree in the management of their health, dress or education'; and finally he demanded 'your solemn promise to discontinue all communication whatever with Lord Melbourne'.[6] If she agreed to this last condition it would suggest the 1836 verdict had been a miscarriage of justice.

Caroline agreed to the first three conditions without demur and dismissed the last with contempt: 'With respect to your introduction of Lord M's name, it was scarcely worth while to call it up again to insult and pain me.' Caroline suggested that as George's sister and her husband, Sir Neil and Lady Menzies, were looking after the boys and had become part of their quarrel, they should help decide their financial differences: 'I am quite willing they should be umpires, and that if you are pleased to abide by their decision, I am quite willing to submit to them what is fair you should do about these money matters, as to forward to them the letters which passed between us in 1837.' Caroline ended by politely threatening to act on her lawyer's advice to proceed against him if he did not arrange for her to see the boys within 'a fair and reasonable time . . . because during the four past years you have often led me to believe that all was about to be settled, and then ended in doing nothing'. She looked forward to when he ended his 'obstinate supposition that I am your active enemy, who am so heart-weary of this quarrel'.[7]

George rejected outright her idea of consulting the Menzies, said that his own mention of Lord Melbourne was 'from no motive of "insulting" or "paining" you, but from a proper sense of duty' and stuck to his guns that it would remain one of his conditions. Dragging in Melbourne to complicate the negotiations further clearly angered Caroline: 'you know he was not in any way the cause of our quarrel, and it is therefore a needless and ridiculous insult to make him APPEAR so in any condition between us, especially three years after you had admitted your injustice, and requested my return home'. Caroline told George that so far she had resisted appealing to 'this new law' and remembered a time when there 'was a bond between us instead of a bitterness'. Giving him six weeks' notice, she told him that she was prepared to pursue her right to have custody of her children even though the act did not apply to Scotland, where her boys were being kept from her: 'the law presses a little hard on women, but there is justice to be had; do not drive me to seek it but let me owe it to you at last.'[8]

On 3 April Norton was still resisting any concession unless the issues of money and Melbourne were addressed. He dangled the bait of the boys, who were apparently due to arrive with his mother or sisters in London 'very shortly' for a two-month stay. If Caroline met all his conditions 'they shall visit you constantly' at her home and 'return to me at such times I think proper'. But in the next sentence George admitted he did not know when they would arrive and wrote that the children could be taken to Edinburgh, where he would allow her to go and see them without a third party being present. If she abided by his terms and her visit to Scotland went well, 'further communication between the children and yourself is likely to be attended to without benefit. I shall be disposed to grant it to an extent much greater than the law can under any circumstance give you'. So furious was she made by his vacillation, Caroline took several days to reply. She accepted his financial offer – 'I would rather starve than not have my children' – but would not allow any man's name to be made part of the conditions between them 'because it would appear as if something about my conduct had been the bar between me and my children, and would destroy your own admission of the injustice done me'.[9]

Caroline was now so short of money that she wrote to John Murray urging him to reprint her *A Cry From the Factories*. It would help her 'for I am in many troubles and difficulties from which I look to my pen to extricate me, as the soldier trusts to his sword to cut his way through'.[10] In June Murray agreed it should go to a second edition; and he had it bound with the second edition of *The Dream*, her book of poems published by Henry Colburn earlier in the year.

A couple of days after Caroline sent her exasperated letter, she received a reply from George that dripped with pomposity. He was immovable and scolded her about her language, which was 'discreditable to any woman of decency and respectability'. George threatened to rake up her colourful past if he had to, mentioning that her family would corroborate that she had intended to elope with a man whose name was known to him; accused her of trying to abduct their son Brin and alleged she had tried to 'ruin' him by running up debts which he could not pay. He wrote that he had been kind and 'indulged' her because he hoped that time had 'bettered, if not corrected' her. Caroline dismissed the elopement story: 'Do you suppose I would be idiot enough to brave you, if there was anything to prove in my conduct, or that you can persuade me, that if you could prove anything you would spare me?' However, she admitted she had tried to snatch all of the children, not just Brin.[11]

In May 1840 Caroline had dinner with some of the literary set at a party hosted by the poet Samuel Rogers. She sat next to Charles Dickens, who had received a letter from the artist Daniel Maclise envying his invitation, joking that he hoped Dickens would not have to sit between 'the Heavenly Norton and the Blessed Seymour for this is too much to bear'. Caroline's sisters Helen and Georgy, the latter's husband and the actor-manager William Charles Macready, were also among the guests.[12]

Beyond Caroline's family circle Mary Shelley was one of the few women in whom she could confide the pain of the loss of her children and also her disappointment at being recently presented at Court and finding it something of a disappointment. After months of nagging Lord Melbourne had succeeded in having Caroline and her sister Lady Seymour presented to the Queen at Buckingham Palace. Caroline wore Isle of Wight lace over a white satin gown with a train of pale lilac poplin trimmed with lace; her headdress had lilac flowers and white ostrich plumes.[13] Some of the ladies present had looked at Caroline askance, but her social rehabilitation had clearly begun and she could be invited elsewhere. Although grateful that the Queen had been 'very kind', she told Mary that the occasion had been an anticlimax. 'The petty successes so valued while one is very young and eager and vain fade into vapour afterwards. I feel the "in vain" of every advantage personal or worldly which may accrue to me and I feel it the more now. I fret less, I struggle less but I hope less. What is anything worth in this life if the strongest of all ties is made the one means of poisonous discomfort? I have not seen the boys and I dare say the summer will slip by without my doing so now that shuffling man has put off so much time.'

Caroline clearly cherished her friendship with Mary and promised to let her know 'if ever I have any good news'. Although her own life had become a 'strange mixture of helplessness and power which has become the warp and woof of my destiny', Caroline hoped to be able to 'serve' her friend, 'who has had more of the world's bullets than is good for her'.[14]

Returning to her correspondence with George, Caroline hit back at his pig-headed intransigence: 'you married me to please yourself; there was nothing extraordinary in your falling in love with a very young, intelligent, good-looking schoolgirl, not anything to call for particular gratitude in the fact. You swore to love and protect me: was your "love" shown by violence at a time when most men have compassion on a woman [when she was pregnant]; or your "protection" in suffering me to be dragged through the court of justice for the sake of a friend who <u>you</u> perpetually encouraged, from whom <u>you</u> asked favours to the last, and whose picture lay unchallenged and unquestioned on the table of our sitting-room?'

Caroline told him bluntly that she could not trust him. To tell a man who congratulated himself on being a 'gentleman of the first rank' that he could not be trusted was a profound insult. George was livid, and instead of agreeing to her seeing the children, suggested that she sign a deed of separation. Norton concluded his letter with a tug on Caroline's heart strings by saying that the paintings that he had commissioned of the boys would be sent to her when they were finished.

Caroline then promised that she would not allow him to be liable for more than the four hundred pounds a year allowance he had offered, and that he would not be 'annoyed or called upon for any payment whatever but the quarterly one paid by your bankers'. If he did not trust her, she would ask a 'gentleman of station and character and eminent counsel, what would be fair and reasonable terms of separation for me to propose or accept' and submit these to George and his advisers. Caroline told him she found his offer to send the pictures of the children disturbing: 'while you behave so harshly about the children themselves, it must seem rather a mockery than a kindness to offer them'. George refused her proposal; whenever an independent referee was suggested as an arbitrator, he pulled back. He told Caroline dismissively that she had no chance of having her children brought back to her from Scotland by any court in the land.

At the end of May, undaunted by her husband's legal knowledge and worn out by years of shilly-shallying, Caroline told George she was going ahead with an appeal to the English courts. 'Of course I know I may fail, but at all events my suspense would be over, and in the meanwhile I should not have bound myself to a disadvantage. You are providing for me at the minimum of what you can afford, and I cannot well be worse off. It would be very absurd of me suddenly to bind myself contentedly to what I think a grievous injustice, without any covenant about the boys to compensate me . . . I shall go into court with a clear conscience, and conviction of the necessity of such a proceeding . . . month after month passing away in useless and shuffling letters, which, while still affirming that you do not refuse access, leave things in fact exactly as they were. I am weary, utterly weary of it!'[15]

In the summer of 1840 Caroline Norton's *The Dream*, a book of poems, was published by Henry Colburn, who had launched her career in the 1830s. It was dedicated to the Duchess of Sutherland who had stood by her after the 1836 trial and invited Caroline to ride openly in her carriage in full view of society. She received a clutch of good reviews, consolidating her career as a poet: Hartley Coleridge, son of Samuel Taylor Coleridge, called her 'the Byron of our modern poetesses'. He praised the 'intense personal passion of her work' and the 'intervals of tenderness and forceful expression'.[16] Coleridge's comments in the *Quarterly Review*, which were reprinted in *The Times*, boosted sales, and within months *The Dream* went to a second edition. The *Naval and Military Gazette* praised the book: 'There is nothing more beautiful in contemporary poetry than many of the passages of this delightful composition. Mrs Norton is certainly among the more graceful, elegant and passionate of our female poets and since the loss of Miss Landon and Mrs Hemans she may be considered as having succeeded to what was until then a divided throne'.[17]

The frontispiece is a portrait of Caroline by Edwin Landseer, an artist better known for his painting of dogs and stags. She is seated, her dark hair is dressed and trimmed and flesh is displayed. She is a beauty whose pensive look, with a book discarded carelessly by her fingertips, suggests she has grown wiser. A handsome man who was popular with women, Landseer was linked with some of the great lookers of his day, and Caroline was one of them during the late 1830s. Landseer, in a histrionic mood, had tried to fall out with her in 1838, but she would not allow his sensitivity to spoil their friendship. Caroline wrote to him, 'It would take more to offend me than a huffy note from you, as I have seen too much gentlemanlike and generous feeling in you, not to forgive you for being touchy, even when I did think it unjust.'[18] Landseer loved falling in love, but it seems that his feelings for Caroline were not reciprocated. She liked him as an artist and friend but refused to take his temperamental behaviour seriously. At the time *The Dream* was published he had had a nervous breakdown from which he never completely recovered: his mother had died in January, the Duchess of Bedford had rejected him and a close friend had been murdered.

The Dream is an autobiographical and sentimental celebration of motherhood and maternity by a mother who had not seen her children for more than a few snatched moments for four years. Remembering her own wedding day in 1827, Caroline undermines the idealisation of marriage in the final stanza. 'There was a pause; then, with a tearful smile, / The maiden turn'd and press'd her mother's hand:– / Shall I not bear what thou hast borne e'erwhile? / Shall I, rebellious, heaven's high will withstand? / No! cheerily on, my wandering path I'll take, / Nor fear the destiny I did not make: / Though earthly joy grow dim, though pleasure waneth / This thou hast taught thy child that God remaineth! / And from her mother's fond protecting side / She went into the world, a youthful bride.'[19]

After a brief respite the Nortons were again wrangling with each other with neither giving an inch. George told Caroline that despite her ungraciousness he had sent her the pictures of the children. When Caroline received the portraits they triggered feelings of enormous loss, of the four years of their lives which he had stolen from her: 'you expect me to feel as if you had done me a favour . . . I CANNOT forget . . . that you have contrived that at least one of those boys would not know his mother if he met her by chance in the street.' Caroline felt bitter that George's life was little changed by what had happened because he was the father, whereas she suffered every day from 'the extreme sickness, irritation, and heart-ache'. She had married a man 'to whom motherhood goes for nothing'.[20]

At the end of September 1840 Caroline was staying on the Isle of Wight. George had consented to send the boys to her on the island for half of their holidays while he looked at possible schools for them. They argued over her signing the deed of separation, which she agreed to do but on condition that it was held by a third party until she knew the boys were in England. She rented a house at Yarmouth, close to Freshwater, famous for its 'stupendous cliffs', which soared six hundred feet above the water and down whose 'frightful precipices' the intrepid locals clambered for birds' eggs. Caroline lit fires and aired all the rooms ready for their arrival and waited. After ten days they had still not come. By late October she was devastated that they had not arrived and dreaded how George would react to a questioning letter from her. Nevertheless she wrote asking where the boys were. Norton replied suggesting that she return to London, where he would deliver them to her with their tutor. She packed and scurried back to Bolton Street, but they did not come. Caroline wrote to George again. 'I cannot believe, and indeed it is almost incredible that you have once more led me to expect the arrival of my children only to disappoint me. Nevertheless, as you are suddenly silent on this matter, and I am keeping fires in the rooms I expected them to occupy, and unable to settle my plans, I must beg you will inform me whether I am to look for their arrival or not. The utter carelessness and inhumanity shown me in all this business is so great, that in an invented story, it would be pronounced unnatural!'

On 2 November George sent Caroline a brief cryptic note stating that 'circumstances that have much grieved me have come to my knowledge' which made it 'utterly impossible' for him to send the children to the Isle of Wight or to London. He did not explain what the circumstances were and suggested she apply to the Court of Chancery as she had planned. Caroline was shattered by his 'dogged and cool inhumanity'. She demanded to know what the circumstances were, or whether it was 'a trick of cunning, to delay by fair words any proceedings against you'. Caroline told him that she was prepared for whatever decision the court made about her access to the children, and that she could no longer suffer his tyrannical behaviour. She said she had prepared herself for the possibility of not being able to see the children again until they were adults, when they would learn for themselves how he had persecuted them as children by denying them their mother. Caroline wrote that George had made an 'orphanage' of their little boys' lives.[21]

Caroline's mood was volatile, some days in the depths of despair about 'the great blow' she had suffered, during others 'more cheerful and rational than I used to be'. She thought that time 'dulled the edge of most sorrows', and as she had been parted from her sons for four years hoped the pain would start to fade. As adults they might be her 'nearest friends'. When her eldest son Fletcher came of age at twenty-one she would only be forty-two and could enjoy their time together. She had heard reports of him being 'a sweet creature and very kind and gentle to the younger ones'. Charles, the youngest, now seven, was said to be a child of 'very remarkable abilities'.[22] Around this time Caroline was unwell. Between the middle of November and early December she was spitting blood and unable to leave the house. She wrote to her friend Mrs Gore to ask if she had any friends in Paris who could cheer up her friend Mary Shelley, who was there and feeling miserable. She realised she was asking a lot as Mary's position among the English was awkward, 'but poor soul, she is a "quiet body" and really very agreeable and they ought to be glad of her'. Having been 'tricked and cheated' by George Norton all summer, she told Mrs Gore she felt that she was 'surrounded by blue devils'.[23]

Caroline's celebrity had attracted the attention of a man who now would be described as a stalker. The day before Christmas Eve she and her uncle Charles were summoned to Marlborough Street Magistrates' Court to give evidence against a certain Edward Wentworth Pearce, who said he was a captain on half pay, and was well known to the court. Pearce was charged with 'loitering about her residence with felonious intent'. Caroline found herself having to describe the bare bones of the 1836 case by way of explaining why the prisoner had 'annoyed' her by forcing his way into her life. Pearce was one of several strangers who pestered her in various ways. He had written to her offering his mediating skills in getting her children for her and called at Bolton Street several times. He offered her uncle's butler, the only male servant in the house, a free ticket to the opera, hoping to get him out of the way so that he could 'annoy her in his absence'. Caroline asked for help from the local police, who obliged by sending one of their men to wait for eight nights to take Pearce and any other nuisances into custody. She explained to the magistrate, Mr Dyer, that the 'repeated attacks' by the half-pay captain and others had made her ill, and her 'constitution had been so enfeebled that her life was a burden to her'. A week before, Pearce had been hanging around her home, and when her mother arrived by carriage he entered by forcing his way past the partially sighted Mrs

Sheridan. The policeman waiting inside arrested him. Caroline told Magistrate Dyer that if Pearce promised to leave her alone she would drop the charge. Pearce replied that it was 'solely from feelings of sympathy' for her that he had called to enquire after her health and to help her to see her children. Caroline told the court she suspected that he was in the pay of Lord Grantley, as the newspaper accounts of the trial had not mentioned her sons. She also mentioned having received anonymous letters over a period of three years inviting her to attend meetings at various addresses which her servants discovered were of 'a disreputable character'.

Pearce described how he had been arrested. He had been shown into a room at Bolton Street and had admired a portrait of Caroline's grandfather Richard Brinsley Sheridan, telling Caroline that he had been introduced to Sheridan by his friend Edmund Burke. He was then startled to be bundled out of the house and into custody. The magistrate asked him how he expected to be able to help Mrs Norton; Pearce told the court that he mixed 'a great deal with the first circle at the west-end and I thought it very likely I might meet with someone who might have influence in the affair'. Caroline testified that Pearce had been seen watching her house 'night after night'; to this he 'disclaimed in most vehement terms any intention either of doing anything wrong or annoying Mrs Norton'. Pearce finally agreed not to write to her any more, or annoy her, and she dropped the charge.[24]

Caroline's stalker was certainly strange. In 1828 he was described as a captain and a 'gentleman whose appearance and manner possess a great deal of oddity' who had befriended Dr Vickers and Mr Bradley of Marylebone, often paying calls to entertain them. But they quickly tired of his visits, accusing him of 'paying intrusive calls' on their friends and 'making ridiculous apologies'. There was a quarrel, and Pearce accused Bradley of giving him a kick or a blow in the middle of his back, which he denied, supported by Dr Vickers.[25]

The truth behind the man who called himself a captain was that the white-haired and white-cravated fellow was 'a sly, old vagabond' who lived on his wits. In the past he had served as an assistant surgeon in the army but was pensioned off. His sister, Mary Ann Pearce, who called herself Lady Barrymore, was a notoriously violent drunk who had spent many nights in the cells of watch houses and bridewells, and had served days on prison treadmills all over London for smashing windows, fighting and once 'setting Holborn into an uproar'. She would drink 'frantically' and turn into a 'furious termagent', picking fights with everyone. One morning when she appeared in court after a night in the cells, while being lectured by the magistrate, Sir Geoffrey Alderson, who was unfamiliar with her previous conduct, she reached under her apron and threw what looked like a cannonball at his head. Luckily it only 'discomposed his curls' and proved to be her own petticoat which she had rolled into a hard ball.

Caroline knew Norton and Grantley had sought evidence against her from disgruntled servants, so it took a while for her to believe that Pearce was unhinged and not in the pay of her in-laws. She had been afraid he might break in and steal her papers, and asked her friend William Cowper, 'Would any man watch a house for five weeks in that hard frost from "sympathy" even for mad frolics?' After the case was heard Caroline learned that her stalker, when apprehended, would pretend to be an incoherent eccentric or a puzzled and harmless old gentleman, and often got off unscathed or with a small fine. Mr Dyer, 'the kindest and most gentlemanly person possible and noted for intelligence', who had dealings with his sister in 1823, fell for Pearce's bumbling and earnest persona in 1840.[26]

On 20 January 1841 Caroline received the dreaded letter

from her lawyers confirming that the new Infant Custody Act had no power to order George to bring the children to England. She could go and live in Scotland and apply to see them there, but her advisers counselled against it, predicting she would have 'very great difficulty in preventing evasions of the order and, or vexations in the conduct of those bound to obey it'. Her lawyer put his finger on the problem with the new law: it was symbolic rather than practical; it 'recognised a mother's right' rather than being a 'means of redressing her wrongs'. If she decided to test her case in the Court of Chancery it would be unlikely to succeed and ruinously expensive.[27] She learned from various sources that George was paying to have her house watched to check who visited her and how frequently, and her servants were being questioned.[28]

Even though the Nortons' situation was in a state of 'dull calm' over the winter of 1840–1, Caroline was still being bullied by George, who warned her that if she put him to any expense by litigation her sons would suffer as he would have no money to send them to school or university. Brinsley Sheridan's lawyers were confident they could winkle the boys out of Scotland, but Caroline was not so sure. At the beginning of 1841 Caroline told Augusta Cowell that she was in a state of collapse, having to stay at home and lie on her sofa: 'What a fearful thing to have the soul so clogged by the body and the body so weakened by the soul, as we certainly find it!'[29]

Caroline wrote to Mrs Gore with her memories of meeting the man who would become such a horrid husband. She had been indifferent to George and ambivalent about him: 'It sounds absurd but I never had any romance about him (tho' I believed he had every good quality when I married and meant to be very comfortable).' Nowhere in Caroline's letters does she recall any happy memory of George. As she considered what a 'capricious thing memory is', she shared with Mrs Gore the only recollection she had of her father: a haunting one, of him leaving her on a little bridge near Rossie Priory in Perthshire, the home of their friends the Kinnairds, and saying to her mother 'How sweet all this is.' This would have been shortly before the Sheridans sailed for the Cape, from where Caroline's father returned in a coffin.[30]

Without telling his wife, in the spring of 1841 George Norton sent their sons to Laleham School, near Spelthorne in Surrey. It was the first preparatory school to be established in the country and the prelude to them going to Eton. Co-founder the Reverend John Buckland was the Norton boys' housemaster; Buckland's brother-in-law, Thomas Arnold, father of Matthew, was its other co-founder.[31] The first Caroline heard of this was when her brother-in-law Sir Neil Menzies wrote to her that the boys were to be transferred out of his care to an English school and, mindful of the new law, assumed that she would be able to visit them. But Caroline was kept in the dark as to their whereabouts and only discovered by accident that they had been sent to a school 'remarkable for its scholastic achievements but also for the severity of its discipline', which troubled her. She would have preferred them to go to Harrow, where her paternal grandfather had been schooled, but at least her sister Helen's son Frederick Dufferin was at Eton and would be kind to Fletcher, who had been brought up under his strict aunt Grace's discipline. She hoped her nephew would encourage Fletcher to be 'gentlemanlike in feeling'. Caroline remembered him as 'a very timid child, perhaps he has grown out of it, I hope he has'.[32]

On Sunday 13 June Caroline went by carriage to Laleham School on the Thames to ask if she might visit her children. Buckland wrote to George Norton asking what, if any, intercourse the boys were to be allowed with their mother. Norton replied, 'No one is to see or have any communication with my children except under my express written authority.' George insisted Caroline had to apply to him personally, ensuring another bout of wrangling leading to nothing. Caroline instructed her lawyer to write to him. On 21 June George rejected her lawyer's request, finding it 'painful and irksome to forbid any mother's access to her children' but doing so because 'Mrs Norton's conduct has not been such as to enable her to have intercourse with her children, nor to justify me in permitting it.'[33] By using the excuse of her 'conduct', George's catch-all term for her refusal to bend to his will, he was continuing to accuse Caroline of criticising him, of being unwilling to 'convenience him in pecuniary arrangements' and of refusing to believe that he had acted on his own initiative in his treatment of her. But the legal situation had changed in 1839, and George's years of lies and ludicrous conditions could now be exposed to a judiciary which had accepted that unless the mother was an adulteress she now had a right to see her children. Caroline applied to the lord chancellor to see her sons under the terms of the new law.[34] Twelve years later the publication of *Bleak House* by Charles Dickens would bring the interminably slow and labyrinthine procedures of the Court of Chancery before the public's attention. At least Caroline made a start before her children's childhood ebbed away to adulthood.

In May 1841 the census enumerator called at 24 Bolton Street in London to record the names and details of every member of the household for the first statutory headcount of the population in England and Wales. Caroline and her uncle Charles Sheridan, described as having independent means, were looked after by three female servants, Sophia Burton, Ann Grace and Ann Lawley, and William Gulliver, her uncle's butler. The loyal Sophia, who had not been paid for years, was allowed to live in with her husband Frederick.[35]

In July Caroline's sister Helen Dufferin was in Italy recovering her fragile health when she heard of her husband's sudden death. On 25 July Pricey, fourth Baron Dufferin and Clandeboye, was with his sister the Honourable Mrs Ward on the *Reindeer* steam packet from Liverpool to Belfast on their way to his estate at Ballyleidy when he died of an overdose of morphine. The night before they sailed he had complained of an 'indisposition' and asked the ship's steward for a dose of morphine, which he took straight away. When they tried to wake him the following morning he was dead. The story went that the local druggist had been flustered by the imminent departure of the steamer and made up a prescription that was too strong. This was a time of enthusiastic self-medication, and trips to the chemist for all kinds of opiates were common. It took some time for letters to reach Helen in Italy and for her to come home; she was now the dowager and her fifteen-year-old-son Frederick Temple-Hamilton-Blackwood, the first Marquess of Dufferin and Ava.[36]

In August Lord Melbourne was out of office, the Whigs having lost a general election on the issue of corn duties, and his life at the heart of government and the royal household came to an abrupt end. The cruel treatment of Lady Flora Hastings, a Tory lady-in-waiting to the Queen, had damaged his reputation and helped those who were keen to get rid of him and his government. In 1839 the Queen had become convinced that Lady Flora was having an affair with her arch-enemy Sir John Conroy, who had 'admired' her mother throughout Victoria's childhood. When Lady Hastings began to look pregnant, the Queen insisted she was medically examined and it was discovered that rather than being with child she had a large tumour on her liver. She died shortly afterwards. Lord Melbourne was criticised by the Tories for not managing the Queen better in this matter. Melbourne had also lost influence through the Queen's marriage to Prince Albert of Saxe-Coburg-Gotha in February 1840. Melbourne did not enjoy being supplanted as Victoria's mentor by her serious-minded German husband, and their relationship cooled. There were also tensions over foreign policy. Melbourne's sister Lady Cowper had married the sabre-rattling foreign secretary Lord Palmerston, who wanted to pick a fight with the French over their ambitions in the Middle East. A war with France was avoided in 1840 partly by Palmerston's tough stance and partly by Melbourne's quiet diplomacy in the Cabinet and with the French.

Sir Robert Peel, ten years younger than Melbourne and with experience of high office as home secretary, leader of the House of Commons, prime minister and chancellor of the exchequer, led the Tories' opposition to the Whigs' attempts to deal with the budget deficit by reducing import duties on sugar, timber and corn. On 4 June 1841 Peel won a vote of no confidence called over the government's plan to abolish the sliding scale of duties in favour of a fixed lower rate of duty on imported corn. Melbourne wanted to resign but was manoeuvred into dissolving Parliament and calling a general election, which the Whigs lost. He retired to his family seat at Brocket Hall.[37]

Lord Melbourne took the loss of power badly; his insouciance could not conceal how he minded terribly. A mature statesman, he had had to stand aside for a young husband and a Tory protectionist. Caroline worried about how he was coping with the dramatic changes in his life, although she may have been pleased that the Queen was no longer so demanding of his attention. She wrote to his nephew William, who too was now out of a job, enquiring after Melbourne, mentioning that she had known him to be sometimes 'causelessly depressed' and a man of 'unequal spirits'. Caroline took his fall from power to heart, calling it a 'mortification and an insult'.[38]

She holidayed on the Isle of Wight for much of August.

Chaperoned by her uncle and aunt Sir James and Lady Graham and her brother Brinsley and his wife Marcia, she enjoyed her re-entry into society. Her name is included with those of two hundred other 'elite ladies' who attended the 1841 ball at the Royal Yacht Club at Cowes. Times had changed – even her departure from the island was noted: 'Sir James Graham and the Hon. Mrs Norton are among the fashionable departures for town.'[39] Back in London her brother Frank had been appointed treasurer of the island of Mauritius, an odd appointment for a debt-laden man who had a problem with drinking and gambling.[40] In September a rumour appeared in the gossip columns that Caroline was going to take up her father and grandfather's profession and go on the stage, and would soon be making her debut at Covent Garden. It was correctly but slyly pointed out that there was drama in her family and that she had other skills and qualifications which suggested that her career would not be based solely on 'personal beauty'. Caroline asked *The Times* to advise their readers that this was a 'gross fabrication'.[41]

In the past Caroline had pooh-poohed the idea of editing a miniature almanac and supplying some poems, but now she agreed to do the work. Produced in time for Christmas 1841, the *Bijou Almanack* was an inch in length and half an inch wide and was sold with its own 'eye-glass of miniature dimensions'. Mr Schloss of Berner Street called it 'one of the wonders of modern printing'; the 'fairy publication was one that Queen Mab might carry without being encumbered'. It was illustrated with a very small portrait of Caroline.[42]

For half a dozen years Charles Dickens had been enchanted by Caroline, often praising her poetry and sometimes recommending manuscripts by her friends to publishers. In 1842 Caroline asked the Dickenses to dine with her to meet some new acquaintances of hers who had asked to be introduced to the author. Perhaps a little tactlessly, Caroline asked Mrs Dickens to bring her 'pretty little sister' along. Once at a supper party Dickens and his wife Catherine were attending he was asked whom he thought was the most beautiful of the Duchess of Sutherland and Mrs Norton. His fellow guests were startled when he replied, 'Mrs Norton perhaps is the most beautiful, but the duchess to my mind is the more kissable person.' He sounded infatuated with Caroline when he wrote to an American that Caroline and her sister Georgy were 'sights for the Gods, as they always have been'.[43]

The event which changed Caroline's life was the death of her youngest son, nine-year-old Charles (who she persisted in calling Willie), on Monday 12 September 1842. The boys were at Kettlethorpe Hall, which was run by a skeleton staff as their father was rarely there. Unsupervised, Willie had gone out on Saturday on a pony and wandered two miles from home, where he was thrown and scratched his arm. He found his way to the nearest house, Chapel Thorpe Hall, where he was cared for by the servants of its owner John Dodgson Charlesworth, a coal master and farmer, until George Norton arrived. But the wound was not properly bathed, and lockjaw – tetanus – quickly set in.

Caroline received a note forwarded to her at Tunbridge Wells, where she had gone to take the waters, by her uncle Charles in London, which had been delivered to him by one of her husband's servants. The note warned it was a 'case of danger', so with a maid she took the train from the new station at Tonbridge to Euston Square the next morning and then the first train to Wakefield a hundred miles away. But by the time she arrived Willie had been dead for some hours and was already coffined. His body was kept at Kettlethorpe Hall, which was left empty until after the funeral. George, Caroline, Fletcher and Brin were invited to stay at Chapel Thorpe Hall while they waited for George's elder brother to arrive at Grantley Hall, five miles from Ripon. Caroline was made welcome by the kindly Mr Charlesworth.

Caroline learned that Willie was conscious when he died and had said some prayers and asked for her twice before his jaws locked completely. The doctor who attended told her that Willie bore the painful spasms 'with a degree of courage which he has rarely seen in so young a child'.

Caroline was hugely upset that she had not been told sooner and had not been able to reach Willie before he died. When she did arrive, George had cried 'in a bitter distress' and made promises about the other boys, but Caroline knew he would not stick to his word: 'his impressions are so weak and so wavering that I only tremble'. Caroline felt that she and her remaining sons were in the 'absolute power of one who had no heart'. When Lord Grantley arrived, George left Brin with Caroline and took Fletcher to stay with the Nortons at Grantley Hall. In the days leading up to the funeral George's demeanour changed under the influence of his brother. George and Fletcher visited Caroline and Brin most days, but on several occasions their family prayers were ended by George being summoned to leave immediately to consult with the Nortons' lawyers. George's recriminations did not end and, numbed by her own sadness, Caroline lashed out at him: 'I have had hard words to bear even now but I am too miserable to shrink from them and too broken to resent them.'

Caroline discovered that after the accident Willie had been kept at Chapel Thorpe because there was no one to look after a sick child at Kettlethorpe; there was only the gamekeeper's wife, 'an old woman who opens the gates and locks the doors'. Caroline learned how poorly the boys were cared for. They were left for much of the time on their own, and she was shocked to learn did not have a manservant to look after them and were allowed to go riding on their own. While she was in Yorkshire she was locked in silent resentment: 'It may be sinful to think bitterly at such time and at least I have not uttered the thoughts of my heart – I have choked them back to spare pain to one who has never spared it to me!' It made her even more miserable to return constantly to the thought that 'it might not have happened had I watched over them'. She was incensed by the amount of money spent on the lavish coffin, which she thought would have been better spent paying a man to be 'in constant attendance in their hours of recreation'. Her youngest son had been 'too young to rough it alone as he was left to do and this is the end of it'.

The only concession George made was to allow her to take eleven-year-old Brin with her to London before he returned to Laleham School. Poignantly, having seen their parents crying over the death of Willie, his brothers hoped that George and Caroline would be reunited and asked her to make a list of all their relations so that they could 'make friends' with her family again. Brin had been hysterical when he saw his dead brother but she hoped his 'buoyant temper' would help him recover. Fletcher, who was not yet thirteen, was maturing into a thoughtful and sensitive young man. 'His forethought, tenderness and precocious good sense will, if God spares him, be the blessing of my life. He soothes his father and watches me as if I, not he, was the helpless one and God knows I am helpless, but my child is out of the storm. He is in Heaven, too young to have offended, he is with those whose angels do always behold the face of our Father.'

On his visits to Chapel Thorpe Hall Fletcher became his mother's secretary as they waited for the day of the funeral to come. He wrote a note to Augusta Cowell on her behalf about the 'great misfortune which has happened to us'. Caroline added a line at the bottom of his note: 'I cannot write today but I will by and by.'

The bereaved mother's angriest thoughts spilled on to the black-edged pages she wrote to her mother, revealing her 'state of terror that Grantley will interfere to complete the ebbing tide of kindness about my remaining boys'. She told her mother that when she arrived and had George on his own, he had 'promised everything for the future' and had even spoken to her 'humbly' about himself and their reconciliation. But since his overbearing brother had arrived George had been kept away from her as much as possible, at Grantley's beck and call. When she did see him, Caroline had had to hear her husband's grievances, complaints and accusations of the past decade trotted out all over again. She noted how quickly George recovered from the 'broken-hearted distress' she had found him in and returned to his old self. Caroline used what little influence she had to persuade him to send Fletcher and Brin to another school, as she thought the Reverend Buckland a brute, who 'ill-used' them. After Willie's funeral and burial at Sandal Magna – of which she left no account – but before she returned to London with Brin, she spoke to Lord Grantley about Buckland's behaviour; ignoring his obvious dislike of her she pleaded with him to take the boys away from Laleham. Caroline was surprised when Grantley said he would warn Buckland personally, and if the harsh discipline persisted the boys could leave. Brin had received such a sudden blow to the head there he had become temporarily deaf. Caroline came up with another idea, begging to be allowed to keep the boys with her for six months with a tutor, after which Fletcher would be ready to go to Eton and Brin might return to Laleham, but this was refused.

Caroline proudly told her mother that Fletcher had intervened at an awkward moment between his parents while they were discussing where she would stay. Although Mr Charlesworth was happy for Caroline to remain at his home, George had oddly suggested that Caroline stay at a nearby inn. Tactfully

Fletcher pointed out to his father the preposterous discourtesy of the idea: if Caroline stayed there she would have to walk through the taproom, where men smoke and drank all day. She wrote to her mother how she felt broken by the story of her nine-year-old's last words to his father: 'I'm certainly dying – I shall soon be strangled, pray for me.' Ten days after she arrived in Yorkshire Caroline and her servant made their way back to London.[44]

The boys spent three weeks with her in London before they returned to Laleham, so Caroline was able to enjoy the company of her boys for the first time in six years. The death of Willie hit Fletcher especially hard: he was so unwell he stayed with his mother for an extra week. On 8 October 1842, a month after the accident, Caroline told the poet Samuel Rogers about her sons. 'My boys are nice creatures, intelligent, free-spirited and true. They are so happy to be re-knit with me that I can scarcely think of it without weeping. Little Brin is brimful of gratitude and love to all who ever loved or were kind to me. The elder is quieter, more thoughtful, less spirited, but seems like an angel to me and his whole care is to keep watch over his father's kindness that it may not flicker or go out for me. Young though he is, he is allowed the greatest influence over his father's mind and uses it with a tenderness and tact very unusual at his age.'

Now, finally, George Norton seemed to have mellowed, writing to the Reverend Buckland that in future Caroline was to be considered an equal to him in terms of access and was to be allowed to visit the boys as often as she wished. For the first time in years Caroline wrote tenderly of him – 'George is very sorry for his little one: and very proud of these two' – although Brin had written her a letter which revealed the extent of his emotional neglect. The eleven-year-old told her he would die of grief if he was parted from her again. 'You can't think how changed I am. I love you and my brother ten times more than I used to do – I love you, and Papa and Fletcher beyond any thing or person I ever did before.' For the first time in a long while Caroline seemed happy. 'I cannot tell you how his letter touched me – I think I feel as he does, that I love everyone better since I received his dear scrawl of affectionate writing.'[45]

On 14 October 'a most daring burglary and extensive robbery of valuable plate' took place at Mrs Sheridan's apartments in Hampton Court Palace. Ten days earlier Mrs Sheridan had confronted her cook, nineteen-year-old Mary Ann Goatley, with her suspicions that she had stolen a number of things and dismissed her. Mrs Sheridan was due to go to London the next day so told her servants to gather all her plate and valuables and lock them into a 'plate cupboard' and lock that inside another cupboard in the parlour. The following morning the apartment was secured and Mrs Sheridan handed her keys to Mrs Gundry, the housekeeper of the palace, and set off for town. She returned early when Mrs Gundry sent a note saying her home had been 'broken open' and all her plate stolen. All that remained of the contents of the cupboard was the list of plate, which revealed that a silver teapot and seventy pieces of silver cutlery, much of it with the Sheridan crest, had been stolen, as well as several pairs of stockings, two pairs of which were black silk and had never been worn. The thieves had also gone into Helen Dufferin's rooms and stolen three shawls, a cashmere dress, a satin handkerchief, three pairs of white stockings, white kid gloves and an Indian gold brooch. The thieves had broken in by removing a pane of glass in the kitchen window which looked onto Tennis Court Lane. Mrs Sheridan had repeatedly asked Mary Ann Goatley to ensure the windows were always locked, but she had seemed reluctant to do this. It soon transpired that Goatley had two accomplices, Martha Grover and her husband Henry, a gardener in Mortlake, a village downriver from the palace. The footprints of a man and a woman's boots were found in flower beds underneath the window; the man's prints bore the marks of six nails on the ball of his right foot. The next day Goatley and Martha Grover, who was heavily pregnant, took their swag to a pawnbroker in the Old Kent Road, where Goatley explained that she worked for a lady named Duffnell, who was 'a very gay one and that her husband was travelling on the Continent'. Mrs Duffnell supposedly needed to pay some of her accounts before he returned. The pawnbroker advanced them twenty-three pounds (now two thousand). Witnesses had seen them behaving suspiciously leaving Hampton Court and making their way to Kingston, loaded down with a couple of bulky bundles. After their visit to the pawnbroker they had also been seen in various taverns enjoying the proceeds of their crime. They were quickly apprehended, and Grover's boots matched the footprints, although the nails had mysteriously disappeared from his boot. Goatley and the two Grovers were committed to be tried at the Old Bailey and imprisoned in Newgate until the trial on 24 October. Almost all of the stolen goods were returned to Mrs Sheridan and her sister.

Mrs Sheridan and Helen attended the court, where Martha Grover, in tears, begged Mrs Sheridan for mercy. Goatley and Henry Grover offered no defence and did not make a plea for clemency. Mary Ann Goatley was found guilty of 'feloniously and burglariously breaking and entering the dwelling-house of our Sovereign Lady the Queen', and stealing silver plate from Mrs Sheridan and items of apparel from Lady Dufferin, and sentenced to be transported to Van Diemen's Land (Tasmania) for ten years. On 26 November she was transferred to the prison ship *Margaret* to be transported on Christmas Eve 1842, one of a hundred and fifty-six female and twenty child convicts, exiled for between seven and fourteen years for theft, larceny, pickpocketing and shoplifting. Four women died before the *Margaret* reached Hobart on 19 July 1843. Martha Grover was found guilty, but because of her pregnancy was only sentenced to six days in prison. Her husband was found guilty of house-breaking and theft and sentenced to ten years' transportation. He served the first eighteen months on the prison hulk *York* off Gosport, was transferred in 1844 to the hulk *Thames*, and then transported to Bermuda.[46]

For the first time in seven years Caroline spent Christmas with her children at Frampton. It had taken the death of one of them to make the breakthrough.

VIII

A Storm of Expostulation
(1843–51)

How strange it seems to be so much and so little to anyone.
                                                    Caroline Norton

Everything was different but nothing had changed Caroline's fear. George's new-found reasonableness could suddenly end. Caroline relished the work that was needed to install Fletcher at Eton in September 1843 and Brin in November 1844. There were six years of mothering to catch up on.

In January 1843 Caroline took Fletcher and Brin to one of Charles Dickens' Twelfth Night parties. Edwin Landseer had told her about the 'exciting conjurations' the author performed. Dickens dressed up as a magician and performed illusions helped by a young man called Ivory. Recently Dickens had bought some new tricks and had also improved some of his old favourites, which included producing from a 'wonderful and mysterious bag' a little figure who was supposed to be a personal friend of his. This magical friend told funny stories in an eccentric voice and made miraculous appearances and disappearances. The highlight of the evening was making a plum pudding in a hat: 'all the raw ingredients were boiled in a gentleman's hat and out tumbled a pudding before the eyes of the astonished children'. Dickens' Boxing Day and Twelfth Night parties were famously good: supper would be served with crackers and speeches, and the evening would end with a country dance. Dickens was moved when Caroline told him she dreaded the boys going back to school and would wake every morning 'fearful that they might forget her'.[1]

To Caroline's irritation one of her friends and a most loyal ally, 'dear Willie' Cowper, now thirty, married Harriet Alicia Gurney on 27 June at St James's Church in Piccadilly. She was nineteen years old and the daughter of Daniel Gurney from a Quaker banking family; her aunt was the prison reformer Elizabeth Fry.[2] They honeymooned at Brocket Hall. Caroline sent an unhelpful note to Cowper addressed to 'Wisp', a reference to what she considered his will-o'-the-wisp elusiveness, inviting him to come and spend some time with her on the Isle of Wight. Caroline would have wanted to have been a wedding guest but that was out of the question. She wrote to Willie, 'Your inconstancy and coldness remain unexplained and I am proportionately irritated.'[3]

After only two months of marriage William Cowper was a widower: his new bride died on 29 August of 'irritative fever', also known as Plymouth Dockyard Disease. It was septicaemia caused by an infected wound. It is not known how Harriet got the cut that gave her the deadly infection, but the treatments her physician could deploy were futile. He might have bled her, given her laxatives, had poultices made up laced with mercury and antimony, or applied bark and sulphuric acid to the wound. The only respite was heavy doses of laudanum, brandy and opium to dull the pain. Harriet died at home at North Runcton Hall.[4] The announcement of her death in *The Times* on 31 August may have given Caroline a moment to regret her unkind letter to a good friend of ten years' standing.

Later in the autumn there was bad news from Mauritius: Frank Sheridan had died after 'a short illness' on 11 September

1843. The family did not hear about it for several weeks. Announced in the newspapers on 1 December, the cause of death was perhaps tuberculosis, his physical well-being also undermined by years of hard drinking. Caroline told Nathaniel Ogle, 'I am undressed and beat and wretched and not fit to receive anyone . . . we are in heavy distress indeed. I fear my uncle will not recover.'[5] The only image known of Frank is a lithograph by Richard James Lane of a dandy, a handsome fellow with an aquiline nose, lots of dark hair and cheekfuls of Dundreary whiskers. The eleventh of September was now the anniversary of three deaths in Caroline's family: her father's, her son Willie's, and now Frank's.

On 29 November Caroline's 'good, kind uncle and friend' Charles, with whom she had lived since the collapse of her marriage, died of an 'apoplexy'. On 13 November they had returned together from visiting the Marquess of Lansdowne at Bowood Park in Wiltshire, and Charles was 'in his usual health and cheerful spirits'. A week later he complained of 'languor'. He fussed about his health but Caroline summoned their physician, who prescribed some medicine, and Charles seemed to recover. On the night of 22 November, when Caroline checked to see that his candles were snuffed out after midnight, Charles told her he was 'tired but comfortable'. He rarely dressed before eleven in the morning, but when Caroline tried to rouse him at noon the following day he was in 'a state of stupor and apparently suffering from an attack of paralysis'. Five days later Charles died 'without pain or struggle, in perfect tranquillity' without recovering consciousness. A post-mortem found evidence of 'disease and inflammation of the brain', which perhaps explains some of his anxiety about his health and that for years he had 'great absence of mind on important subjects'.[6] Everything Charles owned was bequeathed to his stepbrother Tom's widow, Caroline Sheridan, the mother of his nieces and nephews

Caroline, Brinsley, Helen, Georgy and Charlie.[7] When he died it was not just the loss of a good friend Caroline mourned, she knew that in the coming months she would have to find somewhere else to live.[8]

The Sheridan family was so affected by the 'white plague' of tuberculosis that it was a constant fear. As soon as Caroline started to spit blood she would take to her sofa and worry until it stopped. In the holidays after Fletcher's first term at Eton, the autumn of 1843, his weak chest was a cause for concern, and she took him to Brighton to convalesce. Before he returned to school in early 1844 she consulted Dr Latham, physician extraordinary to Queen Victoria, but the doctor insisted that all Fletcher had was a 'casual cold and of no consequence'. Latham was a highly experienced doctor and a devotee of the stethoscope who knew more than most about wheezy chests and breathing difficulties. His own health was delicate, and in 1841 Latham's emphysema and chronic asthma had forced him to resign his duties at St Bartholomew's Hospital, although he continued in his private practice.[9]

Caroline was not reassured by Latham's years of experience and brisk diagnosis. Grieving for her uncle, she was worried that Fletcher was not strong enough to remain at Eton and thought she should bring him home and have him taught by a tutor. By February she had packed her books ready to leave 'dismal' Bolton Street as soon as she could let it: 'I shall be so happy to leave it.' There had been no 'last words, no direction, nothing but goodnight' from her uncle before he died.[10]

In August 1844 Caroline took her sons to the Isle of Wight, where she hired a drawing master for Fletcher, who was good at landscapes. They stayed in a 'neat, clean cottage' with a garden and view of the sea at Ryde. Brinsley had started at Eton during the summer term while Fletcher was still at home, not well enough to return to school. Caroline started a correspondence with their master, the Reverend Edward Coleridge, who was the same age as their father and the nephew of Samuel Taylor Coleridge, whose own time at Eton had been 'rough and too severe a trial for many a boy'. Edward went to the school in 1813. 'It was neither moral, decent nor cleanly . . . Such food as we had was badly cooked . . . and the college provided neither breakfast nor tea, nor any eatable supper. There was no means for washing for any but the sixth form and those of the meanest sort and provided by their own fags . . . All were locked up after Latin prayers in the lower school at 8.30 and left to themselves, or to the tender mercies of the sixth form until 7am. Evil songs were sung and there were many things done which one cannot but remember with horror and regret. And yet there was a kind of safety in the indecent publicity of our lives and in our numbers were the grounds of much amusement and friendship.'[11]

Life at Eton had since improved – otherwise Caroline would not have agreed to send her boys there – and twelve-year-old Brin made a good impression on Coleridge. Caroline insisted her son was 'very intelligent' and assured Coleridge he was 'more manly in mind than in his looks'. She offered a clue as to the diffidence Brinsley may have shown when Coleridge met him: 'he has been sitting up late in London and perhaps was tired and low parting with his brother'. Fletcher's health was such that his return to the school seemed in doubt as her doctors were reluctant to give her any 'sanguine expectations' of him recovering completely.[12]

At the end of their holiday on the island, during which the boys had caught whooping cough, Caroline had the tricky task of replying to her uncle, the Reverend Thomas Le Fanu, Dean of Emly at Abington Glebe, in County Limerick, who had written on behalf of her cousin Alicia Le Fanu, a poet and novelist in her fifties, who had money troubles. Caroline replied that the

Sheridans had recently sent Miss Le Fanu twenty-five pounds and that Caroline had tried to get Alicia a pension from the Royal Bounty Fund, but she did not want to be asked to give any more to a relation she had never met. Explaining that she herself was the poorest of Tom Sheridan's family and had little hope her request from the fund would be successful, she would forward his letter to her brother Brinsley, who might be able to help. Caroline told the dean that she was trying to increase her own income, now all the more urgently, since her late uncle used to help her out financially.[13] Caroline's own mother, she wrote, had for years been a template of 'steady economy and self-denial'. She asked her uncle to refrain from asking for any more help. 'I have long ago learned that <u>no one</u> here has a superfluity of fortune and poor Alicia Le Fanu cannot expect from my family any assistance which I myself have <u>never received, never looked for and would not accept</u>.' To her surprise Caroline managed to get a one-off payment of a hundred and fifty pounds from the fund for her poor relation.

Caroline later wrote to her cousin William, son of the dean, reminding him she too was short of funds and had to eke out a living from her 'literary labours' to supplement the 'very moderate allowance' her husband gave her. She pointed out that such a grant <u>'would never happen again'</u>, and that Alicia would 'indeed be mad to rely upon it' and would have to look to her own 'prudence' in future.[14]

On the Isle of Wight she was spotted with Sidney Herbert, and their friendship became the subject of gossip. They strolled on the sands and went sailing on a yacht called the *Fanny*. A couple of years younger than Caroline and the unmarried son of the eleventh Earl of Pembroke, Herbert's family seat was Wilton House in Wiltshire. He had studied at Oxford, excelled at public speaking, had a 'graceful character' and was handsome and eligible. A Tory, in 1832 he had been elected to Parliament, and for the past three years had been secretary to the Admiralty. Caroline and Sidney became very close, and from the summer of 1844 many were convinced they were lovers. But even if Herbert had wanted to marry her, and his parents had sanctioned it – which was unlikely – Caroline was not free.[15]

By September 1844 talk of their friendship had reached William Cowper and a couple of indignant letters passed between them. She did not take kindly to being questioned about her behaviour when she had written to Cowper asking about Lord Melbourne's health. Since Melbourne had left office, Caroline had taken to calling him her Dearest Old Boy. Caroline would have spent more time with him, but his sister and Cowper's mother, Lady Palmerston, kept her away from Brocket Hall.[16] In October 1842 Melbourne had a stroke, which paralysed the left side of his body. A companion, Miss Cuyler, was employed to keep him company, which did not please Caroline: 'corresponding by proxy with the Cooler is vague and unsatisfactory'.

Born in 1799, Harriet Fanny Cuyler of Welwyn in Hertfordshire was the daughter of General Cornelius Cuyler, of Albany, New York, whose vivid career in the British army had earned him a baronetcy in 1814. One of five daughters, Harriet never married; her sisters all married clergymen. She was eccentric and became a formidable obstacle, thwarting Caroline's many attempts to play a part in Melbourne's final years. For years Harriet had lived as a companion in the grand homes of aristocratic Whigs. She would never get into a carriage unless the driver assured her that he was a Whig, that it had not been used to carry anyone with an infectious disease and that he was not a Puseyite.[17] Lady Palmerston had chosen her for her stubborn and proprietorial personality. Caroline bombarded Harriet with notes about Lord Melbourne's health and was driven mad by her reticence.

Nowhere in any surviving letters does Caroline commiserate with Willie Cowper over the horrid death of his wife; she seems more concerned with her own hurt feelings than with his loss. Caroline told him she was affronted by the tone of their most recent conversation, explaining that she had held back because 'if one's tongue slips its cable one may say things that never can be recalled and make no difference to the argument'. Caroline took offence at the hypocrisy of those in Willie's wide and influential family circle whom she suspected were critical of her friendship with Sidney Herbert when their own arrangements would hardly stand close scrutiny. If Cowper's family had rallied round her in 1836, when she had been 'falsely and grossly wronged for your uncle's sake, you would not have had to lecture me about a later male friendship on the sands at Ryde this autumn'.[18]

Fletcher's health continued to cause concern, so his mother took him to enjoy the bracing air of St Leonard's, a new town adjacent to Hastings. Caroline responded peremptorily to her uncle, the dean, when he wrote asking where Alicia Le Fanu's money was. Accusing Alicia of being 'deplorably rash', Caroline suggested that the best way forward was to 'strictly and almost sternly rule what she <u>shall</u> do'. She thought it would be no hardship for an 'upright mind to submit to advice' rather than suffer 'the galling disgrace of insult and threat from inferiors on account of debts which cannot be liquidated'. Caroline knew about the embarrassment of being harassed by creditors, and had had to give up some of her independence in return for the help her brother and brother-in-law had given her. She thought Miss Le Fanu should be expected to do the same.[19]

Caroline and Fletcher stayed at St Leonard's until the end of November, when he was well enough to return to Eton. During this quiet time, uninterrupted by the social round, she completed work on *The Child of the Islands,* a long poem dedicated to her brother Brinsley, but had to retire to bed with attacks of migraine she treated with leeches, which she called her 'pillow-fellowes'. Writing to Brinsley about the fourteen-year lease she proposed signing on her new home in Mayfair, at 3 Chesterfield Street, she said she would live there on her own, or rent it out for three hundred pounds a year if she found she needed to live more economically or went abroad. Relations with George were easier, but when it came to money Caroline did not trust him. She dreaded him finding out about the property in Chesterfield Street, whose rental value would be 'highly agreeable to him.' Recently she had had a stroke of luck: a publisher gave her five hundred pounds for a novel she had started some time ago. She confided in her brother that she felt weighed down by responsibility for her sons, their health and their future prospects, and that she 'cried over the fire' when they had gone to bed. At St Leonard's she hired a 'gentle, earnest, pious' curate to give Fletcher lessons and, mindful of how easily her brothers the late Frank and Charlie had come off the rails, was glad that Fletcher had met a man leading 'a <u>real</u> humble useful life'.[20]

A Mayfair location was socially essential but some streets were better than others, and with her reputation Caroline was nagged by her family to be mindful of the address she chose. She recommended a correspondence with Mary Shelley, who a couple of years before had been looking for somewhere to live. Mary had found a place in Berkeley Street but then heard that a fie-fie, her term for a courtesan or mistress, had lived there. Caroline thought it was absurd to turn it down for that reason; otherwise how could one find a 'small cheap and pretty house at the west end of the town, for such houses are the prey of such persons'. Caroline told Mary to live where she wanted but, to avoid any confusion, recommended that she behave 'modestly, paint the rails dark green and don't buy a parrot', and keep her geraniums indoors rather than putting them on the balcony – thus 'the barrenness of virtue will be apparent'.[21]

Caroline moved into her new home in Chesterfield Street in the summer of 1845. The house been rebuilt after a fire in 1830 and was rented from a Mr Harland, who had been the Member of Parliament for Durham. Her health and mood were not helped by grey smoggy days. She felt like a doll stuck all over with pins: 'if the days of witchcraft were not past, I should think someone had made a wax figure of me to roast before the fire'. Her friends, the Ladies Gordon, Sutherland and Errol called on Caroline every day, but she was so exhausted by their visits she was glad to see them go. She had an abiding fear of debt, very aware how much Brinsley had helped her with legal expenses and what a drain Frank's 'hopeless entanglements' had been. A letter went off to Brinsley in Dorset: 'It is a hard thing to feel legally so helpless and dependent, while in fact I am as able to support myself as an intelligent man working in a moderate profession.' Because she was a woman she could not make a contract with anyone, as no one would accept a woman was 'a responsible party'. This was the first time she had lived on her own and she could not sign the tenancy agreement.[22] Her brother was happy to stand security for the payment of her lease; he could see that her earnings were healthy, and another five hundred pounds was due for *The Child Of The Islands* in the spring.[23]

For Caroline to live alone was socially risky and did not help her reputation, although a growing circle of literary and artistic friends visited her in her new home. Dining at Chesterfield Street were her new special friend Sidney Herbert, Charles Dickens 'de Pickwick von Chuzzlewit' and his 'dear little wife', the poet Samuel Rogers, author and politician Richard Monckton-Milnes, Lady Duff Gordon, who naughtily sometimes dressed in men's clothing, Lord Melbourne, and the historian and travel writer Alexander Kinglake. Some accepted her invitations, others did not; some accepted but their wives were not allowed to attend. Kinglake, who paid Caroline a great deal of attention in 1845, took her to the opera with other friends, gave her yards of beautiful fabric from his travels in Algeria with which to make a turban headdress and hosted a whitebait dinner which included Sidney Herbert. Caroline's rehabilitation was complete: 'she visits everywhere'. Her beauty had not faded, and she was widely regarded as 'decidedly pretty . . . a nice person, very unaffected, a shade of the free-and-easy, but it seems only the overflowing of an easy disposition'. When people were introduced to Mrs Norton and the memory of her scandalous past for the first time, they assumed they were in the presence of a dangerous woman and looked for clues as to her waywardness. A clergyman friend of Thackeray noted her easiness but during the course of the evening was satisfied that this was a sign of her 'open personality' and not a sign of lax morals.[24] There is no evidence that George now made any criticism of her 'conduct' or living arrangements, or used her unchaperoned circumstances to prevent their boys living with her for half of the year.

In April 1845 came the first reviews of her long poem *The Child Of The Islands*, which originally had been planned for 1842, to celebrate the first birthday of Queen Victoria's son Prince Albert Edward, the future King Edward VII. Caroline explained in the preface that the delay was because 'the recurrence of domestic affliction in two consecutive autumns compelled me to relinquish the task'. *The Times* described it as a 'very beautiful poem upon the great domestic question of the day, the condition of the people'. The child referred to in the title may well be the young prince, whom Caroline respectfully urged 'never to forget the poor who were so often exploited by the privileged'. In the context of the decade, which became known as the Hungry Forties, this was a powerful piece on a sensitive subject, the social question of the day. 'It overshadows everything, and disturbs men's minds with deep anxiety. Strange, that among a people beyond all doubt the wealthiest and most powerful on the face of the earth, and considered by themselves the most civilised, there should be found, not individuals but whole classes, oppressed by the utmost misery, and steeped in brutish ignorance. Things may be mending, but the progress is slow; and the degrading question is perpetually recurring – how were they ever permitted to arrive at such a state in a country possessing so many boasted advantages?'

In four sections named after the seasons of the year Caroline's moral message was wrapped up in a series of 'remarkably pleasant pictures from Nature'. She asked for more open-handed charity for the poor, open-hearted sympathy rather than condemnation of their plight, 'more intimate union between all classes' and that the impartial justice which was dispensed to the rich also be handed down to the rest of society. *The Times* praised the fact that the tough conditions to which her poem referred were 'freed from all repulsiveness of harshness' by the strength of her 'sweet imagination'. The opening apparently sentimental verse landed its blow in the last two lines. 'Of all the joys that brighten suffering earth, / What joy is welcome like a new-born child? / What life so wretched, but that, at its birth, / Some heart rejoiced, some lip in gladness smiled? / The poorest cottager, by love beguiled, / Greets his new burden with a kindly eye; / He knows his son must toil as he hath toiled; / But cheerful Labour, standing patient by, / Laughs at the warning shade of meagre Poverty!'[25]

By the time it went into its second edition the following year, the book had gathered further positive reviews, which were quoted in *The Times*: the *Quarterly Review* declared, 'it bears the stamp of extraordinary ability' and had 'bursts of genius'.[26] Caroline spent the publication day with Lord Melbourne at his home in London and was saddened by his exhaustion, upset that he hardly spoke. He thought he might die soon and asked her if he should send for a clergyman. Caroline requested that if he did so he would make 'a solemn declaration respecting the falsehood of the grounds of proceedings taken by Norton'. She also asked her sister Georgy, who was soon to visit him, to remind Melbourne of her wish. Caroline explained that this was not because she wanted 'the world's favour' but for her boys' sake. She needed 'the solemn words of a dying man' to support her 'living denial'. Caroline was worried that if Melbourne recovered he would not send for the clergyman, and she might not have the chance to ask him again, so she asked Georgy to say, '"I hope you will remember my sister's request" or something of that kind'.

Caroline knew she was pushing the boundaries of acceptable behaviour towards a dying man, but continued to drive home her point. 'If you knew the amount of lethargy, and supineness of his character, you would see that it is necessary even in this, to remind and to appeal and I am asking you to do a nervous thing, but it is a thing that I am feverish about.'[27]

The dogged insistence and forceful tone of her letter to her sister helps explain why Lord Melbourne's family never relinquished their antipathy towards the woman they accused of almost destroying his political career. If he had been found guilty in 1836 it would have rebounded on all of their lives to some degree.

Worryingly, Fletcher was ill again with 'fever' and she took him to Richmond to convalesce. Dr Edward Craven Hawtrey, headmaster at Eton for the past ten years, wrote Caroline a flattering note about *The Child Of The Islands* and politely enquired when her son might be returning to school. She assured him 'most heartily and seriously' that her 'great anxiety' was to send Fletcher back very shortly. The boy had been 'very feeble' and it would have been 'a mockery' to send him to study as he would have been a 'tax on Mr Coleridge's patience which I am sorry to say has already been tried in that way'. Caroline used a respectful but friendly tone with Hawtrey, telling him that her friend Samuel Rogers had had to lend Coleridge's chum William Wordsworth a dress suit to wear to one of the balls at Buckingham Palace.[28]

Apart from having the boys for six months of the year, the greatest improvement in her circumstances was the better relations she was enjoying with her husband. George also visited the boys when they were with Caroline in London, a change in the dynamic of their marriage which she could not have imagined possible in the time leading up to the death of her youngest son.[29]

In November Caroline jumped at the chance to take on a role in Lord Melbourne's social life, an involvement she had hankered after for years. In poor spirits and failing health, her Dearest Old Boy was coming to London to take his seat in the House of Lords. Keen to meet old friends and make the acquaintance of new men, Melbourne asked Caroline to invite Anthony Panizzi, keeper of printed books at the British Museum, and William Makepeace Thackeray to dine with him. He already knew Panizzi but was confused about the novelist: 'he persists very obstinately that Mr Thackeray is a clergyman with whom he ought to be acquainted'. She would also write to close friends they had in common, 'since he is invalided he takes great pleasure in receiving his friends', asking them to pay a call.[30]

On 4 December 1845 the closeness of Caroline's friendship with Sidney Herbert landed her in trouble and saw her being blamed for a story in The Times that Prime Minister Sir Robert

Peel and his Cabinet had decided to introduce a bill to repeal the Corn Laws in six weeks' time when Parliament reassembled. Rumours flew that Herbert, secretary at war with a seat in the Cabinet and one of its three members to support Peel's decision to repeal the laws, had told Caroline in confidence and that she had sold the story to the paper's editor, John Thaddeus Delane. When the news broke, Peel felt his position was impossible and resigned, but resumed the premiership when the Whigs could not form a government. Caroline was not responsible for the leak but was blamed for it years after the event; Lord Aberdeen, foreign secretary in Peel's government and a keen supporter of repeal, had been the source.

Early in the new year forty-three-year-old William Augusta Ann Norton married her cousin James Johnstone of Alva in Stirlingshire at the Norton family home in Abbey Hill, Edinburgh.[31] They had been in a coy and pious correspondence since the mid-1820s, she agonising about not being religious enough and he trying to convince her she was.[32] The Johnstones were notable merchants, profits from the slave trade being the source of much of their wealth. A match with awkward Augusta kept the wealth within their extended family.[33]

Down in London Caroline was not to be invited to the marriage of her childhood friend Sophia Armstrong to the Honourable Colonel George Cadogan of the Grenadier Guards, second son of Admiral George Cadogan, third Earl of Cadogan, on 19 February at St George's, Hanover Square. Caroline and Sophia had grown up together at Hampton Court Palace. Embargoed from inviting Caroline, Sophia was embarrassed to have to offer 'kindly excuses' about why she could not let her attend. Caroline understood that she could not be a guest and gave Sophia a gilt malachite dish from herself and an inkstand from Lord Melbourne as wedding gifts.[34]

Fletcher had an attack of 'ague' in the spring of 1846 and

academically fell behind his precocious brother Brin. Caroline had written to Edward Coleridge, hoping Fletcher was 'less absent and bewildered' and paying more attention: 'I assure you it is not idleness, still less stupidity.' However, once he settled in Fletcher started to shine and in two terms had been 'sent up for good' seven times to the headmaster, Dr Hawtrey, to show him his work.[35] The boy who coughed a lot and missed out on much of the life of the school had 'the sweetest disposition', enjoying his brother's successes 'as if they were his own'.[36]

Caroline struggled to cope with comments made within her hearing concerning the persistent rumours about what was supposed to have passed in bed between her and Sidney Herbert about the Corn Laws repeal. She tried to convince William Cowper that she was phlegmatic about how she was viewed: 'I mean for the future to let every story take its own chance and permit every one to build their own castle of cards to amuse themselves with respect to my actions. I have an existence separate from "the world" and shall be remembered and dreamed of, when the gossiping women of my day have ceased to talk, and are a handful of dust.'[37]

In a letter to her mother Caroline was concerned about how the trial ten years ago still affected Fletcher. 'The growing impatience and weariness and disgust, which has crept up on me especially this last year, the perpetual abuse, interference, and comments to which I have been subjected, the hunted feeling, of never being able to take a walk or ride in peace, without a storm of expostulation . . . Fletcher has been a weight on my heart. I have lain awake whole nights, staring into the dark, at a vision of his large brown eyes, full of an expression they often have, of wistful enquiring, when I look up suddenly from my employment and find him watching me . . . I have never had courage to ask him whether anyone has been cruel enough to give him the trial

<u>to read</u>, or merely that <u>now</u> he is old enough to comprehend <u>why</u> there should be a bar to degrees of intimacy.'[38]

As Fletcher prepared to leave Eton in the summer of 1846 Caroline explained to the headmaster that he 'wanted to spread his wings'. George planned to send him to live with a tutor who would prepare him for Oxford. Before his brother left, clever cheeky Brin got on the wrong side of the French master, Mr Tarver, who flogged him, and his father withdrew both boys from the man's lessons. Caroline was more measured in her response to Brin being beaten. Although she 'believed every syllable of his [Tarver's] explanation', she thought that he had 'a difficult temper for boys to yield to' but may have been pushed to the limit: 'it is impossible not to make an allowance for Mr Tarver who has to teach a number of careless and mocking, insubordinate boys'. Believing that George, who often acted 'rashly', had prevented their son from learning a valuable lesson, Caroline assessed how the situation might have been better handled: 'there must be necessarily so much injustice, so much undeserved considering and misconstructions of motives, that it is rather interrupting the education of the mind and disposition to attempt to control these petty instances and accidents in boyhood and bring up a boy to imagine he can meet them <u>all</u> in a spirit of defiance and resistance. I think it as an especial mistake to allow this in Brin's case.'

Caroline recognised something of herself in the fifteen-year-old Brin. She admitted that they shared petulance, 'his leading fault', and a determination that they would 'bear nothing which he thinks is not strictly deserved'. There was a high-handedness in him which felt familiar: 'there is scarcely any exertion of authority that does not appear to him bordering on tyranny'.[39]

Caroline was now learning from Fletcher and Brin how she was perceived in the Norton family, and how they made sense of the jagged ties between their parents. She was jealous of the

time the boys were to spend that summer in the Highlands with
their Norton relations, invited by their cousin Sir Robert Menzies
to his castle in Perthshire. Their clergyman uncle James and his
wife, who were childless, laid claims to Fletcher's time in London,
which Caroline found galling as for years they had had unlimited access to her sons which she had been denied. She did not
take kindly to James taking Fletcher to his home and 'over-
whelming him with civilities', felt patronised when James loaded
her son with gifts of bread and asparagus for her, and was livid
that he took Fletcher out for walks around London 'sometimes
leaving him to finish his walk alone'. This caused her to 'fidget'
because while the boys stayed with her she would accompany
them all the time, 'making it physically impossible' for Fletcher
to 'get into bad habits, or bad company'. On one occasion
Fletcher's response to being scolded for returning late from a
day with his uncle was to send their servant to buy cigars to
give his mother by way of apology.

Brinny was quite different to his brother. George had been
ambivalent about him in the past, sometimes convinced that
Lord Melbourne was his father as well as Willie's. Brin had a
good 'mind and character' and a 'sturdy earnestness and unself-
ishness about him and is very loveable'. He may not have been
the best-looking boy: 'Except the gift of beauty, which is after
all only a temptation, I think no woman ever had a more hopeful
son than my Brin in everything that nature can bestow.' He
reassured his mother that Fletcher was not thinking of 'bad
women', if that was the reason why she would not let his brother
go out on his own.[40]

On 22 June 1846 Caroline's obsessive admirer Benjamin
Haydon killed himself, mired in debts and deep despair. That
morning he bought a pistol in Oxford Street and went to his
studio nearby in Edgware Road. His death certificate recorded,
'he committed suicide with a razor by cutting his throat after

The first Baron Herbert of Lea and Caroline Norton were close friends, some said lovers, in the 1840s, until his sudden marriage in 1846. He was said to have been driven to an early grave aged fifty-one by Florence Nightingale's excessive demands when secretary-at-war during the Crimean campaign.

The Norton's eldest son Fletcher Norton was born in 1829. He died of tuberculosis in Paris in 1859.

Profession.	Object.	Remarks and Complaints.

Caroline's impression of a summer holiday at the home of Edward Ellice at Glenquoich which she left in the visitors' book in 1857.

Against a London studio set-up of a country idyll, Caroline's mother Mrs Sheridan is trimmed in fur with her son Brinsley and his wife, the heiress Marcia Grant, with whom he eloped in 1835.

Mrs Norton attracted diverse opinions. Many praised her looks and intelligence, others could be hostile. Lord Malmesbury found Caroline amusing, but her beauty and manners were not feminine enough for his taste, and her conversation was 'often coarser than even a man's should be'.

As the editor of *Fisher's Drawing Room Scrap Book*, which was aimed at the Christmas market of 1847.

In 1849 the Irish artist Daniel Maclise unveiled his fresco *Spirit of Justice* in the Chamber of the House of Lords (it is still there). Caroline Norton was Maclise's model thirteen years after the trial held nearby in Westminster Hall, now representing Justice in the same building where the laws of divorce were re-made.

William Etty painted Caroline after her Infant Custody Act
became law in 1839.

Caroline wrote to a friend ten years after this portrait:
'It is the affair of the artist how far he wishes to make a
resemblance ... I see all the little improvements in my actual
face going on the canvas with great interest and curiosity. I am
anxious to meet some painter who will be matter of fact enough
to copy what they see. It is the vice of modern art to shrink
from all that is not prettiness in painting.'

Sir William Stirling Maxwell and Caroline Norton had known each other thirty
years before they married on 1st March 1877. She died three months later.
He died of typhus in Venice the following year.

shooting a pistol ball at the upper and back part of his head'. Haydon was buried in Paddington near the graves of five of his children, the highs and lows of his career summarised in the epitaph on his headstone: 'He devoted forty-two years to the improvement of the taste of the English people and died broken-hearted from pecuniary distress.'[41]

The romance with Sidney Herbert came to a jolting end at Whitsuntide when 'stormy discussions about my affairs and what was said of me in the world' reached such a pitch that Caroline decided that 'some of the positions I had taken up were wholly untenable'. Herbert's family was also deeply concerned at the amount of time he was spending with the scandalous Mrs Norton, and the rumours swirled about them like spun sugar. A marriage was arranged with one of his child-hood friends, a twenty-four-year-old society beauty, Mary Elizabeth A'Court, daughter of General Charles Ashe A'Court of Amington Hall in Warwickshire. With sadness she and Herbert 'talked matters over', and she left London for her first visit to Ireland to stay at her sister Helen's home at Ballyleidy in County Down. She was heartbroken and lashed out in a letter to Samuel Rogers, 'I do not think I have "lost my friend", but if I have, God forbid I should desire that it had rather been by his death – with all his relations in anguish, than by his happiness – with all his relations rejoicing.'

Caroline admitted that she was bitter at losing Herbert to another woman: 'it was a struggle in the doing and it is not a sorrow done'. She was 'dog-sick and heart-weary' at the gossip and the manoeuvres which had led to his engagement and marriage, likening herself to 'a rose shut out by thorny briars'.[42] It was hard enough to lose him, but to hear 'coarse' stories that she was being represented as 'the forsaken and lamenting mistress of a man whose marriage I could not prevent' was especially galling. Caroline asked another of her admirers, Alexander

Kinglake, to stop telling the world that she was 'weak, nervous, shaken by many worries and would grieve many a day' for her 'lost companion' – which was true, but she did not want it broadcast to 'the world'.

She was told that Herbert's friends had been trying to get him to marry Miss A'Court for two years, and that he had asked her even though he had not seen her since Easter. He had invited Miss A'Court to Wilton House to meet someone else he expected her to marry, but events overtook them and it was Sidney's proposal of marriage that was accepted. His half-brother Lord Pembroke, who was married to a Sicilian and lived abroad, was childless, and Sidney was the second son. The family was concerned about heirs, hence the haste to get Sidney married. It all sounds a little odd, but it was all Caroline was offered, and she clung to it.[43]

On the day of the wedding Caroline was at her sister's in Ireland, working with Helen on *The Drawing Room Scrap Book*, which was due for the Christmas market and for which Helen had written 'some capital poems'. Fletcher, who had left Eton, spent a fortnight at Ballyleidy during which time he fell in love with a young girl staying there. On his return to England he wrote her a 'passionate and melancholic letter', which she showed to Caroline 'her eyes sparkling with enchantment' even though Fletcher had told her to burn it. Brin recovered from his wobble with the French master and was 'sent up three times for good' to the headmaster but now stuttered. Caroline planned to take the boys to Paris in the winter to 'furbish them into elegant gentlemen'. Feeling cut off from London life, she asked Bear Ellice to send her political news and gossip. She told him she had seen evidence of the famine at Ballyleidy, where the surrounding fields were filled with the potato crop 'blackened' in the ground with 'hopeless spades' stuck in it.[44]

Caroline had arrived in Ireland feeling 'beat and weary', and when she looked out at the 'drizzling rain' had not imagined there would be 'any prospects of being cheerful'. She ventured out on visits, soaking up all the Irishness she could, connecting with her grandfather's eighteenth-century past. The abandoned houses and gardens in the wake of the famine seemed to mirror her own choked feelings: 'the fat roses crushing each other's cheeks, and nestling down in the long, dank grass, on the paths and in the borders'. Caroline had been pleased to receive 'long kind' letters, which Lord Melbourne sent her every day she was away, but felt guilty about leaving him when he told her he was 'pretty well but very lonely'.

The stream of visitors had been entertaining, and Caroline preferred country house etiquette to that of London visiting, although being confined in the same house with someone who took a dislike to her was awkward. She complained that a fellow guest, an unnamed admiral, who appeared to be a good-natured and gentlemanly man, was unkind to her and 'took a scythe and mowed me down like long grass that was making the path damp and tanglesome'. Caroline asked Bear Ellice to write to her as soon as he could, explaining that she felt like a 'silk worm who requires to be lifted on to a fresh mulberry leaf, which you know they are too lazy to do themselves'.[45]

Caroline was still at Ballyleidy in the middle of October, having stayed three months longer than she had planned. The 'blustering' weather delayed her party sailing for Liverpool. Helen's health was delicate, and as she 'suffered most dreadfully from the sea' they sat out the storms before embarking at Belfast. The weather changed but the crossing was still terrible: on board there were eighty cattle, a flock of sheep and a flock of geese, which helped 'to lurch the vessel one way or the other', and Helen was so seasick Caroline thought she would die. Despite her nephew's reassurances that his mother's health was no worse than usual, Caroline worried that the damp Irish climate was bad for Helen and feared she might be consumptive. Helen had been 'poorly' all the time Caroline was at Ballyleidy, rarely coming downstairs before lunch and sometimes 'not then and often in a dressing-gown to dinner'. Caroline wrote to their sister Georgy about how 'very feeble and shadowy and hob-chickenish' Helen looked.

In Paris Caroline's youngest brother's broken health was remarked upon by English visitors to the British embassy, where Charlie was attaché to the ambassador, Lord Normanby. In the summer the family heard he was weak and emaciated, needing to 'pick up flesh and strength'. At the end of November Charles Dickens wrote to friends from Paris that he had seen Charlie Sheridan, who was 'dying of a consumption'. Dickens knew Charlie 'very well': he had enjoyed seeing him in amateur productions of his grandfather's plays, and in the past they had gone sightseeing together, but given the snowy weather and Charlie's wasted condition, there would be none of that on this visit.[46]

On Christmas Day 1847, which Caroline spent at Frampton, her two new potboilers, *Fisher's Drawing Room Scrapbook*, which included portraits of Queen Victoria, Prince Albert, Richard Cobden and Caroline, and *Aunt Carry's Ballads: Adventures of a Wood Sprite – the Story of Blanche and Brutikin*, were given as presents in many households.[47] Readers of the *Scrapbook* could see how Caroline looked to the artist Thomas Heathfield Carrick. The famously dark hair, eyes and perfect eyebrows were still there, but fashion had changed and her voluptuousness was hidden under fine textiles and sculpted by whalebone corsets. Although around this time the novelist Thackeray called her 'a bare bodkin', there is little flesh on show in this portrait.[48]

Even though Lady Palmerston disliked Caroline Norton intensely, she was prevailed upon by her brother Melbourne to invite her to her soirées and assemblies. There were enough people around for the Palmerstons and Lambs to avoid her, but Caroline often felt cut by her hostess's inner circle. His family was convinced Melbourne was a dying man and were prepared to tolerate Caroline's presence for his sake.

On 1 May 1847 Charlie Sheridan's health forced him to resign from his position in Paris. Twenty-nine days later he died in the hotel of the British embassy, not yet thirty years old. His body was returned to England and placed in the Sheridan vault at Frampton. The popular young Charlie had made his mark and was given a short but warm eulogy in *The Times*: 'Society has lost one of its choicest favourites and ornaments who combined all the gifts and qualities that distinguish his remarkable family – wit, beauty, accomplishments, the graces of manner, and the charm of a cordiality most sincere and genial. His conversation was full of liveliness and zest; his wit was light, easy and managed with good taste and feeling. His talents were excellent and all that he wanted was the energy for their application, which his health, perhaps, refused him, the threatening symptom of which was a prevailing languor when unexcited. The premature end of one so young and so gifted seems to bear out the thought . . . "Heaven sends its favourites an early doom".'[49]

In September, before she made a visit to Netherby Hall, the Cumberland seat of her uncle Sir James Graham and her aunt Fanny, Caroline accompanied Fletcher and his tutor to Southampton to see them off to Lisbon, where he was to pursue his studies in a warmer, dryer climate. His academic career at Oxford was postponed because of his health. Consumptives routinely travelled to places such as Lisbon to recover their health and strength. His tutor was thirty-year-old Otto Frederick Wilhelm Ludwig von Wenck, a political journalist and translator who had arrived in England in 1845. He liked to be known as Otto von Wenckstern, but the English found his name a mouthful and shortened it, to match his diminuitive size, to Mr Winks.[50]

Caroline visited Lord Melbourne at Brocket Hall before setting off north and found him 'pretty well but much fidgeted by that nevertheless useful torment Miss Cuyler'. Irritated by Cuyler's closeness to Melbourne as companion and amanuensis, Caroline found her extravagant, mad and sometimes funny: 'she <u>will</u> press me to her bosom; during which operation I feel like a drowning sailor on a plank, and since Sinbad's old man of the sea there has been no one like her'. From Cumberland she went to see Bear Ellice at Glenquoich in Invernesshire, a trip that had been years in the wanting and wishing. These were the early days of rail travel and it was comparatively dangerous. There were dozens of accidents and fatalities, and Caroline would have preferred to go by foot or by carriage: 'there are so many horrible accidents that I really am afraid I shall never reach you with whole bones'.[51]

During the summer George Norton went back to haggling, trying to raise money on a trust fund ostensibly for the benefit of his wife and two sons, but his underlying motive was to reduce the allowance he was obliged to pay Caroline for her expenses and those of their sons, and to wriggle out of his liability for her debts. Caroline saw this as an opportunity to get the deed of separation she had long wanted. She agreed to his wishes in return for the deed and an annual income of six hundred pounds, content to pay the rest of her sons' expenses out of her literary earnings. George was determined to shave a hundred pounds off the allowance and used Fletcher to persuade his mother to agree. Caroline had waited a long time to get her children back and George knew she would not want to return to haggling. Brinsley's lawyers criticised her verbally agreeing to the deed being prospective for her but retrospective for him, and Brinsley refused to act as guarantor. Without a guarantor the deed would be 'informal'.

Sir Frederick Thesiger, who had acted for Lord Melbourne

in 1836, met George Norton and advised Caroline to accept her husband's terms, which were that a deed of separation would be drawn up without guarantors, and Norton would give her five hundred pounds a year in return for her agreement that for the past ten years and in the future he would not be liable for her debts. She signed it, but it was invalid in law as Caroline as a married woman had no legal right to sign a contract with her husband or anyone else. This vital fact was well known to George, but in Caroline's haste to be done she overlooked it. George had used Fletcher as a go-between, out manoeuvring Caroline and her legal counsel. It seems that Thesiger was remiss in the advice he gave Caroline; he knew that she had already verbally agreed to George having the retrospective advantage. Thesiger knew Norton well and it is surprising that he believed he could be trusted. It was a muddle.[52]

Caroline made plans to visit Scotland in the autumn, wanting to 'refresh myself among romantic scenery', and also saw Lord Melbourne as often as she was allowed. Caroline complained that sometimes his 'nurse' Miss Cuyler overstepped the mark. Melbourne spoke to her about it, and she told Bear Ellice that Miss Cuyler 'lies like a tinker – why are tinkers slandered by this proverb?'[53] Much of her contact with Melbourne was via pen and ink: she would write him gossipy letters that she knew would amuse him. This got her into trouble with Melbourne's sister-in-law Lady Beauvale, who had married his brother Frederick in 1841 and was thirty-five years younger than her husband.[54] Caroline sent Melbourne a letter containing gossip this young German lady, who had taken charge of his care, considered 'coarse' and was reprimanded for it.

Thin-skinned, Caroline fired off a panicky letter to William Cowper, afraid that her letters to Melbourne would be stopped, explaining that she had meant no harm and had been 'anxious to amuse him in <u>his own way</u>'. Melbourne had complained to

Caroline that Lady Beauvale had rebuked him for 'this sort of thing' and that in his changed circumstances the reprimand 'worried and depressed him'. Caroline had always gone along with whatever Melbourne wanted – this was the dynamic of their relationship: 'I have never opposed his fancies and never thought I could do any good by it.' She asked Cowper to look at her letters and speculated that Melbourne had shown his strait-laced sister-in-law Caroline's letter 'precisely because it amused him and was written for that purpose'. Caroline gave Cowper the tricky task of speaking to his aunt, a woman seven years younger than him, to plead her innocence.[55]

Because of Fletcher's health, plans for him to go to Oxford were abandoned, and a junior appointment at the British legation in Lisbon was obtained for him. Caroline set off with him for Southampton to board a boat to Portugal, but he was taken ill and fainted before he got on the train and they had to turn back. He was 'very bad' and she was 'much alarmed'. She called Dr Travers, who tried to reassure her that Fletchy's newly diagnosed heart problem was nothing to worry about and that his own had been so bad 'he used to be carried fainting from the lecture-room'. Fletcher was 'better but very weak' and Caroline nursed him at home.

Meanwhile, Brin had gone up to Oxford and had a nervous collapse. He had had a 'hysteric attack' and spent the night in the 'open air in his shirt and trying to knock up people to attend to him – which seemed natural to him but utterly wondrous to the Dons'. Roaming around in the damp cold air gave him a chill, and he was laid up under the care of a surgeon, who was sure he would make a full recovery. Comforted by the fact that he did not drink or smoke, Caroline confided to her sister Georgy that she was worried but had not told George Norton how much she feared for Brin. Afraid of being accused of 'morbid nervousness', she had not revealed 'what I fear and feel'. Letters from his dons and doctors saying that they knew how clever he was but 'could not understand his ways' added to her anxiety.[56] However, in the middle of October she was touring Scotland, 'refreshing her London eyes with strange purple shadows on the hills, foaming torrents and glassy lakes'. She stayed with old friends at Inverary Castle and with new acquaintances, including a stay at Keir, near Dunblane, the seat of William Stirling, art historian and bibliophile.[57]

November saw George Norton ask her to take Fletcher to Madeira for the winter. The idea went down badly: her father had made a journey there to try to cure himself of consumption, the same disease which threatened her son. Caroline had read the letters Tom Sheridan had written to her mother, which 'contain depression of heart enough to make one hang oneself'. Also, the other Caroline Norton, one of George's 'wild sisters', was living there, and to Caroline's over-protective mind 'would take a pleasure whenever my boy was well enough in dragging him out and over-fatiguing him'. She fancied taking Fletcher to Cannes for a peaceful winter instead of somewhere under 'the cloud shadow of any Norton'.[58]

Fletcher's condition improved enough for him to travel to Lisbon, but when he arrived he had a relapse and was very ill. Because there was cholera in the city Caroline would have to wait for the quarantine to end in December before she could go there. Letters brought frightening news: 'all I hear sounds like a dismal echo of all that used to be said about Charlie'. She was told that 'care and watching may see him a strong man yet but it all hangs on a thread'. There was also a sudden deterioration in Lord Melbourne's health. In October he had another stroke and epilepsy was diagnosed. Melbourne assured his entourage epilepsy was not painful but he knew how 'fearful it was to see', as he had witnessed his son Augustus having seizures throughout his life.

Caroline received a 'kind' letter from William Cowper saying that his uncle was indeed dying and promising that he would write and tell her when it happened. She replied, 'it is a sort of satisfaction to me that I shall hear it from <u>you</u> and not from a stranger'. But she was saddened to be an 'exile' from the events that were to unfold, minding that she was 'only an acquaintance'. The thought of Melbourne's death felt like 'cold lead'.[59]

On 21 November 1848 William Cowper married for the second time. His bride, Georgina Tollemache, ten years his junior, was the daughter of the late Admiral Richard Tollemache. They were both religious enthusiasts and busy philanthropists. It was to be a happy but childless marriage. Three days later William Cowper wrote and told Caroline of Melbourne's death. After a private funeral on 1 December he was buried in the Lamb family vault at Hatfield church. Caroline was not able to attend.[60] The man whose life encapsulated everything it meant to be a Whig from the golden days of the party was gone; an era was over. *The Times* printed a lengthy and robust obituary befitting a Whig prime minister with a colourful private life, which mentioned the 1836 trial but 'declined to examine the details', which would have been 'a painful and profitless task'. Even in death Lord Melbourne and Mrs Norton were tied together.[61]

When Caroline returned to London from Scotland there was a letter waiting for her from Lord Melbourne dated 9 November. Caroline wrote to Cowper, 'so strange and terrible to me . . . I cannot believe I am never to have a letter from him again.' Thanking Willie for his 'kindness' in keeping his promise to her, and conscious of the shadow over everyone at Brocket Hall, Caroline was at pains to congratulate Cowper on his marriage to his 'lovely bride'. Willie's letter touched her and stopped her feeling 'grieved and sorrowful outside the gate as it were, of that home where I have never been anything but a stranger, except in feeling towards him as I do'.[62]

Bear Ellice was one of the two executors of Lord Melbourne's will, a queer choice as they were not close friends and indeed had been political enemies at various times. He was appointed in the last year of Melbourne's life to punish Lord John Russell, to whom Melbourne had been close, because Melbourne was angry with his old ally. The other executor was Lord Brougham, another eccentric choice given that they had been at loggerheads on some matters.[63] Caroline wrote to Bear, asking him to retrieve all the letters she had written to Lord Melbourne from his papers. This was the start of a long battle to get them back which she did not win. Poignantly, she asked Ellice to 'give me those spectacles he wore. I gave them to him – no one will care to have them so much'.[64]

Three days before the funeral Caroline wrote to Cowper, also asking him to return any letters of hers he found among his uncle's papers. The last letter Caroline wrote to Melbourne, which arrived the day after he died, was returned unopened by Miss Cuyler. His death hit her hard. 'I am amazed at the difficulty I feel in taking this event as a <u>reality</u> . . . the old days come back again – as I sit here alone – old days when I was very young and very proud of his liking me. Old fragments of what he used to say and read and old scenes, with my children there, all of them, and life before me.' Caroline comforted herself that it could never happen again: 'that is a sorrow whose last dregs are in this cup'.[65]

Although she was not mentioned in the will, news of Melbourne's letter asking his brother Lord Beauvale to make Caroline an annual allowance of two hundred pounds revived the rumours of their adultery a dozen years before. Lady Branden, the other lady who had landed him in criminal conversation trouble, was remembered in the same way. Lord Melbourne had also asked his brother to put into writing for him that what he had instructed the attorney general to say at his trial in 1836 about Mrs Norton's purity was true. This was a welcome boost to Caroline's desire to clear her name, but many saw it as a cosmetic gesture and, coupled with the rumours of her bequest, dismissed it as untrue.[66]

During the first week of December Caroline fretted about Fletcher as she waited to start her journey to Lisbon. He wrote her breezy letters, but they did not comfort her. She believed his 'present attack' was over and that he would be 'tolerably well till the next one, but that this pattern would be his future 'career of ill health'. The best prognosis the most optimistic doctors could offer her was,'"he may outgrow it" and "they have known it curable"'. Brin, who had made a strange start to his studies at Oxford, asked to travel with Caroline to visit his sick brother in Lisbon, to which George Norton objected in the strongest terms, accusing him of 'black heinous ingratitude'. This put Caroline in a quandary. George seemed unlikely to compromise, and she did not want Brin to spend Christmas with George while she was in Lisbon with Fletcher. 'I know well what would be the result.' Caroline found her position as 'the nominal wife of a man one never sees, and who never (even with his son in peril of his life) can think except of himself' maddening.

She wrote candidly to Ellice, who had already set about his executor's duties, of her impressions of the last months of Lord Melbourne's life at Brocket. Caroline painted a dark picture of the frightened demise of a once-powerful man. 'His death itself was scarcely so mournful and shocking to me as the first day I saw his handsome careless head combed smooth by his servant's care; the first day I saw that though he wanted to be waited on by Miss Cuyler he feared her, or rather feared a scene, and his doleful look at me when speaking of her, and the impatient helplessness with which he said: "I have no choice – it is such a damned helpless life."'

Caroline continued to deny that she had been Melbourne's

mistress. There are dozens of angry and loving letters to him from the early 1830s, yet still she denied that their relationship had been anything other than platonic. This was the line they had both pursued from the moment the criminal conversation suit was threatened, and they had to persist with it or Caroline would never have got back into society. In her letter to Bear Ellice, she again denied it: 'I was not his mistress, but I would rather have been what I was, his favourite female companion, than any other man's wife or mistress I have ever known.' He had been the love of her life, and she held to her belief that 'he liked me better than any other thing in his world of vehement likings'.[67]

By the middle of December Caroline was on her way to Lisbon. She and her maid travelled with Sir Charles Napier on his flagship, HMS *St Vincent,* a hundred-and-twenty-gun first-rate battleship with a crew of nine hundred men dispatched to suppress pirates operating off the Moroccan coast.[68] Caroline enjoyed her time at sea, stored away the 'odd clever conversation of the amphibious old hero' and went down to listen to the sailors sing, gathering ideas and tunes for the songs she wrote with Augusta Cowell. *St Vincent* was leading a convoy of other warships and merchant vessels, Caroline marvelling at the sight of the ships 'who walked after Admiral Napier over the ocean, as if they had been ladies in a procession'.[69]

Caroline spent most of 1849 in Portugal nursing Fletcher back to health. When she first arrived he was 'stronger but not strong', although apart from his health he was 'in every other respect all I could pray for'. Brin was now doing well at Oxford.[70] In early March his father agreed to allow him to join them in Lisbon, George's mind changed by a friend's offer of a free return passage. News of Brin's arrival was tempered by recent confirmation that Fletcher had a heart condition and consumption in both lungs. The twenty-year-old had altered dramatically: 'he is wasted to a pale shadow'. The view from the terrace in Lisbon filled Caroline with fear: they could see 'heaving clumps' of cypress trees that marked the boundary of the 'English burying-ground'.

Caroline again wrote to Ellice for the letters she had written to Melbourne. The family said that they had been destroyed by Lord Melbourne before he died, but she would not be fobbed off. She had seen them for herself when she visited him: they were 'creased and tossed about while they amused him, and then dropped like leaves from a dead tree, no one cared much where'. Caroline knew that her letters were read by his family and missed him: 'poor soul it seems so strange now not to have to correspond with him, after writing to him all my life'. She was so used to telling him about her travels and trials that she was having to check herself from thinking '"Oh that will amuse Lord Melbourne"' and 'writing it to him, till I recall the blank'.[71]

Brin arrived after a month. Caroline's brother Brinsley had sent an airbed for the frail Fletcher to sleep on more comfortably, while Brin was learning to play the guitar and serenaded them with his 'very pretty' voice. Caroline employed a drawing master to teach her perspective but she found herself to be 'stupid – which fills me with astonishment'. Gradually Fletcher improved – the large doses of cod liver oil routinely prescribed for delicate patients seemed to be working. Caroline's appetite returned: 'I eat like a silk worm all round the edge of the leaf I am upon.'[72]

By the middle of May Caroline's maid had packed up the airbed and their trunks and they were living in Sintra, twenty miles along the coast from the capital. It was a stunning place where the kings of Portugal spent their summers. Lord Byron had visited forty years before and called it Glorious

Eden, the most beautiful village in the world. But Fletcher's condition was erratic: it 'wavers and varies so to keep me on tenter-hooks'. When his night sweats returned Fletcher blamed the cod liver oil and refused to take any more.[73] Sir Hamilton Seymour, the head of the British legation, was an 'indulgent and kindly *chef*' and did not ask Fletcher to resign his position, so a career was still possible.[74] Caroline remained in Portugal, wanting to humour Fletcher's wish to travel home through Spain in the early autumn: 'he has so few enjoyments, poor fellow, living at his age the life of an invalid, that I do not like to thwart him'.

It was six months since Melbourne had died and it seemed to Caroline that his relations were being obstructive. All she wanted was for them to gather her letters and return them, as was the convention when anyone died, but it is possible that his family believed Caroline would publish the letters and reveal things that might damage his reputation. Caroline told Lord Eddisbury, under secretary for foreign affairs, a friend and protégé of Edward Ellice, 'the one thing they cannot take away from me is the conviction that Lord M liked me better than anyone else'. Caroline was bombarding Eddisbury with questions, thirsty for political gossip. She considered Queen Victoria's position peculiar, thinking it 'an absurd anomaly, where all women are null by law, this one enthroned example of authority! Or rather, how absurd that women should be so completely null in all respects!'[75]

Caroline and her son continued to pin their tattered hopes on the therapeutic qualities of sunshine. This belief dated from Cicero's trip to Egypt in 86 BC, which was said to have cured him of tuberculosis. Thereafter hundreds of thousands of consumptives, hopeful of a cure and fearful of cold and damp, went in search of hot dry climates. By the middle of the eighteenth century there was an English-speaking consumptive colony in Nice. Some countries in Europe were convinced, correctly, that tuberculosis was contagious and had strict laws on the passage of consumptives, but as the nineteenth century progressed the enforcement of regulations became lax. Other jurisdictions – including Florence, Naples and Nice – were sceptical about the dangers of contagion. Caroline and Fletcher were fortunate that the Portugese tolerated the presence of consumptives in their country. Chopin and his lover George Sand had made the mistake of going to Majorca in 1838. Sand described their nightmarish experience. 'Phthsis is scarce in these climates and they regard it as contagious! . . . The owner of our small house threw us out immediately and started a suit to compel us to re-plaster his wretched house which we had contaminated. We then went to take up residence in the uninhabited monastery of Valdemosa . . . but could not secure any servants or help of any kind from the local peasantry, as not even the poorest wretch wants to work for a phthisitic. We begged to be given a carriage to take us back to Palma, but even this was refused. So we had to go three leagues [nine miles] on neglected, deserted roads on a birlocho [a wheel-barrow]. When we arrived in Parma Chopin had a terrifying haemorrhage. We had to leave at once, but the only boat that would give us room was one transporting pigs to Barcelona. Even there our presence had to be kept secret: we spent the journey in the smelly, stifling hold among the cargo.' Among the pigs, Chopin had another haemorrhage and coughed up basins full of blood.[76]

During her self-imposed exile from damp England, Caroline wrote a tender, bleakly autobiographical poem about the role of the sun in their hopes for recovery, 'The Invalid's Mother: To The Sun, At Lisbon.'

I loved thee, as a careless child,
Where English meadows spread
Their cowslip blossoms sweet and wild
By Thames' translucent bed!

Now, with a still and serious hope,
I watch thy rays once more,
And cast life's anxious horoscope
Upon a foreign shore.

* * *

O sun! that many an eager heart
With false hope hath beguiled,
Deal gently with me, ere we part,
And heal the alien's child!

* * *

And daily in thy heavenly glow
Our sick and weak we set;
Watch for the end of anxious woe,
And sigh, 'Not yet – not yet!'

O sun! look down on me and mine
From that o'erarching sky;
Emblem of God's great glory shine,
And His all-pitying eye:[77]

Fletcher's condition was unstable: 'after being weaker than water' he made a 'great rally' and although 'very thin but in good spirits' was still intent on touring Spain. Brin was still there but his name is rarely mentioned in Caroline's letters.

One of Caroline's correspondents in Lisbon was a new acquaintance, William Stirling, a handsome Scot ten years younger than her. He was a book collector and art historian, and an authority on Spanish art. He was in Spain 'wallowing in pictures' and said he would visit her when he had 'done' the country, but she was afraid he would be bored in Portugal: 'there are no pictures and only one tableau vivant by way of society'. Perhaps the shortest sentence she ever wrote in a letter was: 'I hope he will come.'[78] After finishing at Cambridge in the late 1830s, Stirling had gone on the Grand Tour and begun a lifelong love affair with art and architecture. In 1841 he failed to become Tory candidate for Perth and set off in a huff on a tour of the Middle East. He published *Songs of the Holy Land* in 1846. His three-volume *Annals of the Artists of Spain* was well received in 1848.

In July 1849 Caroline wrote to Edward Ellice, livid about the Lamb family's refusal to hand over her letters to Lord Melbourne. 'If his family choose to make the occasion of Lord Melbourne's death a declaration of war with me, let them – they will find they have shown more courage than perhaps they themselves are aware. If I have lost my only friend amongst them, I have also lost in him the strong check that kept me back in hours of exasperation, as my children's existence kept me back in matters concerning Norton. Can they believe they have a right to detain or offer my own letters as an equivalent of his?'

Caroline told Ellice that she wanted her letters back to be able to show some of them to her sons, and wondered if Lord Beauvale thought they had a monetary value and she would publish them. She was indignant that Beauvale had demanded the return of his brother's letters to her in return, confident that he was not making the same conditions to other people who had written to him. 'Where among Lord Melbourne's correspondents is there a position parallel to mine? Did one ever hear of so monstrous a request to a woman, to surrender letters written by a man of whom she had to go through a divorce case? How do they know I choose them to see a line of those letters? . . . They would have done better with me by kind words . . . than by a crowning insult, to all I have gone through on Ld Melbourne's account, all I <u>still</u> go through, daily and hourly, in my whole position in life.'

Caroline was more troubled than pleased by the small legacy that Melbourne had directed be given to her, and considered declining it 'out of pride'. But she was not in a position to refuse as George Norton had heard about it and reduced her allowance by a corresponding two hundred pounds. There was an impasse with the Lambs, with Caroline refusing to hand Melbourne's letters back and at the same time insisting that her letters to him were returned to her.

Back in Lisbon Fletcher was 'utterly exhausted' by the three-hour journey from Sintra. His condition 'was a terrible disappointment' – he was spitting blood again. The local doctor thought the journey back to England might kill him 'unless we had a sea of glass all the way home'. For herself she was 'dying to get home, it is frightful to be here without any good medical man'.[79] On 25 July it was announced in *The Times* that Mrs Norton had boarded the steam packet *Pacha* for Portsmouth. As well as her son and her maid, the other passengers included three crates of leeches, ten oxen, thirty-five chests of lemons, four casks of wine and six bales of silk.[80] In London Caroline wondered where her son's illness would take them next – to Madeira or the Cape of Good Hope 'to see my son die as my father had died'.[81]

On 9 August Caroline Norton's friend and composer Augusta Cowell was married to the Honourable Reverend Paul Anthony Irby, rector of Cottesbrooke in Northamptonshire, at St Mary's Church in Marylebone. The bride was forty-eight, the groom sixty-five, twice widowed, the father of ten surviving children. It is unlikely that Caroline was a guest at her friend's wedding, although their collaborations continued after Miss Cowell's marriage.[82] For the rest of 1849 Caroline was living at home in Chesterfield Street working on a novel to be published in 1851. George refused to make a contribution to her Portuguese expenses and so there was an added urgency to the hack work she was obliged to do. She had to repay the money she had borrowed from Fletcher's boss, Sir Hamilton Seymour, to pay the medical bills and for their tickets home.

Meanwhile Caroline had the satisfaction of entering the House of Lords. The Palace of Westminster had been largely destroyed in a fire in 1834 and Daniel Maclise won a competition in 1846 to paint the murals of *Chivalry* and *Justice* for the new chamber. Caroline had been the model for the spirit of justice. The fresco is still there. Caroline's good looks and personal history made her an excellent choice to some, but others heartily disapproved.

At the end of 1849 Fletcher's health improved and Caroline marvelled at how well he was despite the 'hard weather', having started the new year in 'higher spirits' than she had ever seen him. He had 'fattened' and was energised enough to 'pen a little article on the growth of Russian power in one of the papers'. Brin was in the final year of his studies at Oxford and was 'flourishing', but Caroline worried at the prospect of having to leave him behind while she escorted Fletcher abroad in search of a suitable career in a healthy climate.

Caroline had arranged for Brin to lodge during the Christmas vacation with a newly married curate living near her brother in Dorset. The young clergyman was inexperienced but 'able', and his 'very pretty and good-natured' wife gave Brin a 'little stray instruction' in music and they sang duets together. Away from his parents, the Oxford dons and his rumbustious friends, and some miles from his uncle, tinkling on the curate's piano and trilling away with his lovely wife, diverted the nineteen-year-old before he returned for his final term before matriculation and a career in the diplomatic service. High jinks at college had preceded the trip to deepest Dorset, and Caroline hoped to keep him out of trouble: 'we trust his thoughts will not wander from the domestic circle'. She was particularly anxious to keep him away from the capital and certain women, the most troubling being a 'London madam' who was 'made up of paint, false hair and artificial teeth'. Caroline hoped the wholesomeness of the sweet young couple would rub off on her excitable son.

Caroline would have preferred to stay in London but felt she had to accompany Fletcher and to make ends meet had to let the house and packed her 'much-loved knick-knacks away', fearful her tenants would 'utterly destroy them'. She dreaded feeling the same loneliness she had felt in Lisbon, abroad with no friends. Before heading for Naples, she bowed to Fletcher's wish to sail first to Lisbon, then visit Cadiz and Seville, places he had wanted to see but had previously been too weak to reach.[83] Caroline's life with Fletcher would become a ten-year dither. Plans would be made, trunks packed and then all would change on her son's whim. Because his mother had nursed him and thought he could die at any time she acceded to all his wishes, no matter how inconvenient they might be.

Fletcher then took it into his head he wanted to work at the British embassy at Paris, which she dissuaded him from, and instead they ended up in Brussels that winter, which Caroline found 'outrageously dull'. There were too many temptations in Paris but in Brussels there was nothing to do. Caroline would have liked Fletcher to do some studying before going to Naples as he was not yet 'a man of the world'. She parodied herself as a fussy mother bird: 'anything so like a hen who has hatched ducks there never was, as I am become'. Now that Fletcher was more than six feet tall, her lectures were 'less imposing as I have to give them with my chin in the air looking up to him who ought not to look down upon me'.[84]

Still in Brussels in July, they had done the rounds of all their acquaintances, had dined with old friends, the King of Belgium and his wife and had made friends with a sickly Dutch baron. Caroline and Fletcher considered going to Switzerland with the aged Baron de Wykerslooth and his pretty young wife. She was 'a handsome merry and dear little thing', who was 'heavily painted in the richest colours' to conceal three 'red claret marks' on her face and she fell in love with Fletcher. The naive young lady skated over the matter of her elderly husband, told Caroline she was sure she loved Fletcher, and Caroline promptly 'adopted her'. The cold winter evenings had given way to midsummer merriness, and Caroline took to her role as chaperone, enjoying herself in her son's 'juvenile society'. She wrote to Helen that they spent their days in 'open carriages careering through the forest with the lightest-limbed of the party dancing alongside'. Caroline said that her 'dignity of matronhood' had not been compromised by the playing of blind man's buff in the evenings and flirting and frolicking with 'fire screens for wings stuck in the dresses of the dancers'. An older 'bepaunched' member of the party, who 'jumped over a lace scarf' in rivalry with a 'slight young man' and made 'desperate efforts at unquenched activity', fell for Caroline, who was now in her early forties, and declared his feelings. 'I have never been able to look at him without laughing since and we have three times taken an eternal and irritated farewell of each other.'[85]

In August Caroline and Fletcher toured Europe: after a visit to Turin, they sweltered in the heat of Aix-en-Savoie, where Fletcher wooed a 'fascinating lady'. Caroline was unimpressed with the 'hot and hideous' town, whose only attraction was a 'kursaal of magnificent proportions'. Her friendship with William Stirling had developed, and he made appearances in letters to her mother and friends. She envied Stirling's unfettered freedom to take off for Russia: 'I should like to be able to be a bachelor and do the same, but alas I am an encumbered female!'[86] Back in Belgium Fletcher got into the habit of going out at breakfast and not returning until late at night. On one of his jaunts around Brussels Fletcher found his mother's little dog, which had been snatched by a gang of thieves. William Stirling's long letters to Caroline charmed her. She admired his turn of phrase, while his tales of Moscow were 'very entertaining' and so vivid she could visualise the Kremlin, and hear the Gypsy bands and the squeals of the little pink pigs as they were chased around the billowing campfires.[87]

At the end of October Caroline was summoned to England when her mother became ill. She wanted to take Fletcher with her but he refused to go. In trepidation she left him in Brussels installed in his new career at the British embassy, but stubbornly devoted to an unhealthy lifestyle. On 2 November 1850 she was escorted home by Richard Monckton Milnes, her poet friend whom she called 'the Bird of Paradox', and William Stirling. As soon as her tenants had gone Caroline and her almost blind mother moved into 3 Chesterfield Street.[88] Some weeks later Fletcher arrived back from Brussels unwell and, defying his mother's wish that he stay in bed until he recovered fully, he went out on the town with Brin and became worse.[89]

In the spring of 1851 Caroline produced a book of new ballads, dedicated to the Duchess of Montrose. *Music on the Waves,* inspired by her sea journeys of the past couple of years, was reviewed kindly by the *Morning Chronicle*. Charles Dickens had a long association with the newspaper and may have had a hand in helping the book get noticed. 'Certainly no ship should put to sea without this pleasant little book either for the ship's company or for that of friends in foreign lands.'[90]

In the census of 1851 Caroline was recorded as being at Chesterfield Street with her son Fletcher. Her occupation is described as 'wife of the Hon. G. C. Norton', and her son is noted as a 'diplomatist'. Their five servants included two men: her coachman, thirty-seven-year-old William Childe, who had been with her for five years, and James Dillon, twenty-two. She also employed a cook, Catherine Lacroix, whom she brought home with her from Brussels, Elizabeth Coe, her lady's maid, and a kitchen maid, Sarah Lawrence, who was thirty. Caroline's mother was staying with her elder daughter, Helen, at the Dufferin townhouse in Grosvenor Place and is described as 'blind'. Caroline lied about her age: she said she was thirty-nine but was in fact forty-three.[91]

Fascination with Caroline Norton's looks was undiminished, although comments on her beauty often remarked on her age now that she was over forty. Lady Eastlake, a pioneer female journalist and writer on art, was only one year younger than Caroline when she suggested that Mrs Norton's looks should be reconsidered. 'Her beauty is, perhaps, of too high an order to strike at first, especially now that she is over forty. It did not give me much artistic pleasure, but I could see that I should probably think her more and more beautiful. Also I did not see her speak or smile, as she was listening to music. Lady Lyell was in great beauty; to my mind she has far more beauty of a legitimate kind than Mrs Norton, though she does not use her eyes so ably and wickedly.'

Some friends seemed unable to see beyond the looks she had possessed in her youth. An older gentleman who had known her for more than twenty years accompanied her to the theatre, 'which sounds gay', but Caroline found it 'as saddening a way of passing an evening as I could find'. He was depressed by the loss of her looks: she was still a 'glorious creature to look at', but her beauty had 'faded' and her life had 'foundered', and it showed on her face and in her demeanour.[92]

Caroline took her mother to Brighton for a week in May, hoping the bracing sea breezes would restore her health and her own flagging mood. Mrs Sheridan was 'ailing and weary', Caroline wrote to a friend. The town looked 'bleak and dismal', and even the sunshine was wrong: it had a 'cheerless vacant staring sort of brightness'. The clouds were also at fault: she was surprised they 'had the heart to chase each other across the flat sea and the treeless downs as if they were in a pleasant county'.[93]

Fletcher Norton was now champing at the bit, eager to return to Portugal and gather intelligence about the revolution that had broken out there for a second time. He told his mother he was 'sick of having nothing to do, with no aim or end'. He was bored with reading books, comparing himself to a tiger who 'having once tasted human blood, disdains all humbler game'. He had taken his career into his own hands and written to Lord Palmerston asking to be sent to Oporto to spy on the rebel headquarters, breezily confident that he would be better able to do that than his old boss, Sir Hamilton Seymour. Fletcher wrote to Caroline that he was already 'feeling better, a lot less moony ever since'. 'I hope, dearest, what I have done will not grieve you – God knows I love you as much as anything in the world can be loved – and I feel I ought to be as contented, cheerful and happy as the day is long. I have broken through old habits of thinking and doing, but having done so, I am in a state of complete prostration, and vague idleness. I feel like a ship that has stopped her course towards the breakers, but which is not making off with her former speed in the opposite direction, only laying to – motionless and undecided.'

Fletcher revealed something of his opinion of his father when he told Caroline he had been to a concert with George, 'the worthy magistrate', who thought her new novel was connected to the recent House of Commons committee report on the laws of divorce. The end of marriages in general and his in particular must have been on George's mind. Careful not to get involved in his parents' rows, Fletcher assured Caroline that he had 'maintained a most diplomatically stupid reserved air' on the subject of her book.[94]

There were warm reviews for Caroline's first novel in several years, *Stuart of Dunleath: A Story of Modern Times*. Readers familiar with her work would have felt at home in her wild romantic Scottish landscapes, and recognised the odd kindly and twinkly gentleman, dastardly male behaviour and stoical women. Ugly scenes during her own marriage and wrestling with the law gave her the raw material to inform readers about wives' inequality before the law. Like Eleanor Raymond, the heroine of the novel, Caroline had been ignorant of her legal and financial position.

Eleanor marries Sir Stephen Penryhn, a man she does not know, because she thinks she has no alternative. He accepts her without a dowry. After eight years the marriage ends when her jealous husband learns that Eleanor still loves her former guardian, David Stuart, who is ten years older than her, assumes she has been unfaithful to him and breaks her arm. 'He rushed towards her . . . and seized her arm with his right hand, he grasped her shoulder with his left, and he shook her as passionate nurses shake a rebellious child . . . she staggered to the nearest chair, and dropped into it; her eyes fixed on his face with speechless amazement and horror.'

Eleanor turns in on herself, unafraid of her husband and indifferent to the possibility that he could kill her. She learns that her money, which had been lost but repaid to her husband, is his alone, and that she has none to call her own. Penrhyn might be using George's words when he turns on Eleanor: 'No married woman has a fortune of her own that is not especially settled on her. There's no such settlement in your case . . . I'm your husband, and it's mine.' Eleanor leaves her husband to live with her brother but remains afraid her husband will force her to return to the marital home for the restitution of his conjugal rights as he is legally entitled to do.

It is a melodrama in its emotional language and breathy

style, but it was a provocative book. If George Norton had read *Stuart of Dunleath*, it would have done nothing to ameliorate his dealings with Caroline.

The *Morning Chronicle* had expected 'clever work from a very clever woman' but was 'astonished' by its execution, which would require the skill of some of the best writers – 'the pathos of Dickens, the wit of Sheridan . . . and the story of Scott' – to approximate. The *Weekly Chronicle* declared it the best novel of the season and 'one of the most brilliant productions in modern literature' with its 'original and dramatic story, character painting of the highest order, sparkling dialogue, wit, poetry . . . and just views of society and a high moral purpose eloquently and unobtrusively enforced'. According to the *Examiner*, Caroline's new work shone among the new novels of the year, 'pre-eminent and peerless'.[95]

On 9 June 1851 Mrs Sheridan, who was sixty-eight, died of stomach cancer at her eldest daughter's London house, 39 Grosvenor Place.[96] Five days later her body was taken to be interred in the Sheridan family vault under Frampton church in Dorset close to her youngest son Charlie. The *Examiner*'s obituarist described a woman who had lived a 'patient and energetic life much marked by earnestness, energy and self-sacrifice' but with the 'wit and genius which are forever associated with the name of Sheridan'.[97]

The pretty, clever young woman who had married the scallywag son of Sherry had managed to keep her brood together after his untimely death at the Cape. Mrs Sheridan had experienced more trials than her siblings and most other women in her privileged caste. Caroline was numbed by her mother's death. She went to visit her body and came away feeling 'ill, chilled and faint', but also moved to see all the 'pain and restlessness' gone from her mother's face. Caroline almost envied her place in the coffin, where she was 'safe from storm and wrong of any kind'. Caroline had had 'a wild nervous hope' that her mother would say 'some little thing' to her before she died, and had kept a long vigil by her bedside, which she was afraid might have been construed by her sisters as 'selfishness'. The visit to Brighton was the last time they were alone together and Caroline clung on to the intimacy they had shared: 'she was very kind to me . . . I feel very miserable'.[98]

'The Clouded Moon of the Sun' (1851–9)

My husband can cheat me because I am his wife.
                    Caroline Norton, 18 August 1853

Obituaries of Mrs Sheridan were brief but respectful, underlining what a template for femininity, economy and stoicism her life had been. Her novels *Carwell* and *Aims and Ends* were praised for their 'graceful style, unaffectedness and good breeding'. As a widow Mrs Sheridan's conduct had been exemplary, her devotion to the education of her children and her 'reappearance in society solely for the sake of her daughters, and on whose marriages she had again withdrawn' were noted. Caroline's mother was held up as a model of the ideal wife, mother and widow, whose life had been 'marked by earnestness, energy and self-sacrifice' as much as by 'qualities of wit and genius which are for ever associated with the name of Sheridan'.

The contents of her will, which was proved on 3 July 1851, would provide a new source of conflict for George and Caroline Norton. Written in 1847, when the situation with George was very difficult, Caroline's name appears throughout the document. Mrs Sheridan's determination that her daughter's inheritance, the interest on her father's pension of fifty-seven pounds plus four hundred and eighty pounds a year, should be protected from her avaricious husband is clear: 'for the sole and separate and unalienable use and benefit of my said daughter Caroline Elizabeth Sarah Norton independent of her present or any future husband and so that in the same way in nowise be subject or liable to the power and control, debts, interference or engagements of her said present or any future husband'.[1] Her son Brinsley was the sole executor. Only Caroline's children were named in the will; Brinsley, Helen and Georgy's children could expect to be comfortably off, and Mrs Sheridan's concern for her grandson Brin was evident. If Lord Grantley remained childless, George Norton would inherit the title if he outlived his brother, and subsequently the title would come to Fletcher when his father died. As the second son and third in line to the title of Lord Grantley, Brin seemed unlikely to inherit, and Mrs Sheridan was concerned about his prospects.

In August it was announced in *The Times* that Fletcher was to be transferred from his post at Brussels to a similar position at the British mission at Naples, and he left England.[2] Caroline enjoyed the social whirl of the Isle of Wight, went yachting at Cowes and was pursued by an elderly German prince. When Brin returned to Oxford she went to Scotland with her friend the translator and travel writer Lady Duff Gordon to stay at William Stirling's house at Keir near Stirling. This was Lady Duff Gordon's last summer in England: diagnosed with consumption, she went to live at the Cape, and then to Egypt.

Caroline's friendship with Stirling was already close enough for her to be able to ask him to pick up a pair of corsets for her sister Georgy in Paris, which he collected in 'an indelicate and slightly covered parcel'. Work had been under way on the house at Keir since 1849 by the architect Alfred Jenoure, who turned it from a 'neo-classical pile' into a building that expressed Stirling's taste and scholarly interests. A bibliophile of his calibre needed a library to reflect the importance of his collection, and a cedar-lined chamber carved with mottoes on every surface was the high point of the house. Caroline was not as impressed with her friend's new library as she might have been: 'it is a very odd room, all built of cedar and smelling like a little girl's workbox, two storeys high and an immense bow window as large as a room'. Stirling was an awkward man at times and 'inordinately humble', she thought, although she found him 'less cheerless than he used to be'. When she tried to comfort him or reassure him about something 'it merely produced grumpy shrugs and heavy moans'. Caroline Norton and William Stirling were quite different people: she was a Whig and he was a Tory and sometimes pious. Caroline was interested in Stirling in a romantic way but knew her position was difficult and may have been wondering who he might marry when she told her sister Georgy about Keir's lovely garden: 'I sigh to think that perhaps some female pig will inhabit it and priggishly do the honours.' Stirling was a man for whom differences in social class could be painful. He was fond of his factor and thought that by rights the young man should be laird of the estate and Stirling should chop the wood and draw the water.[3]

After her visit to Scotland Caroline set off for Naples, and took Brin, on yet another break from his studies, with her. The last leg of the journey on the steamer from Civitavecchia was hair-raising: there was a sirocco headwind with heavy rain throughout the voyage, and the boat was 'leaping about and twirling'. Brin was 'less querulous and more punctual than usual', although he lost his baggage at Boulogne. By the beginning of December they had settled in, delighted to see how the Neapolitan sun and life and a trip to Capri suited Fletcher. He had grown into 'a vivacious young man'. There was a Scottish doctor in Naples who gave him iodine, 'which agreed with him'. Fletcher was more lively than Caroline had ever seen him, describing Naples as paradise and Capri as 'seventh heaven'.

Brin was a serious worry to Caroline so she hired him a singing master as one of several strategies to keep him out of trouble. Although he was 'very fond of music', she was saddened by how, having been a very clever child, he showed no interest in academic study. Caroline hoped that his 'fine voice may make him useful and acceptable in society'. She was relieved that Brin's French was so poor that he could be kept away from 'fast men', with whom happily Fletcher did not mingle.[4]

In the middle of December Caroline travelled north with the Honourable Cecil Duncombe, the nineteen-year-old son of a cousin, who had never been abroad before. She and Cecil travelled in a diligence, a stagecoach, which gave them stunning views. Snow lay on the Alps, and the 'cold pink sunsets' bathed the jagged peaks. When the snow became too deep for the wheels of the coach, sledges were fitted underneath and they crawled up Mont Cenis, nearly seven thousand feet high. After the crawl up, the descent was exhilarating: 'With so fearful and whisking a rapidity, that I felt as if I knew the sensation of a bullet shot from a pistol.'

Night journeys were slow and cramped. Fortunately Cecil, a 'good, innocent-hearted, gentle lad', was a companionable chap; they divided the diligence between them, and when she woke in the morning he looked 'pink and fresh' and was scraping at the icy window with his paper knife to look at the views. However, Caroline ached all over and was 'truly miserable'. When they stopped to change horses they bought a pound of chocolate and 'scraped it into milk' because they trusted no other food. At Turin she felt like 'a wasp that somehow has been hit with a breakfast knife, which is not killed, but escapes to the window, where it crawls, with its poor body somehow heavier, and more awkward, than usual'.[5]

She was back in Naples for Christmas and confided to her sister Georgy how disappointed she was by Fletcher's condition. He had been overdoing it and looked dreadful. The doctor advised him not to get up until four in the afternoon and not dine out in the evenings or do 'any of the things he has been attempting . . . the old shadow of Lisbon has fallen over my heart – of the doubt of his getting well at all anywhere and I feel very low'.[6] A small consolation was that Mrs Emma Gaggiotti Richards's head of her had been exhibited at the Royal Academy and admired.[7]

In August she took Fletcher with her when she went to Scotland to visit William Stirling, now elected Tory Member of Parliament for Perthshire, whose book *The Cloister Life of the Emperor Charles the Fifth* would be published shortly.[8] From Keir they went to Dunrobin Castle in Sutherland and then across the Irish Sea to Lismore Castle in Waterford in October. Caroline learned that her presence, as suffocating as it might be to Fletcher, was necessary to keep him well. He was a typical man in his twenties, who wanted to have the kind of life an attractive young Englishman abroad might expect to lead. He wanted to party and have romantic liaisons, like any beau of his age and class, but he promised her that he would be 'a strong man yet'.

Caroline had decided to abandon writing 'fancy things': she now lacked the interest to work on anything other than 'writing upon the law and I will see it changed'. Divorce was due to be debated in the next parliamentary session, and that was something about which she had a great deal to say.[9] In early November she sailed alone for Naples as Fletcher had insisted on going ahead on his own. When she arrived he looked well and was turning into a 'very fine man, although his beard be rather meagre' – 'the joy, the peace and comfort of my life'. Brin was in bed with 'Naples fever'. There would be few times when both her sons were simultaneously well.[10]

Brin was still in bed in February 1853. Frederick Chichester, Earl of Belfast, a young man who had visited them several times, succumbed to scarlet fever. Belfast was to come to dinner and sing a song he had written for Caroline but died the day he was due. He was 'delicate in complexion . . . the air oppressed him' and hoped he 'should catch nothing', but the smell was 'so heavy' outside his lodgings – which were in the best part of Naples – that Frederick could 'cut it with a knife'. Caroline felt vulnerable. 'I look at my own Fletcher, and know what it would be like, all coming so suddenly; four days, no time to warn, or to send for anyone, this dreadful distance.'

She thanked God that 'pale shadowy Brin' had survived his nine-week fever: 'he might have had one of those dreadful rapid fevers and been lost to us altogether'. Caroline took him to Rome for a change of air, although she had heard reports of sickness there. She started a letter campaign supported by her uncle Sir James Graham to have Fletcher transferred to an embassy nearer England. There was no time or inclination for Caroline to do any drawing or write anything other than letters home: 'this winter like the last, nothing but sick-nursing and sickness'.[11]

A distressed letter from Caroline to her sister Helen written on 5 March and others to her sister Georgy suggest that Brin had stolen money from her and that she had accused and presumably dismissed their servants. Fletcher got dragged in, loyally believing his brother's version of events, insisting 'it is much more likely that the woman lied'. At Helen Dufferin's urging, William Stirling was involved. Although he was unmarried and had no children, he was cast in the role of surrogate father or uncle. He believed Brin's story, or rather he told Caroline he believed her son. When Caroline wrote to her sisters she sounded as if she was trying to convince herself of her son's innocence even though the truth was that he had stolen the money. 'As to my believing him, I cannot do otherwise. He was excessively agitated, wept, and asked for a glass of water, while he was reciting what had happened; there could not be so much acting in any one, as to affect a confession in such a manner, and at such a time, that was not real.'

Brin's dishonesty turned the house upside down and shocked his aunts. When Caroline learned the facts all she said to him by way of admonishment was '"Good God! and you allowed me to accuse the servants."' She showed him the letters from his aunts to make Brin understand for himself 'what a blight such a circumstance is to his character and what all must think of him'. She wanted him 'shielded from the contempt of others'. Caroline was not sure about the tone of a letter of apology Brin wrote to his aunt Helen and worried, 'I hope he has written nothing to you that seems ungrateful, after all your trouble and kindness.'

Caroline was grateful to Helen for suggesting she take William Stirling into her confidence: 'I know many men have liked me, but no one ever was such a real friend.' None of her men friends liked her sons as much as he did, and Caroline knew she could trust Stirling to 'keep silent about it all'. Caroline tried to understand Brin's mood and behaviour in Naples, blaming it on his 'morbid state of nerves and health' caused by the life he led in London, which were so bad he was 'scarcely in a condition to act for himself'. He was now recovering from his fever and was better in 'mind and temper'. She had not dared to leave him in London, where 'I would only have heard that he was ill of delirium tremens or fever.'

Brin had not felt able to ask her for money since the recent troubles, so Fletcher asked George Norton for help with his doctor's fees and provided his younger brother with 'pocket money' by buying clothes (that did not fit him) from Brin's 'glutted wardrobe'. Her younger son's misbehaviour put Caroline's elder son in a glowing light: 'there can be nothing to wish altered in Fletcher – I never saw a nicer creature!' Caroline paid a call on the Count of Syracuse, Prince Leopoldi Beniamino Guiseppe of Bourbon-Two Sicilies, who put on plays in his own apartment and had a studio where he dabbled in sculpture, using 'models of all ranks'. Bulky and bearded, he was parted from his prudish wife and lived an extravagant life in Naples, installing his own monumental sculptures about the city. Dangling from the ceiling of his studio was the skeleton of a favourite valet, who in death served his master by improving the count's knowledge of anatomy.[12]

A confrontation in the courts with George Norton loomed in 1853. In March 1852 the cheques which Caroline wrote drawing on her quarterly allowance were not honoured because George had not paid the necessary monies into her bank account. When Norton learned of the contents of Mrs Sheridan's will he claimed that as her husband he was entitled to the interest on Caroline's father's pension of fifty-seven pounds a year, plus the four hundred and eighty pounds a year that her mother had bequeathed Caroline. Discovering that Mrs Sheridan had left the larger sum to her daughter in such a way that he could not legally get his hands on it, he reduced Caroline's annual allowance by this amount, which left only twenty pounds a year to pay. Despite the fact that he was now comfortably off – his annual income was more than three thousand pounds plus rents from his property in Yorkshire – George Norton refused to make a contribution to Fletcher's medical bills or to give Caroline any help in paying off Brin's debts incurred at Oxford. He also reminded her of the worthless deed of separation which she had signed, against her brother's wishes, in September 1848.[13]

In June Caroline and her sons returned to their London house, stopping at Paris on the way. She came back to prepare for another public legal joust with her husband, and Brin returned to Oxford. Fletcher was transferred from Naples to become second attaché at Vienna.[14]

After weeks of wrangling, on 18 August an action brought by the brothers Thrupp of Oxford Street, coach builders to the Queen, against George Norton for Caroline's unpaid debt was heard at Westminster County Court in St Martin's Lane. The judge was Francis Bayley, son of the Sir John Bayley who had been on George's legal team in 1836, and brother of the John who had represented Norton but subsequently swapped sides to become Caroline's attorney.

The Thrupps were owed forty-nine pounds four shillings and sixpence for repairs to her brougham, a carriage she had bought with her earnings from *The Dream*. The work was carried out between 1843 and 1850. The original bill had been for a hundred and thirty-five pounds, of which Caroline had paid eighty-five over the years, but when George stopped her allowance in 1852 she had ceased the payments. The Thrupps were in court that day and made a point of saying that they 'had nothing whatever to do with the private difference between the defendant and his wife'. The room was crowded 'to excess' with up to three hundred people. George was there and deliberately sat very close to Caroline to intimidate her. She had not realised he would be present and at first her 'courage sank, the horrible strangeness of my position oppressed me . . . my heart beat and the crowd of people swam before my eyes . . . my throat felt as if it were full of dust'. At one point George said, 'Let the witness speak, I cannot hear her.' The judge was asked by several 'legal gentlemen' if it was correct for the defendant to sit so close to such an important witness, but he allowed her husband to stay where he was.[15]

Caroline told the Thrupps' solicitor Charles Dod – really addressing the judge – that even though she had supplied all the necessary paperwork to her husband's lawyers, they had subpoenaed her to appear in court, implying she was there against her will. The judge told her to confine herself to answering the questions, but Caroline would not. Boldly, with the dramatic and rhetorical skills of her family, with George Norton in her eyeline and a captive audience, she said, 'I am here for justice, and as this is a court of justice, I insist upon stating what I have to say. Those tradesmen would have been paid if Mr Norton had not performed the greatest breach of faith that was ever accomplished by man.'

Judge Bayley reminded Caroline that what she was doing was 'irregular' but she replied 'with determination', 'I will speak.' When Mr Joseph Needham, the barrister appointed by Norton's lawyers, admonished her for not fully answering his questions, she fired back, 'You are afraid of my answers when I give them.' When he tried to discover her earnings and what monies George had given her over the years, she snapped back after he implied she was a consistently high earner. Caroline said that some years she could earn a thousand pounds a year but in others she earned nothing, and told the well-heeled Needham, 'I have worked as hard as any lawyer's clerk in this court.' She added that her husband had claimed all her copyrights from her publishers as his own. George Norton interrupted to quibble that his lawyer had done this, not him, to which Caroline asked him directly, 'with indignation', 'Does he act without knowing what your wishes are sir?'

Caroline deflected George's counsel's questions brilliantly. Her scornful quips were worthy of a play by her grandfather; she was cheeky and nimble on her feet. When Needham persisted with his questions about her earnings – 'May we take it as five hundred pounds a year?' – she told him, 'You may take it for what you like.' She reminded him, and the judge and jury, that for several years she had had to rely on help from her family and friends.

Caroline's past was dragged up, as she knew it would be, when Needham asked if two of the friends who had helped her were the late Lord Melbourne and his brother Lord Beauvale. She became 'much excited' and jumped to her feet determined to nail any insinuations about Lord Melbourne's bequest to her. 'I do not receive an income, for his property was strictly entailed. He left his solemn declaration, as a dying man, and gave his word of honour that Mr Norton's accusation against me, when I was a young thing . . . was a false one. He left his request to his brother, and to his solicitor, that as "this young woman" – young enough, and more than young enough to have been his child – would on account of such accusation, undergo great suffering, great misery, the loss of a home and the wreck of her whole life. I stand here a blasted woman from that day, because those people knew me, and Lord Melbourne left me nothing but his letter swearing that I was falsely accused.'

There was a burst of applause from the public gallery, which Judge Bayley rebuked, and Caroline continued, 'My husband can cheat me because I am his wife.' George Norton burst out angrily, 'God forbid!' and then remembered where he was and asked the court, 'Is it regular for me to say one word?' Before the judge could say anything, Caroline replied, 'It is all irregular.' Bayley told her to sit down.

Needham continued to press her about her finances, and Caroline admitted that a year before some money had been paid into her bank by Lady Palmerston, the late Lord Melbourne's sister, and also in the current year, but insisted that it was not a regular arrangement – 'no one is bound to give me anything'. Caroline was then drawn into agreeing that in January and July of 1852 she had received two hundred and ninety-one pounds, which she only later learned had been drawn on Lord Melbourne's account. Caroline reproached Needham for asking her the same question five times: 'and upon my oath each time I have answered you "No"'. Lord Melbourne had left Caroline an annual allowance, but she was not prepared to admit that she knew the ultimate source of the money paid into her bank account by his family as she did not see that was relevant to the bigger issues over which she had been wrestling with Norton since 1836.

Sixteen years after George had menacingly signed letters to her 'Greenacre', she had her revenge and told the court that her estranged husband had 'entreated and adjured' her to return to him, signing himself 'after the man who murdered the woman and cut her body into pieces'. George interrupted, asking the judge to be given the chance to explain. Before Bayley could give his direction, Caroline held up the letter in which he had asked her to meet him in an empty house. She told the court she had not gone, fearing it was a trap, but had bided her time ever since, 'patiently concealing those circumstances but they have at length come out today when my character was attacked'.

It suited George Norton for the court to think that Caroline was a 'kept woman': it would get him off having to pay the Thrupps' bill and her annual allowance, and it satisfied his vindictive personality to smear his wife's reputation further. At the beginning of the saga she had been a twenty-eight-year-old mother of three with a reputation as a flirt, but the woman in court now was forty-five, a writer and poet of note, and a reformer of the law whose Infant Custody Act would inform family law thereafter. The long wait for her day in court was over, and she made the most of it. 'I told you to be aware of your questions if you were afraid of my answers. For seventeen years I have concealed these things, but they come out today because you bully me; and I am ashamed for your client if he does not feel ashamed of himself. My own means will perfectly suffice now that I know Mr Norton can cheat me, and I have no doubt that my friends will assist me more than ever when they learn that the man who calls himself a magistrate, a barrister and a gentleman, and who can also cheat a poor tradesman. I do not ask for my rights. I have no rights – I have only wrongs.'

When she finished her speech there were cheers in court – sympathy had been building steadily throughout her evidence. One of the witnesses George called, James Leman, the solicitor who drew up the 1848 deed, contradicted Norton's assertion that Lord Melbourne, who was then still alive, was a factor in the discussions prior to her signing the deed. George's decision to call Leman as a witness was bizarre and in the end disastrous. However, the Thrupps lost the case against Norton on a technical point: the money they were owed was for a debt that had been incurred before her allowance was withdrawn by her husband so he was deemed not liable for it. It was unfair that the firm which had fixed her carriage in good faith had been caught up in the Nortons' messy marriage, and unless she paid the bill, which she did not as she was not legally commanded to, they had lost a lot of money.[16]

Although George won the case he was livid about her devastating attack on his integrity and asked the judge for a hearing so that he could refute her allegations. When Bayley refused, George lost his temper, 'vehemently addressed' his wife, the judge and the press, accusing Caroline of the 'grossest falsehoods', walked right up to her, clenched his fist and threatened her. The *Dundee Courier* reported that while he was berating Caroline he was hissed by the crowded room and also 'hissed as he walked out of the court'. There was such a hubbub that

Caroline could not hear exactly what George had said, but she understood that he would be out for revenge.[17]

When Mrs Norton returned to Chesterfield Street, against her family's wishes, she wrote a letter to the editor of *The Times,* which she knew would be picked up and repeated verbatim by newspapers all over the country and reach a far greater audience than the one she had had in court. She denied that her friendship with Lord Melbourne had played any part in the discussions surrounding the deed of separation of 1848 and wrote that the solicitor who had drawn up the document had contradicted Norton's assertion under oath in court. 'To save himself from the payment of five hundred pounds a year . . . Mr Norton has uttered this falsehood, and raked up from the past an old, refuted slander, on which for two hours yesterday he himself in person, and the counsel he employed, examined and cross-examined me on topics which had nothing to do with the case, but which were to imply degradation and shame.'

Norton had indulged in muck-raking to 'pain and insult' her and to divert attention from the fraud he was committing against the Thrupps. Caroline's letter was a broadside against her husband in particular and English law in general. Bravely she went public with some of the details of her marriage, using them to make a larger point about women's inequality before the law: 'This case, though it is life and death to me may not interest the public. But what does interest the public is the law.' As the law stood, her husband could dodge any covenant he signed with her because a husband could not make a contract with his wife. She could also legally defraud a creditor by claiming couverture – as she was a married woman the creditor could not recover the debt from her either. By this law unscrupulous or estranged married couples could legally avoid the debts a wife incurred. Caroline believed that the validity of the deed she and George had signed in 1848 should have been examined; it was surely of interest that it had been drawn up by her husband, a magistrate and barrister who would have known it was invalid.

Caroline also wrote about the case to new acquaintances like William Cowper's wife Georgina. She told that philanthropically minded lady how shocked she had been when George questioned her in court, telling her to '"speak up" when my voice choked'. She described her reaction when she heard him whisper to his barrister Mr Needham 'strange and unexpected questions'. The most galling thing was to have to endure his 'falsehoods . . . he knowing and I knowing and <u>we alone in all the court</u> knowing that they were the most utter lies'.[18] James Leman also wrote to *The Times*, reiterating the evidence he had given under oath in court – his letter was published alongside Caroline's on 20 August. Although George had won the case his reputation was further damaged.[19]

Five days later George Norton replied in *The Times* with a mix of basic facts bulked out with lies and an extraordinary rewriting of the story of his marriage. He primly said he had a 'public character to sustain' and that his 'private one is safe in the hands of those who know me'; if he did not speak out it would be 'treason to my character and fair fame to leave all these accusations unanswered'. Norton lashed out at everyone in court, including the judge – even his own legal team for being 'overwhelmed' by his wife – 'those who had a turn for the drama (of whom unfortunately my solicitor was one) were suspended in breathless, helpless inaction'. He sneeringly dismissed Caroline's evidence as 'the most splendid piece of acting ever exhibited' – she had turned the court into the 'stage of Drury Lane'.[20]

A 'disagreeable account' of the Nortons' battle in court reached Charles Dickens in Boulogne, which he mentioned in a letter to his friend Miss Burdett Coutts three days after

George's letter appeared in *The Times*.[21] On 2 September Caroline wrote another letter to *The Times* refuting the more outlandish assertions George had made. In particular she was determined to deal with the insinuation that a girl whose education she had paid for in Suffolk was her illegitimate child, the inference being that Lord Melbourne was the father. Sickened by Needham's questioning in court she told readers that her husband had long ago met the child and knew about her circumstances. Needham's interrogation had been an out-and-out smear. Wounded and weary, she spoke for many wrongly accused women. 'There are also those in whose eyes the accusation of a woman is her condemnation, and who care little whether her story be true or false, so long as there is or was a story against her. But juster minds will pause and review the circumstances Mr Norton himself has published, will perhaps think the fate of that woman a hard one whom neither the verdict of a jury nor the solemn denial of a voice from the dead, nor the petition for her husband for reconciliation and oblivion of the past can clear from a charge always and utterly untrue. I did not deserve the scandal of 1836 and I do not deserve the scandal of 1853.'[22]

Throughout September national and local press covered the Nortons' private affairs. Caroline felt 'sore and miserable' for her sons, who were 'unconscious children when the scandal was first mooted and are now men'. George's 'confused, contra-dictory, shambling letters' were bad enough, but that intelligent people might believe him 'pained' her more than 'than the letters themselves'.[23] The judge's brother, Sir John Bayley, who had inherited their father's baronetcy in 1841, wrote from Scotland, delayed by the terminal illness of his wife Charlotte, who had been so concerned about Caroline's plight she had pleaded with George Norton to let his wife see her children. Bayley had found Norton 'treacherous', and believed that 'there never was a more deeply injured woman' and that George's conduct was the 'grossest cruelty . . . that ever any man displayed'.[24]

Caroline was delighted with Bayley's letter. She thought him 'a kind, earnest soul' to whom she felt 'eternally grateful and ever shall'. She turned her attention to pamphleteering, writing *English Laws For Women In The Nineteenth Century* 'on the hoof' for publication in 1854. Caroline hoped to attract an influential readership in the aftermath of the deliberations of the Royal Commission on Divorce, which had been set up in 1850; its report was due to be published in 1853. During the 1840s there had developed a growing consensus that separation and divorce proceedings were complex, unfair and expensive. Lord Campbell, the attorney general who had defended Lord Melbourne in the 1836 trial, chaired the royal commission. He had been criticised in 1842 for publishing his boastful *Speeches of Lord Campbell*, which revived painful memories of the scandal. Rough and ready with biographical details and sloppy about acknowledging his sources, Campbell was a curious choice for chairman but had a wealth of experience. His three-volume report of 1853 recommended no change to the law regarding separation and divorce but proposed dismantling local ecclesiastical courts and replacing them with secular courts.[25]

In September Fletcher was back in London, and with Caroline he set off for Dublin, taking his manservant and her maid. They stayed at Gresham's Hotel for several days before travelling to see his godfather, the Duke of Devonshire, at Lismore Castle.[26] Caroline was able to relax in Dublin, as she was 'more than half an Irish woman'. Travelling to Lismore would be a 'ripple disturbing the duckweed floating on our pondish minds, and the idea of moving will dawn on us like the limbs of tadpoles'. Fletcher seemed to enjoy himself, but his mother still worried he might do something silly and damage his health.[27] At Lismore the rain poured 'incessantly' and Caroline became despondent about continuing coverage of her problems in the Irish press. She had an 'odd insane feeling of being a spectator and no longer concerned . . . it wrings my heart and makes me sick and angry'.[28] Fletcher's barking cough returned, and was so bad that he left Ireland to see his doctor in London about whether he should go to Naples for the winter. Caroline stayed on at Clandeboye with Helen until the end of the year before returning to London to sort out her affairs.[29] Fletcher's doctor told him there would be a 'very great risk' to his health if he stayed in England for the winter, and at the end of November he was on his way south. His planned move to Vienna was postponed until the spring.[30]

On 13 November in Rome Charles Dickens wrote to Miss Burdett Coutts that Caroline's son Brin had married Maria Chiara Elisa Federigo, a fisherman's daughter. Dickens called it a 'wretched business'. Brin had converted to Catholicism in order to marry a 'peasant girl at Capri who knows nothing about anything – shoes and hairbrushes included – and whom he literally picked up off the beach'. There was also a rumour, which turned out to be ill-founded, that Fletcher was to marry one of Maria's sisters 'with whom he had been intimate'. Dickens was shocked: 'altogether it seems to be a most deplorable affair'. Dickens, who had ten children, was perhaps thinking of how he would have felt if his sixteen-year-old son Charley had done such a thing. The next day he wrote to his wife that Capri girls were a magnet for young Englishmen 'with nothing particular to do'. It was known that Fletcher gave Brin an allowance of two pounds a week, and it was also known that before the wedding Brin had 'fulfilled all matrimonial conditions except the ceremony'. Dickens could not bring himself to call the new Mrs Norton by her married name, instead calling her Mrs Brin. He described the newly-weds: 'Mrs Brin has no idea of a hairbrush and is said to be extremely dirty – which her young husband particularly admires, observing that it is "not conventional". He was described to me as usually sitting on a rock, translating Longfellow's poems for the entertainment of his wife, who has not the least desire to hear anything about them. He appears to be a Young Ass, with certain incoherent inherited ideas concerning the Mantle of Sheridan.'

Dickens waspishly imagined how Caroline Norton's new relation would look in her drawing room in Mayfair. Maria usually wore a billowing white blouse, tight velvet bodice, wide black skirt, white stockings and black boots.[31] All Caroline knew was that Brin's wife was one of the 'Capriote beauties'. If it was true, she thought, it was at least better that he had done it abroad than in England, 'the only grain of satisfaction in the matter'. His age and 'stupid dreams of love without companionship' had caused him to risk his future. Unaware of the rumours about her new daughter-in-law's sister, she was pleased that Fletcher's 'health revived the moment he got into that lovely sunshine and good climate. He wrote in much better spirits, poor fellow.'

While Caroline was at Clandeboye, she received a letter from George's lawyers asking that their affairs be submitted to a referee, as in 1837. She agreed but had no hope of anything good coming from it, as if the decision did not suit him he would 'simply break his word as he always does and refuse to be bound by the arbitration'. When she heard that Lord Grantley was the proposed referee she declined.[32] While Fletcher was travelling to Naples Caroline wrote to lawyers there, Mr Lowther and Mr Wreford, and painted a frank picture of what they should and should not expect of her 'reckless' son Brin whose affairs they were being asked to resolve. She asked the lawyers not to spare her any details: 'do not be afraid of vexing me, it is better for us that I know the clear truth'. Caroline wanted the unvarnished facts about 'the girl': 'her age, her disposition and her conduct – these are things which cannot alter what is done – but which will shape what I can or ought to do'. But 'if the girl be a good girl, then the worst will be spared'.

Caroline asked Lowther and Wreford to deploy their expertise and local knowledge in order to assist Brin's plan to become a farmer and find out how much it would cost to rent a farm for six months or a year on Capri. If such a place was available it was to be put into Fletcher's name, 'as Brin would pawn it or do something wonderfully foolish. I entreat of you utterly to disregard all notions of my younger son being a responsible agent in this matter. He has not a farthing in the world that is not dependent on his father's pleasure . . . I cannot too strenuously impress upon you the necessity of considering Brinsley as one complete cipher in any matter of business.'

Caroline predicted that when her 'cruel and dastardly husband' learned of the marriage it would 'of itself form a plea for continuous severity, if not the utter casting off on his father's part, [and] will greatly increase his difficulties'. That his father would disown Brin seemed a distinct possibility. Caroline also warned Wreford not to be swayed by Fletcher's kindly optimism about his brother's plans. Feeling she had no option but to help, Caroline reluctantly asked a consular official to give Brin a hundred pounds on her account; Fletcher also gave him the same amount. Caroline was concerned that her naive elder son was in danger of getting sucked into supporting his feckless brother. She had opened Brin's letter to Fletcher and learned that Brin expected his brother to buy a farm as soon as he arrived in Capri. Caroline had heard that in addition to an outbreak of war and the risk of a change of government, which might make an English owner's title to a property void, Neapolitan land and houses were 'extremely insecure and burdened with debt and likely to be faulty in title'.[33]

Caroline remained with her sister Helen until March, then set off for Florence where Brin was now living with his new bride. In January she was still not aware of all the facts, and her letters were surprisingly calm: 'it is not a wise thing he has done'. She had still not heard rumours of Fletcher's dalliance when she wrote, 'he leans to being an old bachelor'. She felt that her elder son would not make the same mistakes as her younger as he was 'made of other metal'.[34]

Caroline returned to London to publish *English Laws for Women in the Nineteenth Century*. On the title page of the pamphlet, which she wrote for private circulation, she included a remark by the utilitarian thinker Jeremy Bentham, 'If the Poor had more Justice, they would need less Charity.' Mrs Norton added, 'If women had more Justice, they would have no need of appeals of sympathy.' In the hundred and forty-six pages of the pamphlet Caroline chronicled her own sorry marriage and used her blighted life as a case study to underpin her demand for married women to be visible before the law and protected by fairer laws. This was her second campaign which drew on personal experience to bring about legislative change.

Caroline Norton gave readers an insight into her Sisyphean struggle against George Norton's belligerent intransigence.[35] She argued that, as the law stood in England, married women were 'non-existent': 'except for the purpose of suffering, as far as the law was concerned, it could oppress but never help me'. Wives could not own property in their own names and could neither sue nor be sued as they had no legal identity. When Caroline left her husband she had not been able to sign a lease on a house because in law her signature was worthless. When she had been libelled by John Mitchell Kemble, she could not bring a suit for libel against him, and had to rely instead on her husband and 'protector' to take such action, which she knew he would not consider. Every year George Norton pocketed the interest on her father's small pension, and demanded the money her mother had left her, which he was legally entitled to do. Caroline was advised that she could not make a will of her own because a married woman could 'not bequeath anything as she can possess nothing', and that her property was that of her husband, with whom she was legally still one even after seventeen years of separation. Husbands were entitled to any money their wives might earn. While they were together George had lived off her earnings for years, and he was still entitled to them and could also benefit from her copyrights in the future. Wealthy women whose family lawyers drew up complicated trusts before they married were able to retain some of their wealth. No such trust had been drawn up for Caroline or even considered necessary.

Caroline ended her tract with an impassioned plea for justice. 'If this pamphlet be an appeal to English justice, it ought not to be disregarded because it is a woman's appeal or because it is MY appeal. On justice only, let it rest. Think, if the smallest right be infringed for <u>men</u>, – if the rent of a paddock remain unpaid, or a few angry words of libel be spoken, how instantly the whole machinery of law is set in motion to crush out compensation; and think what it must be, to spend all one's youth, as I have spent mine, in a series of vain struggles to obtain <u>any</u> legal justice! Or do not think at all about me; forget by whose story this appeal was illustrated (I can bring you others, from your own English law books); and let <u>my</u> part in this, be only as a voice borne by the wind – a cry coming over the waves from a shipwreck, to where you stand safe on the shore – and which you turn and listen to, not for the sake of those who call – you do not know them, – but because it is a cry for HELP.'[36]

Caroline attempted to gain political support for her latest campaign by appealing to Lord Brougham – who had opposed her Infant Custody Bill – describing to him how the trouble with Norton had affected her children. Despite the eventual success of the act in 1839, her sons had been left with a 'base and cunning and careless father'. She told Brougham, who had founded the Law Amendment Society in 1844 and had a reputation as a liberal reformer, that 'tender-hearted' Fletcher had also converted to Roman Catholicism at a time of institutionalised anti-Catholic prejudice in England. Though Caroline hoped Brin would become a 'distinguished man' he was currently a 'wayward spinning boy who would have been the better for much wise control'. She reminded Brougham her youngest son was dead and that she had not been able to see him before he died.[37]

In April Caroline departed for Florence with her maid Josephine. She was unwell during the journey, left Paris with a feverish cold and had 'broken down' with bronchitis in Marseille. She could hardly speak and had a 'desperate pain' in her chest and throat. A doctor 'blistered' her, but the treatment drove her 'wild' and did no good. She felt as if she was wearing the 'Shirt of Nessus', the poisoned shirt that had killed Hercules. She worried that Fletcher was ill, and she was so poorly she could not go to him: 'it is all very dismal here'. Impatient to start on the next leg of the journey to Leghorn (Livorno), Caroline was not sure she would be able to travel for at least a week – 'I am a much beat and sick cat' – and knew nothing 'more dismal than being ill at an inn quite alone'.[38]

She arrived in Florence in the first week of May, had rounded up her elusive sons by the twenty-first and learned how Brin's life had spiralled out of control over the past few months. Fletcher's dilly-dallying had by chance saved his life – he had been due to sail on the steamer *Ercolano*, which had been wrecked off Genoa, rammed by another ship, with the loss of thirty-six passengers and twelve sailors. Sir Robert Peel, eldest son of the late prime minister, had been on the boat and survived by swimming ashore.[39] Fletcher was living in a hotel with a friend she could not bear, George John Cayley, whom Caroline saw as trouble. Three years older than Fletcher, he was years ahead of him in experience of life. He had been to Eton and Trinity College, Cambridge, where he won a gold medal for his poetry but did not graduate. Cayley became a barrister and was called to the bar in 1852. Like Fletcher Norton, he suffered from poor health and was sent in search of the sun to Spain, where he started another career as a travel writer. He was a bearded fair-skinned young man in his late 'twenties with a bohemian appearance, and a cigarette smoker before it became fashionable'.[40]

Caroline focused much of her anger and frustration on George Cayley, to whom she took a 'positive loathing'. He was creepy, and followed Fletcher about like a 'dog on a string', gatecrashing her son's invitations 'as his own'. He had lived off her elder son for the past year and walked into her rooms without knocking. When Cayley went to stay with Fletcher and Brin in Capri, he had moved his mistress, a 'donkey girl', in as well. Brin saw through him and would not allow Cayley's lady friend in the same room as his wife but found himself manoeuvred into leaving the house their mother was paying for and taking Mariuccia to a local hotel, while Fletcher was bamboozled into allowing his friend to take over Brin's rooms. 'A more presumptuous and affected creature, I do not think lived. He saunters about with tactless intrusion; came into my room, where I was without my gown, putting leeches onto Brin's head, and actually had to be told to go and 'wait in the sitting room'. He is always huffed, if he is not asked out with Fletcher, and is certainly a desperate hypocrite, since having abandoned the donkey girl, and pretending to Fletcher that he is to become a sincere penitent, and an embryo Catholic – the first thing I hear is a scandalous row in the hotel because he got into some maid's room at night!'

Caroline wrote to her sister Helen that she was 'low and anxious' about Brin. His wife Mariuccia was six months pregnant and they were living in a couple of 'hot rooms' that cost ten shillings a week which Caroline was paying for. Brin looked thin and pale and 'extremely grave'. He regretted his marriage but felt honour bound to stay with his wife because their child was due to be born in August. Caroline wrote, 'He obviously feels that he did a madness in marrying' and now realised that 'seeing her dressed as a lady, and among other people, is very different from the costumed peasant girl, among the rocks of Capri . . . Even if he left off loving her (which he affirms to be impossible) he would never forsake her.' Brin told his mother that he had never expected his wife to be received in society like other wives, and that she did not want to be; they were both content for her to be his 'home companion'. He reassured Caroline he knew lots of literary men who were married to women who did not go out with them.

From the reports Caroline had received she had expected Brin's wife to be a pretty girl but was disappointed: 'she is scarcely pretty . . . and very old-looking for her age'. She had a ruddy, freckled face – Victorian ladies aspired to an alabaster complexion – and a 'good many moles on her neck'. Mariuccia did have some redeeming features: her hands and feet were small and her voice, manner and 'way of moving' were 'gentle'. She appeared to be helpful and intelligent but 'utterly ignorant' and illiterate, and could not tell the time by the clock. Her needle-work was confined to making Leghorn ribbon and tatting lace.

The Neapolitans were not impressed with Brin or the marriage; even though he had done the right thing by marrying

Mariuccia, they had 'cut him dead'. Perhaps they suspected he would abandon her and ruin her life. His wild scheme to become a farmer on Capri had been dropped, but Brin promised Caroline he would work hard and asked her to set him up in 'a mercantile house or anything' so that he could 'prove he was sincere in "redeeming the evil days" '. In the two weeks she had been in Florence she had not seen him laugh. Caroline could not believe the change in him: he was 'pained and worried' about the baby and had been 'very poorly' for a few days with a severe pain in his head and spine. The doctor put leeches on his head, but Caroline was told by an eminent Irish surgeon, Sir Philip Crampton, who was visiting Florence that Brin should not be bled because 'the congestion of his brain is nervous'.

Brin and his wife had married secretly at Salerno in a Catholic ceremony, but he had since learned that secret marriages were forbidden and considered void, so they would have to go through an official ceremony before the child was born to ensure its legitimacy. Worry about this had pushed him close to the edge, a place he was never far from. He could neither eat, sleep nor rest, but Caroline was impressed by how his pregnant wife looked after him. She was 'very careful and clear-headed and minded no fatigue'.

Caroline was sure Brin was unfit for any kind of work. To her irritation Fletcher had 'whisked off' to his new posting in Vienna with Cayley, where she would join them as soon as she felt it was safe to leave Brin. Mariuccia was not the daughter-in-law she would have chosen for Brin, but Caroline warmed to her and was aware that the girl was terrified of being a burden. She went to great lengths to persuade Caroline and Brin that she did not need anything. Caroline empathised with her. Mariuccia could not speak her husband's language, and his grasp of hers was sketchy, and she was many miles from her mother and sisters in the middle of a big city. Having heard what Brin's life had been on Capri, Caroline was sure they could not return there. His wife's people did not like Brin and nor did any of the locals. The young marrieds seemed helpless, which Caroline found maddening. Mariuccia did not know what to buy for the baby and was incapable of making it any clothes. 'Little I thought ever to sit and see the wife of a son of mine write her name as a triumphant proof of advancement! Brin does teach her, but is dis-spirited about that, as about everything – though she is evidently quick at learning. If Brin was but well, and quiet, I should not feel so unhappy; she is a good little creature I think, and evidently thinks him a demi-god.'

Brin tried to economise and refused to have any kind of hired help, but Mariuccia was not adept at cooking or cleaning, and as far as their landlady could see the apartment was 'left to the beetles to clean'. There were no regular meal times, and when Brin did come home his wife would take a bit of meat and 'poke it anxiously into the fire or into a saucepan, and he eats it and smokes his cigar'. They had no bath and no one to fetch any water, so far removed from Caroline's well ordered life in Mayfair.[41]

Brin's messy ménage was not the only difficulty. Caroline was detained in Italy until July, stuck at Leghorn because of trouble with her maid Josephine, whom she dismissed early in her stay at Florence, because she had lost (Caroline suspected she had stolen) her mistress's things, tried to seduce Brin and insulted his wife. The disgruntled maid said her mistress owed her fifty pounds, which she did not; Caroline had paid her wages plus travel money to return to England. There was a tussle and Josephine bit Caroline's finger in an attempt to stop her writing letters to find out what had happened to her property. Josephine went to a local tribunal, which eventually found in Caroline's favour, but her passport was blocked and she was caught up in a 'curious cobweb of Tuscan laws' trying to reactivate it. The plan she had made to visit Fletcher at Vienna was on hold, but Caroline was able to seek the help of William Cowper's uncle, Sir William Temple, British ambassador to the Court of Naples. She drew a picture of the irascible person she had become: 'If it were not ridiculous it would be wildly provoking . . . I am now going home to London with my feathers all broken, like an old raven who has been out in bad weather . . . I remember the day when I was an intelligent being – but very vaguely. Also, when I was cheerful and good company, but all is evaporated. I am fierce, sullen, and rather vulgar. I hunch my shoulders, and say 'What' when I am spoken to, not immediately catching what is said, from sulky abstraction of mind.'[42]

In June the lord chancellor Lord Cranworth had introduced a bill into the House of Lords to transfer the granting of marriage separations from ecclesiastical to new civil courts and end the system of divorces being granted by private acts of Parliament. Now sixty-four, the lord chancellor was not an impressive advocate, but had a reputation as a courteous and conscientious fellow who knew the law well. His cautious personality and lack of flair was going to make the task of steering such a controversial issue past their lordships a difficult one.[43]

In Cranworth's bill there was no proposal to make it any easier for women to end their marriages. At this time a husband could divorce his wife for adultery, but for a wife to get a divorce she had, in addition to establishing her husband's adultery, to prove bigamy or incest – which included him having sexual relations with her own sister. Cranworth rejected the idea that wives should be given the same legal rights as husbands, asserting it was harsh to punish a husband who was just 'a little profligate'. A wife was expected to tolerate adultery, but a husband could not be expected to condone an act which threatened his wife with the loss of 'station in society'. This double standard was embedded in every discussion of matrimonial matters. The essence of the proposed reform was not fairness but a transfer of jurisdiction, and if it had been passed it would have increased the cost of divorce while leaving the troublesome criminal conversation actions untouched. However, it became clear that the bill was unsatisfactory and unpopular with the Lords, while Gladstone insisted that the working class was 'unanimously opposed' to the spirit of the measures the lord chancellor was urging. Cranworth withdrew the bill and announced it would be reintroduced in March 1855 with amendments.

Caroline Norton was one of three distinct voices promoting legal reform in the area of divorce and legal separation. Lord Lyndhurst was in his eighties, had been lord chancellor at various times in the late 1820s, 1830s and 1840s, and was her most prominent ally. He articulated her ideas and some controversial ones of his own in the Lords in 1854. Speaking from a wheelchair and clearly thinking of George Norton, Lyndhurst drew attention to husbands who seized their estranged wives' property, and the fact that wives could not appear to defend themselves in criminal conversation trials where they were accused of adultery. He actually went beyond what Caroline Norton called for, by raising the issue of women's unequal access to divorce. Lyndhurst cited three previous lord chancellors who had favoured equal access to divorce for both sexes. Lyndhurst wanted change that went beyond bureaucratic tinkerings and a new secular courts; he asked for a law which would protect married and separated women's property, allow wives to defend themselves in trials and give women access to divorce on the same terms as men. The very rich could protect their daughters' property interests using trusts, but this was costly and beyond the reach of most women affected by the unjust laws which Caroline Norton's pamphlets had illustrated. Unfortunately Lord Lyndhurst's proposals were so radical that he may have helped to delay changes to married women's property rights for years.

Caroline Norton had no interest in attacking the institution of marriage and did not wish to make divorce easier; she simply wanted to safeguard women who were legally separated from their husbands by establishing their existence in the eyes of the law so that their property, earnings and bequests could be protected from avaricious husbands who were legally entitled to raid their wives' assets.

Barbara Leigh Smith (in 1857 she married and added Bodichon to her name) was another activist in divorce reform. With her supporters in the Langham Place Group, she worked with Lord Brougham's Law Amendment Society to protect married women's property. The ladies of the Langham Place Group, predominantly a generation younger than Caroline, did not approve of her 'personal as political' approach – laying bare the details of the Nortons' marriage – and accused her of calling for a change in the law for selfish reasons rather than the wider good of all married women. They were also nervous of her ragged reputation. Opponents of any easing of the means by which couples could divorce included married women who feared that it would encourage more men to get rid of their wives, clergymen wary of having to marry people who had been divorced, and conservative Christians for whom any kind of divorce was against the teachings of the Bible.[44]

While Caroline was wending her way back to London through Germany, Brin and his wife were married again before Caroline's first grandchild was born in Florence on 26 August 1854, named Carlotta Chiara Mary Norton. Meanwhile, in yet another shift, Fletcher had been appointed second attaché at the British embassy in Paris.[45] Caroline stopped in Paris to help Fletcher unpack, finding him 'thin and very much worked but well'. His rooms were close to where her brother Charlie had lived and died during his time at the embassy. It was a tough job for someone who was not really used to working: couriers arrived all day and night, and Fletcher would have to get up to write the dispatches and send them on.[46]

In June 1855 *A Letter to Queen Victoria on Lord Chancellor Cranworth's Marriage and Divorce Bill* was published by Caroline, addressed to the most powerful woman in the country and the 'ruler of millions of men' round the world. Addressing the Queen as Madam, Caroline pointed out the 'grotesque anomaly which ordains that a married woman in England shall be "non-existent" in a country governed by a female Sovereign'. She further pointed out that every year when the country's legislators met to begin their business in Parliament they were addressed by the Queen, who was head of state, head of the Church and head of the law. They 'reverently listened' to her 'clear voice, rebellion against whose command is treason'.

Caroline described what a married woman's legal non-existence meant. A wife might have been deserted by or separated from her husband for years but was still regarded in law as being one with him. Unless she could get a divorce in the House of Lords she was tied to him for ever and disabled by the legal fiction of her marriage. She was not entitled to keep any of her possessions unless by a special settlement. In England a wife had no right 'even to her own clothes or ornaments'; her husband may 'take them and sell them if he pleases even if they be the gifts of relatives or friends before the marriage'. An English wife could not make a will. Any money she earned belonged to her husband. If she was paid for her work and he had not agreed to the payment, he could insist that a second payment was made to him.

A married English woman was not allowed to move out of her husband's house. If she did, he could sue her for the restitution of conjugal rights, could enter the place where she was and 'carry her away by force, with or without the aid of the police'. If a wife tried to separate from her husband for reasons of cruelty, it had to be 'cruelty that endangers life or limbs'. If she had forgiven him in the past for such treatment, the law considered she had condoned his offences, and could not complain of subsequent cruelty. If a woman's husband started divorce proceedings she had no means of contesting his allegations as she was not allowed to have an attorney or to be considered a party in the suit between her husband and her alleged lover. If a wife was guilty of adultery her husband could divorce her *a vinculo*, meaning that he could marry again, but no matter how 'profligate' a husband might be, a wife could not divorce him in this way. When the House of Lords considered private bills seeking to end marriages they granted them 'almost as a matter of course to the husband but not the wife'.

English wives could not sue for libel, sign leases or do any business which involved signing a contract. Separated wives were not entitled to financial support as a matter of right, and when a husband deserted his wife and was living off her money, if he could prove her friends and relations had the means to help her, he could legally avoid making any payment to her. When a marriage failed it was the wife who suffered most; even a 'spotless character' gave them no advantage in the eyes of the law. 'She may have withdrawn from his roof knowing that he lives with "his faithful housekeeper", having suffered personal violence at his hands; having "condoned" much, and being able to prove it by unimpeachable testimony: or he may have shut the doors of her house against her: all this is quite immaterial: the law takes no cognisance of which is to blame. As <u>her husband</u>, he has a right to all that is hers: as <u>his wife</u>, she has no right to anything that is his. As her husband, he may divorce her (if truth or false swearing can do it), as his wife, the utmost "divorce" she can obtain, is permission to reside alone, married to his name. The marriage ceremony is a civil bond for him, and an indissoluble sacrament for her; and the rights of mutual property which that ceremony is ignorantly supposed to confer, are made absolute for him, and null for her.'

Caroline answered the inevitable objections about 'bad, wanton, irreclaimable women'. She argued that as well as the power of social condemnation, there were 'severe' laws in existence to punish and restrain wicked women. But there was no adequate law to punish 'vicious, profligate, tyrannical men', and in her opinion the law 'holds out a sort of premium on infidelity'. The woman who divorced a husband for a lover and married him suffered 'less, except in conscience – than the woman who <u>does not deserve to suffer at all</u> – the wife of a bad husband who can inflict what he pleases, whether she remain in her home, or attempt to leave it.'[47]

Caroline again used herself as a case study. For the past three years, since her mother had died, George had refused to pay her any of her allowance. He also persisted in holding on to her possessions, her manuscripts and one manuscript which Lord Melbourne had written as a young man. She could not divorce him and had to remain married to <u>his name</u>, and because of that he had 'a right to everything I have in the world'. Caroline had no more claim on him than a complete stranger. 'I never see him – I hear of him only by attacks on my reputation and I do not receive a farthing of support from him.'

It was a powerful piece of lobbying in which Caroline deployed her wide reading in and around the law and eighteen years of bitter experience. The letter took a personal turn when she brought the Queen's former mentor and close friend Lord

Melbourne into the discussion. Caroline referred to the fact that Norton had invoked his status as a magistrate when he slandered the late prime minister in 1853, and respectfully asked Queen Victoria to regard Caroline's quarrel with George as of more importance than a 'private matter'. Surely it was no light matter for Norton, who had been repeatedly accused of lying by his own previous legal counsel, to slander a man who could not defend himself of 'adultery, bribery, malversation, corruption and baseness of every kind'. 'I am, as regards my husband, in a worse position than if I had been divorced. In that case . . . some chivalrous-hearted man might perhaps have married and trusted me, in spite of the unjust cloud on my name. I am <u>not</u> divorced, and I cannot divorce my husband; yet I can establish no legal claim upon him, nor upon any living human being! My reputation, my property, my happiness, are irrevocably in the power of this slanderer. I cannot release myself. I exist and I suffer but the law denies my existence.'[48]

Caroline was keen to reassure the Queen that she was no feminist, not part of the burgeoning campaign of Miss Barbara Leigh Smith.[49] Caroline's remark 'The natural position of woman is inferiority to man. Amen!' may seem an illogical position for her to take up, but her campaign for a mother's right to have custody of her children and now her desire for a married woman to have a legal identity were about justice, not equality with men. Like many of her female contemporaries Caroline believed a woman's position in society was by God's appointment, 'not by man's devising'. Caroline promised the Queen she had 'never pretended to the wild and ridiculous doctrine of equality' and agreed with the fourth Song of Solomon in the Old Testament: *Uxor fulgit radiis Mariti* – 'The spouse shines in her husband's rays.' She described herself as Mr Norton's inferior, 'the clouded moon of that sun', but pointed out that George could not libel his housekeeper with impugnity, could not ill-treat an apprentice, could not refuse to pay his scullery maid, could not say that a contract he signed with a man was worthless. They all had the protection of the law, which Caroline did not because she was his wife. She pleaded with the Queen to put her under some protection of law and 'not leave me to the mercy of one who has never shown me mercy'.[50]

On 1 October Caroline's second grandchild was born in Florence and christened Richard. That month she planned to visit Fletcher again. His health was troubling his doctor, who thought 'badly of him', said he was not strong enough to carry on with his job and recommended he go to Madeira. Fletcher preferred Capri, where he had got better in the past.[51] Caroline was in Paris in the middle of November, troubled with rheumatism and preoccupied with Fletcher's well-being, convinced like his doctor he was overworked. His new boss, Henry Richard Charles Wellesley, first Earl Cowley, was not as 'gentle and good-natured' as his former master, but the extra work gave Fletcher the opportunity to demonstrate his abilities.[52]

With her sister Helen Caroline indulged in gossip about the clothes and fashion she saw in Paris. She wrote about the new fad for wearing shag, a plush velvet: Caroline liked the new soft textures, which meant her 'fellow creatures are become agreeable to the touch'. As a result, she speculated that romantic poetry and prose would be more realistic; heroines could truly 'repose in the arms' of their loved one and be 'clasped in a soft embrace' as the new textiles made everyone 'smoother and eider-downey'. In the past heroes might have been 'repulsed' by 'buttons, hooks, pins and horrid rough braids and jet and bugle beads – in fact you might as well have embraced a barberry tree, a moss rose or a thorn bush as the prettiest friend you had.'

In March Mrs Norton's new ballad, *The Murmur Of The Shell*, was available and her last novel, *Stuart Of Dunleath*, was republished.[53] Caroline was back in Paris, 'a whirligig city', for

Easter 1856, on her way to see Brin in Florence, and hoped to catch up with Fletcher at Naples in April before he returned to his post at the embassy.[54] She was therefore out of the country when Lord Cranworth's divorce bill, delayed by the Crimean War, was reintroduced in Parliament in May 1856.

Mindful of Lyndhurst's sweeping proposals, the House of Lords Select Committee recommended that a separated wife's property and earnings be protected from seizure by her husband, giving women the freedom to make contracts, and allowing them to sue their husbands for cruelty in addition to adultery aggravated by incest or bigamy. They dodged the issues of criminal conversation actions and punitive damages. Reluctantly the government accepted the changes, but the situation was more complicated when Sir Erskine Perry introduced the Married Women's Property Bill into the House of Commons. This was the work of Lord Brougham's Law Amendment Society informed by the demands of Miss Barbara Leigh Smith's Langham Place Group and backed up by a petition of twenty-five thousand signatures of men and women. Erskine Perry, who was the same age as Caroline, had been a judge in India before returning to England in the early 1850s, becoming the Whig Member of Parliament for Devonport in 1854. But his bill was too radical, troubling MPs of all shades of opinion with its proposals that women, whether married, separated or deserted, be responsible for their own property and dispose of it as they wished, be liable for their own debts, and be able to make contracts and write their own wills. Brimming with feminist conviction, it was a direct attack on patriarchal law and the values by which generations of British families had conducted their lives. It was fiercely defeated, sunk by the government, which preferred its own measure steered by Cranworth.

There was no widespread popular demand for any change to the law concerning divorce or legal separation. Within the political establishment, the prime minister Lord Palmerston said he wanted to tidy divorces and separations into a cheaper and more efficient bureaucracy and 'bring divorce which had been a privilege within the reach of the rich man only, to the doors of the humblest classes'. This was a lie: there was no wish in any political party to make divorce or legal separation available to the poor. Even if the bill became law, unhappily married working-class couples would have to carry on as they had before: part company amicably or desert their wives or husbands, commit bigamy or go in for an old illegal practice, wife-selling.[55] What the government wanted was to put all matrimonial litigation into one secular court in London in order to make full divorce easier and cheaper for the upper middle class, to reduce the number of couples separating legally by making it more expensive, and to keep separation and divorce inaccessible to the lower middle class and the poor.[56] However, Parliament ran out of time in 1856 and Cranworth's bill was postponed until the following year.

Caroline had a maddening and miserable time with Brin and his family in the ground floor of a 'comfortless villa' outside the gates of Florence. Brin barked out orders, sending servants scurrying off for milk or a piece of carpet as the fancy took him. There was never any food in the house; meals were not prepared until he was hungry; a chicken pecked at Caroline's heels wherever she went in the house. No account books were kept as Brin was the only literate person in the household and watching pounds and shillings had never been his strong point. Creditors called constantly hoping to be paid, and Brin usually tried to borrow money from Tennyson's brother's wife, who lived upstairs. He was unwell: his nerves were worse and he believed himself 'to be dying every ten minutes'. He was prone to fainting and panicked that every swoon was his last. 'It is impossible to argue with him on any subject or to fix his attention. He cannot sleep and gets up and wanders over the country at 3, 4, 5 in the morning. He gets very irritable and ill at the smallest opposition and I am really beside myself with worry and alarm.'

Caroline had grown very fond of Mariuccia, who was as 'nice a creature as you could imagine'. Her only defect was her freckled face. She found her daughter-in-law intelligent and eager to learn, kind, and most important when faced with Brin's mood swings, 'cheery'. With her acute writer's ear for what people said, Caroline heard grace and originality in Mariuccia's newly learned English. Mariuccia wanted Brin to teach her but he was too self-absorbed to be bothered. Caroline wrote, 'I really like her extremely well and as far as manner or look goes, I defy any one to guess she was not a lady.' Caroline's granddaughter Carlotta looked like a 'gipsy child' with her black eyes, and Richard, known as Riccardo, was 'a pretty fair boy'. Caroline moved them all to Boulogne for a time, where she hoped the sea air would be good for Brin.[57]

At the end of 1856 Caroline heard that a young girl with whom Fletcher had fallen in love had died. Judith de Palazieux Falconnet expired in Rome. The marble sculpture of her by the American Harriet Hosmer in the church of St Andrew the Apostle in Rome suggests she may have suffered from consumption. Fletcher's Italian maid told Mariuccia that Fletcher was sometimes racked with remorse, at other times uncomfortable about 'his connection with her'. It is not known why the relationship ended so abruptly; it may have been because they were both consumptive and her mother had forbidden their relationship or because Fletcher's financial prospects were considered inadequate. Caroline feared the shock of Judith's death might send Fletcher off to a monastery, where the monks would be 'enchanted if they could clutch him'. She felt sorry for 'poor pretty Judith', whose life had been cut so short, but 'would have disliked beyond all belief her marrying Fletcher. I always hoped to hear she had found a rich husband, instead of an early grave.'[58]

Caroline was in London for Christmas 1856. George had abandoned his earlier refusal to meet his new daughter-in-law, and early in December he visited Fletcher in Paris to arrange the meeting. Meanwhile Caroline tried to interest the publisher of her new poem *The King of Denmark's Ride* in Fletcher. She was more sure of his literary talent than he was: 'he is as diffident of his own powers as his brother is the reverse'. It was a source of regret that Fletcher was 'a humbly-inclined man'; Caroline often urged him to become 'conceited'.[59]

In January 1857 the forthcoming session in Parliament would be dominated by the government's wish for a successful conclusion to the three-year debate over divorce. Such was her reputation that at least two anonymous pamphlets were incorrectly attributed to Caroline. Ahead of the political debate scheduled for the summer she sought to put her mark on some current ideas. Writing to *The Times* she endorsed the idea of establishing a 'Divorce Court' to decide the disputes of married couples who were at war with each other. She believed such a body would reduce, not increase, the number of divorces and legal separations granted, which would be a good thing. As someone who knew a great deal about the law and could summarise it well she made a surprisingly deprecating remark about herself and her sex: 'I consider a marriage tribunal would help . . . by controlling the disputants who now fight their own battles and by bringing these battles to speedy, certain, and summary conclusion. I do not pretend that a woman can argue on a great legal reform otherwise than defectively . . . Men would judge how far a wife deserved punishment or support . . . I never argued for the facility of divorce.'

Caroline believed a divorce court should have the right to

interfere with warring couples in the same way that the Court of Chancery did with fathers and wards. So optimistic was she about the potential for reconciliation such a court might possess that she did not approve of including the word divorce when the tribunal was given a name. If a tribunal had existed when she and George had had their problems 'the subsequent storms, struggles, pamphlets and public scandals would have been avoided'. Caroline believed she would have been awarded an allowance and custody of her children and she and George may have even been reconciled. At the end of her letter Caroline said that she was not arguing for the rights of women, but for one right alone 'based on nature, equity and religion, to the protection of man'. New laws were needed to protect women, 'which it is admitted by all that the law has not the power at present to do'.[60]

At the meeting arranged by Fletcher, George Norton and Brin were reconciled; George met his daughter-in-law and grandchildren for the first time. To Caroline's relief he agreed to give Brin three hundred pounds a year but was ashamed of the 'misalliance' and refused to allow the family to live in England. This prevented Brin from taking up a profession for which he might have been qualified. George 'took to the poor little children more than we dared hope'. Caroline was besotted with her grandchildren, 'the poor darlings', and 'passionately in love' with Carlotta, who was 'the oddest, dearest, cleverest little thing'. One day while Caroline was writing letters and the little girl was perched in the folds of her dress, there had been an accident. A servant lighting lamps dropped a burning taper on Caroline's dress and Caroline had been burned on her throat causing her a month's pain and some scarring.[61]

Lord Palmerston's government was determined to get the revised bill, broader in scope and more favourable to married women than originally intended, passed in 1857, and from June three months of parliamentary time were devoted to that end. Palmerston showed his authority by bringing the seven-year-long debate to a tidy conclusion. There was opposition to all the clauses from all directions, but by the end of August much of it had evaporated and the government's dogged persistence paid off. The bill got through by the smallest of margins. On 28 August the Matrimonial Causes Act was passed and would become law on 1 January 1858. The late Lord Melbourne's brother-in-law had got the groundbreaking measure on to the statute book.[62]

Four of the sixty-eight clauses of the act originated in Caroline Norton's pamphlets. Separated and deserted wives with property could seek protection from a local police magistrate (someone like George Norton!) or the new Divorce Court from husbands raiding their earnings and assets. The new court could also award custody of children to either parent, guarantee visiting rights and award alimony to a wife. Henceforth, a separated wife was to be regarded as a *femme sole*, a woman who had never been married, widowed or divorced in the eyes of the law, and would be entitled to make contracts, to sue or be sued, and to inherit property and dispose of it as she wished.[63]

The act also stipulated that when a wife was accused of adultery and her alleged lover was sued for damages, she could appear at the trial and be represented by a lawyer who could call witnesses to defend her reputation. While husbands still only needed to cite their wives' adultery to seek a divorce, women could now cite cruelty as an aggravating factor. Although the act was a patchwork quilt of ideas and far from perfect, it took away all matrimonial matters from the Church. By replacing the ecclesiastical courts and divorces granted by act of Parliament with a new civil, secular court, it made divorce more affordable for numbers of women who were stuck in unhappy marriages.[64]

Caroline had followed the debate through a haze of neuralgia and rheumatism. Brin and his family were in Paris waiting for George to decide whether he would allow them to visit Cowes, the price they had to pay for Brin's allowance. If her husband forbade the visit to the Isle of Wight, Caroline would join them in Paris and go to Italy.[65] George decided he would not allow his son to set foot on English soil, and instead they went to Florence. Before she set off, Caroline asked her doctor, whom she addressed as Leech, for some pills and a prescription for more in case she ran out: 'Let me have something (not strychnine) in my stores ready to recover me, for I dread strange medicines and strange medical men in strange lands.' She did not plan to be away for long and was wondering about bringing two-year-old Carlotta back with her.[66] In England by the end of September, Caroline went with Helen and her son Lord Dufferin to Edward Ellice's estate at Glenquoich in Invernesshire for a month. It poured with rain the whole time. When the sisters signed the visitors' book, Caroline described herself as a 'scrivener' and added two pen-and-ink drawings of their soggy stay.[67]

In 1858 Caroline was fifty. Much of that year was spent trying to extricate herself from her marriage via a deed of separation. Thanks to the new Matrimonial Causes Act she and other separated wives now existed in the eyes of the law and could sign contracts and deeds with their husbands without guarantors. A friend, Henry Pelham-Clinton, Duke of Newcastle, was nominated by her as her trustee; George named Sir Fitzroy Kelly as his. Newcastle had domestic worries of his own. In 1850 he had divorced his wife for her scandalous behaviour, while the estates he inherited in 1851 were debt-ridden. He was forced to resign in disgrace from his position in charge of military logistics during the Crimean War, and his eldest son, now twenty-three, was a wastrel who ran up large gambling debts.[68] As soon as Caroline got George Norton's signature on the deed – never likely to be an easy undertaking – she would be free. This freedom was partial, and unless George died before her, Caroline could not think of remarriage. Because she had left George and gone back to him, albeit more than twenty years ago, she would never be able to divorce him.

During the late summer and throughout November she toured the Highlands, stopping at Keir, the home of William Stirling, where she discussed 'that martyr Brinny'. Caroline shared her worries with Stirling, hoping her host would be able to offer a solution. Their discussions were amicable but boisterous, with her pulling 'all the hair out of Stirling's head and he half the hair out of mine'. William and Caroline were close friends but could not be as close as she would have liked. In an undated letter she told Edward Ellice, 'I want to be Mrs Stirling of Keir.'[69] The man she wanted was forty, unmarried, very eligible and unaware of an aged aunt's efforts to hunt down a wife for him. William Stirling would have been a perfect husband for Caroline: he was kind, gentlemanly, erudite and well off.

Brin and his family had returned to Paris from Florence in October for medical treatment, as his Capri doctor had 'made a mess of him'. Although they had been invited to Frampton for Christmas – a first trip to England and presumably a secret from George – Brin was too unwell to leave his Paris room and all plans went to 'smithereens'. Caroline was unable to go to Paris, detained in London with her 'law business' of separating from George, and felt like 'a wounded snake that drags its slow length along'. Brin's French surgeon was confident he could cure him, and 'kind and tender' Fletcher was on hand to help. Fletcher was in the midst of a drama of his own, announcing to Caroline and George that he intended marrying a woman who had followed him from Vienna four years ago. Both parents were outraged. The 'lady' in question, who was forty-five, just five years younger than his mother, had a scandalous reputation, having 'lived with three men to their knowledge', and was said to have been married. Caroline wrote Fletcher 'long frantic letters' saying that she would never meet his intended, but would have accepted a 'virtuous maid servant' as a daughter-in-law. She warned him that all hopes of a career as an ambassador would have to be abandoned if he lived in such a ménage, and that, after his father, Fletcher was the heir-in-waiting to the Grantley title. If Fletcher persisted with his plan Caroline felt sure his uncle would take steps to disinherit him. Now as a zealous Roman Catholic, Fletcher had been advised by his priest that to marry the woman was a religious duty. George Norton refused to speak or write to him, and Fletcher was eventually persuaded to give the woman up.

When Caroline wrote to Henry Newcastle from the Highlands she was weary. 'I can do nothing . . . I think the angels have changed me. I do not write, read, sing, count, walk or think except through a dreary mist . . . perhaps I am like the spiders who are said by naturalists to have only a certain length of web in them and my ball of cotton is spun out. I am cracked and old like a bell that has hung in an old steeple. My sole occupation is writing to lawyers and my energies devoted to a puff of anger at their replies.'

Caroline hoped Newcastle would be able to find Brin a position of some kind somewhere. They had clearly discussed him before as she told Newcastle she 'pardoned' him for not thinking her son was 'a deserving object' and thought he judged Brin 'too harshly'. A proud mother's blind spots were in evidence as she asked for one more chance: 'he is saucy and wayward but not ungrateful or unaffectionate'.[70]

In December Sir Fitzroy Kelly made Caroline an offer of four hundred pounds a year and a thousand pounds for arrears, which she considered accepting but rejected when Henry Newcastle read the terms more closely and discovered the lack of a provision stipulating that if ever her husband inherited his brother's title the allowance would be increased. Caroline was raising the money to buy 3 Chesterfield Street, the house she had rented for the past ten years, for three thousand guineas by borrowing a thousand pounds each from two old friends, one of whom was Sidney Herbert. Her brother Brinsley agreed to guarantee a thousand-pound bank loan against her literary earnings from a novel and poem she was writing. It was hard for her 'bemused and bemuddled head and feverish mind' to concentrate.

At the end of 1858 Caroline was in London alone. Her sons were in Paris; her sister Helen was in Alexandria with her son; Georgy and Brinsley were in the country, and the lawyers were 'twirling their thumbs and doing nothing'. Caught up in the law, borrowing money and trying to write all made her gloomy and anxious; she hoped she would not hang herself before Helen returned to London.[71] In the spring George appointed a new set of lawyers. Everyone agreed that she should hold out for a clause about what would happen to her allowance if George inherited the Grantley title: 'I might as well be a pensioned-off mistress (instead of a fettered wife) if my position was not to change with his.' Caroline was relieved that George had softened his harsh stand on Brin's wife and was allowing the family to stay with him in London, but she dreaded Brin being dragged into the dispute.[72]

Caroline kept her trusty trustee up to date with developments, although Newcastle was not involved in any of her dealings with her lawyers. She was finding it hard to persuade them to get to grips with Norton and his tactics: 'nothing will get these gentlemen to understand who they are dealing with . . . One thing I cannot say to them is how glad Norton would be to make a public fuss about you being my trustee because he would know I should dread it and so likely to agree.' Some progress had been made with the deed but it had recently become 'overgrown with mushroom clauses about nothing at all'. She dreaded her attorney, Mr Ouvry, saying to her like Mr Leman had said in 1853, '"Well I am very sorry – I see I was wrong but I thought I was dealing with a <u>gentleman</u>."'[73]

At the end of July Fletcher was staying with Caroline in London. He was en route to a new position in September as secretary of Her Majesty's legation in Athens.[74] Caroline wrote to Newcastle that she had recently obtained another legal opinion, which advised her that if George made over his Yorkshire property to an unnamed woman, presumably his mistress, he could still evade his financial responsibilities, and so if he inherited any money he could say he was no wealthier than he had been before. Although Caroline did 'not trust Mr Norton one inch', she was sensitive to the fact that his sister Augusta was dying and felt it was 'not a good moment for war – though he thought little of abusing my dead brother [Charlie] and mother in *The Times*'. Augusta Johnstone died on 21 July of a 'tumour in the abdomen' at Alva House, leaving James Johnstone, a son of twelve and a daughter of ten.[75] In August Caroline thanked Henry Newcastle for 'all his trouble . . . it will be pleasant to me to owe any security of peace and independence to your friendly help and steady kindness'.[76]

George Norton was adamant that Brin could not live in England permanently and ordered him to take his family to Dinan in Brittany. When Caroline went to a steam packet office to buy their tickets an extraordinary scene unfolded. She met George 'by accident', there doing the same thing. They found themselves doing something they had not done for twenty years, talking to each other civilly: 'We talked matters over without lawyers and agreed to sign and seal and settle and have done with grievous battling and uncertainties.' Caroline told Newcastle the only people who would be disappointed that she and George had agreed terms were the lawyers. She reckoned that Fladgate, Fynmore and Clarke had squeezed four thousand pounds from George in the twenty-odd years the firm had acted for him.

Relieved that 'the restless part of this life quarrel' was over, she resigned herself to the fact that her son and his father would 'not draw a little closer'. George invited Caroline plus Brin and his family to breakfast at Wilton Place, the first time they had all eaten together since Brin was a five-year-old at Storey's Gate, twenty-three years before. 'I was besides myself with anxiety to conciliate him about Brin.' Caroline wrote to Newcastle, 'they parted friends', although George would not 'rescind the sentence of exile with a vague hint of future recall'. As Brin settled in Dinan during August, she again begged a favour for her son of Henry Newcastle, who was now colonial secretary: 'My whole hope is that you will not let this really clever and energetic son of mine rot there doing nothing but pine.' Drawing on the capital of their friendship, she reminded him how she understood the difficulties he himself had experienced in the past: 'knowing all sorts of troubled wishings and burning disappointments you will be pitiful to me and give him a vice-consulate in France or Italy'.[77]

During the week leading up to Caroline signing the deed on 2 September, Fletcher prepared to go to Paris and then Athens via Vienna to take up his new position. Caroline was to accompany him on the journey. On 27 August he and a friend went to Brighton for a few days, but Fletcher was so unwell he had to return to London the next day. On 31 August Fletcher almost fainted in the street and decided to leave London immediately to visit his physician, Dr Andral, in Paris. The doctor recommended he go to Madeira or Cairo. Andral listened to Fletcher's chest, heard a *plaie* or wound in his lung, and said that his 'immense and perpetual expectoration' was not the result of bronchitis. Caroline had written to ask the doctor not to tell her son that he should give up his career as he would think he was dying.[78]

Caroline signed the large vellum deed, eaten up with concern about Fletcher's relapse and Brin's exile. It should have been a time of celebration, but her thoughts were across the Channel, where Fletcher was coughing and Brin was brooding. The terms of the deed were straightforward. Caroline was to receive four hundred pounds a year in quarterly instalments and a one-off payment of a thousand pounds to settle any arrears. Caroline's legal existence was asserted and her freedom from interference from him was recognised in the eyes of the law. 'Caroline Elizabeth Sarah Norton shall live separate and apart from him as if she was sole and unmarried, free from the powers and command, restraint, control, authority and government of him . . . and shall and may live and reside in such place or places . . . and he shall not molest or disturb her in her person or in her manner of living nor compel her to cohabit or live with him or enforce any restitution of conjugal rights . . . nor use any force or violence or restraint or sue any person or persons whomsoever for harbouring, receiving, lodging, protecting or entertaining her but that she may in all things live as if she was sole and unmarried, without the restraint of George Chapple Norton.'

In the event of George dying before her, Caroline was entitled to retain her own property and was not liable for any debts he left. George Norton agreed that if in the future his annual income rose by more than a thousand pounds, the Duke of Newcastle and Sir Fitzroy Kelly should decide if Caroline's annuity would increase, and if so by how much. Mr and Mrs

Norton's confident signatures and seals formalised and legalised the end of a marriage that had collapsed more than twenty years before.[79]

Before Caroline travelled to Paris, she received a letter from Fletcher assuring her that he was better but admitting that he had been spitting blood and had been advised that if he 'kept quiet' he might be able to start his journey to Athens at the end of September. On the ninth he wrote to say he was much better and getting 'quite like himself again' but two days later a letter to his father suggested Fletcher knew he might be dying. 'I am just able to crawl from bed to sofa, not allowed even to speak owing to the spitting of blood that has set in. In the long dreary nights I wander with you on the garden terrace by the beck in Yorkshire or better still smell the heather and see once more the larch and birch and rowan of Rannoch! Shall I ever be there in the flesh again? . . . The doctor talks confidently of bolstering me up for the journey to Athens by the end of the month and that is the outside of my hopes.'[80]

By the time Caroline reached Paris on 19 September Fletcher had taken a terrible turn for the worse. He was suffering from diarrhoea, 'alarmingly ill, weak and thin'. Fletcher 'was much shaken at seeing me and wept for some minutes'. Caroline was confronted by the pitiful sight of her ill son trying to play a guitar he had just bought. Fletcher insisted he would be able to make Athens but conceded he might have to alter his route. Every day he got weaker and thinner, 'constantly coughing and expectorating and suffering in many ways, tormented by a raw and burning state of his throat and tonsils, which made swallowing anything great pain and even <u>torture</u> at times. And from his wasted thinness, his bones were chafed by long lying in bed and that became a new torture . . . He <u>never</u> slept and that wore him away.'

One day he told his mother he was 'too weak to live' and

never spoke again of Athens; instead Fletcher asked her to plant 'a beautiful tree' near the family vault in Yorkshire, where he would be buried with his brother.

On 28 September Caroline hired some Tyroleans to sing to him from the next room, but Fletcher cried and she sent them away. George came from London and Brin arrived from Brittany, and Fletcher sang and played his guitar, but even hearing Brin in an outer room was too much for him. Caroline read to Fletcher from *Tom Brown's Schooldays*, which reminded him of Eton. The last book he held in his hands was one about British birds she had given him at school. He communicated by writing on a slate. In the evening of 13 October he lost the sight of one eye and then the other. 'But I see – oh, what is it I see? So many, so many, so beautiful, beautiful, beautiful! Oh!' He lay on her bosom, 'breathing fainter and fainter', turned his head and said 'in a soft sad tone "Mother"' and died at ten to eight in the evening. Two days later Fletcher Norton's body was taken to be buried at Kettlethorpe.[81]

Brin was 'not at all well' at the interment ceremony at the family vault. George was 'very kind to him and anxious to be kind' to Caroline, but it was difficult to grieve with George, 'we feel so differently'. The loss of a second son was the 'bitterest trial' of Caroline's 'tossed and troubled life', and she blamed herself for his death. Two months after signing her deed of separation she wrote to Henry Newcastle, 'unless you could look into my mind, as they do in a glass beehive, and see how the black thoughts crawl over each other like drones making no honey, you could not know what a blank all is with me. I keep eternally reproaching myself and I seem to have lived a blind life – not seeing that Fletcher was unfit for employment and unfit for Cowley's scoldings and faggings and that I killed him with that stupid idea that he should have a profession.'[82]

In December Caroline went to Dinan to stay with 'sad and

poorly' Brin and his family. She was 'stunned' in her 'body and soul' by Fletcher's death, feeling that the future had been 'lopped off' her life. With his death had gone 'all the pleasant part of life'.[83]

X

Life After George (1860–77)

One of the women of our time who have left a name not soon
to be forgotten.

Athenaeum obituary, 23 June 1877

Caroline Norton's sister Helen died of breast cancer on
13 June 1867 at her house in Highgate, London. 'There
is some new surgical treatment of tumours. A small
sharp instrument, as delicate as a needle, injects some acid
under the skin, and by withering the swellings prevents the
pain which the pressure on the nerves creates. But of course
the swellings may recur in one place as fast as they are
conquered in another. The only certain thing is that the operation has failed to eradicate the evil, as we all hoped and
expected it had done. It would have melted a heart of stone
to see her when she broke to me the opinion of her doctor
as to the impossibility of her recovery.'[1]

A mastectomy had not worked, nor did the acid injections,
and Helen had only six months to live from the date of Caroline's
letter. In the autumn before Helen died Caroline hovered in
London half-ready to travel to Capri, where her son Brin was
physically and mentally unwell, but afraid to leave England.
The family watched Helen fade away: 'she is terrible to see, her

406

beautiful arm is swelled and much discoloured and all is pain'.[2] Large doses of morphine offered little relief from the cancer, which had spread to her bones: 'Even Dufferin [her son] and I had to leave her, she was in such dreadful pain.'[3] Caroline wrote 'A Regret', celebrating her sister. 'You never clasped her hand; not knew how much / Of cordial welcome lived in that light touch! / Nor saw her, with a fluttering swiftness come, / And stand all radiant on the steps of Home; / Her eager lips – her cheek and brow / Suffused and rosy with a wakening glow – / As though some inner flame began to burn, / Greeting the festival of your return; / Some innocent lamp of Gladness, newly lit, / And she the Priestess who attended it. / Oh dark blank Life – how bear your desolate pain? / Never again that welcome. NEVER again!'[4]

Widowed since 1841, Helen had married an old friend, George Hay, Earl of Gifford, on his deathbed on 13 October 1862. Hay, thirteen years younger than Helen and Member of Parliament for Totnes, had proposed to her many times. Helen did not deny him his last wish. He had been with a gang of workmen clearing the grounds at Neidpath Castle in the Scottish Borders when he saved a man about to be crushed by a falling tree, thereby fatally injuring himself. Gifford was brought to Highgate, where Helen nursed him. He died two months after the wedding on 22 December.[5] Seven years later Helen was buried with him in the churchyard at Friern Barnet.[6]

During the 1860s Caroline became the full-time carer of her grandchildren, as Mariuccia had her hands full with Brin, with whom they were both having serious trouble. His wild and feckless behaviour had previously been manageable, but now his mood darkened and his behaviour took a turn for the worse. He would get drunk, berate Caroline and even hit her. As physical and mental collapse set in, his frustration was taken out on his wife and mother.

George Norton had not allowed Brin and his wife to stay in England but even he had to relent when Brin became unstable and Caroline could not travel to Dinan. Caroline paid for them all to be brought home but had to 'promise Mr Norton that they shall not live in London'. Brin improved: he was 'infinitely better for the change'.[7] Caroline arranged for him and his family to live at Hampton Court Green.[8] Macmillan published her poem *The Lady Of La Garaye* in time for Christmas 1861, bringing in funds to pay Brin's medical bills. She confided in her publisher that she wished she did not have to be so concerned about 'pecuniary advantage' but that 'a chain of evil circumstances, family disputes and my son's imprudent marriage' made her earnings so important that she could not be 'indifferent to all but the pleasure of success.'[9]

The time Caroline spent in Dinan with Brin in 1860 gave her the material for the new book. In the first half of the eighteenth century the Countess of Garaye and her husband had founded the Hospital for Incurables at Dinan after she survived a riding accident. Caroline assured readers her poem was not a 'fiction . . . nothing is mine in the story but the language in which it is told'. *The Lady Of La Garaye* tells the tale of a beautiful young wife injured in a hunting accident with her husband and taken home to her chateau unconscious. Her husband, Claud, fears that she will die or survive 'in a state of deformity'. The lady recovers but has lost her looks, cannot have children and dreads she has lost her husband's affection. The couple plunge into despair but recover by seeking 'the moral enjoyment of life', becoming devoted to feeding, clothing and serving the sick.

As a publication for the Christmas market, *The Times* said, 'it is a surprise to get a tragedy when we expect a Christmas pantomime; but the tragedy yields a pleasure as real as that of any comedy'. So well known was Mrs Norton's own story that autobiographical allusions were read into everything she wrote: 'the force of feeling which she has thrown into the poem . . . may have been inspired by her own personal suffering'. Her 'pithy' writing had a 'power' that was 'peculiar to her' and portrayed the arc of the story with her 'rare talent for mental analysis'. *The Lady Of La Garaye* remained in print until the end of the century.[10]

During the autumn of 1862 Brin had an operation on his spine and was under the care of two eminent surgeons, Mr Caesar Hawkins and Mr Prescott Hewett, for nine weeks. Brin had been 'taken with a most dangerous inflammatory attack threatening mortification'. Years before at Oxford Brin had been thrown from his horse, striking the pommel of the saddle with the base of his spine. Now a tumour was found on his spine, and if he was not operated on Hawkins and Prescott told Caroline he would die. They chloroformed him because Brin was 'such a nervous irritable subject'. Caroline nursed him back to health 'in terror and sorrow,' afraid that he might die; George Norton went shooting in Scotland. Brin recovered from the operation and took Mariuccia and the children to Malta to convalesce.[11]

From Malta they sailed to Capri, where Brin's bizarre behaviour soon meant they were not welcome. Caroline received 'startling letters' about her 'poor Brin' which kept her in a 'state of perpetual restlessness and fear'. She wrote to her contact in Naples, Mr Wreford, asking him to make a donation of twenty-five pounds a year to the schools in Capri 'for Mariuccia's sake' and to visit Brin to 'talk to him and see if he is happy and comfortable or restless or sad restless and discontented'. His mother wanted Brin to know that 'it frets me more for <u>him</u> than for <u>me</u> his not writing to me – because I never know what to think if I hear anything by chance'.[12] But things were not going well in Capri and the restless family was forced to return to England at the end of 1862. Buried in a letter to her doctor in May 1863 there is a remark which dates the beginning of Brin's darkest behaviour towards her to 1860 or 1861. Recently she had been shaken up when the brougham in which she was travelling overturned. She only suffered a bruised hand, but the accident triggered a 'memory of a horrid fear'. Caroline confided, 'I have never felt quite well since that hurt two years ago from Brin.'[13]

Caroline's new novel *Lost And Saved* provoked mixed reviews during 1863. It is set in Wales and tells the tale of the naive and beautiful Beatrice Brooke, who is seduced by a predatory cosmopolitan toff, Montague Traherne, with whom she lives 'in sin' and is then left with a baby boy, Frank, who dies while the bounder Traherne abandons her to marry a woman for her money. It is the story of a fallen woman but with a twist: Beatrice rebuilds her life by selling her sketches, being an artist's model and making lace, and refuses to be bowed down by her shame in the eyes of society. She marries and becomes a mother again. Beatrice's life undermines the moral conventions Victorian parents were inculcating into their daughters. The *Athenaeum* pronounced *Lost And Saved* 'a work of such excellence that it would cause a stir among novel readers even if it did not have Mrs Norton's name on the title page' and the *Examiner* said it was 'distinctly original as every work of true genius must be, its place is beside the best contemporary fiction' and concluded it was the author's 'best prose work'. The *Illustrated London News* and others disliked Caroline's proposition that Beatrice could be saved, and she was drawn to defend her book in letters to *The Times*.[14]

During the summer of 1863 Brin clamoured to return to Capri. Although she could ill afford it, Caroline took the family of four out there and set them up in a new home, although it was thought better for the two children if she took them away with her when she left. As a result Caroline got into trouble with her bank, who told her not to draw any more money 'until she was square with them', and she wrote to Henry Newcastle. Apologising for her 'very selfish unexpected note', she begged for an immediate loan of twenty pounds by noon 'at the latest' the next day. She explained that she had been counting on her publishers, Macmillan, to publish a coffee-table book she had proposed, but they had declined, and she was in a muddle.[15]

Then came terrible news from Capri. Caroline was 'miserably agitated' by a letter telling her that Brin had been stabbed in the groin and thigh by a man whose wife Brin had struck. The woman was protecting her daughter, whom Brin was pursuing. The people 'were up in arms against him . . . everybody has to be paid and compensated and pacified'.[16] In August and September 1864 Caroline spent six weeks in Germany recovering her health. Soon after her return, Henry Newcastle, friend and trustee of her deed of separation with George Norton, died of a stroke, aged fifty-three.[17]

On 26 April William Stirling Maxwell (he inherited a baronetcy from his uncle in 1865 and added Maxwell to his name) married a distant cousin, Lady Anna Maria Leslie Melville, at the British embassy in Paris. Caroline made a firm friend of the woman who had got the man she had been so fond of for fifteen years, describing her as 'decidedly handsome, with delicate, regular features, fair hair and high-bred, gentle manners'.[18] Lady Anna was thirty-nine and the daughter of the Earl of Leven. In two years she had two sons, John and Archibald; Caroline was godmother to John. Caroline would write candid letters to her new friend about the abuse she suffered from her only surviving son.

Caroline needed to plan a trip to see Brin in November but it was not safe to travel to Naples as there was cholera in the city, so grandmother and her two charges did not reach there until the end of January 1866. Caroline wrote to her ailing sister Helen with travellers' tales and some family news. George Norton had grown fond of his ten-year-old grandson, writing Richard a letter 'in terms of the tenderest affection you ever read!' George had told Caroline that a doctor had put him 'through the most exquisite torture' of an operation. He was getting well, but his brother, the odious Lord Grantley, was also ill. 'I don't care' was Caroline's response. She heard en route that 'my poor lad [Brin] has really been very bad, partly his own fault, and he has been blind but is much better'.[19]

Caroline and her grandchildren Carlotta and Richard returned to London for the summer of 1866 as the gravity of Helen's condition was obvious. Caroline was torn, fearful for her son's sanity and life and dreading her sister's imminent death. At the beginning of 1867 she and 'her little chicks' made a quick trip to Capri to see Brin, writing Helen a cheery chatty letter from Genoa in January. Although the children were 'as good as possible', Caroline, who was now almost sixty and had rheumatism, found it 'a great drag and fatigue' to be travelling with them without her usual maid. Unhelpful Brin sent her a note to say he was 'suffering and cannot stir a step to meet us'.[20] During the two months Caroline was there she enjoyed Capri, thinking it 'the strangest place I have ever been in'. On her first day she paid her respects to Mariuccia's parents, meeting them for the first time. Her father was a 'regular old peasant, stone deaf with a very sweet and kindly countenance, staring smilingly and sweetly' at the grandchildren, and her mother was 'slender and strong bearing the unmistakeable impress of past loveliness in her skinny but still graceful throat and great dark disapproving and scornful eyes'. Brin paid his wife's family to look after them, perhaps because no one else would. Mariuccia's sister was their cook and housekeeper; a nephew was his valet, a brother was his 'game-keeper' and looked after Brin's four dogs. Unhappily for Carlotta and Richard, their father was 'too poorly' to show much interest in them: 'they have felt disappointed in waiting like two little breathless dogs for walks and drives that never come off after hours of expectation'. To relieve the children's boredom Caroline took them to see the excavations at Pompeii and to the Blue Grotto, where they sang 'glees'. Richard filled the place with his 'little treble voice'. Caroline and the children were glad to leave in the middle of March: 'very few and far between have been our pleasant hours'. Brin was in a 'sad state of health and very moody and uncomfortable' the whole time they were there.[21]

At the end of July 1867, after thirty-six years on the bench, George Norton retired as magistrate of Lambeth Street Police Court in Whitechapel because of 'failing health'.[22] Caroline and her grandchildren went to Cowes, sailing on the Dufferin yacht, which added to their collective sadness over the death of Helen. During the year Caroline's novel *Old Sir Douglas,* her last and darkest, was published to mixed reviews. *The Times* was not impressed: 'We regret that Mrs Norton, who is a poet of repu-tation and a practised writer of prose had not written a better book.' The novel had offended the reviewer with its sensational tales of vulgar behaviour, wanton but unabashed women, murder, secret marriages, hidden identities, implausible escapes and prejudices.

Caroline responded confident that her readers had greater imagination and empathy than her reviewer. 'I can only trust I may find "simple readers" who do not live in so Arcadian a "world of facts" that they consider all treachery, wickedness and undeserved hatreds to be inventions of sensational writers; who do not believe that all parents of good conduct and Christian principles are sure to have excellent children . . . and that all the members of a family are exactly alike who have been under the same parental care; nor doubt that many wicked youngsters have found pardons from fathers and uncles, instead of the rigorous justice of changeless alienation.'

The *Athenaeum* however recommended it as a 'thoroughly readable and wholesome book of fiction'. The reviewer was confident that fans of her work would admire it, coming from a writer who 'has been a witness of much that is brilliant in human society and much that is most sad in human life, and describes with equal candour and vividness the things that she has seen and the sorrow she has felt'. The *Express* brushed the spat with *The Times* to one side, as 'very amusing to those who had time for it', believing it would be 'too terrible if writers of fiction had a right to criticise at length every unfavourable review of their work: Mrs Norton's example is not to be made a precedent'. The reviewer for the *Pall Mall Gazette* liked it, noting how Caroline's colourful life and its harsh lessons had entered into her latest work. It was a 'thoroughly readable and wholesome book, a graceful and touching story'.[23]

In January 1868 Caroline took Carlotta to Yorkshire for a month to stay with her cousins the Fevershams at Duncombe Park. In her sixties, Caroline found it hard to keep up the rhythms of her life, describing herself 'a crumbling old ruin of an aunt', but somehow found the strength and mobility to go to Paris and Geneva in the summer. The Highland tours which had been such a big part of her life were harder to manage as her joints got creakier, although Carlotta, now aged fifteen, was a useful pair of hands, sometimes doubling up as her maid. Late-summer pilgrimages to the graves of her two sons at Wakefield were important dates in her calendar; 1869 was the tenth anniversary of Fletcher's death. When Brin and his wife arrived from Capri he was not as ill as Caroline had feared, although he was in a 'mournful condition' of mind. Brin imagined he needed more surgery on his spine but his surgeon assured Caroline that 'no other operation is required or would do him any good'. Caroline also had to contend with Mariuccia's 'sobbing explanation of all she has to go through attending to his very real sufferings.'[24]

Caroline did not leave the country in 1870; the year was spent in London and on a stately progress to Dorset, Yorkshire and Scotland. Caroline paid for her grandson Richard to go to Harrow School, proud that he would be a pupil where her grandfather had studied. During his time there Richard 'outraged Harrow and society' by returning to school with a loaded six-barrelled revolver in his coat pocket. Caroline took the news calmly: 'what things boys will do and what risks they run'.[25] At the end of March Caroline and the Stirling Maxwells attended a dinner at the American legation, where the Queen of the Netherlands, a friend of the Sheridans of Frampton, was present. Also in the company were Charles Dickens, Wilkie Collins and Robert Browning.[26] In August Augusta Cowell died, and Caroline fell down some stone steps at Cowes, which prolonged her stay there.[27]

Caroline's political pamphlets were a thing of the past. On 9 August 1870 the Married Women's Property Act was passed, and she had played no part in the debate. The act allowed married women to keep their own earnings and to inherit property after they were married if it was not part of a trust, to inherit up to two hundred pounds, to hold and inherit rented property in their own name, and made them liable, like their husbands, to pay for the maintenance of their children out of their earnings and assets. However, the notion of property rights was not addressed: the new law was not retroactive, and many married women did not benefit, as any property a wife owned prior to marriage remained that of her husband. The act was important in that it recognised a married woman's right to own her own property and keep her own earnings, but it took another twelve years for the law to recognise that a wife was entitled to her own legal status equal to that of her husband and to address the issue of property law.[28]

In April 1871 Caroline was summoned to appear at Marlborough Street Magistrates' Court for not paying her parish rates. She had refused to pay the thirty pounds demanded, saying that the damp in her house was caused by the leaky pavement in front of it. Her plea was rejected and she was ordered to pay in full.[29] Her indifferent health made for gloomy moods: she described how she felt like a fly who had fallen into 'the grouts and lukewarm water of a slop basin after breakfast' and was having 'great difficulty drying my wings'.[30] At the end of 1871 Caroline started to put her affairs in order, looking through old papers and drawing up 'several contradictory wills and codicils' before taking the grandchildren to Keir for Christmas with the Stirling Maxwells.[31]

In 1873 Brin and his wife were back in the country, always a nerve-racking time for Caroline. On his next birthday Brin would be forty-two, but he was the most untypical and reluctant husband and father of two teenage children.[32] Caroline saw Brin and Mariuccia in Scotland when her son and his wife paid a call on, but were not invited to stay with, his father at Rannoch Lodge near Pitlochrie, George Norton's sister's home. Brin looked better but had 'intervals of intense melancholy'. George insisted his son and wife accompany him to Yorkshire a week later but would not confirm any plans in case he was summoned to Wonersh, where Lord Grantley was ill. Caroline, Brin and Mariuccia stayed at the Rannoch Hotel for a few days, which was a 'blessing in some ways' – if 'things went wrong between me and my son . . . then only I would bear the brunt of "the dree of shame" with inn keepers and inferiors'. Her son and the locals would expect George to be 'the one accountable for Brin's vagaries'. While there Caroline was informed that even though her new cook in London had come with good references she had proved to be a 'most drunken and disreputable creature' and had disappeared with the cheque Caroline had sent to pay for the coal and the other servants' board wages.[33]

A few days later Caroline wrote a despondent letter about Brin to her cousin William Le Fanu in Dublin. 'He never quite emerges from the strange confused hypochondriacal state of mind in which he has long been. I watch him with mournful compassion. He is almost always restless, suspicious and downcast, thinks his nearest and dearest are plotting something; that he has unknown foes; that he is being poisoned . . . It poisons the very well of my life to see him, poor dear, and we never know what his mood will be from one day to another.'

Looking after Brin's children made up for the way their father had turned out and the 'strange empty life' he led. Richard, who was nearly eighteen, was 'not industrious' but 'extremely intelligent', serious, shy and fortunately 'quite steady', and seemed likely to become a diplomat. Carlotta, a year older, was 'very short and very brown' with 'no grace' for dancing and no skill for working, but was 'as good as gold and sensible and helpful'.[34] One day Mariuccia and Carlotta wanted to meet Richard and Brin when they were fishing, but the walk took longer than they expected and they missed each other. Persuaded by George that it was Caroline's fault – who had not been on the walk – Brin flew into a rage and was so 'disturbed' that Caroline dared not go down to dine.[35]

Caroline returned to London in the middle of November, where she did some reviewing, 'turning a penny' as she called it. She wrote to her friend Lady Anna Stirling Maxwell, whose husband had been to dinner one evening, about what happened when their guest left. 'I know that to you and such as you . . . among women, separations between man and wife seem very awful and inexplicable and I can scarcely give you a better idea of the life I led with my <u>husband</u> than by describing my life with my <u>son</u>. The causeless rages and contradictions are like a dreadful echo of my youth and of the unhappy days at home.'

After Sir William had left, Caroline remembered she had forgotten to post an important letter, a character for a servant who needed employment, and asked Brin, who was in the study smoking a cigar, to take the letter to the pillar box at the end of the street. Brin was rude, said he 'would not stir' and told her to send the servant with it. Caroline explained the woman was in bed 'dog tired' and she did not want to disturb her. Brin lost his temper: 'Tell her to get out of bed and dress herself. I shan't stir be sure of that.' Caroline called him 'very selfish' to insist on waking the woman, and told him, 'You must go!' Brin refused: 'I wonder you <u>dare</u> contradict me! Shift for yourself with your folly.' Caroline told him that she was not well enough to go, had a bad pain in her side, had 'spit blood that morning' and asked if Mariuccia would take it. He refused to let her and told his mother to do her own errands. When Caroline returned from posting the letter she confronted Brin again, telling him that no gentleman, especially the son of a mother who was unwell, would have refused to help, and this made Brin even angrier. 'He pushed me violently from the study door to the bottom of the stairs and said: "Get out of my sight or it will be worse for you I can tell you. Get out. Get away!"'

The next morning after a sleepless night Caroline told Mariuccia that she and Brin would have to stay in lodgings, which she would pay for, until they left for Capri. Mariuccia burst into tears, told Caroline that she had put up with such behaviour for twenty years – 'He does not know what he says or does' – and begged Caroline to let them stay until the day of departure. Caroline remembered when her son Fletcher would come to stay, how they would rush to greet each other 'to be sooner in each other's arms', and now in contrast all she could hope for was a promise that Brin 'shall not stay to torment and terrify us beyond the week'. Caroline wrote to Lady Anna that she had had little experience of men in her life before she was married at a young age: her father was long dead and her elder brother Brinsley was in India. 'Men were all strangers to me and hard was my first acquaintance with the specimens that fell to my lot.'[36]

In February 1874 Sir William Stirling Maxwell was elected the Tory Member of Parliament for Perthshire. Nine months later, on 21 November while he was out hunting, Lady Anna had an epileptic fit and fell into a fire at Keir House. Her hand was badly burnt and had to be amputated. She died seventeen days later on 8 December.[37] Caroline and Carlotta were in Scotland and due to make their annual visit when they heard the news.

On 24 February 1875 George Norton died of liver disease at Lord Grantley's house at Wonersh. He was buried at Sandal Magna church near Wakefield with his two sons. Caroline was with Carlotta in Capri visiting Brin at the time. Notices in *The Times* and elsewhere of George Norton's death were brief: he was remembered chiefly as being 'the husband of the well-known authoress Mrs Norton'. The *York Herald* reminded its readers the marriage had not been a happy one and that in 1853 there had been a correspondence in the press of a 'not very edifying character but public opinion generally was on the side of the lady'.[38] In April Caroline and Carlotta were back in England, mindful that Lord Grantley's health had been poor for years, and now that George was dead Brin might soon inherit the title. When George's will was proved in June it was more vindictive than Caroline had predicted. 'I have passed a most dreary and revolted time. My husband's will has been a sad torment to us all – as if he wished to make it painful . . . he forbids Brin to go to Kettlethorpe Hall "so long as his mother lives" and orders the house to be let.' Caroline could not understand why George had gone out of his way to prevent his son being the squire at Kettlethorpe and was outraged that he had left all his papers, including her letters to him and to Fletcher, to his unnamed mistress, when the letters should have been returned to her.[39]

Caroline and her lawyers were still unpicking the terms of George's will when Lord Grantley died at Wonersh on 27 August of liver disease, aged seventy-seven.[40] Other than being at the battle of Waterloo, George's brother had made such little impact on the world that notices of his death were even briefer than those of his younger brother, but they again mentioned he was connected by marriage to the 'well-known authoress' and 'brilliant Caroline Norton'. For all the years the brothers had plotted and schemed against her, it was her success which padded out and gave some colour to their feeble obituaries.

At the time of her marriage Caroline believed that Lord Grantley's property was entailed and that her sons would inherit his title and estate, but in February 1876 she and her lawyers were shocked to learn that Grantley had broken the entail in 1824 – when George had first set his cap at Caroline – and disinherited her boys, insisting they were passed over for their own sons and ensuring there was very little money to support the peerage for at least a generation.[41] Caroline was now resolved to embark on another legal battle, this time on behalf of her ungrateful and high-handed son Brin, who sent orders from Capri as to how she should proceed.

On 15 June 1876 Caroline asked her old friend Willie Cowper to go into court with her to contest the will. Grantley's dastardly omission of Brin from his will she interpreted as 'an act of enmity and vengeance for being jeered the day of that false action against your uncle [Melbourne]'. Caroline hoped there would be 'a lingering interest in my luckless destiny in your friendly heart and that if you can spare the time you will not refuse the feeling I am with friends'. She had been told the case would be a brief discussion as to whether Grantley's will would be allowed to stand and 'pauperize the peerage for a genera-tion'.[42] If it was upheld, Richard would inherit the title, which would be held in trust until the late Lord Grantley's wife, the Dowager Lady Grantley, died. It was an unusual arrangement. Brin was to be leap-frogged by his twenty-year-old son, who was left very little money to pay for what he inherited. It was a delicate situation: Richard, now heir-in-waiting, was with his father in Capri as the implications of Grantley's will became clear.

In July 1876 Caroline's attempt to contest the will on Brin's behalf failed when the court upheld Lord Grantley's will. Brin was too ill to come to London and may have been more of a liability than a help.[43] Caroline felt overwhelmed by her son's breezy orders – 'I do feel so helpless . . . my son writes to me as if I could be a sort of second Providence to set all his affairs to rights' – and even her grandson treated her like a steward, telling her airily to put all things in their proper order and on the most profitable footing. Her own lawyer was infuriating, 'making as much business and gives as little intelligible informa-tion as he can'.[44] Caroline, now in her late sixties, did what she could, but rheumatism forced her to retreat to her house in Mayfair 'grunting and groaning', where she remained house-bound for the rest of her life. She could not stand up and had to be carried downstairs. Carlotta became her secretary.

Less than a year after the horrid death of Lady Anna, the rumour had started that Caroline was to wed the recently widowed Sir William Stirling Maxwell. The *Aberdeen Journal* said the stories were 'quite correct', others 'could hardly believe it'. The rumour did not go away, and on 1 March 1877 they were married in his house at 10 Upper Grosvenor Street by special licence. The bride was sixty-nine and the groom ten years younger. All the witnesses, except a Maxwell cousin, were from her family, including her brother Brinsley and his wife Marchy.[45] Caroline and William had been friends for thirty years, and during that time he had 'never swerved from good gracious acts to me and mine'. William told Caroline he wanted to make a home for her, his sons and her grandchildren, and give her 'peace and happiness' after a long life of struggle and torment. Caroline and he had been discussing it for some time and she knew his family were against her, but 'if it adds to his happiness the opinion of others ought not to touch me'.[46] Caroline wrote, 'it is very, very late in life to welcome happiness and peace. If you knew the years and years of alienation, of being ashamed of one's name and persecuted to the last only because he could not rid me of it . . . to live in dread, and then suddenly to change to real "Home" and real love and be proud and grateful, after so much suffering – you would not wonder I have accepted my good lot and cling to the Giver. The doctors say I shall get well.'[47]

It was brief. Caroline died fourteen weeks later on 15 June 1877 of jaundice and peritonitis.[48] Brother Brinsley and Marchy sat with her for several nights and did not expect her to die: 'she talked as pleasantly and as cheerfully as ever'. But Caroline sensed her life was coming to an end and told them of her fear of losing her new peace so soon after finding it. Her husband wrote, 'we were buoyed up with false hope till the night before she died. The constancy and cheerfulness with which she bore her agony were worthy of her life.'[49] On 20 June Sir William, Carlotta, Richard and Caroline's brother Brinsley escorted her body to Scotland for the funeral and interment in the vault at Lecropt at Keir. Brin was too ill to attend.[50]

Carlotta, now twenty-three, felt 'a terrible blank' in her life.

While her brother's future had some kind of shape hers looked awkward and uncertain. She went to Keir, where Sir William was 'so kind and good to me'. A return to Capri did not seem likely.[51]

Six weeks after Caroline died, her son Brin was also dead. On 24 July he expired while 'undergoing a painful procedure to which he had been compelled to submit'. His son Richard, now the fifth Lord Grantley, travelled to Capri. *The Times* was tactful in its brief notice of Brin's death: 'a man of considerable talent . . . had he remained in England under the healthier intellectual social influences of his country he might have played a valuable part in life. He has for some years been laid aside as a confined invalid.'[52] In November 1877 Sir William escorted Carlotta to Capri for her to spend the winter with her mother.[53] On 6 January 1878 Sir William called in on friends in Venice on his way home to England. Seven days later he died from typhus, seven months after Caroline.[54] His body was returned to England and buried with Caroline at Keir. Thirty years of deep friendship and fourteen weeks of married life were over.

Caroline Norton's obituaries decorously revisted her 'friendship' with Lord Melbourne and her struggles with the ghastly George. Her battles with her husband had often got in the way of her creative life, and even after his death the terms of his and his brother's wills meant the struggle did not end. Caroline Norton is a heroine to every woman who has made a mistake in judging a man. Her miserable marriage drew her out of private life and into the sphere of law. Her Infant Custody Act was the first piece of feminist legislation, and her pamphleteering informed the 1857 Matrimonial Causes Act and the 1870 Married Women's Property Act. She was an exceptionally strong woman and an accidental feminist who changed women's lives for the better.

Today Caroline Norton's name and work are not widely known, but every time a mother is granted custody of her children, or is successful in her application for financial support, Caroline's struggle with her dreadful husband and her eventual success should be saluted. Many women have had bad marriages and have suffered in silence, terrified to speak out for fear of violence or society's disapproval, but Caroline Norton would not and did not. The Infant Custody Act opened the debate on wives' and mothers' invisibility before the law.

George Norton died in 1875, but there have been many George Nortons since, and this kind of behaviour persists.

Tell Johnny that is my face Kissing him by Archie.

Abbreviations

BL British Library
HO Home Office
NLI National Library of Ireland
NLS National Library of Scotland
JMA John Murray Archive
Old DNB *Old Dictionary of National Biography*
ODNB Oxford Dictionary of National Biography
PROB Probate
PRONI Public Record Office of Northern Ireland
WO War Office

Notes

Prologue

1. *Morning Chronicle*, 23 June 1836, p.2; Meteorology Archive, Royal Society, 22 June 1836, MA/238
2. *The Times*, 23 June 1836, p.1
3. *The Satirist and the Censor of the Times*, 22 May 1836, p.162
4. *ODNB* online, Sir William Follett; John Bayley; Richard Crowder; Dr Mark Collins, Parliamentary Estates Archivist and Historian
5. *ODNB* online, Sir John Campbell; Serjeant Thomas Noon Talfourd; Frederic Thesiger
6. *ODNB* online, Queen Caroline
7. Lord Campbell, *Speeches of Lord Campbell at the Bar and the House of Commons*, A. & C. Black, London, 1842, p.2
8. Lawrence Stone, *Road To Divorce: A History of the Making and Unmaking of Marriage in England*, 1995, pp.256–66
9. *The Times*, 30 August 1875, p.9
10. *ODNB* online, Lord Wynford
11. *The Age*, 26 June 1836, pp.209–13
12. WO 97/850/16

Chapter I

1. *ODNB*: Thomas Sheridan; John Watkins, *Memoirs of the Private and Public Life of the Rt. Hon. Richard Brinsley Sheridan with a Particular Account of His Family and Connexions*, 1817, p.126
2. Percy Fitzgerald, *The Lives of the Sheridans*, 1886, Vol. 2, 1886, p.325
3. *ODNB* online, Elizabeth Ann Sheridan, née Linley; Lord Edward

Fitzgerald; Fintan O'Toole, *A Traitor's Kiss: The Life of Brinsley Sheridan*, 1997, pp.261–70

4. Ibid., pp.309, 311
5. Ian Kelly, *Beau Brummell: the Ultimate Dandy*, 2005, p.60
6. Thomas Moore, *The Memoirs of Richard Brinsley Sheridan*, Vol. II, 1825, p.314
7. *Old DNB* online, Thomas Sheridan
8. *Old DNB* online, Caroline Henrietta Sheridan, née Callander
9. Marriage register, St George's, Hanover Square, 29 November 1805. In addition to it being the fashion for people of their rank to marry with more privacy by the more expensive mode of licence, this strategy was necessitated by her advancing pregnancy.
10. Cecil Price (ed.), *The Letters of Richard Brinsley Sheridan*, Vol. 2, p.249
11. *Old DNB* online, Caroline Sheridan née Callander; Fitzgerald, 1886, Vol. 2, p.333
12. *The Times*, 28 May 1806, p.2
13. *Morning Post*, 8 July 1807; 'The Proceedings Against Thomas Sheridan, Esq, for Criminal Conversation With The Wife of Peter Campbell, Jun, Esq, July 1807', 1807, pp.1–7; *Journals of the House of Lords*, 49, GEO III, 1809
14. Letters from Thomas Sheridan to Richard Peake, BL Eg 1976, f.7 and f.11; Kelly, 2005, p.292
15. Letter from Caroline Sheridan to George Callander, 30 March 1808, PRONI, D1071/B/E3/2
16. Ben Weinreb and Christopher Hibbert (eds), *The London Encyclopaedia*, 1983, pp.291–2, 445–6, Letter from Thomas Sheridan, June 1808, BL 3518, f.1179
17. O'Toole, 1997, pp.430–31
18. Baptism record, Jane Georgiana Sheridan, St Peter's Church, Petersham, 1815
19. Letter from Thomas Sheridan to Charles Ward, 13 February 1809, BL Eg 1976, f.26; Thomas Dormandy, *The White Death: A History of Tuberculosis*, 1999, p.41, pp.44–6
20. Price, 1966, Vol 3, pp.66-8
21. *The Times*, 20 July 1810, p.3
22. Jane Gray Perkins, *The Life of Mrs Norton*, 1909, p.2
23. Baptism record, Thomas Berkeley Sheridan, St Peter's Church, Petersham, 1815
24. Price, 1966, Vol. 3, pp. 147–51

25. Letter from Tom Sheridan to Richard Peake, 1812, BL Add. 35118, f.117
26. Ibid. and f.181
27. Price, 1966, pp.175–78; Letter from Richard Brinsley Sheridan to the Earl of Lonsdale, July 1814, Cumbria Record Office, LONS L/2/27
28. Dormandy, 1999, p.39
29. John McAleer, *Representing Africa: Landscape Exploration and Empire in Southern Africa, 1780–1870*, 2010, pp.39–41
30. Price, 1966, Vol. 3, p.217
31. *The Times*, 8 July 1816, p.3; 15 July 1816, p.3
32. Will of Thomas Sheridan, PROB 11/1678. Brief and simple though the document was, things were never easy or straightforward for Tom or his widow; the will would not be proved for another six years.
33. Letter from Charles Brinsley Sheridan to Thomas Le Fanu, 1817, King's College, Cambridge, Le Fanu 2/24
34. Madeline Masson, 'Birds of Passage', unpublished typescript, Chapter 9, p.9
35. *The Times*, 27 January 1818, p. 2; Dr J. McAleer, National Maritime Museum, Greenwich, London. There is no captain's log for the *Abeona*.
36. 'In memory of Thomas Sheridan the eldest son of the Right Honble. Richard Brinsley Sheridan by his first wife Elizabeth Brinsley who was buried in the cathedral of Wells . . . and was buried by the side of his mother.' Society of Genealogists, DO/M34
37. Moore, 1825, Vol. II, p.315; *The Times*, 1 July 1819, p.3
38. Sarah E. Parker, *Grace and Favour: A Handbook of Who Lived Where in Hampton Court Palace 1750–1950*, 2005, pp.11, 14; Lucy Worsley and David Souden, *Hampton Court Palace: The Official Illustrated History*, 2000, pp.98–9
39. Perkins, 1909, pp.4–5
40. Alice Acland, *Caroline Norton*, 1948, pp.21–2
41. Perkins, 1909, p.6
42. *The Times*, 5 November 1822, p.4. In May 1823 he attended a public meeting at the Crown and Anchor Tavern in London to raise money 'to assist the Greeks in their present efforts to establish their independence'. (*The Times*, 16 May 1823, p.3)
43. IOR/J/1/37/f.288. In the end George Canning did not take up his post as governor general of Bengal; in September 1822 he was appointed foreign secretary (*ODNB* online, George Canning).

44. Letter from Charles Sheridan to Georgiana Sheridan, 20 September 1823, D/RA/A/2B/5/1, Buckinghamshire Record Office; Letter from Caroline Sheridan to Randall Callander, 23 May 1823, PRONI, D1071/E3/10/1
45. Letter from Caroline Norton to Mrs Gore, 26 October 1836, Yale University, Beinecke Library, Gen. MSS 260, Box 2, folder 60
46. Perkins, 1909, pp.9–10; Acland, 1948, p.23
47. Letter from Helen Pricewood to Mrs Sheridan, September 1825, PRONI, D/1071/F/A3/1
48. Caroline Norton's songs and ballads, King's College Archives, Cambridge, LEF/1/4
49. *Morning Post*, 13 July 1826
50. Perkins, 1909, p.14
51. *ODNB* online, Fletcher Norton, first Baron Grantley; James Grant, *Old And New Edinburgh*, Vol 5, pp.127–28
52. Guidebook of Markenfield Hall, p.26
53. Scotland's People website, Norton family birth and baptism records
54. *ODNB* online, Ultra Tories

Chapter II

1. Simon Bradley and Nikolaus Pevsner, *The Buildings of England, London 6: Westminster*, 2003, pp.479–80, 534
2. Lucy Johnston, *Nineteenth-Century Fashion Detail*, 2005, p.50
3. Mark D. Heber, *Ancestral Trails: The Complete Guide to British Genealogy and Family History*, 2000, p.220
4. Marriage register, St George's, Hanover Square, 30 July 1827. Several years before his marriage to Caroline, George had 'adopted' a deaf and dumb girl, which had caused problems. There were questions about his intentions towards the girl and he had 'some difficulty removing other impressions about her when I married'. Letter from George Norton to Lord Melbourne, 26 July 1831, Hertfordshire Archives, D/ELb/F39/13
5. A cabriolet was a two-wheel carriage drawn by a single horse with two seats and a folding top. The word cab derives from cabriolet. *The Times*, 9 April 1836, p.2
6. *The Times*, 15 October 1937, p.17
7. *ODNB* online, James William Douglas Kinnaird
8. *ODNB* online, Charles William Vane (formerly Stewart)
9. Perkins, 1909, p.10

10. Charles Dickens, *The Pickwick Papers*, 1837, 1999 edition, pp.418–19

Chapter III

1. *The Times*, 11 May 1837, p.1
2. Perkins, 1909, pp.16–7; Caroline Elizabeth Sarah Norton, *English Laws for Women in the Nineteenth Century*, 1854, 2010 reprint, p.25
3. Clarke Olney, 'Caroline Norton to Lord Melbourne', *Victorian Studies*, Vol. 8, No. 3, March 1965, p.258
4. *The Times*, 15 August 1822, p.3; 9 October 1822, p.3
5. *The Edinburgh Annual Register for 1823*, 1824, pp.108–24. Lord Portsmouth lived at Hurstbourne Park until he died in 1853 aged eighty-six. There is a strange tale of Lord Byron meeting the earl at John Hanson's house in 1799 – they were both in effect wards of Hanson when he was eleven. The earl, a man in his thirties, pinched the sensitive boy's ears. Byron was so outraged he threw a shell at Portsmouth and smashed a mirror. 'I will teach the fool of an earl to pinch another noble's ear.' Fourteen years later he got his revenge. (Paul McNeil, 'Vampyre Lord', *Mensa Magazine*, August 2008, pp.8-10.) The Earl of Portsmouth's younger brother, who had gone to so much trouble to save his title and wrestle the family fortunes from the Hansons, had to wait a long time to become the fourth earl, inheriting it in 1853 but dying in 1854. (1851 Census return, Hurstbourne Priors, Hampshire.) Caroline Norton, *English Laws*, p.25
6. Caroline Norton's Songs and Ballads, King's College Archives, Cambridge, LEF/1/4
7. Caroline Norton, 1854, p.26
8. Perkins, 1909, pp.15–16
9. *ODNB* online, William George Spencer Cavendish, sixth Duke of Devonshire; Frances Anne 'Fanny' Kemble
10. *ODNB* online, Henry Richard Fox, third Baron Holland of Holland
11. *The Times*, 26 December 1828, p.3
12. *ODNB* online, William Lamb, Lord Melbourne
13. *ODNB* online, Lady Caroline Lamb
14. Leslie G. Mitchell, *Lord Melbourne, 1779–1848*, 1997, p.214
15. Ibid., p.217
16. Caroline Norton, *The Undying One, and Other Poems*, 1830; *The Times*, 20 May 1830, p.3

17. *The Times*, 8 February 1832, p.3

18. *ODNB* online, Princess Adelaide of Saxe-Meiningen, Queen of England

19. Letter from Caroline Norton to Richard Bentley, 1830, Yale University, Beinecke Library, Gen MSS 260, Box 2, folder 89

20. Letter from Caroline Norton to Richard Bentley, 1830, New York Public Library, Berg Collection, Maggs 7.32.62

21. Caroline Norton, 1830, pp.178–9

22. *The Times*, 2 February 1832, p.7

23. Edward Adolphus Seymour (ed.), *Letters, Remarks and Memoirs of Edward Adolphus Seymour, Twelfth Duke of Somerset*, 1893, p.23; *The Times*, 16 June 1830, p.5

24. *ODNB* online, Edward Adolphus St Maur (formerly Seymour), twelfth Duke of Somerset

25. Marriage register of St George's, Hanover Square, 1830

26. *ODNB* online, Sir James Robert George Graham; Marriage register of St Marylebone Church, 1819

27. *Letters, Remarks and Memoirs of Edward Adolphus*, 1893, pp.26–7; Frances Anne Kemble, *Record of a Girlhood*, Vol. II, 1878, p.139

28. *Letters, Remarks and Memoirs of Edward Adolphus*, 1893, p.23; Perkins, 1909, pp.29–30

29. Ibid., p.31

30. Kemble, 1878, p.136

31. *The Times*, 30 August 1830, p.7

32. Letter from Charles K. Sheridan to Lady Seymour, 1830, Buckinghamshire Studies Centre, D/RA/A/2B/5/4

33. The portraitist Henry William Pickersgill asked her to sit for him in the summer of 1830. She was keen to oblige but because of the uncertainty around the general election and then the loss of her husband's seat, she was unable to do so. (Letter from Caroline Norton to Bulwer Lytton, 7 July 1830, New York Public Library, Carl Pforzheimer Collection, Misc 1594.)

34. J.C. Sainty, *Office Holders in Modern Britain, Admiralty Officials 1660–1870*, Vol. 4, 1975, p.54

35. Letter from Charles Sheridan to Lady Seymour, 22 August 1831, Buckingham Studies Centre, D/RA/A/2B/5/2; Letter from Francis Sheridan to Lady Seymour, 15 July 1831, Buckingham Studies Centre, D/RA/A/2B/8/1/1; Letter from Caroline Norton to Captain Price Blackwood, 13 September 1831, PRONI, D1071/F/E1/9; *ODNB* online, Daniel Maclise. Daniel Maclise was born in Ireland of Scottish

parents. After leaving the army his father ran a tanning yard and shoemaking business where he would display his son's drawings. Daniel had a precocious talent and studied at Cork drawing academy. In 1827 he entered the Royal Academy School in London and soon established his reputation as a portrait draughtsman, producing lithographs of the celebrities of his day.

36. Kemble, 1878, p.284

37. *The Times*, 31 May 1831, p.3

38. Kemble, 1878, Vol. III, p.36

39. *The Newgate Calendar* was a popular book from 1750 to 1850. Subtitled *The Malefactors' Bloody Register*, its lurid tales of lives of loose morality ending in criminality and the gallows, where redemption was often granted, made it a compulsive read.

40. *The Times*, 1 June 1831, p.5

41. *The London Gazette,* 24 June 1831, p.7; Fitzgerald, 1886, p.360

42. Letter from George Norton to Lord Melbourne, 26 July 1831, Hertfordshire Archives, D/ELb/F39/13

43. Perkins, 1909, pp.39–40

44. James O. Hoge and Clarke Olney (eds), *The Letters of Caroline Norton to Lord Melbourne*, 1974, pp.28–30

45. Letters from Caroline Norton to Lord Melbourne, 1831, Hertfordshire Archives: 11 July, D/ELb F47/47; 1 August, D/ELb/ F47/8; 4 August, D/ELb/F47/43; 7 August, D/ELb/F47/10; 9 August, D/ELb/F47/44; 12 August, D/ELb/F47/12; 21 August, D/ELb/F47/15; 25 August, D/ELb/F47/17; 26 August, D/ELb/F47/18; Perkins, 1909, pp.41-2

46. Chris Cook and John Stevenson, *The Longman Handbook of Modern British History 1714–1980,* 1983, pp.56, 62, 96; Boyd Hilton, *A Mad, Bad and Dangerous People? England 1783–1846,* 2006, p.424

47. Edward Pearce, *Reform! The Fight for the 1832 Reform Act,* 2003, p.69

48. Leslie G. Mitchell, *The Whig World 1760–1837,* 2005, pp.136–40

49. *ODNB* online, Lord Melbourne; L.G Mitchell, 2005, pp.118–125; *The Cabinet Register for the Year* 1831, pp.28–30

50. Letter from Caroline Norton to Lady Seymour, 7 November 1831, PRONI, D1071/F/E/1/2; *The Times,* 29 November 1831, p.4; 7 January 1832, p.4; 10 January 1832, p.6; Old Bailey Online reference: t18320105-22

51. Letter from Caroline Norton to Augusta Cowell, 5 January 1832, Carl Pforzheimer Collection, Misc. Ms 3997

52. Perkins, 1909, p.42
53. Letter from Caroline Norton to Captain Price Blackwood, 13 November 1831, PRONI, D1071/F/E1/8
54. *The Times,* 4 January 1832, p.2
55. *The Times,* 12 March 1832, p.1
56. Sainty, 1975, Vol. 4
57. *ODNB* online, Constantine Henry Phipps, first Marquess of Normanby
58. Hilton, 2006, pp.422–25
59. *The Times,* 14 July 1832, p.6
60. Perkins, 1909, p.46
61. Letter from Caroline Norton to Lord Melbourne, undated September 1832, Berg Collection
62. Letter from Caroline Norton to Richard Brinsley Sheridan, 18 September 1832, BL Mss Add. 42767, ff.1–2; *ODNB* online, Henry Bingham Baring
63. Letter from Caroline Norton to Lord Melbourne, 21 September 1832, Berg Collection, Maggs 11.23.60
64. Letter from Caroline Norton to Lord Melbourne, 29 September 1832, Berg Collection, Maggs 11.23.60
65. Acland, 1948, pp.62–3
66. Perkins, 1909, p.49
67. Caroline Norton, 1854, p.26
68. Letter from Caroline Norton to Lady Seymour, January 1832, PRONI, D1071/F/E1/3
69. Sainty, 1975, p.54
70. Correspondence between George Norton and Sir James Graham, February 1833, BL MSS Add. 79270 f.125; f.127; f.129; f.133; f.135; f.139 and Add. 79722 ff.129–130
71. *The Times,* 27 March 1833, p.2
72. Letter from Frank Sheridan to Lady Seymour, 20 May 1833, Buckinghamshire Record Office, D/RA/A/2B/8/4; Letter from Frank Sheridan to his mother, 3 August 1833, Buckinghamshire Record Office, D/RA/A/2C/12/2. In 1834 slavery was abolished throughout the British empire, except in Ceylon, St Helena and the territories in the possession of the East India Company. Forty thousand slave owners were compensated a total of twenty million pounds for the loss of their property, forty per cent of the government's annual expenditure. The passing of the act did not mean that slavery ended immediately; it would last until the last tranche of 'apprentices' was released in 1840.

73. Perkins, 1909, pp.53–4
74. Letter from Caroline Norton to Lady Seymour, 18 October 1833, PRONI, D1071/F/E/1/2
75. Perkins, 1909, pp.56–57
76. Letter from Frank Sheridan to Sir James Graham, 20 December 1833, BL MSS Add. 79722, f.108
77. *The Times*, 18 December 1833, p.1
78. Letter from Caroline Norton to Lady Holland, 14 March 1834, Buckinghamshire Record Office, D/ELb/F47/9
79. *ODNB* online, Lord Melbourne
80. *ODNB* online, Earl of Mulgrave
81. Perkins, 1909, p.59
82. Letters from Caroline Norton to John Murray, 2 and 6 August 1834, National Library of Scotland, JMA Ms 42507 and Ms 41910, f.151
83. Letter from Caroline Norton to Francis Cowper, 22 August 1834, Berg Collection, Maggs 11.23.60
84. Perkins, 1909, p.63
85. *ODNB* online, William Francis Cowper-Temple Letter from Caroline Norton to William Francis Cowper, 2 November 1834, Berg Collection, Maggs 11.23.60; Mitchell, 1997, pp.218–19; Hoge and Olney, 1974, p.117
86. Perkins, 1909, pp.65–6
87. Letter from Caroline Norton to Augusta Cowell, 1835, Carl Pforzheimer Collection, Misc. Ms 4007. The son of John Cowell of Bedford Square, John Welsford Cowell was born in 1796 and educated at Eton and Trinity College, Cambridge. In 1821 he helped found the Political Economy Club with James Mill, father of John Stuart Mill, and served on the Poor Law Commission and factory commissions in the early 1830s. In 1834 he was agent at the Bank of England's Gloucester Branch, having first provided personal financial security of ten thousand pounds. In 1837 he was sent by the Bank of England to Philadelphia to collect debts owing to British firms and creditors.
88. *The Times*, 26 March 1835, p.5
89. *ODNB* online, Benjamin Robert Haydon
90. Paul O'Keeffe, *A Genius for Failure: The Life of Benjamin Robert Haydon*, 2009, pp.160, 217, 334
91. Willard Bissell Pope (ed.), *The Diary of Benjamin Robert Haydon*, Vol. 19, 1963, pp.47, 57, 97, 102, 105, 109

92. Ibid., pp.334–56
93. Letters from Caroline Norton to William Francis Cowper, 1835, Berg Collection, Maggs 11.23.60
94. Letter from Caroline Norton to Mary Shelley, Bodleian Library, Ms. Abinger c.49, ff.12–14; Perkins, 1909, pp.70–75; *The Times*, 2 June 1835, p.7; *The Times*, 26 September 1835, p.7
95. *The Times*, 3 August 1835, p.5; Caroline Norton, 1854, p.30
96. *ODNB* online, Sir Colquhoun Grant
97. Perkins, 1909, p.67
98. *The Times*, 1 June 1835, p.3
99. *Court Journal*, 5 June 1835, Vol. 7, p.357; *ODNB*, Lord William George Bentinck
100. Letter from George Norton to George Bentinck, 25 June 1835, BL Ms 42767, ff.44–6
101. Letter from Caroline Norton to William Cowper, 1835, Berg Collection, Maggs 11.23.60
102. Caroline Norton, 1854, pp.30–1
103. *The Times*, 19 September 1835, p.3; 24 December 1835, p.3
104. *ODNB* online, Edward John Trelawny
105. David Crane, *Lord Byron's Jackal: A Life of Edward John Trelawny*, 1998, pp.12–13, 34, 313
106. House of Lords Minutes of Evidence, Trelawny's Divorce Bill, 1819, House of Lords, 59 GEO III, 1819
107. Crane, 1998, pp.46–50
108. Perkins, 1909, p.84
109. Crane, 1998, pp.313–14
110. Ibid., p.313
111. Florence A. Marshall (ed.), *The Life and Letters of Mary Wollstonecraft Shelley*, 1889, pp.272–3
112. Letter from Caroline Norton to Mrs Sheridan, 16 October 1835, PRONI, D1071/F/E1/4
113. Letter from Caroline Norton to Lady Seymour, undated, 1835, PRONI, D1071/F/E1/3
114. Letter from Caroline Norton to Edward Trelawny, 20 October 1835, PRONI, D1071/F/E/2/7
115. *ODNB* online, Charles Kemble
116. *The Times*, 20 October 1835, pp.3, 4; 21 October 1835, p.6
117. *The Scotsman*, 18 November 1835, p.4
118. Letter from Caroline Norton to Edward Trelawny, 13 November 1835, PRONI, D1071/F/E/2/7

119. Marriage of Maria Campbell Norton to Edmund Phipps, third son of Henry Phipps, Earl of Mulgrave, 15 May 1838, Peerage.com

120. Letter from Caroline Norton to Edward Trelawny, 29 December 1835, PRONI, D1071/F/E/2/7

121. Letter from Frank Sheridan to Lady Seymour, 29 December 1835, Buckinghamshire Record Office, D/RA/A/2B/8/6

Chapter IV

1. Letter from Caroline Norton to Edward Trelawny, 4 January 1836, PRONI, D1071/F/E/2/7

2. *ODNB* online, Edward Ellice

3. Letter from Caroline Norton to Edward Ellice, 6 January 1836, NLS, Ms 15037, f.86

4. Letter from Caroline Norton to Edward Trelawny, 19 January 1836, PRONI, D1071/F/E/2/7

5. Letter from Caroline Norton to Edward Ellice, 23 March 1836, NLS, Ms 15037, f.91

6. Letter from George Norton to Edward Ellice, 23 March 1836, NLS, Ms 15037, ff.208–11

7. John Goodchild, *Attorney at Large*, 1986, pp.23–4

8. *ODNB* online, Charles Fitzgerald Leicester Stanhope

9. Letter from Caroline Norton to Edward Ellice, April 1836, NLS, Ms 15037, ff.105–108

10. Letter from Caroline Norton to Lord Melbourne, 2 April 1836, Hertfordshire Archives and Local Studies, D/ELb547/30

11. The Reverend John Barlow became secretary of the Zoological Society in 1838 and succeeded Michael Faraday, of whom he was a close friend, as secretary of the Lectures Committee at the Royal Institution. He lectured in the practical application of science and was interested in the management of the insane, publishing *On Man's Power Over Himself To Prevent or Control Insanity* in 1849. From 1854 to 1859 he was chaplain-in-ordinary at Kensington Palace. (Wikipedia and Royal Institution websites)

12. Letter from Caroline Norton to Lord Melbourne, 4 April 1836, Hertfordshire Archives and Local Studies, D/ELbF47/28

13. Letter from Lord Melbourne to Caroline Norton, 6 April 1836, cited in Perkins, 1909, pp.85–6

14. Letter from Caroline Norton to Edward Trelawny, 6 April 1836, PRONI, D1071/F/E/2/7

15. Letter from Caroline Norton to Augusta Cowell, 12 April 1836, Carl Pforzheimer Collection, Misc. Ms 3999

16. Letter from Lord Melbourne to Caroline Norton, 8 April 1836, cited in Perkins, 1909, p.85

17. Letter from Lord Melbourne to Caroline Norton, 10 April 1836, cited in Perkins, 1909, p.86

18. Letter from Caroline Norton to Lord Melbourne, late April 1836, Hertfordshire Archives and Local Studies, D/ELbF47/36

19. Letter from Caroline Norton to Lord Melbourne, April 1836, Hertfordshire Archives and Local Studies, D/ELbF47/55

20. Letter from Caroline Norton to Lord Melbourne, April 1836, Hertfordshire Archives and Local Studies, D/ELbF47/37

21. Letter from Lord Melbourne to Caroline Norton, 19 April 1836, cited in Perkins, 1909, p.86

22. Letter from Caroline Norton to Lord Melbourne, April 1836, Hertfordshire Archives and Local Studies, D/ELbF47/27

23. Letter from Caroline Norton to Edward Trelawny, 5 May 1836, PRONI, D1071/F/E/2/7

24. Letter from Caroline Norton to Lord Melbourne, 6 May 1836, Hertfordshire Archives and Local Studies, D/ELb/F50

25. Philip Whitwell Wilson (ed.), *The Greville Diary Including Passages Hitherto Withheld From Publication*, Vol. 1, 1927, p.474

26. *ODNB* online, Emily Mary Temple, née Lamb, Viscountess Palmerston

27. Letter from Caroline Norton to Edward Ellice, 11 May 1836, NLS, Ms 15037, f.171

28. Edward H. Buxton Forman (ed.), *The Letters of Edward John Trelawny*, 1910, p.199

29. *ODNB* online, Barnard Gregory

30. *The Satirist*, 22 May 1836, p.162

31. *ODNB* online, William Cavendish, seventh Duke of Devonshire; *ODNB* Thomas Slingsby Duncombe

32. *The Satirist*, 29 May 1836, p.172

33. Letter from Caroline Norton to Augusta Cowell, June 1836, Carl Pforzheimer Collection, Misc. Ms 3992

34. Letter from Lord Melbourne to Caroline Norton, 9 June 1836, cited in Perkins, 1909, p.93

35. *The Satirist*, 12 June 1836, p.186

36. Letter from Caroline Norton to Augusta Cowell, 19 June 1836, Carl Pforzheimer Collection, Misc. Ms 3993

37. Letter from Caroline Norton to Lord Melbourne, 20 June 1836, Hertfordshire Archives and Local Studies, D/ELb/F47/62

38. Letter from Caroline Norton to Lord Melbourne, 20 June 1836, Hertfordshire Archives and Local Studies, D/ELb/F47/45

39. Since the Reformation the Church of Scotland had accepted divorce on the grounds of adultery, and later added the grounds of desertion for more than four years. From 1830 Scottish divorces were handled by the Court of Sessions, like other cases in civil law in Edinburgh. Both men and women could seek divorce for adultery or desertion, which was different from English law, under which men could divorce their wives for adultery but women did not have the same right until 1923 unless other serious offences were involved. Scottish divorces were cheaper than English ones and not confined to the upper classes. Very poor people could claim financial help from the Poor Law authorities if they had a good cause against their spouse. (University of Glasgow Scottish Way of Birth and Death: Divorce website)

40. Letter from Caroline Norton to Lord Melbourne, 21 June 1836, Hertfordshire Archives and Local Studies, D/ELb/F47/46

41. Letter from Caroline Norton to Lord Melbourne, 21 June 1836, Hertfordshire Archives and Local Studies, D/ELb/F47/26

42. Letter from Caroline Norton to Edward Trelawny, 21 June 1836, PRONI, D1071/F/E/2/7

43. Letter from Caroline Norton to Augusta Cowell, 21 June 1836, Carl Pforzheimer Collection, Misc. Ms 4004

44. Letter from Caroline Norton to Richard Brinsley Sheridan, 22 June 1836, BL, Mss Add. 42767, f.5

45. Fitzgerald, Vol. 2, 1886, pp.417–18

46. Madeline House and Graham Storey (eds), *The Letters of Charles Dickens*, 1965–2002, Vol. 1, 1965, p.153. Recently married, on 2 April 1836, over twenty years later Dickens fell out of love with his wife Catherine, mother of his nine children, and in love with Ellen Ternan, an actress whom he met in 1857 and employed in his amateur theatre company. But for a man of his starry reputation and champion of many good causes, making use of the brand new 1857 Matrimonial Causes (Divorce) Act was not an option. (*ODNB* online, John Macrone; *ODNB* online, Ellen Ternan)

47. Letter from Caroline Norton to Augusta Cowell, 24 June 1836, Carl Pforzheimer Collection, Misc. Ms 3994

48. Fitzgerald, 1886, Vol. 2, pp.421–22

49. Letter from Lord Seymour to Richard Brinsley Sheridan, 23 June 1836, BL, Ms Add. 42767, ff.13–14; Mitchell, 1997, pp.224–5

50. *The Times*, 25 June 1836, p.4

51. *The Satirist*, 26 June 1836, p.206

52. Letter from Caroline Norton to George Norton, 26 June 1836, cited in Caroline Norton, *Letters Etc. Dated from June 1836 to July 1841*, privately printed, pp.7–9

53. Letter from Caroline Norton to Richard Brinsley Sheridan, 28 June 1836, BL, Ms Add. 42767, ff.26–7

54. *The Times*, 28 June 1836, p.7

55. Letter from Lord Seymour to Richard Brinsley Sheridan, 28 June 1836, BL, Ms Add. 42767, ff.22–3

56. *The Times*, 29 June 1836, p.2; *ODNB* online, Edmund Thomas Parris; *The Times*, 5 July 1836, p.4

57. Letter from Caroline Norton to Lord Melbourne, 1 July 1836, Hertfordshire Archives and Local Studies, D/ELb/F47/50

58. Letter from Caroline Norton to Augusta Cowell, 7 July 1836, Carl Pforzheimer Collection, Misc. Ms 3998

59. Dormandy, 1999, p.37; Bronchiectasis: Wikipedia website

60. Letter from Caroline Norton to Lord Melbourne, 8 July 1836, Hertfordshire Archives and Local Studies, D/ELb/F47/49

61. *The Times*, 11 July 1836, p.6

62. Letter from Caroline Norton to Lord Melbourne, 13 July 1836, Hertfordshire Archives and Local Studies, D/ELb/F47/31

63. Letter from George Norton to Caroline Norton, 15 July 1836, cited in *Letters Etc.*, p.9

64. Ibid. 20 July 1836, p.11

65. Letter from Caroline Norton to Augusta Cowell, 21 July 1836, Carl Pforzheimer Collection, Misc. Ms 3990

66. Letter from Caroline Norton to Charles Jennings, 25 July, BL, Ms Add. 42767, ff.36–7; letter from Charles Jennings to Richard Brinsley Sheridan, July 1836, BL, Ms Add. 42767, f.38; letter from Caroline Norton to Richard Brinsley Sheridan, 25 July 1836, BL, Ms Add. 42676, ff.40–1

67. Letter from Caroline Norton to Lord Melbourne, late July 1836, Hertfordshire Archives and Local Studies, D/ELb/F47/35

68. Perkins, 1909, p.105

69. Letter from Caroline Norton to Lord Melbourne, late July 1836, Hertfordshire Archives and Local Studies, D/ELb/F47/24 and 25

70. Perkins, 1909, pp.106–7
71. O'Keeffe, 2009, p.368
72. Letter from Caroline Norton to Edward Ellice, 5 September 1836, NLS, Ms 15037, ff.95–7
73. Letter from Caroline Norton to Augusta Cowell, 22 August 1836, Carl Pforzheimer Collection, Misc. Ms 3986; Perkins, 1909, p.100
74. *The Times*, 12 August 1836, p.1; letters from Caroline Norton to Mary Shelley, 17 August 1836, Bodleian Library, Ms Abinger C51 ff.58–9 and f.59, old shelf mark Dep c538
75. Perkins, 1909, p.101
76. Letter from Caroline Norton to Lady Seymour, September 1836, PRONI, D1071/E/1/2
77. Letter from Caroline Norton to Edward Trelawny, 21 September 1836, PRONI, D1071/F/E/2/7
78. Forman (ed.), 1910, pp.201–2
79. Norton, *Letters Etc.*, 27 September 1836, p.12; *ODNB* online, Dr Stephen Lushington
80. Fitzgerald, 1886, Vol. 2, pp. 426–8
81. Letter from Caroline Norton to Thomas Le Fanu, 13 October 1836, NLI
82. Norton, *Letters Etc.*, pp.13–15
83. Letter from Caroline Norton to Mrs Gore, 26 October 1836, Yale University, Beinecke Library, Gen. Mss 260, Box 2, folder 60
84. Letter from Caroline Norton to Edward Ellice, 3 November 1836, NLS, Ms 15037 ff.97–9
85. Perkins, 1909, p.99
86. Norton, *Letters Etc.*, pp.16–17
87. Letter from Caroline Norton to Augusta Cowell, 22 November 1836, Carl Pforzheimer Collection, Misc. Ms 4003
88. Letter from Caroline Norton to Mary Shelley, 5 December 1836, Bodleian Library, Abinger Papers, C.49, ff.54–55, original shelf mark, Dep c538
89. Letter from George Norton to Edward Ellice, 4 December 1836, NLS, Ms 15037, ff.210–11
90. Caroline Elizabeth Sarah Norton, *A Cry From the Factories*, 1836; *ODNB* online, Anthony Ashley-Cooper, seventh Earl of Shaftesbury
91. Letter from Caroline Norton to Mary Shelley, 5 December 1836, Bodleian Library, Abinger Papers, C.49, ff.54–5, original shelf mark Dep c538

92. Letter from Caroline Norton to Edward Ellice, 6 December 1836, NLS, Ms 15037, ff.99; PRONI, D1071/F/E/2/2
93. Letter from Caroline Norton to Edward Trelawny, 25 December 1836, PRONI, D1071/F/E/2/2

Chapter V

1. Letter from Caroline Norton to Augusta Cowell, February 1837, Carl Pforzheimer Collection, Misc. Ms 4100
2. Letter from Caroline Norton to Edward Ellice, 1 January 1837, NLS, Ms 15037, ff.101–4
3. *Freeman's Journal*, 4 January 1837; letter from Frank Sheridan to Lady Seymour, 19 February 1837, Buckinghamshire Studies, D/RA/A/2B/8/8/1–3
4. *The Times*, 2 February 1837, p.3; Perkins, 1909, p.138; *ODNB* online, Alexander Hayward
5. Letters from Caroline Norton to Mary Shelley, 5 January and 14 February 1837, Bodleian Library, Abinger Ms c.49, f.100 and ff.105–6, original shelf Dep c538
6 Letter from Richard Brinsley Sheridan, 8 January 1837, BL, Ms 42767, ff.51–2
7. Perkins, 1909, p.136
8. Letter from Caroline Norton to Lord Melbourne, 6 March 1837, Hertfordshire Archives and Local Studies, D/ELb/F47/56
9. Norton, *Letters Etc.*, pp.18–19
10. Ibid., pp.21–2
11. Ibid., p.21
12. Ibid., pp.22–3
13. Letter from Caroline Norton to Lord Melbourne, 17 March 1837, Hertfordshire Archives and Local Studies, D/ELb/F47/40; Hoge and Olney, 1974, p.117
14. Letter from Caroline Norton to Lord Melbourne, 19 March 1837, Hertfordshire Archives and Local Studies, D/ELb/F47/42
15. Declaration made by Richard Brinsley Sheridan, April 1837, BL, Ms. 42767, f.55
16. Letter from Caroline Norton to Lord Melbourne, late April 1837, Hertfordshire Archives and Local Studies, D/ELb/F47/32
17. Letter from Caroline Norton to Lord Melbourne, late April 1837, Hertfordshire Archives and Local Studies, D/ELb/F47/48

18. Letter from Caroline Norton to Lord Melbourne, late April 1837, Hertfordshire Archives and Local Studies, D/ELb/F47/52

19. Letter from Caroline Norton to George Norton, 19 May 1837, Norton, *Letters Etc.*, pp.26–7

20. Letter from George Norton to Caroline Norton, 20 May 1837, ibid., p.28

21. Letters from George Norton to Caroline Norton, 23 and 27 May 1837, ibid., p.29

22. Letter from George Norton to Caroline Norton, 29 May 1837, ibid., pp.30–1

23. Letter from Caroline Norton to George Norton, 29 May 1837, ibid., p.32

24. Letter from George Norton to Caroline Norton, 30 May 1837, ibid., pp.32–3

25. Letter from Caroline Norton to George Norton, 30 May 1837, ibid., pp.33–6

26. Letter from George Norton to Caroline Norton, 30 May 1837, ibid., pp.36–7

27. Letter from George Norton to Caroline Norton, 1 June 1837, ibid., pp.37–9

28. Letter from Caroline Norton to Lord Melbourne, 3 June 1837, Hertfordshire Archives and Local Studies, D/ELb/F47/34

29. Letter from Caroline Norton to George Norton, 3 June 1837, Norton, *Letters Etc.*, pp.39–41

30. Letter from George Norton to Caroline Norton, 4 June 1837, ibid., pp.41–2

31. Letter from George Norton to Caroline Norton, 7 June 1837, ibid., pp.42–3

32. Letter from Caroline Norton to George Norton, 7 June 1837, ibid., pp.43–4

33. Letter from George Norton to Caroline Norton, 7 June 1837, ibid., pp.45–6

34. Letter from Caroline Norton to George Norton, 7 June 1837, ibid., pp.47–8

35. Letter from Caroline Norton to Lord Melbourne, 7 June 1837, Hertfordshire Archives and Local Studies, D/ELb/F47/53

36. Letter from George Norton to Caroline Norton, 8 June 1837, Norton, *Letters Etc.*, pp.48–9

37. Letter from Caroline Norton to George Norton, 9 June 1837, ibid., pp.50–1

38. Letter from George Norton to Caroline Norton, 12 June 1837, ibid., pp.52–3
39. Letter from George Norton to Caroline Norton, 12 June 1837, ibid., pp.53–4
40. Letter from George Norton to Caroline Norton, 14 June 1837, ibid., pp.54–5
41. Letter from Caroline Norton to George Norton, 14 June 1837, ibid., pp.55–7
42. Letter from Caroline Norton to Lord Melbourne, 15 June 1837, Hertfordshire Archives and Local Studies, D/ELb/F47/33
43. *ODNB* online, Sir Benjamin Collins Brodie
44. Letter from Caroline Norton to George Norton, 16 June 1837, Norton, *Letters Etc.*, pp.58–9
45. Letter from Caroline Norton to George Norton, 16 June 1837, ibid., pp.61–2
46. Letter from George Norton to Caroline Norton, 18 June 1837, ibid., p.63
47. *ODNB* online, Queen Victoria
48. Perkins, 1909, p.139
49. Letter from Caroline Norton to 'Miss A', probably Augusta Cowell, August 1837, Norton, *Letters Etc.*, pp.63–4; letter to Edward Ellice, 28 August 1837, NLS, Ms 15037, ff.167–9
50. Letters from Charles Jennings to Caroline Norton, 15 and 17 July 1837, BL, Add. 42767, ff.58–9 and ff.60–1
51. House and Storey, 1965–2002, Vol. 1, p.303; Charles Dickens, *The Posthumous Papers of the Pickwick Club*, 1907, pp.464–88. In her biography of Charles Dickens, Claire Tomalin wonders if Charles Dickens's father, John, said to be the posthumous child of a servant William Dickens, and his wife Elizabeth, might in fact have been the illegitimate son of either his mother's employer John Crewe, a Cheshire landowner, or Richard Brinsley Sheridan, who often visited John Crewe at Crewe Hall and in Mayfair. Sherry was well known for his eye for the female sex. John Dickens was a curious fellow: well read, the owner of many expensive books, favoured with lordly patronage and profligate with his own and other people's money, more of a toff in his behaviour than might be expected of the son of servants. If Sheridan was John Dickens' biological father this would have made John a half-brother of Caroline's uncle Charles, with whom she lived, and uncle to her, and Caroline and Charles Dickens would have been cousins. There is no suggestion that they

knew anything of this possible connection. (Claire Tomalin, *Charles Dickens: A Life,* 2011, pp.5–6)

52. Letter from Caroline Norton to Edward Ellice, 28 August 1837, NLS, Ms 15037, ff.167–9
53. Norton, *Letters Etc.*, p.64
54. Letter from Caroline Norton to Mary Shelley, 31 August 1837, Bodleian Library, Abinger Ms Collection, C49, f.71, original shelf mark Dep c538
55. *The Times*, 5 September 1837, p.1; 12 September, p.7
56. Letter from Richard Brinsely Sheridan to Charles Jennings, 9 September 1837, BL, Add. 42767, ff.71–2
57. Letter from Caroline Norton to Brinsley Sheridan, 5 September 1837, BL, Add. 42767, ff.66–7
58. *Pigot and Co's National Commercial Directory*, London, 1835, pp.794–5
59. Letter from Caroline Norton to Richard Brinsley Sheridan, BL, Add. 42767, ff.68–70
60. Letter from Caroline Norton to Miss Le Fanu, 1 October 1837, King's College Archives, Cambridge, LEF/2/17
61. Letter from Caroline Norton to Edward Ellice, 1 October 1837, NLS, Ms 15037, ff.114–16; letter from Caroline Norton to Mrs Caroline Henrietta Sheridan, 17 October 1837, PRONI, D1071/F/E1/4
62. Letter from Caroline Norton to Brinsley Sheridan, 26 October 1837, BL, Add. 42767, ff.79–80
63. Letter from Caroline Norton to Helen Dufferin, 7 November 1837, PRONI, D1071/F/E/1/1; Letter from Caroline Norton to Miss Le Fanu, 8 October 1837, King's College Archives, Cambridge, LEF/2/17
64. *The Times,* 28 December 1871, p.7
65. Letter from George Norton to John Bayley, 23 November 1837, Norton, *Letters Etc.*, pp.3–4
66. Perkins, 1909, pp.119–22
67. Letters between George Norton and John Bayley, 30 November 1837, Norton, *Letters Etc.*, p.9
68. Letter from Caroline Norton to John Bayley, 30 November 1837, ibid., p.10
69. Letter from Caroline Norton to Brinsley Sheridan, 1 December 1837, BL, Add. 42767, ff.87–8
70. Letter from John Bayley to Caroline Norton, 1 December 1837, BL, Add. 42767, ff.89–90

71. Letter from John Bayley to George Norton, 2 December 1837, Norton, *Letters Etc.*, pp.12–14
72. Letter from Caroline Norton to Mary Shelley, 2 December 1837, Bodleian Library, Abinger Ms C49, ff.4–5, original shelf mark Dep c538
73. Letters from John Bayley to George Norton, 2 December 1837, Norton, *Letters Etc.*, pp.14–15
74. Letter from Caroline Norton to 'A', undated, ibid., p.15
75. Letter from George Norton to Mrs Bayley, 5 December 1837, ibid., pp.17–18
76. Letter from George Norton to John Bayley, 11 December 1837, ibid., pp.25–7
77. Letter from John Bayley to Caroline Norton, 30 December 1837, ibid., pp.46–8
78. Letter from John Bayley to Caroline Norton, 30 December 1837, ibid., pp.46–8
79. Letter from Caroline Norton to John Bayley, 31 December 1837, ibid., pp.48–50
80. Perkins, 1909, pp.119–22

Chapter VI

1. Letter from Brinsley Sheridan to Lord Seymour, 22 December 1837, BL, Add. 42767, f.140
2. Letters from Frank Sheridan to Brinsley Sheridan: 31 December 1837, Buckinghamshire Archives, D/RA/A/2B/8/10; 3 February 1838, BL, Add. 42767, ff.161–2
3. Letters from Charles Jennings to Brinsley Sheridan: 16 January 1838, BL, Add. 42767, ff.151–2; 5 February 1838, ff.163–4
4. Letter from Georgy Seymour to Brinsley Sheridan, January 1838, BL, Add. 42767, ff.143–4
5. Letters from Caroline Norton to Brinsley Sheridan, 16 and 18 January 1838, BL, Add. 42767, ff.126–7; f.128
6. Letter from Caroline Norton to Mrs Le Fanu, 5 March 1838, King's College Archives, Cambridge, LEF 2/17
7. Letter from Caroline Norton to William Cowper, March 1838, Berg Collection, Maggs 11.23.40
8. Anon., *The Separation of Mother and Child By The Law of 'Custody of Infants' Considered*, Roake and Varty, London, 1838, pp.1–9

9. Letter from Caroline Norton to William Cowper, March 1838, Berg Collection, Maggs 11.23.60

10. Letter from Caroline Norton to William Cowper, March 1838, ibid., Maggs 11.23.60

11. Letters from Caroline Norton to William Cowper, March 1838, ibid.

12. *ODNB*, Edward George Earle Lytton Bulwer-Lytton; *ODNB*, Rosina Anne Doyle Bulwer-Lytton. Except for four months in 1858 Rosina was not allowed to see her son Edward Robert from 1838 until she died in 1882. Also denied access to her daughter Emily, she needed a special dispensation from her husband in 1848 to be allowed to visit her daughter before she died of typhoid.

13. Letter from Caroline Norton to Brinsley Sheridan, 12 April 1838, BL, Add. 42767, ff.96–7

14. *The Times*, 23 May 1838, p.1

15. Perkins, 1909, pp.145–6

16. *The Times*, 22 June 1838, p.7

17. Letter from Caroline Norton to Lord Brougham, 21 June 1838, University College London Library Special Collections, Brougham Papers, 9093

18. *ODNB*, Henry Peter Brougham

19. Letters from Caroline Norton to Lord Brougham, 1838, University College London Library Special Collections, Brougham Papers, 9094

20. House of Lords Debates, 30 July 1838, Vol. 44 cc772–291

21. *ODNB*, William Draper Best, first Baron Wynford

22. Letter from Caroline Norton to Lord Brougham, August 1838, University College London Library Special Collections, Brougham Papers, 9095

23. Letter from Caroline Norton to George Norton, 4 August 1838, Bodleian Library, Ms Eng Lett c.4 ff.40

24. *Pigot's Directory for Hampshire*, London, 1828 and 1844

25. Letter from Caroline Norton to Lady Seymour, 25 August 1838, PRONI, D1071/ F/E/1/2

26. *The Times*, 29 August 1838, p.5; Perkins, 1909, p.149

27. Letter from Caroline Norton to Lady Seymour, 31 September 1838, PRONI, D1071/F/E/1/2; *ODNB*, Madame Vestris

28. Letter from Caroline Norton to Mrs Caroline Sheridan, 8 October 1838, PRONI, D1071/F/E1/4

29. Letter from Caroline Norton to Lady Seymour, 13 October 1838, PRONI, D1071/F/E/1/2

30. *Crim Con Gazette,* 10 November 1838, p.1. In 1838 and 1839, the years the *Crim Con Gazette* was in print, it was involved in numerous libel actions. In April 1840 its publisher James William Hucklebridge was found guilty of libel at the Old Bailey, in a charge brought by the Society for the Suppression of Vice, and also of publishing an obscene publication.
31. Pearce Stevenson, *A Plain Letter to the Lord Chancellor on the Infant Custody Bill,* James Ridgway, London, 1839; *ODNB,* Charles Christopher Pepys, first Earl of Cottenham
32. *The Times,* 23 January 1839, p.5
33. Letter from Caroline Norton to John Murray, January 1839, NLS, JMA, Ms 42507
34. *ODNB,* John Mitchell Kemble
35. Letter from Caroline Norton to Lord Conyngham, January 1839, Yale University, Beinecke Library, Gen. MSS 260, Box 1, folder 3; *ODNB,* Albert Denison, formerly Conyngham, first Baron Londesborough. Messalina was the infamously promiscuous wife of the Roman Emperor Claudius.
36. Letter from Caroline Norton to William Cowper, January 1839, Berg Collection, Maggs 11.23.60
37. Letter from Caroline Norton to Lord Melbourne, 6 February 1839, Hertfordshire Archives and Local Studies, D/ELb/F47/1
38. Letter from Caroline Norton to Lord Melbourne, February 1839, ibid., D/ELb/F47/63
39. Letter from Caroline Norton to Lord Melbourne, 25 February 1839, ibid., D/ELb/F47/66
40. Letter from Caroline Norton to William Cowper, 10 March 1839, Berg Collection, Maggs 11.23.60
41. Letter from Caroline Norton to Lord Melbourne, 15 March 1839, Hertfordshire Archives and Local Studies, D/ELb/F47/60
42. *ODNB,* John Hardwick
43. Lady Kirkwall was born Anna Maria de Blaquiere. She married John Fitzmaurice, Viscount Kirkwall, in 1802 and had two sons. Theirs was a difficult divorce, and she was made a ward of the Commission of Lunacy until she died in 1843; he predeceased her in 1820.
44. Letters from Caroline Norton to Nathaniel Ogle, March 1839, Yale University, Beinecke Library, Gen. MSS 260, Box 1, folder 18
45. Public Acts, Act to Amend the Law Relating to the Custody of Infants, 1839, Acts 2 & 3, Victoria, Chapter 54, pp.581–2; Mary

Lyndon Shanley, *Feminism, Marriage and the Law in Victorian England*, Princeton University Press, New Jersey, 1989, pp.136–7

46. Letter from Nathaniel Ogle to Caroline Norton, 29 July 1839, Norton, *Letters Etc.*, pp.53–5

47. Letter from Caroline Norton to Lady Seymour, October 1839, PRONI, D1071/F/E/1/2

48. Letter from Caroline Norton to Helen Dufferin, 14 November 1839, PRONI, D1071/F/E/1/1

49. *Medical Examiner*, 1839, London, Vol. 2, p.64

50. Letter from Caroline Norton to Lord Melbourne, 19 December 1839, Hertfordshire Archives and Local Studies, D/ELb/F47/69

51. *The Times*, 24 December 1839, p.7; Custody of Infants Bill, *Hansard*, 18 July 1839, Vol. 49, cc.485–94; *ODNB*, Lord Denman

52. *The Times*, 10 April 1839, p.4

Chapter VII

1. Letter from Charles Brinsley Sheridan to Thomas Le Fanu, 26 March 1840, King's College Archives, Cambridge, Le Fanu, 2/34

2. Letter from Charles Brinsley Sheridan to Thomas Le Fanu, 10 February 1840, ibid., Le Fanu 2/34; *ODNB* online, Sir Benjamin Collins Brodie

3. Letter from Caroline Norton to William Cowper, 1839, Berg Collection, Maggs 11.28.60

4. Letter from Caroline Norton to Augusta Cowell, February 1840, Carl Pforzheimer Collection, Misc. Ms 4015

5. Letter from Caroline Norton to William Cowper, 23 February 1840, Berg Collection, Maggs 11.28.60

6. Letter from George Norton to Caroline Norton, 19 March 1840, Norton, *Letters Etc.*, pp.4–5

7. Letter from Caroline Norton to George Norton, 21 March 1840, ibid., pp.6–7

8. Letters between Caroline Norton and George Norton, March 1840, ibid., pp. 8–13

9. Letters between Caroline Norton and George Norton, April 1840, ibid., pp.13–18

10. Letter from Caroline Norton to John Murray, 15 April 1840, NLS, JMA, Ms 42507

11. Letters between Caroline Norton and George Norton, April 1840, Norton, *Letters Etc.*, pp.19–22

12. House and Storey, 1965–2002, Vol. 2, p.73; *ODNB* online, William Charles Macready; *ODNB* online, Samuel Rogers

13. Perkins, 1909, p.178

14. Letter from Caroline Norton to Mary Shelley, May 1840, Bodleian Library, Ms Abinger, c.51, ff.65–6, old shelf number Dep c538

15. Letters between Caroline Norton and George Norton, May 1840, Norton, *Letters Etc.*, pp.22–9

16. *ODNB* online, Caroline Norton

17. *The Times,* 17 July 1840, p.8. Miss Letitia Elizabeth Landon, 1802–38, whose admirers included Daniel Maclise and Edward Bulwer-Lytton, had a vivid personal life and a successful career as a poet and writer before she killed herself, aged thirty-six, with prussic acid a few months into an unhappy marriage with George Maclean, governor of the British post at Cape Coast, west Africa. (*ODNB* online, Letitia Elizabeth Landon.) Mrs Felicia Dorothea Hemans (1793–1835) was a best-selling author and poet who separated from her husband. Her workaholism enabled her to support her five sons while her husband exiled himself in Rome. She died in Dublin aged forty-two of consumption apparently triggered by scarlet fever. (*ODNB* online, Felicia Dorothea Hemans.)

18. *ODNB* online, Edwin Henry Landseer

19. Caroline Norton, *The Dream*, 1840, p.71; Randall Craig, *The Narratives of Caroline Norton*, New York, 2009, pp.182–3

20. Letters between Caroline Norton and George Norton, August 1840, Norton, *Letters Etc.*, pp.29–31

21. *Pigot's Directory for Hampshire*, 1844; letters between Caroline Norton and George Norton, October and November 1840, *Letters Etc.*, pp.34–7

22. Letter from Caroline Norton to Edward Ellice, November 1840, PRONI, D1071/F/E/2/1–12

23. Letter from Caroline Norton to Mrs Gore, 2 December 1840, Yale University, Beinecke Library, Gen. MSS 260, Box 2, folder 60

24. *The Times*, 24 December 1840, p.7; 25 December, p.3; 28 December, p.6

25. Ibid., 19 January 1828, p.3

26. Letter from Caroline Norton to William Cowper-Temple, 2 January 1841, Berg Collection; *The Times*, 1 September 1819, p.3; 31 July 1823, p.3; 29 August 1823, p.3; 30 August 1824, p.3; 25 September 1824, p.3. Mary Ann Pearce, aka 'Lady' Barrymore, died in a 'miserable attic' in October 1832 after a fearful gin binge-drinking session.

The Times reported that much of the fifteen years she lived in London had been spent in prison. Caroline Norton thought Edmund and Mary Ann Pearce were brother and sister, but *The Times* suggested they were husband and wife. Apparently she had been a mistress of the eighth Earl Barrymore, who abandoned her, got one of his servants by the name of Pearce to marry her, and paid them off. But they bickered a great deal, which led her to 'adopt the miserable course of life the irregularities of which obtained for so much notoriety'. (*The Times*, 10 October 1832, p.3.) Edmund Pearce died in London in 1848.

27. Letter from Caroline Norton to Mary Shelley, 9 January 1841, Bodleian Library, Ms Abinger C.50, ff.9–10, original shelf mark Dep c538

28. Letter to Caroline Norton from unnamed lawyer, 20 January 1841, Norton, *Letters Etc.*, pp.37–8

29. Letter from Caroline Norton to Augusta Cowell, 1841, ibid., pp.39–41

30. Letter from Caroline Norton to Mrs Gore, 1841, Yale University, Beinecke Library, Gen. MSS 260, Box 2, folder 60

31. *ODNB* online, Reverend John Buckland; *ODNB* online, Thomas Arnold

32. Letter from Caroline Norton to Helen Dufferin, 6 October 1840, PRONI, D1071/F/E/1/1; census return for 1841, Laleham, Surrey

33. Letter from George Norton to Caroline's lawyers, 21 June 1841, Norton, *Letters Etc.*, p.41

34. Letter from Caroline Norton to Augusta Cowell, summer 1841, ibid., pp.41–3

35. Census return for 1841, 24 Bolton Street, London

36. *The Times*, 26 July 1841, p.6

37. *ODNB* online, Lord Melbourne; Mitchell, 1997, pp.240–6; *ODNB* online, Sir Robert Peel

38. Letter from Caroline Norton to William Cowper, undated 1841, Berg Collection

39. *The Times*, 19 August 1841, p.6; 20 August 1841, p.6

40. Ibid., 21 August 1841, p.3

41. Ibid., 7 September 1841, p.5; 10 September 1841, p.4

42. Ibid., 11 December 1841, p.5

43. House and Storey, 1965–2002, Vol. 3, pp.32–3; pp. 297–8

44. Letter from Charles Brinsley Sheridan to Thomas Le Fanu, 17 September 1842, King's College Archives, Cambridge, Le Fanu, 2/24;

letter from Caroline Norton to Samuel Rogers, September 1842, University College London Library Special Collections, The Sharpe Papers; letter from Fletcher Norton to Augusta Cowell, 15 September 1842, Carl Pforzheimer Collection, Misc. Ms 4016; letter from Caroline Norton to Caroline H. Sheridan, 19 September 1842, BL, 42767, ff.104-7; death certificate of William Charles Chapple Norton

45. Letter from Caroline Norton to Samuel Rogers, 8 October 1842, University College London Library Special Collections, The Sharpe Papers

46. *The Times*, 21 October 1842, p.3; 26 October, p.6; Old Bailey, 24 October 1842, t18421024–2840; PCOM2/208 Newgate Prison Calendars; Hulk Registers, HO 9/15; HO 11/13, p.253

Chapter VIII

1. House and Storey and Tillotson, 1965–2002, Vol. 3, pp.437–8; Tomalin, 2011, p.151
2. *ODNB* online, Daniel Gurney
3. Letter from Caroline Norton to William Cowper, July (?) 1843, Berg Collection, Maggs 11.23.60
4. Death certificate of Harriet Alicia Cowper; John Butter, *Remarks on Irritative Fever, commonly called 'The Plymouth Dock-Yard Disease: with Mr Dryden's Detailed Account of the Fatal Cases*, 1825
5. Letter from Caroline Norton to Nathaniel Ogle, November 1843, Yale University, Beinecke Library, Gen. MSS 260, Box 1, folder 18
6. Statement concerning the death of Charles Brinsley Sheridan, University of Nottingham Manuscripts and Special Collections, Nec. 13,068
7. Charles Brinsley Sheridan was buried in Old Windsor Churchyard. Last Will and Testament of Charles Brinsley Sheridan, 12 January 1844, PROB 11/1992
8. Letter from Caroline Norton to Thomas Le Fanu, 30 November 1843, NLI
9. *ODNB* online, Peter Mere Latham
10. Letter from Caroline Norton to Augusta Cowell, 18 February 1844, Carl Pforzheimer Collection, Misc. Ms 3995
11. Edward Coleridge, 'The Autobiography of the Reverend Edward Coleridge', transcribed by Richard J. Smith, 1992, BL, Add. Mss, 47555

12. Letter from Caroline Norton to Edward Coleridge, August 1844, Yale University, Beinecke Library, Gen. Mss 260, Box 1, folder 29

13. Letter from Caroline Norton to Thomas Le Fanu, 30 August 1844, King's College Archives, Cambridge, LEF/2/17

14. Letter from Caroline Norton to William Le Fanu, 26 September 1844, NLI

15. *ODNB* online, Sidney Herbert

16. Mitchell, 1997, p.229

17. George William Erskine Russell, *Collections and Recollections,* 1898, p.40. The theologian Edward Bouverie Pusey wanted a return to more ceremony and Catholicism in the Anglican Church.

18. Letter from Caroline Norton to William Cowper, 4 September 1844, Berg Collection, Maggs 11.23.60

19. Letter from Caroline to Thomas Le Fanu, 30 October 1844, King's College Archives, Cambridge, LEF/2/17

20. Letter from Caroline Norton to Richard Brinsley Sheridan, 13 November 1844, BL, Ms 42767, ff.109–11

21. Perkins, 1909, p.184

22. Letter from Caroline Norton to Richard Brinsley Sheridan, December 1844, BL, Ms 42767, ff.119–20

23. Ibid., ff.115-18

24. Perkins, 1909, p.195

25. Caroline Norton, *The Child Of The Islands,* 1845

26. *The Times,* 28 November 1845, p.10

27. Letter from Caroline Norton to Lady Seymour, 30 April 1845, PRONI, D1071/F/E/1/2

28. Letter from Caroline Norton to Edward Hawtrey, May 1845, Yale University, Beinecke Library, Gen. Mss, 260, Box 1, folder 9

29. Letter from Caroline Norton to Augusta Cowell, 18 May 1845, Carl Pforzheimer Collection, Misc. Ms 4013

30. Perkins, 1909, p.196

31. Marriage record of James Johnstone to the Hon. William Augusta Ann Norton, 9 January 1846, Edinburgh

32. Letter from Augusta Norton to James Johnstone, 3 February 1824, Clackmannanshire Library, PD 239/9/19; 5 May 1838, PD 239/10.27

33. Emma Rothschild, *The Inner Life of Empires: An Eighteenth Century History,* 2011, pp.1–10

34. Letter from Caroline Norton to Lady Seymour, February 1846, PRONI, D/1071/F/E/1

35. Eton School Lists 1843–8, Eton College Archives; Letter from Caroline Norton to Edward Coleridge, 14 October 1845, Yale University, Beinecke Library, Gen. Mss 260, Box 1, folder 29

36. Letter from Caroline Norton to William Cowper, May 1846, Berg Collection, Maggs 11.23.60

37. Letter from Caroline Norton to William Cowper, 12 May 1846, ibid.

38. Letter from Caroline Norton to Mrs Caroline Sheridan, June 1846, Buckinghamshire Studies, D/RA/A/2C/11/6

39. Letter from Caroline Norton to Dr Hawtrey, June 1846, Yale University, Beinecke Library, Gen. Mss 260, Box 2, folder 63

40. Letter from Caroline Norton to Mrs Caroline Sheridan, June 1846, Buckinghamshire Studies, D/RA/A/2C/11/1–4

41. *ODNB* online, Benjamin Robert Haydon

42. Letter from Caroline Norton to Samuel Rogers, 23 July 1846, University College London Library Archives, Sharpe Papers

43. Letter from Caroline Norton to Alexander Kinglake, July 1846, University of Cambridge Library, Kinglake Papers, Add. 7633/7/35

44. Letter from Caroline Norton to Edward Ellice, 19 August 1846, NLS, Ms 15037, ff.117–120

45. Letter from Caroline Norton to William Cowper, 11 October 1846, Berg Collection, Maggs 11.23.60; Letter from Caroline Norton to Edward Ellice, 19 October 1846, NLS, Ms 15037, ff.120–123; Letter from Caroline Norton to Lady Seymour, October 1846, PRONI, D/1071/F/E/1/2

46. Katherine Tillotson, House and Storey (eds), 1965–2002, Vol. 4, pp.669–72

47. *The Times*, 21 December 1846, p.11

48. *ODNB* online, Thomas Heathfield Carrick

49. *The Times*, 14 June 1847, p.5

50. Letter from Caroline Norton to Lady Seymour, February 1847, PRONI, D1071/F/E/3. Fletcher's tutor was seriously overqualified for this appointment but by now had a wife to support. In 1848 he wrote for *The Times*, in 1854 about the Crimean War for the *Daily News* and Charles Dickens's periodical *Household Words*.

51. Letter from Caroline Norton to Edward Ellice, 6 September 1847, PRONI, D1071/F/E/2/1

52. Acland, 1948, pp.184–5

53. Letter from Caroline Norton to Edward Ellice, June 1848, PRONI, D1071/F/E/2/1

54. *ODNB* online, Frederick James Lamb, Baron Beauvale and third Viscount Melbourne
55. Letter from Caroline Norton to William Cowper, summer 1848, Berg Collection, Maggs, 11.20.60
56. Letter from Caroline Norton to Lady Seymour, September 1848, PRONI, D1071/F/E/1/2; letter from Caroline Norton to Mrs Caroline Sheridan, undated, 1848, Buckinghamshire Studies, D/RA/A/2C/11/8/1
57. Letter from Caroline Norton to Mr W. Le Fanu, 11 October 1848, King's College Archives, Cambridge, LEF/2/7
58. Letter from Caroline Norton to unnamed woman, 3 November 1848, Carl Pforzheimer Collection, Misc. 3703
59. Letter from Caroline Norton to William Cowper, 9 November 1848, Berg Collection, Maggs 11.23.60
60. Mitchell, 1997, p.272
61. *The Times,* 25 November 1848, p.5
62. Letter from Caroline Norton to William Cowper, November 1848, Yale University, Beinecke Library, Gen. Mss 260, Box 1, folder 5
63. Mitchell, 1997, p.257
64. Letter from Caroline Norton to Edward Ellice, November 1848, NLS, Ms 15037 ff.143–7
65. Letter from Caroline Norton to William Cowper, 28 November 1848, Berg Collection, Maggs 11.23.60
66. Perkins, 1909, p.213
67. Letter from Caroline Norton to Edward Ellice, 7 December 1848, NLS, Ms 15037, ff.177–9
68. *ODNB* online, Sir Charles Napier
69. *The Times,* 15 December 1848, p.7; letter from Caroline Norton to Mr W. Le Fanu, 29 May 1849, NLI
70. Letter from Caroline Norton to Mrs Le Fanu, February 1849, NLI
71. Letter from Caroline Norton to Edward Ellice, 19 March 1849, NLS, Ms 15037, ff.123–31
72. Letter from Caroline Norton to Richard Brinsley Sheridan, 9 April 1949, PRONI, D1071/F/E1/5
73. Dormandy, 1999, p.45
74. *ODNB* online, Edward John Stanley, second Baron Stanley and first Baron Eddisbury
75. Letter from Caroline Norton to Lord Eddisbury, 19 May 1849, PRONI, D1071/F/E/2/12
76. Dormandy, 1999, p.108

77. Caroline Norton, 'The Invalid's Mother: To The Sun, At Lisbon', 1849, Dorset Archives, D/SHE/11

78. Letter from Caroline Norton to Mrs Caroline Sheridan, 9 June 1849, Buckinghamshire Archives, D/RA/A/2C/11/7/1

79. Letter from Caroline Norton to Edward Ellice, 3 July 1849, NLS, Ms 15037, ff.135–40; *The Times*, 25 July 1849, p.5

80. Perkins, 1909, p.213

81. *The Times*, 9 August 1849, p.9; Peerage.com website

82. Letter from Caroline Norton to Henry Pelham-Clinton, fifth Duke of Newcastle, 12 January 1850, University of Nottingham Manuscripts and Special Collections, NeC12986

83. Letter from Caroline Norton to Henry Pelham-Clinton, 19 March 1850, ibid., NeC12987

84. Letter from Caroline Norton to Helen Dufferin, 9 July 1849, PRONI, D1071/F/E/E1/5

85. Letter from Caroline Norton to Abraham Hayward, 10 August 1850, Carl Pforzheimer Collection, MISC 3706

86. Letter from Caroline Norton to Helen Dufferin, 22 September 1849, PRONI, D1071/F/E1/5

87. Perkins, 1909, p.215

88. Ibid., p.214

89. Letter from Caroline Norton to Helen Dufferin, 1851, PRONI, D1071/F/E1/5

90. *The Times*, 10 March 1851, p.11

91. 1851 Census, 3 Chesterfield Street, London

92. *ODNB* online, Lady Eastlake; Perkins, 1909, pp.217, 222

93. Letter from Caroline Norton to Mr Lockhart, May 1851, NLS, Ms 930, f.83

94. Letter from Fletcher Norton to Caroline Norton, 6 May 1851, PRONI, D1071/F/E1/4

95. *The Times*, 9 May 1851, p.8; 24 May 1851, p.8; 26 May 1851, p.5; Caroline Norton, *Stuart Of Dunleath*, 1851; Craig, 2009, pp.115–18

96. Death certificate of Caroline Henrietta Sheridan

97. The *Examiner*, 14 June 1851, p.5

98. Letter from Caroline Norton to Lady Seymour, 19 June 1851, PRONI, D1071/F/E1/6

Chapter IX

1. The *Examiner*, 4 June 1851, p.3; will of Caroline Henrietta Sheridan, PROB, 11/2136
2. *The Times*, 4 August 1851, p.4
3. Letter from Caroline Norton to a niece, 1 September 1851, Buckinghamshire Studies, D/RA/A/2C/22
4. Letter from Caroline Norton to Helen Dufferin, 5 December 1851, PRONI, D1071/F/E1/10
5. Letter from Caroline Norton to Mrs Brinsley (Marcia) Sheridan, 13 December 1851, ibid., D1071/F/E1/11
6. Letter from Caroline Norton to Lady Seymour, 29 December 1851, ibid., D1071/F/E/1/2
7. *The Times*, 17 July 1852, p.4; 12 January 1853, p.2
8. Ibid., 14 May 1852, p.6
9. Letter from Caroline Norton to Lady Seymour, 4 October 1852, PRONI, D1071/F/E/1/2
10. Letter from Caroline Norton to Lady Seymour, 28 December 1852, ibid., D1071/F/E/1/2
11. Letter from Caroline Norton to Lady Seymour, 11 February 1853, ibid., D1071/F/E/E/1/3; *ODNB* online, Frederick Richard Chichester, Earl of Belfast
12. Letter from Caroline Norton to Helen Dufferin, 5 March 1853, PRONI, D1071/F/E/1/1; Leopold, Count of Syracuse, Getty Museum website
13. Perkins, 1909, p.227
14. *The Times*, 18 July 1853, p.2
15. Perkins, 1909, pp.228–9
16. *The Times,* 19 August 1853, p.10; *Bury and Norwich Post and Suffolk Herald*, 24 August 1853, p.2
17. Perkins, 1909, p.232; *Dundee Courier*, 24 August 1853, p.1
18. Letter from Caroline Norton to Georgina Cowper, August 1853, Berg Collection, Maggs 11.23.60
19. *The Times*, 20 August 1853, p.8
20. Ibid., 24 August 1853, p.7
21. Storey, Tillotson and Angus Easson (House and Storey, 1965–2002), Vol. 7, pp.132–3
22. *The Times*, 2 September 1853, p.8
23. Letter from Caroline Norton, 9 September 1853, Carl Pforzheimer Collection, Misc. 3698
24. *The Times,* 17 September 1853, p.9

25. Stone, 1995, p.369; *ODNB* online, Sir John Campbell

26. Letter from Caroline Norton to Mrs Le Fanu, 17 September 1853, King's College Archives, Cambridge, LEF 2/17

27. Letter from Caroline Norton to William Le Fanu, 20 September 1853, NLI

28. Letter from Caroline Norton to William Le Fanu, September 1853, NLI

29. Letter from Caroline Norton to William Le Fanu, 29 October 1853, King's College Archives, Cambridge, LEF/2/17

30. Letter from Caroline Norton to Mrs Le Fanu, 30 November 1854, King's College Archives, Cambridge, LEF/2/17

31. Storey, Tillotson and Easson (House and Storey, 1965–2002), Vol. 7, p.195

32. Letter from Caroline Norton to William Le Fanu, 18 December 1853, King's College Archives, Cambridge, LEF/2/17

33. Letters from Caroline Norton to Mr Lowther and Mr Wreford, November and December 1853, Markenfield Hall, Ripon, private papers

34. Letter from Caroline Norton to William Le Fanu, 18 January 1854, King's College Archives, Cambridge, LEF/2/17

35. Caroline Norton, *English Laws for Women in the Nineteenth Century*, 1854, p.128

36. Ibid., pp.160–3, 169–70

37. Letter from Caroline Norton to Lord Brougham, 1 April 1854, University College London Library Special Collections, Brougham Papers, 12,902

38. Letter from Caroline Norton to Richard Brinsley Sheridan, 27 April 1854, Buckinghamshire Studies, D/RA/A/2C/30/3

39. *The Times*, 3 May 1854, p.12

40. *ODNB* online, George John Cayley

41. Letter from Caroline Norton to Helen Dufferin, 21 May 1854, PRONI, D1071/F/E/1/1

42. Letter from Caroline Norton to Sir William Temple, 5 July 1854, Berg Collection, Maggs 11.28.60; *ODNB* online, Sir William Cowper Temple

43. *ODNB* online, Robert Monsey Rolfe, Baron Cranworth

44. Stone, 1995, pp.368–77. Married women's property was not secured until 1882 and equal access to divorce was made law in 1923.

45. Peerage.com

46. Letter from Caroline Norton to Lady Seymour, 29 October 1854, PRONI, D1071/F/E/1

47. Caroline Norton, *A Letter to Queen Victoria on Lord Chancellor Cranworth's Marriage and Divorce Bill,* 1855, pp.3–14

48. Ibid., pp.84–8, 96

49. *ODNB* online, Caroline Elizabeth Sarah Norton; Barbara Leigh Smith Bodichon

50. Norton, 1855, pp.98–100; Matthew Henry and J. B. Williams, *Exposition of the Old and New Testament,* Vol. 2, 1828, p.637

51. Letter from Caroline Norton to Lady Seymour, October 1855, PRONI, D1071/F/E/1/2

52. *ODNB* online, Henry Richard Charles Wellesley, first Earl Cowley

53. *The Times,* 13 March 1856, p.13; 7 January 1856, p.9

54. Letter from Caroline Norton to Sir William Cowper Temple, 21 March 1856, Berg Collection, Maggs 11.20.60

55. Stone, 1995, pp.371–2, 377. The illegal practice of wife-selling persisted in rural areas of England until the early twentieth century. A practical solution to unhappy marriages and no possibility of divorce, a wife was often sold in an amicable way to a man whom she already knew and was happy to marry. (Samuel Pyeatt Menefee, *Wives For Sale: An Ethnographic Study of British Popular Divorce,* 1981, pp.1–3)

56. *ODNB* online, Sir Thomas Erskine Perry

57. Letter from Caroline Norton to Helen Dufferin, autumn 1856, PRONI, D/1231/D/2/3

58. Letter from Caroline Norton to Helen Dufferin, autumn 1856, ibid., D/1231/D/2/4

59. Letter from Caroline Norton to Mr Parker, 22 December 1856, Carl Pforzheimer Collection, Misc. 3919

60. *The Times,* 30 January 1857, p.7

61. Letter from Caroline Norton to William Le Fanu, 14 January 1857, King's College Archives, Cambridge, LEF/2/17

62. Stone, 1995, pp.378–82

63. An Act to Amend the Law Relating to Divorce and Matrimonial Causes in England, Public Acts, 20 & 21 Victoria, Chapter 85, 1857, clauses 21, 24, 25, 26

64. By 1861 the number of divorces being granted had shot up from four to a hundred and fifty a year. By 1914 the figure was eight hundred a year. Caroline was unable to divorce George because she had returned to the marital home in 1835 and had 'condoned' the situation. Unable to benefit from the change in the law, she pressed for a deed of separation, which would grant her some, though not

total, freedom and enable her battles with George Norton to draw to a close. (Stone, 1995, pp.388–90)

65. Letter from Caroline Norton to William Le Fanu, August 1857, NLI
66. Letter from Caroline Norton to Dr Locock, August 1857, Yale University, Beinecke Library, Gen. MSS, 260, Box 1, folder 15
67. Visitors' Book of Edward Ellice, NLS, Dep. 356
68. *ODNB* online, Henry Pelham Fiennes Pelham-Clinton, fifth Duke of Newcastle
69. Letter from Caroline Norton to Edward Ellice, undated, PRONI, D1071/F/E/2/1–12
70. Letter from Caroline to Henry Newcastle, 2 November 1858, University of Nottingham Manuscripts and Special Collections, NeC 13001
71. Letter from Caroline Norton to Helen Dufferin, 16 December 1858, PRONI, D1071/F/E/1/1
72. Letter from Caroline Norton to Henry Newcastle, March 1859, University of Nottingham Manuscripts and Special Collections, NeC 13013
73. Letter from Caroline Norton to Henry Newcastle, July 1859, ibid., NeC 13008
74. *The London Gazette*, 16 July 1859, p.5
75. Record of the death of the Hon. William Augusta Ann Johnstone, 21 July 1859, Scotland's People website
76. Letter from Caroline Norton to Henry Newcastle, July 1859, University of Nottingham Manuscripts and Special Collections, NeC 12992
77. Letter from Caroline Norton to Henry Newcastle, August 1859, ibid., NeC 12991
78. Letter from Caroline Norton to Helen Dufferin, undated, PRONI, D1071/F/E/1/1
79. Deed of Separation of the Honourable Mr and Mrs Norton, 2 September 1859, East Sussex Record Office, Acc. 7755/33/4
80. Letter from Fletcher Norton to George Norton, 11 September 1858, Markenfield Hall, Ripon, private papers
81. Letter from Caroline Norton to William Le Fanu, 6 November 1859, King's College Archives, Cambridge, LEF/2/17
82. Letter from Caroline Norton to Newcastle, undated, 1859, University of Nottingham Manuscripts and Special Collections, NeC 13033
83. Letter from Caroline Norton to Edward Ellice, 8 December 1859, NLS, Ms 15037, ff.160–61

Chapter X

1. Letter from Caroline Norton to Lady Anna Stirling Maxwell, 1866, Mitchell Library, Glasgow City Archives, Ms 119.15.1
2. Letter from Caroline Norton to William Le Fanu, 24 May 1867, King's College Archives, Cambridge, LEF/2/17
3. Letter from Caroline Norton to Lady Anna Stirling Maxwell, June 1867, Mitchell Library, Glasgow City Archives, Ms 119.15.36
4. Caroline Norton, 'A Regret', 1867, Dorset History Centre, D/SHE/11
5. Letter from Caroline Norton to Lord Houghton (Richard Monckton-Milnes), October 1862, Trinity College, Cambridge, Houghton 18, p.180; *The Times,* 23 December 1862, p.10
6. *ODNB* online, Helen Selina Hay, née Sheridan, Countess of Gifford
7. Letter from Caroline Norton to William Le Fanu, 15 July 1860, King's College Archives, Cambridge, LEF/2/17
8. 1861 Census, Hampton Court Green
9. Letter from Caroline Norton to Macmillan and Co., October 1861, Berg Collection
10. *The Times,* 1 January 1862, p.10; Caroline Norton, *The Lady Of La Garaye,* 1862, pp.8–13
11. Letter from Caroline Norton to Lord Houghton (Richard Monckton-Miles), 1862, Trinity College, Cambridge, Houghton 18, p.15; Letter from Caroline Norton to John Murray, January 1862, NLS, JMA, 40884; *ODNB* online, Caesar Henry Hawkins; *ODNB* online, Sir Prescott Gardner Hewett
12. Letter from Caroline Norton to Mr Wreford, 11 August 1862, Huntington Library, California; Letter from Caroline Norton to Sir Charles Locock, 1862, Yale University, Beinecke Library, Gen. MSS 260, Box 1, folder 14
13. Letter from Caroline Norton to Sir Charles Locock, 13 May 1863, Yale University, Beinecke Library, Gen. MSS 260, Box 1, folder 15
14. Caroline Norton, *Lost And Saved,* 1863; *The Times,* 23 June 1863, p.15; Perkins, 1909, pp.276–81; Craig, 2009, pp.48–63
15. Letter from Caroline Norton to Henry Newcastle, 1863, University of Nottingham Manuscripts and Special Collections, NeC 13039
16. Letter from Caroline Norton to Henry Newcastle, 1863, ibid., NeC 13003
17. Death certificate of Henry Pelham Clinton-Pelham, fifth Duke of Newcastle
18. Perkins, 1909, p.284

19. Letter from Caroline Norton to Helen Gifford, 20 January 1866, PRONI, D1071/F/E1/5

20. Letter from Caroline Norton to Helen Gifford, 6 January 1867, ibid., D1071/F/E/1/1

21. Letter from Caroline Norton to Lady Anna Stirling Maxwell, 1–6 March 1867, Mitchell Library, Glasgow City Archives, Ms 119.15.2

22. *The Scotsman*, 29 July 1867, p.3

23. *The Times*, 17 October 1867, p.13; 25 October, p.7; 23 October, p.13; Craig, 2009, pp.66–74

24. Letter from Caroline Norton to Lady Anna Stirling Maxwell, 1869, Mitchell Library, Glasgow City Archives, Ms 119.15.16

25. Letter from Caroline Norton to unnamed friend, undated, Huntington Library, California, Ms 32028

26. *The Times*, 29 March 1870, p.12

27. Letter from Caroline Norton to Mrs Friswell, 7 October 1870, Huntington Library, California, Ms 32022

28. Public and General Acts 33 & 34 Victoria, Chapter 93; Mary Lyndon Shanley, *Feminism, Marriage and the Law in Victorian England*, 1989, pp.77–9

29. *The Times*, 21 April 1871, p.11

30. Letter from Caroline Norton to Edward Coleridge, 17 November 1873, Yale University, Beinecke Library, Gen. MSS 260, Box 1, folder 29

31. Letter from Caroline Norton to Lady Anna Stirling Maxwell, 15 December 1871, Mitchell Library, Glasgow City Archives, Ms 119.15.33

32. Letter from Caroline Norton to Lady Anna Stirling Maxwell, 7 September 1873, ibid., Ms 119.16.1

33. Letter from Caroline Norton to Lady Anna Stirling Maxwell, September 1873, ibid., Ms 119.15.48

34. Letter from Caroline Norton to William Le Fanu, 12 September 1873, NLI

35. Letter from Caroline Norton to Lady Anna Stirling Maxwell, 12 September 1873, Mitchell Library, Glasgow City Archives, Ms 119.15.50

36. Letter from Caroline Norton to Lady Anna Stirling Maxwell, December 1873, ibid., Ms 119.15.61

37. Record of death of Lady Anna Stirling Maxwell, 8 December 1874, Scotland's People website; *Birmingham Daily Post*, 8 December 1874; *The Times*, 10 December 1874, p.10

38. Death certificate of George Chapple Norton; *The Times,* 26 February 1875, p.5; *York Herald,* 27 February 1875, p.5

39. Letter from Caroline Norton to William Le Fanu, June 1875, NLI

40. Death certificate of Fletcher Norton, Lord Grantley

41. Letter from Caroline Norton to William Le Fanu, 8 February 1876, NLI

42. Letter from Caroline Norton to William Cowper, 15 June 1876, Yale University, Beinecke Library, Gen. MSS 260, Box 2, folder 60

43. *The Times,* 7 July 1876, p.12

44. Letter from Caroline Norton to Mr Leveson-Gower, 1876, PRONI, D1071/F/E2/3

45. Marriage certificate of Caroline Norton and Sir William Stirling Maxwell

46. Letter from Caroline Norton to William Le Fanu, 20 February 1877, King's College Archives, Cambridge, LEF 2/17

47. Letter from Caroline Norton to Mrs W. Le Fanu, 4 March 1877, ibid.

48. Death certificate of Lady Stirling Maxwell

49. Letter from Sir William Stirling Maxwell to William Le Fanu, 16 July 1877, ibid.

50. Letter from Richard Brinsley Sheridan, 19 June 1877, King's College Archives, Cambridge, LEF 2/17

51. Letter from Carlotta Norton to Mrs W. Le Fanu, 15 July 1877, ibid.

52. *The Times,* 31 July 1877, p.8

53. Letter from Carlotta Norton to Mrs W. Le Fanu, 14 November 1877, King's College Archives, Cambridge, LEF 2/17

54. Letter from Carlotta Norton to Mrs W. Le Fanu, 31 January 1878, ibid.

Bibliography

Acland, Alice, *Caroline Norton*, Constable and Company, London, 1948

Bradley, Simon and Pevsner, Nikolaus, *The Buildings of England, London 6: Westminster*, Yale University Press, New Haven and London, 2003

Buxton, Edward H. (ed.), *The Letters of Edward John Trelawny*, Henry Frowde and Oxford University Press, London, 1910

Campbell, Sir James, *Memoirs of Sir James Campbell of Ardkinglas*, Vols. 1 and 2, Henry Colburn and Richard Bentley, London, 1832

Cecil, David, *Lord M, or the Later Life of Lord Melbourne*, Constable and Company Ltd, London, 1954

Chedzoy, Alan, *A Scandalous Woman: The Story of Caroline Norton*, Alison & Busby, London, 1992

Craig, Randall, *The Narratives of Caroline Norton*, Palgrave Macmillan, New York, 2009

Crane, David, *Lord Byron's Jackal: A Life of Edward John Trelawny*, Flamingo, London, 1999

Cruickshank, Daniel, *The Country House Revealed: A Secret History of the British Ancestral Home*, BBC Books/Ebury Publishing, London, 2011

Dickens, Charles, *The Pickwick Papers*, 1837, Penguin Classics, London, 1999 edition

——*The Posthumous Papers of the Pickwick Club*, Everyman's Library, London, 1907

Dormandy, Thomas, *The White Death: A History of Tuberculosis*, The Hambledon Press, London and Rio Grande, 1999

Fitzgerald, Percy, *The Lives of the Sheridans*, Richard Bentley and Son, London, 1886

Goodchild, John, *An Attorney At Large*, Wakefield Historical Publications, Wakefield, 1986

Gregory, Jeremy and Stevenson, John, *The Routledge Companion to Britain in the Eighteenth Century*, Routledge, London, 2007

Hammerton, A. James, *Cruelty and Companionship: Conflict in Nineteenth-Century Married Life*, Routledge, London and New York, 1992

Heber, Mark D., *Ancestral Trails: The Complete Guide to British Genealogy and Family History*, Sutton Publishing, Gloucester, 2000

Hilton, Boyd, *A Mad, Bad and Dangerous People: England 1783–1846*, Clarendon Press, Oxford, 2006

Hoge, James O. and Clarke, Olney, *The Letters of Caroline Norton to Lord Melbourne*, Ohio State University Press, Ohio, 1974

Hoppen, Theodore, *The Mid Victorian Generation, 1846–1886*, Oxford University Press, Oxford, 2008

Horstman, Allen, *Victorian Divorce*, Croom Helm, London and Sydney, 1985

House, Madeline, and Storey, Graham et al (eds), *The Letters of Charles Dickens*, The Clarendon Press, Oxford, 1965–2002

Johnston, Lucy, *Nineteenth-Century Fashion Detail*, V. and A. Publishing, London, 2005

Kelly, Ian, *Beau Brummell: The Ultimate Dandy*, Hodder and Stoughton, London, 2005

Kemble, Francis Ann, *Record of a Girlhood*, Vol. 2, Richard Bentley and Son, London, 1878

McAleer, John, *Representing Africa: Landscape, Exploration and Empire in Southern Africa, 1780–1870*, Manchester University Press, Manchester, 2010

Marshall, Florence E. (ed.), *The Life and Letters of Mary Wollstonecraft Shelley*, Richard Bentley and Son, London, 1889

Masson, Madeline, unpublished typescript, 'Birds of Passage', Markenfield Hall, Ripon, private papers

Meneffe, Samuel Pyeatt, *Wives For Sale: An Ethnographic Study of Popular British Divorce*, Basil Blackwell, Oxford, 1981

Mitchell, Leslie G., *Lord Melbourne 1779–1848*, Oxford University Press, Oxford, 1997

——*Bulwer Lytton: The Rise and Fall of a Victorian Man of Letters*, Hambledon and London, London and New York, 2003

——*The Whig World, 1760–1837*, Hambledon Continuum, London, 2007

Moore, Thomas, *The Memoirs of Richard Brinsley Sheridan*, Vol. II, Longman, London, 1825

Norton, Caroline Elizabeth Sarah, *The Undying One, And Other Poems*, Henry Colburn and Richard Bentley, London, 1830

——*The Wife* and *Woman's Reward*, Sanders and Otley, London, 1835

——*A Cry From The Factories*, John Murray, London, 1836

——*The Dream*, Henry Colburn, London, 1840

Norton, *Letters Etc. Dated From June 1836 to July 1841*, privately printed, London, 1841

——*The Child Of The Islands*, Chapman and Hall, London, 1844

——*Stuart Of Dunleath: A Story Of Modern Times*, Henry Colburn and Co., London, 1851

——*English Laws For Women in the Nineteenth Century*, printed for private circulation, 1854, reprinted The Dodo Press, United States, 2010

——*The Lady Of La Garaye*, Macmillan and Co., London, 1862

——*Lost And Saved*, Hurst and Blackett, London, 1863

——*Old Sir Douglas*, Hurst and Blackett, London, 1867

O'Gorman, Frank, *The Long Eighteenth Century: English Political and Social History, 1688–1832*, Arnold, London, 1997

O'Keeffe, Paul, *A Genius For Failure: The Life of Benjamin Robert Haydon*, The Bodley Head, London, 2009

O'Toole, Fintan, *The Traitor's Kiss: The Life of Richard Brinsley Sheridan*, Granta, London, 1997

Parker, Sarah E., *Grace and Favour: A Handbook of Those Who Lived Where In Hampton Court Palace, 1750–1950*, Historic Royal Palaces, London, 2005

Pearce, Edward, *Reform! The Fight for the 1832 Reform Act*, Jonathan Cape, London, 2003

Perkin, Joan, *Women and Marriage in Nineteenth-Century England*, Routledge, London, 1989

Perkins, Jane Gray, *The Life of Mrs Norton*, John Murray, London, 1909

Phillips, Roderick, *Untying the Knot: A Short History of Divorce*, Cambridge University Press, Cambridge, 1991

Pope, Willard Bissell (ed.), *The Diary of Benjamin Robert Haydon*, Vols. 19–22, Harvard University Press, Cambridge, 1963

Price, Cecil (Ed.), *The Letters of Richard Brinsley Sheridan*, Vol. 3, The Clarendon Press, Oxford, 1966

Shanley, Mary Lyndon, *Feminism, Marriage and the Law in Victorian England*, Princeton University Press, Princeton, 1989

Stafford, Alice, Countess of, (ed.), *Leaves from the Diary of Henry Greville*, Smith Elder and Co., London, 1905, reprint by Forgotten Books

Stevenson, Pearce, *A Plain Letter to the Lord Chancellor on the Infant Custody Bill*, James Ridgway, London, 1839

Stone, Lawrence, *Uncertain Unions: Marriage in England 1660–1753*, Oxford University Press, Oxford, 1992

——*Broken Lives: Separation and Divorce in England 1660–1857*, Oxford University Press, Oxford, 1993

——*Road To Divorce: A History of the Making and Breaking of Marriage in England*, Oxford University Press, Oxford, 1995

Tomalin, Claire, *Charles Dickens: A Life*, Viking, London, 2011

Waller, Maureen, *The English Marriage: Tales of Love, Money and Adultery*, John Murray, London, 2009

Watkins, John, *Memoirs of the Private and Public Life of the Rt Hon. Richard Brinsley Sheridan, With a Particular Account of Family and Connexions*, Henry Colburn, London, 1817

Weinreb, Ben and Hibbert, Christopher (eds), *The London Encyclopaedia*, Papermac, London, 1983

Wood, Mary and Alan (eds), *Silver Spoon: The Memoirs of Lord Grantley*, Hutchinson and Co., London, 1954

Zeigler, Philip, *Melbourne: A Biography of William Lamb, 2nd Viscount Melbourne*, William Collins and Son, London, 1976

List of Illustrations

Integrated Illustrations

P 405   The Mitchell Library, Glasgow, by permission of Mr D. Maxwell
Macdonald
P 424   The Mitchell Library, Glasgow, by permission of Mr D. Maxwell
Macdonald

While every effort has been made to contact copyright holders, the author
and publisher would be grateful for information about any material where
they have been unable to trace the source, and would be glad to make
amendments in further editions.

Acknowledgements

I must first thank Caroline Norton for being Caroline Norton. For being such a passionate, witty and caring subject. I also thank her for her handwriting, which made life easier for me and thereby for those around me.

Before the Internet and digital imaging a book from sources scattered all over the world, as Caroline Norton's letters are, was impossible. The three previous books about her were written in 1909, 1948 and 1992, before these innovations. Caroline's letters stood up so well to multiple readings that recipients kept them – even though she sometimes instructed them to burn them – and over the years have ended up in London, Dorset, Glasgow, Edinburgh, Belfast, Nottingham, Cambridge, Dublin, New York, and libraries at Harvard and Yale Universities. I thank the archivists who supplied me with the materials to write this book:

Elizabeth Denlinger and Charles Carter at the Carl H. Pforzheimer Collection of Shelley and his Circle, New York Public Library, Astor, Lenox and Tilden Foundations

Dr Isaac Gewirtz and Anne Garner, the Berg Collection of English and American Literature, New York Public Library, Astor, Lenox and Tilden Foundations

Sheila McKenzie, National Library of Scotland, Edinburgh

Patricia McGuire, King's College Library, Cambridge

Lynne Burton, Hertfordshire Archives and Local Studies, Hertford

Janet Hancock and Liam O'Reilly, Public Record Office of Northern Ireland, Belfast

Gayle M. Richardson, Manuscripts Department, Huntington Library, California

Katherine Cone, Centre for Buckinghamshire Studies, Aylesbury

Nerys Tunnicliffe, the Mitchell Library, Glasgow City Archives

Tessa Spencer, National Register of Archives for Scotland, Edinburgh

Susan Palmer, Sir John Soane's Museum, London

I would like to thank the following for permission to quote from their collections:

The British Library

Public Record Office of Northern Ireland, Belfast

Trustees of the National Library of Scotland, Edinburgh

The Board of the National Library of Ireland, Dublin

Carl H. Pforzheimer Collection for the Study of Shelley and his Circle, New York Public Library, Astor, Lenox and Tilden Foundations

Berg Collection of English and American Literature, New York Public Library, Astor, Lenox and Tilden Foundations

Bodelian Libraries, University of Oxford

Beinecke Library, Yale University

Manuscripts and Special Collections of the University of Nottingham

University College London Library Services Special Collections for access to the Brougham Papers and Sharpe Family Papers

Syndics of Cambridge University Library

Master and Fellows of Trinity College, Cambridge
King's College Archives, Cambridge
Centre for Buckinghamshire Studies
Dorset History Centre
Hertfordshire Archives and Local Studies
Huntington Library, San Marino, California
Cumbria Archive Centre
Mitchell Library, Glasgow City Archives
Marchioness of Dufferin and Ava
Lowther Trust
Sir Raymond Johnstone of Alva
Provost and Fellows of Eton College
Mr D. Maxwell Macdonald
County Archivist of East Sussex

Thanks are also due to:

Lord Baker for the lovebirds cartoon.
Fintan O'Toole for writing such a splendid book on Caroline's grandfather Richard Brinsley Sheridan, *The Traitor's Kiss*.
Anyone wrestling with the huge subject of divorce owes a debt to Lawrence Stone, who made this subject his own so that others did not have to.
My editor Trevor Dolby immediately understood how important Mrs Norton was, and is, appreciated her humanity and beauty of looks and spirit, and made it possible for her story to be told in full for the first time.
Nicola Taplin at Preface for her great work: she turns whirlpools into millponds. It is a joy to work with her.
The publishers and contributors to the *Oxford Dictionary of National Biography* for its pithy and brilliant essays which strongly support the work of biography.
Peggy and Robert Lazenby, former owners of Frampton House

in Dorset, who fed and watered me, and allowed me to rummage through their archive and photograph it to my heart's content.

Lady Deirdre Curteis and Ian Curteis for their hospitality and frankness about their ancestor George Norton, and access to their private papers at Markenfield Hall.

Richard Sheridan for bringing two trunks of family papers to my house and helping sift the contents.

Donna Smith, who did such important work on the images.

Mr and Mrs Brinsley Sheridan for their family history.

Marilyn Imrie and James Runcie for their love and hospitality on many research trips to Edinburgh.

Patrick Hughes has been a rock and a brick, and I am most grateful to him for everything and more.

Index

(key to initials: CN = Caroline Norton; FN = Fletcher Norton (Lord Grantley); FS = Frank Sheridan; GN = George Norton; LM = Lord Melbourne; RBS = Richard Brinsley Sheridan; TS = Thomas Sheridan)